P9-DWM-821

EXIT RIGHT

*The People Who Left the Left and
Reshaped the American Century*

Daniel Oppenheimer

SIMON & SCHUSTER
New York   London   Toronto   Sydney   New Delhi

Simon & Schuster
1230 Avenue of the Americas
New York, NY 10020

First Simon & Schuster hardcover edition February 2016

SIMON & SCHUSTER and colophon are registered
trademarks of Simon & Schuster, Inc.

For information about special discounts for bulk purchases,
please contact Simon & Schuster Special Sales at 1-866-506-1949
or business@simonandschuster.com.

The Simon & Schuster Speakers Bureau can bring authors to
your live event. For more information or to book an event,
contact the Simon & Schuster Speakers Bureau at 1-866-248-3049
or visit our website at www.simonspeakers.com.

Interior design by Lewelin Polanco

Manufactured in the United States of America

10 9 8 7 6 5 4 3 2 1

Library of Congress Cataloging-in-Publication Data

Names: Oppenheimer, Daniel.
Title: Exit right : the people who left the Left and reshaped the American
century / Daniel Oppenheimer.
Description: First Simon & Schuster hardcover edition. | New York : Simon &
Schuster, 2016. | Includes bibliographical references and index.
Identifiers: LCCN 2015028768
Subjects: LCSH: Politicians—United States—Biography. |
Intellectuals—United States—Biography. | Right and left (Political
science)—History—20th century. | Liberalism—United
States—History—20th century. | Conservatism—United
States—History—20th century. | Affiliation (Philosophy)—Political
aspects—United States—History—20th century. | United States—Politics
and government—20th century. | Political culture—United
States—History—20th century. | Social change—United
States—History—20th century. | BISAC: BIOGRAPHY & AUTOBIOGRAPHY /
Political. | POLITICAL SCIENCE / Political Ideologies / Conservatism &
Liberalism. | HISTORY / United States / 20th Century.
Classification: LCC E747 .O67 2016 | DDC 324.2092/2—dc23
LC record available at http://lccn.loc.gov/2015028768

ISBN 978-1-4165-8970-9
ISBN 978-1-4165-9717-9 (ebook)

For Jessica, Jolie, and Asa

"There's one thing I want to tell you, lad. You can't live in two worlds. It's one world or the other. We learned that long ago. And we don't live in two worlds. Our Party is our world. It's the world of the future. Out there," Nolan made a sweeping gesture toward the window, "is the dead world. It's that world or this world."

THE RENEGADE, JAMES FARRELL

Contents

5

The Betrayed: David Horowitz

6

A Man Alone: Christopher Hitchens

Postscript

Acknowledgments

Notes

Index

Introduction

This is a book about why six men changed—why they moved from one set of political beliefs to staunchly different ones. It's also a history of the American Left in the twentieth century, and the rise of the Right. At its most basic level, it's a book about how we come to believe at all. Why is it that each of us holds the beliefs that we do? Why do we follow this set of politics, vote for this party, and associate with these people?

There are obvious answers: Because it's what our mom and dad taught us to do. Because of that professor in college whose insights punctured the bubble of our childhood beliefs, liberating us to discover for ourselves what seems true and right. Because of the faith community in which we were raised, and its stubborn persistence in offering up lives that seem decent and honorable and worth emulating. We act because we're made indignant by injustice. Or because our failures taste bitter, and we project that bitterness onto the world and call it injustice. Age brings responsibility and maturity, and we let go of the utopian fantasies of our youth. Affluence brings anxiety and guilt; its opposite brings anger and blame. Our bodies break down and we grow fearful and angry, or compassionate and wise. We marry an activist because we admire his commitment, then divorce him because of his narcissism. We hate our job. We're inspired by our new job. We're caught up in a movement, or an epoch. We're mugged by reality. Become the victim of history. It's in our genes. It's complicated.

We know all this. We know belief is complicated, contingent, multi-determined. But do we really know it? Do we feel it? Do we act as though it's true, with the humility that such knowledge would entail? Not most of us. Not most of the time. That's one good reason why the stories of Whittaker Chambers, James Burnham, Ronald Reagan, Norman Podhoretz, David Horowitz, and Christopher Hitchens are worth telling. Not because we need to understand them so that we can inoculate ourselves against their heresies, or bask in their enlightenments. Not because the drama of political change in itself is so compelling, though it is. The stories are worth telling because it's during the period of political transition, when the bones of one's belief system are broken and poking out through the skin, that the contingency and complexity of belief become most visible.

"The ex-communist is the problem child of contemporary politics," wrote the eminent Trotskyist writer Isaac Deutscher in 1950, reviewing an anthology of essays by ex-communists.[1] He was right about that, but blinkered in the extent to which he was capable of understanding why. The ex-believers—the heretics, the apostates—are the problem children of any politics, in any time. They are the ones who reveal how shaky the ground beneath us always is.

What if Whittaker Chambers had come of age not in the 1920s and '30s but in the 1960s and '70s, when the intense spiritual energies of young men from repressed and dysfunctional families were as likely to be channeled into the counterculture as they were into radical politics, and when there was more breathing room in the culture for sexual experimentation? Would he have ended up a hippie instead of a communist spy? Would he have come out as gay rather than loathing himself for his dalliances with men? Would he have ended up lecturing at Berkeley rather than renouncing his beliefs and helping put his old comrade Alger Hiss behind bars for espionage? Impossible to say.

Would David Horowitz have stayed on the Left if a colleague hadn't been killed by Horowitz's allies in the Black Panther Party? Probably. His life had been lived so completely within the cosmos of the Left, his identity constructed so completely of its materials, that it's hard to imagine that without a truly catastrophic shock he could have made the journey all the way over to conservatism. But that shock came, and in its aftermath Horowitz became one of the fiercest critics of the legacy of the 1960s counterculture. Would Norman Podhoretz have turned to the Right even if his good friend Norman Mailer had written an enthusiastic review of Podhoretz's memoir, rather than the critical one Mailer did in fact write? Probably. Many of Podhoretz's friends and intellectual allies turned toward neoconservatism over the period of time he did, out of convictions and affinities he shared. But it would have taken longer for Podhoretz to get there, and the kind of person and writer he would have become would have felt very different. What if Ronald Reagan's movie career had been more successful, and he'd never gone to work for General Electric? Would he have remained the New Deal liberal he was to that point? Hard to say. What if the 9/11 hijackers had failed? Or George W. Bush hadn't been interested in connecting the attack with the need for regime change in Iraq? Without the lever of the Iraq War, would Christopher Hitchens have been separated from the Left? Maybe not. Maybe so.

What about us? Could we be wrong about everything? Would we believe differently if we were born only twenty years earlier, or later? Could we be as frail and fallible as these apostates so visibly are, only without the courage or bad judgment to put it all out there for the world to see?

That such questions are impossible to answer should give us pause. Not so much pause that we go about our lives refusing to act or believe passionately. But pause enough to recognize that political belief, if we're to act on it, should be hard-earned. It should bear evidence of confrontation with the abyss, of an awareness that the grounds of our beliefs are more contingent than we could possibly ever account for. And even if we're not political actors in the way the characters in this book are, our political beliefs should have to fight to earn a meaningful place in our lives. They should fight with their opposites, with the possibility of their absence, and with the possibility that there is no ground for them at all.

It is easy to disparage other people's politics by psychologizing, historicizing, biologizing, or sociologizing them. The harder and more important truth to admit is that everyone's politics are resonating on all of these frequencies. Once that point is granted, it casts into relief the problem with one of the charges that is so often leveled against political turncoats, which is that they are acting out personal issues. *Of course* they are. That's what being human entails. The better questions, or at least the ones with which this book is concerned, have to do with what we can learn about the world and ourselves by observing that process with empathy and respect. Also, what does it look like when someone does it well? Or poorly? We can make judgments—we can't not make judgments—but they should be made with an awareness of how hard it is to be a person in the world, period, and how much more confusing that task can become when you take on responsibility for repairing or redeeming it.

Which points to another charge leveled against political turncoats, which is that they turn opportunistically. They follow the money. They join the winning team. See which way the wind is blowing. Sign with the Yankees.

Opportunism is part of human nature. It's there in greater or lesser degree in a number of the stories in this book. And it's true that by the end of the 1930s an anticommunist/anti-Left establishment had come into existence in America that had the resources to fulsomely reward exiles from the Left for their apostasy. But the notion that simple opportunism is at the root of these stories, or most other stories of political transformation, doesn't square with what must be true about almost everyone who has ever turned against his political beliefs, commitments, and allies, which is that it's painful. It is painful to break from what you've cared about and believed deeply, from the institutions and allegiances whose inner laws gave structure to your life, from the friends and family whose regard brought your self into being and sustained it in the face of adversity.

This is the case whether the world you're rejecting is defined by politics or by any of the other meaning-worlds that have the coherence and scale to encompass a human being. Substitute "my faith," "my family," "my community," or "my country" for "the Left" and it becomes clear what was at stake for the subjects of this book when they broke from, and then turned against, their political commitment to the Left. Nothing less than what confronts every man or woman who has ever turned against what defines him or her.

At the moment Whittaker Chambers left the Communist Party underground, at the end of the 1930s, he had no ties to the political Right, no history of publishing with conservative or anticommunist publications, and no good plan to situate his family within a community that would embrace them with a love anywhere equal to the hatred they were likely to incur from the community they were abandoning. He conceived of his break as a jailbreak, and assumed that what lay on the other side of the prison walls was what usually confronts jailbreakers: death in a hail of gunfire or the terrifying contentless "freedom" of the successful escapee, who has no safe place on the outside to stop running and start rebuilding. For Chambers the risk of death, at the hands of a party that had an espionage operation to protect, was worth taking in order to be free of the excruciating fear and hypocrisy that his life as a Communist had become. But that didn't mean he saw great rewards coming, even supposing he did make it out with his life.

James Burnham was in a much better condition when he broke in 1940 from Leon Trotsky's international network of loyalists. Burnham's political comrades were Trotskyists, and he lost those relationships, but his personal friends were mostly his old set from Princeton, none of whom had followed him so far over to the left. The security of his job as a philosophy professor at NYU was only more secure once he severed his radical ties. And he had even managed to cultivate for himself, while working as a party man, a solid reputation as an independent-minded intellectual. He was likely to be able to keep publishing with barely a bump. So there was a visible, plausible life for Burnham on the other side. He wasn't making the leap that Chambers was. But one can't read the letters and essays that Burnham and Trotsky exchanged over the last few months of Burnham's life on the Marxist Left, brimming with anger and hurt, without recognizing how much he knew he would be giving up if he left the party: friends, power, a direct conduit to one of the titans of the twentieth century, and a sense of purpose, situated within a coherent worldview, that had kept him centered during a decade when the whole world seemed in danger of spinning away. It would be another fifteen years before Burnham would be able to reassemble all those elements, as an editor at the conservative *National Review*, in anywhere near as satisfying a form.

When in 1967 Norman Podhoretz published his memoir *Making It*, he believed it would establish him as a writer for the ages, or at least a writer of the moment. When it was panned and mocked by his friends and colleagues, he went into a deep, drink-fueled depression that culminated in a mystical vision and a months-long heightened state of being so alarming that a friend suggested to Podhoretz's wife that he was manic and needed to be committed. The person who came up on the other side of that depression, now dedicated to fighting the New Left movement and ideas he'd once helped birth, wasn't the same man who went into it. His joie de vivre was gone. Podhoretz would go on to acquire serious influence as one of the prime articulators and promoters of neoconservatism, but he would never get that groove back. He was so hurt by what he saw as the betrayal and abandonment of his friends on the Left, at that critical moment, that he's spent much of the remainder of his intellectual life writing memoir after memoir retelling and revising the story, each time insisting with more certitude and less credibility that he's at peace with who he was and what he has become.

David Horowitz's depression and dissolution, following the murder in 1975 of Betty Van Patter, would last a good five years. Paralyzed by guilt and confusion, Horowitz stopped doing politics, which had been his motive force since his teens. He barely wrote. He destroyed his marriage. To this day he speaks of his colleague's death, and his sense of responsibility for putting her in the way of danger, with such evident rawness that any notion of follow-the-money opportunism evaporates in the face of it.

Ronald Reagan and Christopher Hitchens, of all the subjects of this book, are the ones against whom the charge of opportunism can be most credibly leveled. Reagan made his most substantial turn to the Right during the period, from 1952 to 1961, when he was a spokesman for General Electric, which at the time was engaged in perhaps the most comprehensive pro-business, anti-union, anti–New Deal public relations effort ever devised by an American corporation. For years Reagan traveled the country by train, accompanied by ideologically correct GE handlers, reading the pamphlets and newsletters produced by the shop of GE's visionary public relations chief Lemuel Boulware. No one told him he had to let go of the liberal beliefs he'd held when he took the job, or replace them with the latest GE product line. He was hired to deliver not politics but good vibes and the frisson of celebrity to the company's workforce. But there was a system in place around him, a thick ecology of incentives, ideas, and identity that was designed not to coerce individual people into altering the politics they espoused but to do something more subtle and powerful: to move the very grounds of social consensus. Reagan, by nature a company man, was moved, and was rewarded in turn. He also began to perceive during this period how the ideas he was absorbing from GE, and the opportunities he was gaining as its spokesman, might help create a new future for him as a politician.

Christopher Hitchens made his most decisive turn away from the Left (if never quite over to the Right) at a moment when the winds of history were pushing with gale force against the Left, after September 11, 2001. And he was rewarded for doing so. New and more powerful friends and allies. More TV spots. Better sales for his books. More outlets in which to publish. A trans-Atlantic armada of tanks, fighter jets, Apache helicopters, smart missiles, bunker-busting bombs, and hard-faced soldiers set loose as if at his command to liberate Iraqis from the tyranny of a fascist dictator. It wasn't a frictionless moment for him. Friendships and long-standing affiliations were severed. Some distasteful new associations had to be tolerated. But for a while at least it was an exhilarating charge away from the Left.

For Reagan and Hitchens there were obvious incentives to move away from the Left, and very little of the overt trauma that haunted the other men in this book. But to survey their motives and choices and see a betrayal of principles and loyalties, for the sake of lucre, is to miss what was most interesting about the psychology of their turn. It wasn't that they betrayed their true selves for the sake of short-term gain, but that they set different aspects of their selves loose. It was the long-deferred release of energies that had been blocked, diluted, or sublimated by their identification with the Left. In Reagan there was a romantic love of country that had never harmonized comfortably with those elements on the Left drawn to pointing out how far the nation remains from realizing its ideals, to say nothing of those radicals who want to tear down those ideals and erect foreign idols in their place. There was his admiration for businessmen, and his comfort in their ranks. And there was a consistent affinity for localism and individualism that had remained alloyed to welfare state liberalism, in Reagan's political psyche, only by the figure of Franklin Roosevelt, in whose charismatic glow all contradictions were resolved.

For Hitchens it was a return to the family legacy of military valor and service to empire. It was a chance to see force deployed on the side of the downtrodden after so many years of writing furiously about force being applied against them. And it was a glorious not-to-be-missed chance to take a stand, as his hero George Orwell had during World

War II, on the side of Western civilization against the barbarian hordes, even (or especially) if that meant enduring insults and accusations from former allies on the Left.

None of these six men became something alien to who they were. Pieces of who they were, which had been there all along, were given more rein and license, while other pieces, which had been more dominant, were demoted or newly inflected.

Very few of us fit perfectly into the political suit we've chosen or been given to wear. It would be strange if we did, since at any given time the suits on offer are patched together according to complex social, political, historical, and other rather arbitrary patterns that are unlikely to overlay perfectly the equally complex ecosystems we inhabit as individuals. We fall in love with a candidate, and take with him the buzzwords, policy preferences, and talking points that have attached to him in order to bring into an election-winning coalition the greatest possible number of demographic subgroups. We pick a side in the culture war, because it really does feel as if there is a war going on for the soul of America, and with that allegiance comes a whole family of positions and preferences, some of which have very little to do with what motivated us to enlist in the first place.

Most of us pick the suit that fits us best and deny, ignore, or just muddle along with the ways it doesn't feel quite right. Because it feels reassuring to wear the same uniform as so many other people. Because it is good, and necessary, to put aside differences in the name of shared goals so that you can work toward important ends. Because it can bring clarity.

But things change. People change. Pieces of people change, while other pieces stay constant. A political identity is always a negotiation, between what it demands and who we are. This book is about the negotiation of specific left-wing identities (or in the case of Ronald Reagan, a left-of-center identity) and how those negotiations fell apart. The suit fit for a while, for meaningful reasons, and then it grew too tight, or too loose, also for meaningful reasons. It's about the humanity of those who abandoned us, politically, and the fallibility of those who arrived late to our side. And the book is a challenge, to the reader, to wrestle with the ways in which his or her own political suit might strain at the shoulders a bit more than is comfortable to admit.

1

In Spite of Noise and Confusion: Whittaker Chambers

I n the summer of 1923, while sitting outside a café in Weimar Berlin, on semi-voluntary leave from college, Whittaker Chambers noticed a woman walking by crying. As he watched her all the terrifying truths of the twentieth century seemed to collapse into the moment.

"It would miss something to say that she was crying," he remembered. "Tears were streaming down her face—tears which she made no effort to conceal, which, in flowing, did not even distort her features. She simply walked slowly past, proudly erect, unconcerned about any spectacle she made. And here is what is nightmarish: nobody paid the slightest attention to her. The catastrophe was universal. Everybody knew what she signified. Nobody had anything left over from his own disaster to notice hers."[1]

He looked at the woman, at the men and women looking through her, and held in his hands the two perceptions that would possess him throughout the rest of his life, that had, he sometimes felt, been born with him. The first was that Western civilization was most probably dying. The other was that he was called to do something about it.

As a boy there had been only ghostly presentiments of disaster, allied to that sense of great expectation that lonely, bright children often
gather in themselves to give meaning to their alienation. He would do
something heroic someday, in the face of great danger, though what he
didn't know.

In college at Columbia in the early 1920s he found a language to
give form to his perceptions. It was the modernist vocabulary current
in his set of advanced young men, spiced with a hint of Marxism. God
was dead. All that was solid was melting into air. Everything was frac-
turing and fragmentation. All one could do was be manful and clear-
eyed when faced with the dissolution of the old truths, and perhaps
write some good poetry.[2]

As a Marxist, which he became in 1925 and remained until 1938,
he believed the West was dying dialectically, sundered by the force of its
own contradictions. But there was a way through the darkness. There
was a program. If enough men and women toiled hard enough a new
kind of civilization might burgeon up from the remains of the old.

As a conservative, anticommunist, and believing Christian, all
of which he became next and remained until his death in 1961, he
thought the West was dying because it had turned away from God and
toward the prideful illusion that man was the measure of all things. The
Soviet Union was the most overt instantiation of this heresy, but the
United States was its shadow brother in sin, shallow and soft where the
Soviets were cruel and hard. What was left to do, for those who would,
was hold back the fall for as long as possible. When that failed, as it
probably would, there remained the charge to bear witness, and with
such witness to keep lit the flame of hope for future generations.

"It is idle to talk about preventing the wreck of Western civilization," he wrote a friend in 1954. "It is already a wreck from within.
That is why we can hope to do little more now than snatch a fingernail
of a saint from the rack or a handful of ashes from the faggots, and
bury them secretly in a flowerpot against the day, ages hence, when a
few men begin again to dare to believe that there was once something

else, that something else is thinkable, and need some evidence of what it was, and the fortifying knowledge that there were those who, at the great nightfall, took loving thought to preserve the tokens of hope and truth."[3]

There are different ways of reading the arc of Chambers. One is to see it as no arc at all, but rather a loop, an endless staging of the same primal melodrama in which the local setting and color are updated but the themes enacted stay exhaustingly constant. Still and always huddles the lonely, hurting child who projects his inner misery onto the world, armoring himself in stories of heroism and redemptive suffering to deflect or dignify his pain. Communist or conservative, modernist or Christian, the hour is always nigh, the armies of darkness are always massed at the gate, and the fate of the world always depends on the actions of the valiant few.

Alternatively, we might accept Chambers's own reading of the data, see his as a genuine journey of spiritual growth and redemption. He was a lost soul, but one with a strong tropism toward the divine. For a time he channeled his yearnings into the vessels of the world: literature, ideology, revolution. Then he fell low enough for God to find him. He was saved and knew himself at last for the fallen, sinful, endlessly loved creature he was. And with that clearing of his vision he was able to perceive correctly the nature of modernity that before he'd seen distorted.

In the one biography that approaches in literary force Chambers's crafting of his own story, that there's any kind of arc at all in his chaotic-seeming life is unclear at first. Only after much suffering and many missteps does its shape finally begin to assert itself. It's a progression toward maturity, an increasing harmony between the intuitions that drove Chambers, the often snarled grooves of his psyche, and the concrete choices and commitments he made over the course of his days. In the end, in this version of the story, he achieved a kind of grace not because he had the right answers, or chose the right side, or knew himself perfectly, but because he persisted in trying to become himself more fully.[4]

Whittaker Chambers had some truths that were fixed in him young: There was a deep pain in the world. He was called to sacrifice himself in the cause of healing or excising it. These convictions preceded reason. They preceded politics. They were the raw ore he spent his life trying to forge into authentic and correct political beliefs and commitments.

To say that isn't to say that he did a good job of it. Or that it was psychologically healthy to devote his life so urgently to finding the right political forms through which to express his inner being. But it is to say that the task he set himself was the right one. Maybe the only one. It was to live his truths as well and fully as possible.

Chambers is fascinating, among other reasons, because he presented in such distilled form how extraordinarily vexing that task is for all of us. Like him, we're fixed at a young age in core ways of seeing and being. Then we're thrown out into the storm of history, buffeted left, right, and upside down, and forced to spend our lives trying to stagger the right path forward.

The blows don't always land on us as heavily or as often as they did on Chambers. Politics isn't the only realm through which we can choose to travel. We don't all go as far as he did in pursuit of authenticity. But we all go a great distance. We encounter new information along the way, and have to decide whether and how to change in response to it. As we change we pray we're not betraying our deepest convictions in the process. And at the end our fate, in some way, is like his. We die without knowing whether our story, as told by posterity, will be one of triumph, tragedy, or treachery.

> It is the childhood of a poet, a criminal, an ideologue, a spy, a closet homosexual, a scholar, or an informer.[5]
>
> —ELIOT WEINBERGER

"I was born in Philadelphia, on April 1, 1901," wrote Whittaker Chambers in his autobiography, *Witness*. "When my father, Jay Chambers, who was then a young staff artist on the *New York World*, received the startling news, he crumpled the telegram and threw it into the waste basket. He did not believe it and he did not think April Fool jokes were in good taste.

"Mine was a dry birth and I weighed twelve pounds and measured fourteen inches across the shoulders. . . . Other women seem to forget the sharpest agonies of childbirth. My mother overcame her memory sufficiently to bear a second son, my brother, Richard Godfrey. But my terrible birth was fixed indelibly in her mind. Throughout my boyhood and my youth, she repeated to me the circumstances of that ordeal until they were vivid to me. They made me acutely unhappy, and her repetition of them made me even unhappier (for it seemed to imply a reproach). But I never told her so."[6]

The family of Jay Vivian (Whittaker) Chambers was too excruciatingly neurotic to be typical of the new century that was coming into being around them, but it was symptomatic. Chambers's father, Jay, was a talented illustrator and half-closeted gay man whose passion, as his son eventually came to realize, was compressed into a sublimely choked obsession with "ornament, costume, scenery—the minutiae and surfaces of things . . . the spell of the serpentine neck, the elegant anemia and flowing robes, the flight from the actual and ugly into the arabesque and the exotic."[7] Jay spent months every year hand-making the gorgeously embellished Christmas cards he sent out to a select group of appreciative friends. He built miniature, architecturally precise, classical temples out of matchboxes, and seeded the house with artifacts and totems of the Xanadus of his mind.

Chambers's mother, Laha, who had been an actress before she moved to New York and met Jay, shared with her husband a love of the exotic and high—"culture," as they extolled it to their children. She declaimed poetry and dramatic monologues, sang sad songs in three languages, instructed her sons in the glories of music and theater and literature.

Beneath the surface of their artsy communion, however, husband and wife were badly suited to each other. She was overemotional where he was severely contained. Her craving for affection and affirmation was met by him with, at best, an effortful formality, and at worst by emotional and occasionally physical torment. Her domestic ideal—a circulation of warmth and intimacy throughout the home, between parents and children, from room to room—wasn't merely incompatible with what Jay desired, but antithetical. It was refuge he sought, a place of solitude in which to sketch or embellish, away from domestic entanglement. By the time their son Jay Vivian (he wouldn't adopt "Whittaker" until college) was old enough to have a perception of his parents' marriage, it was a suppurating thing, one that would only bleed out further over the course of his childhood.[8]

In 1904 the family moved to the coastal town of Lynbrook, Long Island, about twenty miles outside Manhattan. It was an impulsive and ultimately self-defeating move for Laha, who had made a point of finding the yellow frame house on Earle Avenue. The town looked, on the surface, like the proper setting for the graceful life of which she'd long fantasized, but in truth Lynbrook had little culture and was filled with the kinds of provincials inclined to find both Jay and Laha hard to digest.

Even more corrosively, the move was made over Jay's objections, and was interpreted by him as a door slamming shut on what remained of his dreams of life. He had hoped to stay close to his work, where he was liked and respected, and to his coterie of friends, who shared his appreciation for beautiful surfaces. Instead he was exiled to Long Island, condemned to precisely the life he'd always defined himself against.

Jay took with him to Lynbrook a grudge that manifested, most visibly, in a refusal to spend any of his comfortably middle-class income on repairing the house, which descended into disreputability. The yellow paint on the exterior faded further and "peeled off in an incurable acne."[9] The green shutters wore to a shabby blue. The joining at the roof of the main house and the kitchen (which had once been a separate structure) was badly done, and when it rained, or in the spring when the snow melted, the kitchen would flood. Inside the house, the wallpaper grew stained and cracked. A piece of the ceiling in the dining room fell down, and because Jay wouldn't give her the money to hire someone to repair it, Laha covered it over with a cheesecloth that remained there, ruefully patching the hole, for more than a decade. The house got so dilapidated that Laha finally went to the city and pawned her jewelry for the money to hire some men to fix the most glaring of the problems.

The house, unfortunately, was just one of the symbolic vessels through which Jay and Laha articulated their contempt for each other. Among their favorite bludgeons were their sons, whom Laha would drench in a performative affection that was implicitly reproachful of her husband, and whom Jay would treat with a cool contempt that was meant to reflect onto his wife (and back onto himself). Even their eldest son's name was a site of conflict. Laha refused to let the boy call himself Jay. She declared instead that he would be known by his girlish middle name, Vivian, which she had bestowed on him, over her husband's protests, because she thought it sounded English. Jay called his boy "Beadle" and would "utter the ugly word with four or five different intonations each of which was charged with quiet derision, aimed not at me, but at my mother."[10]

The effect on Whittaker, of his parents' endless struggle with each other and with their own dashed expectations of life, was a marked alienation. He was alienated from his father, who, "At the least loving gesture or word . . . seemed to withdraw in a slow, visible motion that I can compare only to the creepy contraction of a snake into its coils."[11] His mother was a source of love but also anxiety and oppression, who would lash out at her sons if she felt herself abandoned or betrayed. As Whittaker grew older, he began to see something dangerously snakelike in her as well.

The other kids in town found Whittaker (Vivian, as they knew him) strange and unsocializable. It wasn't just his neglected, rotting teeth and poor hygiene that set him apart, or the costume-ish clothes that his mother dressed him in. By the time he started grade school, he was precociously serious and quick to distrust, and burdened by his parents with eccentric manners that were as distant as possible from those of his working- and middle-class schoolmates. He was, as one of his teachers remembered him, "the pudgy little boy standing alone at the sidelines of the school playground, silent and observant, never taking part."[12]

The petty bourgeoisie of Lynbrook assigned a role to the Chamberses. They were "the French family," and over the years both Jay and Laha managed to insert themselves, as messengers of culture, into the life of the community. None of their events, productions, or initiatives, however, made adjusting to Lynbrook any easier for their older son.[13] He was embarrassed by seeing his parents on stage, and by the theatrical flotsam that would accumulate around the house. Particularly mortifying were the roles he was often assigned in his father's productions, including an annual turn as a nearly nude, gauze-draped cherub in the Pre-Raphaelite favorite *The Rubaiyat*.

The consolations that the young Whittaker found were solitary ones. Lynbrook was still a nearly unspoiled place, not so different in its contours from what it had been when populated by the Rockaway Algonquins. It was a landscape of cedar trees and gentle rivers, salt marshes and organic-seeming villages, bounded at its edge by the vast, brooding presence of the Atlantic Ocean. Chambers was uncommonly sensitive to this natural beauty, and he would spend much of his childhood losing himself in it. He went out alone mostly, but also tramped around with his easygoing younger brother, with whom he was close. When he was small he would even take walks with his father, who loved to sketch the sea and the trees and who was occasionally able to discover himself in a mood, and in a setting, in which he could communicate a kind of affection for his son. All this combined in Chambers to produce, from a very young age, a sense of spiritual connection to the land, as well as a feeling that the natural world contained within it secrets and prophecies just at the edge of hearing, that he might understand if only he listened long and closely enough.

"Two impressions sum up my earliest childhood world. I am lying in bed. I have been told sternly to go to sleep. I do not want to. Then I become conscious of an extreme silence which the fog always folds over the land. On the branches of the trees the mist has turned to moisture, and, as I listen to its irregular drip drip pause drip pause, I pass into the mist of sleep.

"The other memory is of my brother. He is standing on our front porch, dressed in one of those shapeless wraps children used to be disfigured with. It is raining softly. I am in the house. He wants me to come out to him. I do not want to go. In a voice whose only reproach is a plaintiveness so gentle that it has sounded in the cells of my mind through all the years, he calls: 'Bro (for brother), it's mainin (raining), Bro.' He calls it over and over without ever raising his voice. He needs me because he knows what no child should know: that the soft rain is sad. I will not understand this knowledge in him until too late, when it has ended his life. And so I do not go out onto the porch."[14]

Whittaker also found solace in stories. His parents had an eclectic library through which he was free to range from an early age, and he read the novels of Dickens, the plays of Shakespeare, biographies of eminent American men like Hamilton and Lincoln, and the poetry of aesthetes like Dante Gabriel Rossetti. Jay and Laha also subscribed, for their sons, to *St. Nicholas Magazine*, which was both an impressively serious magazine for children, with contributions from many of the best authors and artists of the time, and a stunningly earnest monument to the prevailing creed of late Victorian middle-class American aspiration.[15]

Chambers's imagination was nurtured by *St. Nicholas*–style stories of heroism and unflinching virtue, by the books he found around the house, by his parents' flamboyant tastes, and in particular by one story that resonated on all of his frequencies.

"It was an old-fashioned book," he wrote in *Witness*. "The text was set in parallel columns, two columns to a page. There were more than a thousand pages. The type was small. I took the book to the little diamond-shaped attic window to read the small type in the light. I opened to the first page and read the brief foreword:

"*So long as there shall exist, by reason of law and custom, a social damnation, which, in the face of civilization, creates hell on earth, and complicates a destiny which is divine with human fatality; so long as the three problems of the age—the degradation of man by poverty, the ruin of woman by hunger, and the stunting of childhood by physical and spiritual night—are not solved; so long as, in certain areas, social asphyxia shall be possible; . . . so long as ignorance and misery remain on earth, books like this cannot be useless.*

". . . The book, of course, was Victor Hugo's *Les Misérables—The Wretched of the Earth*. In its pages can be found the play of forces that carried me into the Communist Party, and in the same pages can be found the play of forces that carried me out of the Communist Party."[16]

It was a vision that would stay with Chambers, and continue to condition his view of the world, until the end of his life. Not just the melodrama, which appealed to the melodramatic son of Jay and Laha, or the evocation of suffering, which appealed to the suffering little boy. He found deep solace in the novel's conviction that suffering can have great purpose, that without suffering the heroic life is impossible, and that all human stories, no matter how puny they seem on the surface, are part of a grand struggle between light and dark, meaning and de-spair. He was moved by the particular models of self-sacrificing righ-teousness that the novel embodied—by the holy force of the Bishop of Digne; by the holy lies of Sister Simplice, who sacrificed a bit of her own soul so that another could go on to spread justice in the world; and by the self-lacerating heroism of Jean Valjean, the former galley slave eternally haunted by his past, hounded by the law, and driven to do good in a fallen world that conspired at every turn to thwart his noble intentions.

Les Misérables also told a story of the wretchedness of the modern world that made more sense to Chambers than the sunny story of progress and order he got from the adults around him. Life in early twentieth-century America wasn't nearly as wretched as it was in France at the beginning of the nineteenth, but it was still miserable for millions, barely tolerable for millions more, and pleasant for at best a sizable minority of the population.

People died young, suddenly, ridiculously. Bacteria, and its role in the passage of disease, had been discovered only in the last years of the nineteenth century, and the science of antibiotics wouldn't mature until the 1930s and '40s. Any kind of sickness—an infected hangnail, a fever, a cough—might be the first domino in a short cascade that led to death. Epidemics and pandemics rolled across the populace like stampedes. Fires took out cities. Childbirth was always a gamble for the mothers, and often a prelude to early death for the children. Second and third marriages were as common as they would be in the late twentieth century, but it was early death, rather than divorce, that gave men and women their next chances at love. Science hadn't even yet seriously taken up the task of ameliorating common discomforts, and for toothaches (from which Chambers suffered terribly), gout, eczema, arthritis, nausea, the whole panoply of pains, itches, aches, wheezes, sores, and sniffles, there were few better cures than the snake oil remedies, usually made with narcotics, whose advertisements filled the pages of the daily newspapers.

Inflecting all this struggle was a less quantifiable, but no less destabilizing, fear of modernity—of a rapidly accelerating society that, whatever its promise of material abundance, seemed to offer the people of America far less certainty than the old worlds of family, farm, tradition, God, ethnic homogeneity, church, and community.[17]

Making the experience of misery and confusion even that bit more subjectively excruciating was a collective American insistence that the bad things shouldn't be mentioned too often or worried about too openly. To be unhappy was normal, unavoidable, but to dwell on that unhappiness, and to refuse to affirm that it would be absolved by the gains of the future, was a bit queer. As soon-to-be-president Teddy Roosevelt wrote in "The American Boy," published in *St. Nicholas* in 1900, "in life, as in a foot-ball game, the principle to follow is: Hit the line hard; don't foul and don't shirk, but hit the line hard!"[18]

Such currents impinged on Whittaker Chambers's existence in subtle ways. Lynbrook was suburbanizing and modernizing, and although its overt politics weren't particularly nuanced, the rough-and-tumble politics of the schoolyard, the factory, the church pews, and the barber shop were pervaded by an anxiety that Chambers, even as a teenager, could taste.

Less subtle was the disorder of his home. When Chambers was seven, Jay and Laha's animosity finally exceeded the capacity of the house in Lynbrook to contain it, and Jay left, taking an apartment (and a lover) in Brooklyn. The separation was a mixed blessing for Whittaker and Richard. In their father's absence the temperature of the house cooled. There were no more fights between Jay and Laha, no more of Jay's contempt, no more dinners getting cold as they waited to see if he would arrive home on the next train from the city, or the next, or the next. In his absence, however, Laha and her sons endured a kind of half-poverty that was typical of the time, when the middle class hadn't yet embedded itself securely in a thick matrix of social capital, savings, and welfare state benefits.

The money that Jay sent from Brooklyn was usually enough for his family to subsist, and the grandparents were always in reserve in the event of truly catastrophic need, but Chambers was suddenly, undeniably poor. After dark, he and his brother Richard and their mother would steal wooden beams and scraps from construction sites to heat the home. They raised and sold chickens and vegetables. Laha sold cakes to townspeople. Their dinners became peasant-like, with efficient foods like rutabagas, pea soup, spaghetti, and rice displacing their old diet, which had been oriented around the rich tastes of the food-loving Jay.

"One of my mother's ways of managing," wrote Chambers, "was to charge things at the stores. 'Charge it,' I would say as casually as possible, with increasing embarrassment when I knew that the unpaid bill was big. Sometimes, the baker's wife would whisper with him before letting me have a loaf of bread. Sometimes a shopkeeper would say: 'Tell your mother, no more credit till the bill is paid.' Once an angry woman leaned over the counter and sneered at me: 'Your mother is a broken-down stagecoach.' In time the bills were always paid, but I knew a good deal about the relations of the poor man and the shopkeeper before I read about them in Karl Marx."[19]

Jay stayed away for three years, and then returned to Lynbrook. The family resumed the appearance of semi-normalcy, but life inside the home was as awful as ever. Jay no longer even bothered to play at the family game. In New York City, away from his family, he was known to his friends as a funny, generous man.[20] At home he was a sullen child, a tyrant, or a contemptuously bemused bystander. Mostly, he retreated to his room, escaping into the minutiae of his arts and crafts.

Laha's pathology, too, became increasingly a burden to Whittaker as he struggled to construct a self that could bear the weight of his unhappiness in the world. "I felt [her love] around me like coils," he wrote, "interposing between me and reality, coddling my natural weaknesses, to keep the world away from me, but also to keep me away from the world."[21]

As an adolescent, Chambers began to distance himself from his mother, and became more openly antagonistic toward his father. Even his relationship with his younger brother, though it remained intense, was altered, as Laha and Richard reacted to Whittaker's withdrawal by reconstituting as a dyad.

In high school, Chambers became a rebel of sorts. He pushed himself to curse and disobey and under-perform. He barely passed most of his courses, doing well only in English and Latin, where his enthusiasm for the subjects overwhelmed his urge to act out. Among his peers, he was an outsider both by default and by choice.

"Vivian didn't care much about his appearance," a high-school classmate later told one of Chambers's biographers. "The boys used to call him 'Stinky.' His hair was never combed. He usually wore dirty sneakers. He was a butterball, soft and effeminate. None of the kids had much use for him."[22]

Outside of school, Chambers was more forgiving of himself. He expanded the range of his wanderings. "I became a haunter of the woods and the fields," he wrote. "I would set out by myself before the family was stirring in the morning and spend whole days in the woods, which required of me only that I be silent, patient and harmless. . . . I could soon find my way about them even at night, as I sometimes used to do. For I never found the loneliness of the woods at night as disturbing as people by daylight."[23]

Although his parents and teachers couldn't, or wouldn't, offer him much in the way of intellectual guidance, he found other ways to cultivate his garden. Working mostly on his own, he taught himself at least the rudiments of Gaelic, Russian, Spanish, Italian, French, Arabic, Persian, Hindustani, and Assyrian cuneiform. He got up every morning, before school, and studied French and German, eventually acquiring a near-fluency in German that would later serve him well as a professional translator and as a player in the polyglot world of international communism. He initiated a correspondence with George Frazier Black, a philologist at the New York Public Library, who sent him grammars and even sent him out, as a kind of apprentice field philologist, to visit a gypsy camp near Lynbrook and collect vocabularies of the particular dialect spoken there.

By the time he graduated from high school, Chambers had cobbled together his various influences, impulses, and legacies into a proto-political style that would remain constant even as he found radically different vehicles through which to discharge his pent-up political and intellectual energy. His perspective was global, epic, esoteric, romantic. He was more fascinated by world affairs than domestic matters. He measured history in ages and empires rather than in institutions and votes. He sought hints of cosmic significance in the rustle of leaves in the forest, in the chick birthing from its egg in his attic, in the bully picking on the weakling behind the school. He had a weakness for the grand gesture, the spontaneous life-altering act, the doomed but courageous stand. He had, as well, a mystical impulse that only rarely found its way into church or other overt forms of religiosity.

Chambers's political journey of the next few decades would be driven by an authentic pursuit of answers to some of the deep political and existential questions of his time. It would also, however, be fueled by a private desire to quench his loneliness and alienation in the currents of History.

After graduating from high school, and after two months in a job clerking at a local bank, Chambers and a friend, with no warning to their families, snuck out of Lynbrook and began a journey they hoped would eventually take them to Mexico.

Their savings got them to Baltimore, where they found a room in a boardinghouse and, that Monday morning, a job ripping out and laying railroad track near the Capitol. The work was nasty and dangerous, and the housing was spartan, with the veteran laborers receiving a bit of personal space in a boardinghouse and the newer men, like Chambers, getting only a bunk in a collective barracks.

For most of the men it was just another soul-eroding stint in a lifetime of such temporary laboring work. For Chambers, who'd left home precisely in search of the authentic life, it was bracing. The work was uncomplicated and exhausting in a way that soothed him. And there was a kind of solidarity among the men that bypassed his defensiveness.

"They were my first International," he wrote. "Practically every European nationality was represented. Yet they had no nationality, just as they had no homes. . . . They had reached that bleak barracks in the unheroic course of a workingman's everlasting search for work which, as Tolstoy had noted, beggars the wanderings of Odysseus."[24]

Characteristically, Chambers learned as he went. He discussed *Madame Bovary* and the novels of Zola with a Belgian worker who claimed to have once been the overseer of slave laborers in the rubber tree fields in Malaysia. He added to his small Russian vocabulary with the help of

a Russian worker who was overjoyed simply to hear someone say anything in his native language. With Manuel, a Venezuelan native who
was an admirer of Woodrow Wilson and a believer in the necessity of a
League of Nations, Chambers wandered the boulevards of Washington,
practicing his Spanish and debating world politics.

For three months, Chambers labored at the job, outlasting almost
every other worker. When the contract ended and everyone was let
go, he took the money he'd earned and bought a ticket to New Orleans. Unable to find work, he languished there for two months, just
absorbing and observing the desperate lives of the tenants surrounding
the French Quarter courtyard in which he'd rented a room. When his
money finally came to an end, he wired home to his parents—whom
he'd kept apprised, by letter, of his adventures—for the money to buy a
train ticket back to New York.

The typical Columbia University freshman, when Whittaker Chambers arrived at college in the fall of 1920, was much like his fellows at
the other Ivy League schools. He was a polished young man of Prot-
estant extraction with tasteful expectations of going on to a career as
a banker, lawyer, minister, or senator. But Columbia also, and almost
against its will, had a population of students that better reflected
the character of the city—propulsively ambitious, first-generation,
Jewish.

Most of these boys had hopes that weren't very refined. They simply pursued their futures of success, esteem, and wealth with greater
intensity than their gentile classmates did. There were a few, however,
in whom the drive to assimilate and excel was fused with a ravenous desire to know and discover—even to change the terms by which America
understood itself. It was among this lot that Chambers, for the first
time in his life, felt like he belonged.

"Were I forced to attempt a generalization concerning these seven,
I should speak of their extraordinary individuality, sharpened as it is in
each case by a certain lack of adjustment to the conventions of college

and other life," wrote poet Mark Van Doren, in 1927, about the coterie of students with whom Chambers ran.[25]

The article, "Jewish Students I Have Known," was commissioned by the *Menorah Journal* because Van Doren, who was a gentile, had developed a reputation while teaching at Columbia as a friend of the Jews. It described, with a poet's eye, seven of the best students Columbia had ever seen. There was the future art historian Meyer Schapiro, who would pace Van Doren's office discoursing brilliantly on the nature of Byzantine art, and who was, in Van Doren's memory, such a luminous figure, so bubbling over with knowledge and the passion to learn, that he "glowed." There was Louis Zukofsky, whose hyper-cerebral modernist poetry would, within a few years, catch the eye of Ezra Pound. Of Lionel Trilling, who would one day become the first tenured Jewish professor in the Columbia English department, Van Doren wrote, "What he will eventually do, if he does it at all, will be lovely, for it will be the fruit of a pure intelligence slowly ripened in not too fierce a sun."[26] Clifton Fadiman, who would become one of the great emissaries of high culture to the American middle classes, was already so fluent in the byways and catchwords of Western literature that he made many of his professors feel unschooled.

For Chambers, this particular group of Jewish students became more than just good friends; they were portals to a new way of life. He first met them in the gym locker room, where he and other commuter students ate the lunches they brought with them from home. They would sit on the long, narrow benches between the rows of lockers and debate the great issues of the day. Was the war in Europe truly over, or just prologue to another war? With the dissolution of so many old empires, what forms of political organization would emerge to fill the void? Was Lenin's revision of Marxist doctrine a necessary adjustment to the conditions of Russian development or an opportunistic corruption of authentic communism? Did the prosperity of the 1920s conceal a fundamental rottenness at the core of twentieth-century life?

These young men took on, too, the grander and more eternal

questions of life. What place was there for faith and religious ritual after Copernicus, Darwin, Freud, and Nietzsche had so mortally wounded God? What was the nature of the psyche? What was the proper relationship between art and politics? They talked of Russian novelists, the rise and fall of great civilizations, revolution, dialectics, the soul of man under mechanization and mass organization.

"To me they were an entirely new race of men," Chambers wrote toward the end of his life. "Their seriousness was organic. . . . They sat there, that consciously separate proletariat, loudly munching their sandwiches, because they came of a stock that, after God, worshipped education and the things of the mind. They were there, in most cases, by acts of superhuman sacrifice and contrivance on the part of their families. To me that seriousness was deeply impressive."[27]

Chambers had arrived at Columbia without a real organizing principle. By his second year, under the influence of his Jewish friends, he'd become a full-fledged, free-thinking bohemian who looked to the literature of modern angst and social protest for meaning. He fell as well under the influence of Van Doren,[28] soon accepting as his own Van Doren's gospel that the poet's life is the most noble life of them all.

Chambers held his own, too, in the dance of influence. His knowledge of the culture and history of Europe couldn't compare with that of his friends, whose intellectual breadth seemed to him almost genetic. He was, however, as rawly talented and as intellectually intense as his Jewish friends, and he evinced an air of shaggy Americana that impressed them. He was the only one who'd torn up rail in the bowels of Baltimore, dissipated himself in New Orleans, trafficked with Gypsies. Even his family's dysfunction was a badge of experience that the Jewish boys, who were adored (or at least prized) by their families, could admire from a safe distance. Chambers was also Van Doren's favorite student—so compelling a personality, in fact, that Van Doren felt it necessary to slide a few references to him into the essay on Jewish students.

Van Doren didn't name Chambers in the essay, as he did the other students. Nor did he sketch his character as he did with the others, but he was, wrote Van Doren, "perhaps the best one of them all."[29] His presence in the essay is highly charged, testament not just to Chambers's talent but to the gravity-warping effect of his personality.

"I think he saw himself as a center of interest and as a battleground for momentous struggles," wrote drama critic John Gassner (another of Van Doren's beautiful seven) in 1962, a year after Chambers's death. "In a penetratingly quiet way he called attention to himself as a man of destiny. He had a talent for dramatizing himself as an important person with a high destiny, possibly as the hero of a tragedy slowly but inevitably taking shape, as a seeker after faith, and as a seeker after knowledge. He thought hard. He studied hard, he was curious about everything; he was impatient with sloth and he scorned mediocrity in any form. He dressed like a derelict but carried himself like a king."[30]

The style of Chambers's beliefs at Columbia would have been familiar to anyone who'd known him before or would know him after. When he believed in something, he believed it all the way down, or he struggled to do so until a given notion no longer seemed sufficient to carry the burden of his restless energies. The contents of his beliefs, however, were in flux.

Within the broad outlines of his new calling to be a poet, and with his own particular and ineradicable bent toward drama, Chambers absorbed and experimented with many of the ideas and energies that were ricocheting around the walls of Columbia. Along with Van Doren's ironic, subversive humanism, there was the huskier humanism of John Erskine, who in 1920 launched the first of the General Honors seminars that would eventually evolve into Columbia's Great Books curriculum. There was a cadre of young instructors, some of them veterans of World War I, whom Chambers remembered as so cynical and soggy with ennui that they were barely able to muster the energy to sit up straight while teaching their classes. In the philosophy department, the pragmatism of John Dewey prevailed. There were powerful remnants, as well, of the nineteenth century—men for whom the teaching of literature, philosophy, and history was best performed as a series of offerings to the icons of past greatness.

It was also the first years of the manic 1920s, when the political conflicts—between nations, between labor and management, between Left and Right—that had characterized the wartime and postwar years were mostly sublimated into a kind of soft cultural revolution. Sports became a national obsession, and the New York Yankees perhaps the first truly national sports team. Trends of all sorts sprang up and faded away. Petting parties among the young got salacious, and piously scandalized, coverage in the newspapers. Music got earthier, and was disseminated to the masses through the new technology of broadcast radio. Money was being made so fast and so easily, particularly in the stock market, that moneymaking itself became an object of cultural fascination. It was, as Chambers would later write of another brief era of manic overflow, "one of those rare interludes of history where everybody who could possibly do so had a wonderful time."[31]

To Chambers, writing decades later, the cultural eroticism of the 1920s was of a piece with Columbia's intellectual eroticism, which seduced him away from the spiritual and conservative concerns he'd brought with him to college. "I was a boy who, above all, needed firm and wise direction," he later wrote.[32] Instead he got Mark Van Doren, an ironist whose influence on his students was so profound, and so evidently dangerous, that Chambers was once grabbed in the hall by a rival instructor, forced to hold still for the recital of an ominous lyric by the eighteenth-century Scottish poet James Thomson, and then cast off with the injunction: "Be careful of Mark Van Doren. He is clever and he is kind. But his mind has no boundaries."[33]

Later, Chambers would come to agree with this assessment of Van Doren, and he would resent his old teacher for his boundary-dissolving influence.[34]

At the time, however, Chambers was intoxicated by the sense of possibility offered to him by Columbia. Everything old and solid was evaporating, but new forms were emerging from the mist, and he and his friends felt they were poised to be the poets and thinkers who would give them flesh.

Chambers, like generations of college kids before and after him, was also just having a lot of fun. Like his father, he could be joyful and lighthearted around friends in a way that wasn't possible with family. When he didn't get in the way of himself, he was an extremely compelling young man—loyal, sweet, funny, affectionate—and someone who had the capacity to form deep and long-lasting commitments.

In his sophomore year Chambers moved into a dorm on campus, and threw himself even more completely into the literary life. He began publishing poems and stories in the two student literary magazines, *Varsity* and *The Morningside*, and made a splash, in particular, with his story in the March 1, 1922, issue of *The Morningside*.

The story, "That Damn Fool," took up two-thirds of that issue and exhibited a voice that was so confident that it marked Chambers as perhaps the singular literary talent on campus. It told the tale of Everett Holmes, a shiftless dockside clerk in New York City who, after being fired from his job, decides abruptly to make his way to Russia to fight for the White Army against the Bolsheviks. Holmes's long, incident-filled journey to Russia, and his encounters with death on the battlefield, have the effect of transforming him from the mama's boy he was when he embarked into a kind of warrior prophet, a "mad monk" who carried a cross before him as he led his band of Russian soldiers into battle. When he's finally caught by the Bolsheviks—and crucified, tortured, and then dismembered—he dies as a martyr, though to what cause or idea, exactly, is left unclear.

Soon after "That Damn Fool" was published, Chambers was named editor of *The Morningside* for the following year. By that next fall, when he became editor, Chambers and his friends had distilled their philosophical concerns into an aesthetic ideology they named "profanism."

Profanism, as announced in the editorial note of his first issue as editor, was their version of the modernism that was taking mature form, elsewhere, in the poetry of T. S. Eliot, the novels of Joyce, the performativity of the Dadaists, the architecture of Le Corbusier. It was a rejection of what was seen as the sentimental optimism of the nineteenth century—its reliance for comfort on the illusions of God, tradition, and capitalism, and its conviction that history was a natural progression toward greater harmony and justice. It was a cold and clear-eyed embrace of what they saw as the fractured and alienated nature of modern life, a willingness, they wrote, "to wipe away the lactic droolings of the late century and accept something more nearly approaching reality than the ethical, religious and materialistic hypocrisy of modern life."[35] And it was, as well, an exuberant project of a group of students—"the Morningside circle," as one historian would later describe them[36]— who were simply excited to be young and brilliant and in the company of one another.

For Chambers profanism was also the name he gave to his latest, and in many respects his last, wholehearted attempt to find a literary form that was majestic enough to dignify his emotional suffering yet also porous enough to play host to what was more joyous and eccentric in him. His short play in that fall issue of *The Morningside*, "A Play for Puppets," was dedicated, tongue-in-cheek, to the Antichrist, and it consisted primarily of mildly profane banter between two Roman soldiers who were guarding the tomb of Jesus. Mostly, they joke about sex, sparing only a few comments for Jesus, who was interesting to them mostly for his refusal to have sex. Jesus himself makes a quick appearance only at the end of the play, when he plays the existentialist with the angel who's descended to earth to shepherd his ascension to heaven.

ANGEL: *Thou shall stand upon the right hand of the throne of God and intercede for the Souls of sinful men.*
VOICE OF CHRIST: *What is sin? Do not men live and do not men die? I wish to sleep.*[37]

The brief play proved far more explosive than anyone had expected. Faculty and students attacked its author as a heretic, the dean ordered Chambers to recover every copy of the magazine he could find (Chambers refused), and soon the controversy grew so charged that it was covered by the New York papers.

"Student disapproval was excited," reported the *New York Times*, "by the leading article of the magazine, 'A Play for Puppets,' by John Kelly, a nom de plume of the editor-in-chief, Whittaker Chambers, '24, of Lynbrook, L.I. The scene is laid in front of the Holy Sepulchre, and, in the view of the Committee on Student Publications, deals objectionably with the resurrection."[38]

The furor, and the administration's decision to side with the offended parties against the editors of *The Morningside*, took Chambers by surprise. Van Doren had assured him that the play was worth publishing. It was mild in comparison to much of the modernist literature that Chambers was reading, and gentle in its blasphemy. And though his aim had been to provoke, he had no reason to expect that it would provoke on such a scale. The overreaction brought to the surface what had been, to that point, only a lurking suspicion in Chambers that the liberalism of Columbia was simply too shallow to serve as a guide to living. The institution, he rapidly concluded under the duress of its censure, was a fraud. It could neither stand with its students, who after all were doing only as they'd been taught to do—thinking the best there was to think, grappling with the fundamental dilemmas of the modern era—nor could it even respond to his transgression with an authentic religious revulsion. Chambers's sin, so far as he could tell, wasn't sacrilege but bad taste, conduct unbecoming a Columbia gentleman.

After a brief spurt of bravado, during which he claimed to be invigorated by the fight, Chambers crumbled. His class attendance, which had always been spotty, ceased entirely, and by the end of the semester he'd decided that college, for the time being, wasn't for him. He withdrew at the end of the fall, and although he would try Columbia again, briefly, a year later, it was no longer a plausible life for him. His friends

were mostly graduated, his commitment to radical politics had begun
to crowd out his literary energies, and his family and his love life had
grown too unruly for him to recapture the romance of college that had
given him a few exhilarating years of reprieve from the full weight of
his problems.

In the fall of 1924, as Whittaker Chambers's last stint at Columbia was
winding down, he chanced upon a translation of a speech, "The Soviets
at Work," that Vladimir Lenin had given to his fellow Bolsheviks a few
months after their successful revolution.

By this point Chambers was no stranger to radicalism. Even as a
child he'd been drawn to stories of men and women who'd risen up
against corrupt orders and in dramatic fashion changed the world or
registered their protest against its unchangeability. At Columbia, his
radical impulse was given expression through the utopian and dysto-
pian philosophies that circulated like currency in his group, and he
took for granted that society was in need of rescue. He'd spent much
of the year after he first left Columbia searching the stacks of the New
York Public Library for an answer to the crisis of modern life, and he'd
been persuaded that socialist policies were likely to be part of any solution that might emerge. He'd been particularly moved by the tales of
the *narodniki*, late-nineteenth-century Russian revolutionists who'd
turned to terrorism as a way to shock the peasants into rising up against
the czar. For Chambers, their grand acts of terror, and the poetic and
sacrificial spirit with which they carried them off, represented "all that
was soldierly and saintly in the revolution."[39]

What remained missing for Chambers, however, was testimony of
the quality that could carry him through to the only kind of political
commitment he believed worth making—a total one.

On the surface, *The Soviets at Work* was an unlikely catalyst for such
transformation. Its purpose, as Lenin explained in the first paragraph,
was practical. He wanted to focus the minds of his Bolshevik allies and
followers on "the problem of organization."[40] To that end he offered a

survey of the main organizational problems that Russia's new leaders were facing in their struggle to set their gargantuan, preindustrial, politically inchoate nation on a course that was both ideologically sound and pragmatically sustainable.

Lenin defended compromises made with the old bourgeois order (to pay a higher wage to technical specialists, for instance, than to laborers). He addressed the question of how to inspire greater productivity and innovation in workers once the capitalistic incentive system had been discarded. He looked at the comparative difficulties of nationalizing different sectors of the economy. Lenin wrote, even, in the vein of Benjamin Franklin: "Keep accurate and conscientious accounts; conduct business economically; do not loaf; do not steal; maintain strict discipline at work."[41]

In a passage that must have resonated with Chambers, Lenin described the type of recruits upon whom the revolution would rely in managing the rocky transition from the old to the new society. They would be a kind of semi-underground order, able to temper their revolutionary fire with strategic discretion, advancing in increments as they engaged in the subtle work of educating and engineering the masses block by block, brick by brick, cell by cell, soul by soul.[42]

Lenin's rhetoric wasn't delivered with the eloquence that Madison or Jefferson found when they were writing the future of America, but he was following in their wake as a founding father of the modern world, marrying words to power in order to give shape to a new society. As Lenin made the argument that the Bolsheviks were the authentic instantiation of the people's will, he was consolidating his control over the elements of power in the Soviet Union. As he argued that insofar as the Bolsheviks did represent the people, they were invested with the right to rule absolutely, dictatorially, he was in the process of imposing such rule.

Lenin's effect on Chambers was revelatory. Here was a voice, and a model, that spoke to him in a way that Karl Marx, whose cadences had won over so many intellectuals to the cause, had been unable to do.

Until he read Lenin, communism had been embodied for Chambers in the few communists he knew in New York, and in the communists he'd noticed haunting the alleyways of Berlin—"little knots of furtive figures selling newspapers"[43]—when he'd visited Germany during the summer of 1923. These people, for all their admirable zeal, were too obviously marginal to be any answer to the crisis of civilization.

Lenin, with his ruthless practicality and his absolute sense of entitlement to power (not to mention his actual acquisition of power), was an answer. He was an answer, moreover, that arrived at the right time in Chambers's life, which was quickly becoming excruciating even by Chambers family standards. In the previous year, Chambers had left, and then returned, and then once again left college. His paternal grandfather had died in the arms of a mistress. His maternal grandmother had moved in with the family after her dementia rendered living on her own impossible. Chambers had taken up with a married woman and possibly fathered a son with another woman. To top it all off, he had to contend with an emerging sexual attraction to men, which carried with it not just the general stigma of homosexuality but the very particular taint of his father, whose gayness had come to represent, in Chambers's emotional-symbolic calculus, both a betrayal of the family and a symptom of the civilization-wide failure of paternal authority.

"Studied under the lamp of Leninism, things at last fitted into place," writes Sam Tanenhaus in his biography of Chambers. "Chambers could examine himself, Jay, Laha, Richard and see their failures not as aberrations but as symptoms of a wider malady. What was the 'French family' if not a textbook example of the eclipsed middle class, of families that had lost their way in the twentieth century? . . . With its cracks and fissures 228 Earle Avenue was the heartbreak house of a doomed world."[44]

After *The Soviets at Work*, Chambers read through Lenin's more substantial *The State and Revolution*, and Bukharin's *The ABC of Communism*. He found in them the same compelling fusion of dry practicality and grand abstraction, of contempt for the equivocations of liberalism and supreme confidence in the future of the proletariat.

"The reek of life was on it," Chambers wrote. "This was not theory or statistics. This was socialism in practice. This was the thing itself. This was how it worked."[45]

On February 17, 1925, Chambers joined the Communist Party U.S.A. It wasn't, in any apparent way, a match made in heaven. The American Communist Party of the 1920s was a dollhouse version of its Russian model. The same concerns that were debated by Lenin, Trotsky, Stalin, and Bukharin in Moscow were debated by Chambers and his comrades in the States, but in Russia the conclusions to these debates cascaded out to affect the lives of millions of people. In America they bounced around the walls of dingy apartments in Brooklyn or the Bronx. Factional disputes that ended, in Russia, with the losers lined up before a firing squad led in New York to broken friendships or, at worst, to divorce court.

Even as an echo, though, the party had a force that Chambers found compelling. It had charismatic leaders, hard-line rules, sacred texts. It was uncontaminated by irony, tolerance, and most of the other liberal values that had so conspicuously failed to anchor Chambers when he was at Columbia. And it was a community of people who shared with him something that his family and school friends simply couldn't wrap their minds around—the radical willingness to hand over one's identity, autonomy, material ambitions, good name, and even, if necessary, one's life to the cause. There was something rather absurd, viewed from the outside, about a bunch of garment workers, school-teachers, bookstore clerks, and itinerant carpenters arguing about the proper speed with which, say, the future revolutionary government of America should collectivize its farms. Yet what else had revolutionaries ever been but misfits dreaming dreams that seemed impossible until the impossible moment when potentialities were suddenly, violently, made real?

"[I]t offered me," wrote Chambers, "what nothing else in the dying world had power to offer at the same intensity—faith and a vision, something for which to live and something for which to die. It demanded of me those things which have always stirred what is best in men—courage, poverty, self-sacrifice, discipline, intelligence, my life, and, at need, my death."[46]

Chambers wasn't blind to the party's flaws, but he found even in its imperfections the opportunities to practice the revolutionary virtues of humility, submission, and patience. From the romantic heights of editing an avant-garde literary journal at Columbia University he willingly descended to the task of collecting money from the far-flung newsstands that carried the party's newspaper, the *Daily Worker*. At marathon meetings, he kept his quiet while people who couldn't keep even their own lives in order were debating how they would order the totality of American society once the revolution came. As a volunteer writer for the *Daily Worker*, he took his place on the propaganda assembly line, duly swiping content from other newspapers and rewriting it according to the Moscow party line.

Such abnegation offered Chambers a kind of heroic path—he would be a monk of the revolution—and also an escape. At home in Lynbrook, the dismal equilibrium to which the Chamberses had for decades consigned themselves was coming apart for good. His grandmother brought chaos with her, pacing the house at night, knife in hand, convinced that someone (nameless Jews, her sodomite son-in-law, and so on) was out to get her. Whittaker's failure to complete Columbia, and his serial romantic melodramas, were a strain. The running battle between Laha and Jay continued unabated.

It was younger brother Richard, however, who tipped it all over into utter tragedy. He'd left for college in the fall of 1924 in high spirits, but within weeks his apparently easygoing nature had revealed itself to be a flimsy construct. By the time he returned home at the end of the semester, he was in the grips of a full-blown existential/depressive crisis. Like Whittaker, he'd become obsessed with the hypocrisy and shallowness of modern society. Unlike Whittaker, however, Richard could find no solace in politics—or in literature, religion, romance, or any of the other traditional alchemists of despair.

"I came in one night," wrote Chambers, "to find him sitting in the kitchen with my mother—an almost unrecognizably white-faced, taut-lipped boy, arguing desperately . . . that life is worthless and meaningless, that to be intelligent is to know this and to have courage to end it."[47]

Richard refused to go back to school, instead settling in Lynbrook and devoting himself to renovating the family homestead, and to drinking. He built a small shed in the backyard that served functionally as a workshop but emotionally as a kind of tree house from which to pretend to escape from Laha. At night in the shed, he drank and womanized, and then in the morning he confessed his sins to his mother, taunting her with her inability to control his behavior at the same time that he was casting himself directly, destructively, into the psychosexual crucible that she and Jay had made of their lives. Soon, inevitably, Laha called in Whittaker to help.

"'You must go with him,' she said, 'and watch over him. I do not know what he is going to do next. But I am afraid that he is going to try to kill himself.' She wept. 'What have I done that was so wrong?' she said. 'Oh, God, what have I done? I only tried to love you both.'"[48]

For a few months, Whittaker became his brother's keeper. During the day, he worked in Manhattan at the public library. On those nights when he wasn't committed to party activities, he joined Richard and his ne'er-do-well friends as they cruised the speakeasies of Long Island. There was an allure for Chambers in attaching himself to his brother's escapes into "mindless, animal activity," and for a brief while he enjoyed the partying.[49] It couldn't last, though. There was too much pain, paired with too much alcohol, for the brothers' bottled-up resentments to remain bottled up. After a few booze-fueled fights between them, they stopped going out together at night.

"Now my brother was seldom sober even in the daytime," wrote Chambers. "He used to wear a vivid plaid pullover, violent checked knickerbockers and green or red golf stockings. Above this atrocious outfit, which seemed to me to symbolize the whole failure of our judgment, peered my brother's pale, drawn face from which all joy had gone."[50]

Over the next year, Richard deteriorated further. A first suicide attempt—gas in the kitchen—was foiled by Whittaker, who got home from work in the city in time to save him before too much gas was inhaled.

A second attempt—gas in the backyard workshop—was again interrupted by Whittaker, though this time the gas had pervaded Richard's system so thoroughly that he was reduced to lurching around on the floor for hours, his muscles contorted, barking out cries of distress.

On the night of September 8, 1926, Richard went to the train station in Lynbrook to meet Whittaker, with whom he'd spent the previous few nights commiserating about the sad state of the world. That night, however, Whittaker didn't come home. He'd gotten caught up in a conversation with a communist friend and had decided to stay in the city. Richard waited for a while at the station, eventually giving up after none of the trains disgorged his brother. He drove home to the small apartment he'd taken in a nearby town, drank a bottle of whiskey, put a pillow down in the stove, turned on the gas, and lay down his head on the pillow. His body was found by the police the next morning.

Chambers spent the next few months dwelling in his grief. He held himself responsible for failing to save his brother, but also for failing to kill himself at Richard's side (as Richard had proposed many times). He resented Richard for abandoning him, and for killing himself in a way that linked the act so directly to their relationship. As the autumn wore on, and as the sorrow settled, Chambers found a formula with which to transmute the pain into something workable. Rather than blaming himself, or his parents, or Richard, he would blame the world. It was such a toxic place, he determined, that committing suicide wasn't an act in itself so much as it was a refusal to act—a refusal to continue breathing in and out the world's toxins.

He considered following his brother into death, but it wasn't in him. He retained too much of an attachment to life, and to his dreams for himself. What he would do instead was commit himself to the fight to cleanse the world of its corruption. He would kill the world that had killed his brother.[51]

"I had come to believe that the world we live in was dying, that only surgery could now save the wreckage of mankind, and that the Communist Party was history's surgeon," he wrote. ". . . I was already a member of the Communist Party. I now first became a communist."[52]

Once he truly committed himself to the cause, Chambers began to move fitfully toward the heart of American communism. He returned to the *Daily Worker* in 1927, this time as a (badly and erratically) paid writer, and within the year was an editor. The work wasn't much different from what he'd done as a freelancer—along with churning out his own propaganda, he became responsible for editing other people's propaganda—but he was now on the inside, and it was an interesting place to be.

The *Worker* was a kind of depressive version of the fast-talking, cynicism-drenched, Jazz Age newspaper that Cary Grant and Rosalind Russell would inhabit in *His Girl Friday*, with one signal difference: "However unpleasant the Communists on the *Daily Worker* might be as human beings, there was not one of them who did not hold his convictions with a fanatical faith; and there was scarcely one of them who was not prepared to die, at need, for them. That gave them a force."[53]

The editor of the paper, when Chambers joined up, had lunched with Lenin, and had been prosecuted under the Espionage Act by the Department of Justice. A fellow hack was also an old Wobbly from out west, a veteran of many of the Industrial Workers of the World's reckless and noble campaigns for justice.[54] The paper's business manager walked around the office like a stock character out of a vaudeville routine, moaning about money and complaining to the men in the newsroom about their grab-assing of the office girls. Later in life, under his real name (Benjamin Mandel), he would serve as research director for the House Un-American Activities Committee and become one of the staunchest of America's anti-communists.

After 1928, when the paper and the party headquarters moved over to the newly established Workers Center on Union Square, the atmosphere of force only grew thicker. The leaders of the main factions would drop by the newsroom to try to inflect the coverage of a recent conference or protest or resolution. Mysterious men, who spoke in mysterious accents, would be seen climbing the stairs to the upper floors, where secret councils were held and grave decisions made. Painters from the John Reed Clubs, the party's cultural arm, covered the walls of the ground-floor cafeteria in colorfully heroic murals of thick-sinewed workers. Communiqués arrived from Moscow, and the word would suddenly go out that Trotsky was down and Stalin up, or Foster down and Lovestone up. Each shift made itself evident, in one way or another, in the *Daily Worker*. And not just in the pages of the *Worker*, but in its people. Those who'd made the right bets were rewarded while the unlucky or stubborn were purged or forced to confess their counterrevolutionary sins in order to remain in the bosom of the party.

So much of what went on in the rooms of the Workers Center was more than a touch absurd—all the lonely people living out great adventures in their minds. Even so it was an intense existence, a complete life. Members socialized and slept and drank with other members. They were given jobs, barricades to man, and unions to subvert. They raised their kids together and went to classes in theoretical Marxism together. They were told where to move, what music to listen to, what books to read. Binding it all together was an embracing vision of a future in which solidarity would reign.

Chambers's communism was typical in many ways. He went to parties and protests, made friends, hatched a few clumsy intrigues, had a series of dysfunctional/oedipal/kinky/transferentially homoerotic relationships with women from the party. He found comfort in being part of the community, and in giving over some chunk of his autonomy to the party.

In other ways, however, he held himself aloof. Few in the party were so naïve as to believe everything that they were asked to repeat or report, but few were as skeptical of party propaganda as Chambers. And few of Chambers's comrades were as deliberate as he was in the construction of a communist identity. He did what he was ordered most of the time, but always kept his own counsel—silently cataloguing the vices and virtues of his colleagues, sifting through the muck of party life for the rare nuggets of revolutionary wisdom, observing everyone and everything with his acutely literary eye, and even doing some work outside the party, as a translator, to keep his literary and linguistic skills sharp.*

The party, for Chambers, was less a political organization than a crucible for the forging of his own Bolshevik soul. Even Lenin, and the earth-bestriding men who'd conquered Russia along with him, were used by Chambers on his own terms, as material in the ongoing construction of the epic narrative of his life.

No longer content just being a foot soldier, Chambers endeavored to make himself over into a knight of the revolution. He laid down copy as tirelessly as he'd once laid down rail in Baltimore. He sought out friendships with the few men and women he encountered who seemed, in their souls, to have the spark of the true revolutionist. He continued to read widely, and idiosyncratically, in the literature of the Left, preferring history, biography, fiction, and poetry to tracts on theory and ideology. Chambers even found a way, once in a while, to inject a bit of flavor into the mealy pages of the *Daily Worker*. He took on the neglected task of editing and publishing the best of the letters that came into the office from real workers—"the arterial flow between the working class and the Communist Party"—and was rewarded with an

---

* Including the first English translation of *Bambi*.

enthusiastic response from the readership, an official commendation from the powers in Moscow (who usually had nothing but contempt for the *Worker*), and an assistant.[55]

Chambers's ambitions, however, were more often than not frustrated by the failures of the American party. Instead of thinking deeply about the problem of fomenting revolution in a nation as capitalistic and prosperous as America, the leaders of the party, like their counterparts in the Soviet Union, spent an extraordinary amount of their time contending with each other, and with other elements of the Left, for power.[56]

In the Soviet Union, where the power being fought over was immense, these intra-Left fights had a brutal but undeniable logic. Someone was going to wield extraordinary power over the lives of tens of millions of people, so the rewards of power, and the dangers of failing to acquire it, were genuine. But in America, where communism was so marginal, such jockeying for power seemed to Chambers like a disguised form of fatalism. What was needed were organizers and movement builders, people with the vision and endurance to keep plotting, and plodding, through years and decades of failures. What the party got instead were arguers and in-fighters, climbers and power seekers.

The factional intrigue came to a kind of crescendo in 1929, when Stalin, having finally maneuvered Bukharin out of the way, was able to turn his attention to bringing the rest of international communism into line. He ordered Jay Lovestone, the current leader of the American party, to come to Moscow, where he brought him and his delegation in front of an "American Commission." The ostensible purpose of the commission was to resolve certain policy disputes between Lovestone's majority and the minority faction led by William Foster. In fact, Stalin had already decided to make Foster the leader of the American party. He'd called Lovestone to Moscow not to consult with him, but to set him up for a public humiliation—to destroy not just his position, but his reputation and self-respect as well.

"And you, who are you?" demanded Stalin, toward the climax of the last session in which Lovestone was allowed to defend himself against the various charges of counterrevolutionary tendencies. "Who do you think you are? Trotsky defied me. Where is he? Zinoviev defied me. Where is he? Bukharin defied me. Where is he? And you! Who are you? Yes, you will go back to America. But when you get there, nobody will know you except your wives."[57]

After the commission announced its conclusions, Lovestone and his allies were imprisoned in Moscow for a few months, while Foster and his people went about imposing a new order on the party. It was, Chambers later wrote, "the coming of fascism to the American Community Party." Public confessions of imaginary transgressions were demanded, and then published in the *Worker*. Lovestonites were humiliated or expelled (or humiliated and then expelled). Fosterites were elevated. Everyone else was cowed into submission or forced to walk away. The *Worker*'s editorial line, which had always suffered from having to tack according to the winds in the Soviet Union, was brought even more firmly under Moscow's control. Within a short time, the American Stalinists had plugged up every last nook of freedom that had once existed within the party.

Chambers, who'd kept himself aloof from the factional struggle, stayed on at the *Worker* for another few months, but his heart wasn't in it. He didn't object, in principle, to the idea of imposing discipline on the party (in fact, he'd often thought that the party suffered from a lack of discipline), but the specific decisions that were being made seemed wrongheaded to him. The wrong people were being purged. The wrong policies were being dictated.

"I was not looking for trouble and I hoped to ride out the storm in peace," he wrote. "But as it lashed up, I grew more and more restive. I spoke and acted with hazardous freedom."[58]

Lovestone had been shouted down by Stalin in May of 1929. Within a few months, Chambers had acted with hazardous freedom one too many times (among other mistakes, he'd been too sympathetic to one of the recently purged) and was called up to the ninth floor to face a dressing-down of his own. Instead, he just walked away.

On October 29, 1929, within weeks of Chambers's quitting the *Worker*, Laha Chambers found her husband Jay lying dead of a heart attack on the bathroom floor. She called Whittaker to come over and manage the details of his father's death.

"My father lay huddled in his bathrobe on the sea-blue tiles my brother had laid," wrote Chambers. "His body was still warm. Of the bodies I had lifted in the last years, his was the most inert. I could move him only inch by inch.

"Later, the undertakers carried my father downstairs. Without my knowledge, they began the preliminary stages of embalming, in our living room. Unsuspectingly, I walked into the room. My father lay naked on a stretcher. One of his arms was dangling. From this arm, near the shoulder, his blood, the blood that had given my brother and me life, was pouring, in a thin, dark arc, into a battered mop bucket."

On the same day that Jay Chambers died, the stock market suffered the last of the three precipitous tumbles that would bring a sharp end to the great bull market of the 1920s. On Black Tuesday, as it became known, the market lost almost an eighth of its value, the equivalent of more than four times the federal budget for that year. For Chambers, all the upheaval—the death of his father, his exile from the party, the crash of the economy—merged into one overwhelming swell. It was terrifying, and traumatic, but also liberating. There was space for something new to unfold.

"Our line seemed to be at an end," he wrote. "Our family was like a burnt-over woods, which nothing can revive and only new growth can replace. The promise of new growth lay wholly within me."[59]

Over the next two years, as he mulled over what to do next, Chambers conducted himself as an "independent Communist oppositionist." He kept apart from official party activities and publications, but most of his friendships were still with communists, his romances were

mostly with communists, and although the existing party, in his opinion, was proving itself terribly inadequate to the demands that history
was placing upon it, his faith in the program remained firm. He would
bide his time, waiting for the party to come to its senses. The party, for
its part, adopted a comparable attitude toward Chambers; he wasn't
excommunicated, and it was intimated to him, by way of occasional
contacts, that he would be accepted back into the fold under the right
circumstances.

In 1930, he ended the last of his quasi-bohemian "party marriages,"
and began a more conventional wooing of Esther Shemitz, a spritely
painter whom he'd first noticed, a few years before, when she led a
crowd of radical protesters against police lines during an epic textile
workers strike in Passaic, New Jersey. Their courtship, as Chambers
would later describe it in *Witness*, was like something out of a screwball
comedy. Chambers was the cad who secretly cared about the world
so much that he'd adopted a cynical pose precisely to protect himself
against disappointment, while Shemitz was the woman-child who
yearned, beneath her skittishly independent façade, for a powerful man
to take control of her life. Over the many evenings Chambers spent socializing at the small apartment of Shemitz and her roommate, radical
writer Grace Lumpkin, he would play up the romantic-comic aspects
of his tiff with the party, describing his time at the *Worker* as if he were
a charming, naughty boy whose mischief simply couldn't be tolerated
by the stuffed shirts anymore. Shemitz, who was under some pressure
from party friends to distance herself from the rogue Chambers, would
visibly wrestle with her attraction to him.

"One afternoon, my future wife, in a flare-up of her Passaic strike
spirit, was belaboring me with my 'renegacy' and related charges," he
wrote. "I sat studying her. As I watched her climbing around on the
barricades, I was given one of those rare total insights into another soul
that, for good or ill, we sometimes know. I felt like a man on a hilltop,
who bursts through a screen of obstructing undergrowth, and suddenly
sees, spread beyond him, the most tranquil of sunlit countrysides with

its pattern of blown, green and ripening fields, its hedgerows and cool trees, its winding roads and falling brooks. I thought: 'This is not revolutionist at all. This is the most gentle and tender spirit, a child except for its courage and firmness and capacity for love, should someone understand and awaken that love.' I said: 'Why don't you stop drawing those mob scenes and clenched fists and paint the landscapes you were meant to paint.'"[60]

At the same time that he was trying to persuade Shemitz to give over her political art—"terrifying posters in which hatless proletarians with clenched fists were always storming somewhere"—for what he believed was her more authentic, more feminine artistic self, Chambers was on the verge of returning to the world of politics. The times seemed to demand it of him. Since he'd left the *Worker* in 1929, nearly every apocalyptic prediction the Communist Party had ever made about the fate of American capitalism was appearing to come true. The stock market had crashed. Unemployment was sky high. Millions of middle- and working-class people were dropped into the kind of dire poverty that was supposed to be the exclusive preserve of the infirm, the dark-skinned, and the undeserving. A society that had grown used to progressing in predictable ways was faced suddenly with the terrifying truth that the universe made no guarantees that tomorrow would be anything like yesterday.

The moment should have been ripe for communists to step forward with their reassuringly detailed explanations of how, exactly, things had gotten so bad so quickly, and their bold plans for how they were going to get better. But the party, Chambers observed, was being as lead-footed as ever in adapting itself to the American situation. It was still turned inward, obsessed with purity and orthodoxy precisely when it should have been looking for ways to translate its alien-seeming doctrines into a language that Americans, who were desperate for answers, might be able to absorb. Chambers saw the chance he'd been waiting for—to serve the cause in which he believed and to step into the leading role for which he believed himself destined.

"It occurred to me that there was another way than politics to influence policy. I might try writing, not political polemics which few people ever wanted to read, but stories that anybody might want to read—stories in which the correct conduct of the communist would be shown in action and without political comment."[61]

In one long night, Chambers wrote such a story, and in March of 1931, it was published in the *New Masses*. "Can You Make Out Their Voices?" was about a community of small farmers, living out in the dusty, hardscrabble West, who were struggling to survive in the face of drought and capitalist indifference. Over the course of a few months, under the organic guidance of one of their ranks—a man who considers himself a communist but whose deepest code was the ancient one of justice and fairness—the farmers rise up. They cast off their passivity and fatalism and confront the simpering bourgeoisie from the town, taking by force the food and supplies they need to keep their families alive, and then retreating to the hills to plan revolution.

"Can You Make Out Their Voices?" was an instant phenomenon on the literary Left. It was republished as a pamphlet by the official publishing house of the international Communist Party, and translated into a host of other languages. Letters poured in, from intellectuals and workers alike, expressing rapturous enthusiasm for the story. A left-wing playwright adapted it for the stage, and her show was soon being performed for workers around the world. Chambers was almost instantly welcomed back to the party, and was encouraged to write more such stories, which he did.

"You Have Seen the Heads," which came out a month later, traced the political evolution of a young Chinese peasant, as the cruelty of the world—and the state—slowly but inexorably wins him over to communism. "Our Comrade Munn," published in October of 1931, chronicled the life and death of a Christlike communist who transforms an out-of-touch communist local into an efficient machine for organizing factory workers. "The Death of the Communists," the last of Chambers's quartet of stories, told of the martyrdom of a group of communists who use their remaining time on earth, while in prison awaiting execution, to win over the other prisoners to their cause.[62]

With each new story, Chambers offered more evidence that he'd discovered the ability to effectively embed communist ideology and practice in the vehicle of fiction. He drew on the techniques of the pulps—and the great popular novelists of the mid-nineteenth century like Hugo, Dumas, and Dickens—to pour forth an inspired stream of square-jawed heroes, thin-lipped villains, dramatic confrontations, boyish jokes, exotic settings, and exciting climaxes. He created entire worlds, in miniature, full of excitement and conflict, where there were good guys and bad guys, where life and death was at stake, and where regular people, chosen by fate, could suddenly rise as heroes.

Chambers was, by any standards, a good storyteller. For American communists in particular he was potent. Not only were they the ones being mythologized, but they were people whose lives, to an exceptional degree, generated the kind of tension that such fiction was so good at discharging. Had Chambers been a different writer, the stories might have looked directly at the neurotically charged existence of the American communist, its blend of excruciating anxiety and profound hope, delusion and commitment. Instead, as in most good popular fiction, the anxieties were transmuted into fantasies—of empowerment, revolution, manliness, perfect solidarity, and martyrdom.

There was something else there, too, an unapologetic moral vision that resonated with many communists because it was so much of what had drawn them to the party in the first place. In Chambers's stories, injustice was opposed with the righteous anger that it deserved. Solidarity wasn't just a slogan; it was an authentic feeling of brotherhood and shared purpose. None of the stories ended happily, with any kind of concrete victory over the forces of exploitation. But there was a sense in them that the arc of the world wouldn't always bend to serve the powerful. One day, fairness would prevail.

"That is how they died, gentlemen," recalled one of the prisoners in Chambers's last story, describing the Communists' final, noble march to the firing squad, singing "the Internationale" even as the bullets cut them down. "And to tell the truth, I had a feeling, singularly light and unsorrowful, that their deaths made no essential difference to themselves, to what they were effecting, or that for which they stood. Indeed, I felt as I have felt only once before in my life, when I was lying on my back in a small boat, with a cool wind, but a hot sun, playing on my body, and a swell and strong tide carrying me along with no effort on my part.[63]

In the spring of 1932, Chambers was asked to become one of the editors of the *New Masses*. It was quite a feather in his cap. It was also a great relief. The *Worker* had given him community, but at the cost of suppressing his talents and political instincts. His exile had been creatively fruitful, but lonely. Now he'd no longer have to hold himself apart in order to be authentic. He could live the communist dream—fully an individual and also fully integrated into the collective.

His domestic life had achieved a rare equilibrium as well. He and Esther were married in April of 1931, and in the spring of 1932 they allowed themselves to follow their hearts out of the city. Some left-wing friends of theirs owned a farm in western New Jersey, and told the couple that if they were willing to remodel the old barn on the property, they could live in it for free.

For a short while it was an idyllic life, one that seemed to have arranged itself to satisfy every one of Chambers's not easily reconcilable needs. He spent his weeks in the city, sleeping on the couches of communist friends and rising early to labor on the magazine. He edited as a hard-liner, screening the content that came across his desk for revolutionary correctness, and writing, in his own hand, brutal editorials that warned his fellow left-wing writers to join up with the cause or be crushed by History. In the evenings he unwound, spending his time in the cafés and cozy apartments of the Village, musing and arguing with other artists and writers about art, literature, life, and the state of the world. On the weekends he returned to the farm, where he and

Esther tended to their small world. He sanded floors and erected stone walls; she planted vegetables and sewed linens. Together they went for long walks out into the countryside, communing with nature and each other.

The idyll lasted for only a few months. In June of that year, only three issues into his tenure as an editor of the *New Masses*, Chambers got a call from Max Bedacht, a former national secretary of the American party. He was told simply to report immediately to Bedacht's office on the ninth floor of the Workers Center. There was business to discuss.

"What are you doing now, Comrade Chambers?" said Bedacht, after Chambers sat down in front of him.

Chambers answered, and then was told, with little preamble, that he'd been chosen to go into one of the party's "special institutions."

Chambers asked what that meant.

"It is a 'special institution,'" said Bedacht again.

Chambers looked at him quizzically.

"They want you to do underground work," said Bedacht.

When pressed for more information, Bedacht would indicate only that such work was a total commitment. Chambers would have to leave the *New Masses*, and he'd have to remove himself from the normal life of the party. Chambers asked for some time to think it over, and was given until the next morning. He went home to Esther, who pleaded with him not to do it:

"Why not?" said Chambers. ". . . It is the most responsible work the party can offer me. I am a revolutionist."

"'I don't know,' she said sobbing. 'I don't know why not. You must do what you think is right. But I am afraid. Please, dear heart, don't do it.'"[64]

The next morning, when he told Bedacht he wouldn't do it, his refusal was ignored. He could either go underground, said Bedacht, or leave the party entirely. It wasn't much of a choice for Chambers, who was committed to the party and who was powerfully drawn to the romance of underground work. The *New Masses* was satisfying work, but in the end, he told himself, it was just words. The real revolution was calling. This was action, and it was what he wanted.

Or thought he wanted. In going underground, Chambers was forced to let go of the fusion of purpose and community that had met so many of his needs. He'd been singled out, and given a higher purpose, but at the same time cut off. Never again would he be able to root his intensity in the soil of a stable communist community. For the next six years he would have to move constantly, live under assumed names, lie as a matter of course to almost everyone around him, separate himself from many of his friends, and subject his wife and his young children to an isolation that was so extreme it verged on cruelty. To sustain him there were occasional thrills, a sense of mission, a belief in the cause, and a few friendships, forged in the crucible of underground life, that attained a battlefield intensity (including, most significantly, the friendship with State Department official and secret Communist Alger Hiss). But day-to-day, month-to-month, year-to-year, it would prove a bone-wearying existence.

"Now what name did you use there?" asked one of the attorneys for Alger Hiss, in 1948, deposing Esther about the few months that the family spent in Staten Island, in the winter of 1933.

"Arthur Maguire—Arthur Dwyer," said Esther.

"Arthur Dwyer?"

"Arthur Dwyer."

"And who did you know?"

"Nobody," said Esther.

"While you were living there?"

"Nobody except the A&P man."

"Did you have an account at the A&P store?"

"Oh, no, not an account, but just a nodding acquaintance. I just asked him to send things out on occasion, and made purchases there."[65]

For his first two years in the underground, while he and Esther—and soon their daughter, Ellen, who was born in 1933—were bouncing around the boroughs of New York, Chambers's primary task was to act as a liaison between Soviet military intelligence and the American party. That meant, in practice, that he was a courier, one link in a chain that led from Moscow through Germany to New York and back again. Sailors coming over on shipping lines from Germany would deliver their packages—letters written in invisible ink and microfilm concealed behind the faces of small mirrors—to contacts at the dock, who would deliver them to Chambers, who would bring the package to one of the apartments used by the party for such purposes. The letters would then be treated with chemicals to bring out the messages, and the microfilm would be enlarged and printed. Chambers's superior would read them, take some notes, and then burn all the documents. A similar procedure was followed, in reverse, to send messages back across the ocean.

There were other tasks, but they were almost as rote. Exacerbating the tediousness of all the copying, delivering, and enlarging was an exhausting set of practices designed to keep the work hidden from an American counterintelligence apparatus that didn't, in fact, exist. Chambers could spend hours in a single day traversing the city, doubling back, changing trains, circling blocks, simply to make his way to one clandestine meeting, which might last for a few minutes, or even a few seconds, at which point he'd turn around and begin the process of evasion again.

There were aspects of the work that he enjoyed. He was too much his father's son not to revel at least a bit in the exoticism of underground life—all the coded language, the secret bases, the furtive glances and baroque precautions. And he was too much his mother's son not to take advantage, sometimes, of the opportunities he was afforded to perform. He would often go out of his way, in his first few years in the underground, to drop theatrically enigmatic hints to his old friends that he was doing work of grave importance. He liked trying on identities, and even went so far, for a number of years, as to affect a slight accent to convince his comrades in the underground that he was Russian.

The peculiar nature of underground work also gave him the push he needed to explore his attraction to men. He was suddenly dropped into a netherworld where the boundaries between the licit and the illicit, the moral and immoral, were blurred, and where a large part of his job was to act in ways that men like him, in that era, tended to act when they were cruising for anonymous sex with other men. A large part of his job was to move in the shadows, to exchange meaningful glances with strangers, to take midnight ambles punctuated with intervals of purposeful loitering. After a year or two of such a life, the dam that he'd put up, between himself and his sexual attraction to men, finally broke open.

"In 1933 or 4, a young fellow stopped me on the street in N.Y. and asked me if I could give him a meal and lodgings for the night," Chambers confessed to the FBI in 1949. "I fed him and he told me about his life as a miner's son. I was footloose, so I took him to a hotel to spend the night. During the course of our stay at the hotel that night I had my first homosexual experience. There he . . . taught me an experience I did not know existed. . . . It was a revelation to me. As a matter of fact it set off a chain reaction in me which was almost impossible to control. Because it had been repressed so long, it was all the more violent when once set free."[66]

Over the next four years, until he broke from the party, Chambers did a lot of cruising, finding partners in the "parks or other parts of town where these people were likely to be found." It was a double-secret existence, both exhilarating and excruciating. His wife was in the dark about it, as was the Communist Party, whose enlightened attitude toward sex extended only as far as endorsing heterosexual promiscuity. The men he slept with were kept away from any knowledge of who he was outside the bedroom. It was all one-night stands, quick and dirty, exclusively sexual. He never went to gay clubs, made any gay friends, or socialized in any gay scene.

Outside of his one confession to the FBI, Chambers never said anything else about his homosexual experience, and so it's impossible to know what it represented to him aside from the mix of pleasure, pain, excitement, guilt, and shame that are all evident in that one short document. If nothing else, however, the sexual realm was one of the few parts of his life, during his years in the underground, in which he didn't have to live up to his oppressively sentimental standards for himself. In the dark, he was free to be neither the perfectly efficient Bolshevik nor the perfectly devoted husband/father. His secret sex life was also, perhaps, something that was under his control when very little else was.

In the summer of 1934 Chambers was assigned to help manage an elite cell of government workers in Washington, D.C. It was a re-markable promotion. It was also another sacrifice. The family had to relocate again, this time to Baltimore, bringing to seven the total of moves in the two years since Chambers had gone underground. They were now even farther away from what little support they'd had in New York, and they had even less leeway, because of the greater importance of Chambers's new position, to bend the rules of secrecy for the sake of human contact.

Chambers's responsibility, at first, was simply to handle the cell, which was made up of seven of the most high-status Americans the Communist Party had ever recruited, all of them rising young Turks in the Roosevelt administration. He collected party dues, distributed copies of the *Daily Worker*, oversaw their Marxist-Leninist study ses-sions, and passed on to his superiors whatever information his contacts gave him that might be useful. Less tangibly, but as significantly, he was there to be the daily or weekly reminder in the lives of the cell members that their commitment to the party was meaningful, that they weren't just playing at conspiracy but in fact were practicing it. Such psycho-logical maintenance was necessary because, for the time being, they were a "sleeper apparatus," expected to do nothing at all except thrive in their day jobs, acquiring influence and building connections for the day when they'd be called upon to act.

When Chambers assumed supervision of the apparatus, his con-tacts were concentrated in the new agencies of the New Deal, in par-ticular in the Agricultural Adjustment Administration (AAA) and the National Recovery Administration (NRA). Over the next few years, as the cell matured, they spread out. Henry Collins, who struck Chambers as "all that Princeton and Harvard can do for a personable and intelligent young American of good family," moved from the AAA to the Department of Agriculture.[67] Lee Pressman, another Harvard alumnus, went from the AAA to the Works Progress Administration (WPA). Alger Hiss, who soon became Chambers's closest friend in Washington, left the AAA for a Senate subcommittee, then moved over to the Justice Department, and then finally landed at the State Department, where he was an aide to the assistant secretary of state.

As Chambers settled into his role, and as his charges settled into their government work, the activities of the cell increased slightly. Cell members were encouraged to stay on the lookout for potential recruits, and, if they identified good targets, to begin the careful process of cultivating them. Chambers was also introduced to another, parallel cell, and took on some responsibilities for managing it—including assisting with a few early stabs at espionage, which fizzled out when the Soviets showed little interest in the material the Americans were offering them. For those first few years, though, Chambers's professional life in Washington was sleepy. He kept things running smoothly, kept morale up, and waited for something to happen.

In the fall of 1936, Chambers came across a brief newspaper account of the execution, by the Soviet regime, of a former Soviet general. Though he'd never heard of the man, he was unsettled by the idea of such a man—a former hero of the Soviet state—being executed. He approached one of his superiors in the underground and asked him whether there was something going on in the Soviet Union that he should know about. The response was disturbing: Yes, something was going on, and no, he shouldn't know about it, talk about it, or ask anything further about it.

It was Chambers's first intimation of the avalanche of terror and death that was in the process of cleansing the Soviet Union not just of anyone who might plausibly threaten Stalin's supremacy, but of hundreds of thousands of people who looked vaguely like the kind of people who might perhaps threaten Stalin's supremacy, and a few hundred thousand other people thrown in for good measure. Between 1935 and 1938, in what became known as the Great Purge (or the Great Terror), millions of Soviet citizens were executed or sent away to prison camps for no reason other than Stalin's will to power and the inner logic of the purge itself, which, with each new arrest and conviction, produced further false allegations of conspiracy.[68]

For Chambers, as for many other party members around the world, the Great Purge was striking not so much for its scale, which wasn't widely known until much later, as for its targets. Stalin's aggression was directed not at genuine conspirators or counterrevolutionaries, of whom there were no more than a few left by the mid-1930s, but at the heart of the Soviet system. The primary targets were the army, the secret police, the technical classes, the intellectuals, and, most startlingly of all, the old guard of the Bolshevik party. Some of the very men whom Chambers had joined the party to emulate, his paragons of courage and brilliance fused, were hauled in front of the world and forced to confess (falsely, Chambers could only assume) to being enemies of the Soviet Union.

"To the Western world," wrote Chambers, "those strange names— Rykov, Bukharin, Kamenev, Zinoviev, Piatakov, Rakovsky, Krylenko, Latsis, Tukhachevsky, Muralov, Smirnov, Karakhan, Mrachovsky— were merely tongue twisters. To a Communist, they were the men who had made one of the great transformations in human history—the Russian Revolution. The charge, on which they were one and all destroyed, the charge that they had betrayed their handiwork, was incredible. They *were* the Communist Party."[69]

That the Soviet regime could be brutal wasn't news to Chambers. He'd long believed that a new world wasn't likely to emerge without a great deal of destruction of the old, and he'd been drawn to Lenin in no small part because of his frankness about the necessity of violence. But Chambers's conception of the regime's violence, until 1936 or so, had remained conveniently romantic. It was storybook violence, redemptive and thrilling and only incidentally wrought upon the innocent. When Stalin started killing characters in the storybook—its heroes, no less—it shook Chambers.

In his autobiography, Chambers paused, at a few moments, to consider what it was that ultimately caused his break from communism. Why, after so much sacrifice and love and loyalty paid to the party, did he leave? He arrived at two kinds of answers. One was metaphysical: It was the spark of the divine in his soul, the ineradicable immanence of God, that enabled him to eventually recognize that communism wasn't a solution to the crisis of modernity, but in fact its most terrible manifestation.

Chambers's other answer was more contingent. There was no one event, person, epiphany, or betrayal that detached him from the cause to which he had devoted so much of his adult life. There were, instead, many small shocks that over the course of years dissolved his faith from below. There was the accumulated tedium of years of underground work, and how little there was to show for it. There were the sappingly antisocial patterns of underground life, all the dislocations and secrecy and lying. There was the call of the countryside, and his long-deferred dream of putting down roots. There were his children, to whom he could never give a full life if he stayed underground. There was the menagerie of grotesque characters he'd met in the underground, people whose vulgarity and mediocrity made him wonder, despite himself, at the worth of a cause that could hand authority to such types. And there were the astounding facts of Soviet cruelty, which were lying in wait for him, in plain sight, if ever he proved unflinching enough to look at them.

Against all of these reasons to break away was the leviathan fact of his communist faith, which had been his gravitational center for more than a decade. The modern world was sick, and only communism, he'd concluded, contained the possibility of a cure. To abandon communism, for Chambers, would be to abandon any hope of living in a just world. To reject it, also, would be to reject everything of personal importance he'd enmeshed in its web of meaning. He had vowed to his dead brother to avenge him through communism. Under the umbrella of communist purpose, he had formed extraordinarily close bonds with friends (the Hisses, in particular). He'd allowed himself to neglect for years the immediate needs of his family with the understanding that only a communist revolution would enable them, in the long run, to live truly fulfilled lives. To leave the party wouldn't simply entail a change of political ideas and loyalties; it would render meaningless all the sacrifices he'd made in communism's name. And it would, if he proved unable to replace communism with a new and equally substantial belief system, leave him bereft of purpose in the world, an intolerable condition for Chambers.

By the end of 1936, the balance began to tip. The purge, the strain, the secrecy, the danger, the life. It was all too much. It would be another year or so before he was able to say to himself, definitively, that he intended to leave the party. Once the angle of his interpretive lens had shifted, however, he saw evidence against communism everywhere, and he began seeking it out as well.

In 1937, Chambers finally decided to read an anti-Soviet book. The one he found, *I Speak for the Silent*, couldn't have been better chosen to erode what was left of his faith. Its author, Vladimir Tchernavin, was a former scientist with the Soviets' state fishing agency—a man of hard facts and clear-eyed reason—and the book was an unrelenting, unsentimental account not just of Tchernavin's own descent into the Soviet prison system, but of the absolute corruption and almost comic folly of the Soviet government. It was as if Lenin, fifteen years after *The Soviets at Work*, had returned from the dead to survey the dry facts of the government he created, only to discover that everything was the inverse of what he'd promised. Not justice but crass opportunism was the logic of the system. Not the best but the worst were in charge. Not efficiency but disorder reigned.[70]

Chambers had never been impressed with the quality of the people in the American party, or with the wisdom of the party's strategies, but he had consoled himself with the assumption that in the Soviet Union things were better. And even if it wasn't perfect over there, it was at least an imperfect system guided by high-minded leaders and a vision of justice. The Soviet government of *I Speak for the Silent* was devoid of anything resembling high-mindedness. There were decent, intelligent souls in Tchernavin's Soviet Union, but almost without exception they were being shaken down, jailed, or executed. They were the victims of the idiots, thugs, manipulators, and sociopaths who were in charge (who were in turn always victimizing each other).

Just as devastating to Chambers's faith was the story that Tchernavin told of the ruin of the fishing industry by the government's attempt to centralize economic planning. At every level, from the fishing trawlers to the docks to the refineries to the administrative offices in Murmansk to the headquarters in Moscow, incompetence, corruption, and brutality were rewarded while honesty, intelligence, integrity, and efficiency were extinguished. In less than two years, from 1930 to 1931, the secret police (the GPU) and the Soviet central planners took what had been a growing, highly efficient operation—proof, indeed, that a communist economy could prosper—and ran it full speed into the ground. Then, when it became apparent what a mess they'd made, they accused the people like Tchernavin, whose advice they'd ignored, of intentionally sabotaging the operation. Then they killed them or sent them to prison.

"No disaster, no epidemic, no war could destroy with such selection the cream of experienced and active workers in the industries which the GPU attacked," wrote Tchernavin. "This wholesale destruction of specialists could not fail to have fatal results for the fishing business. . . . The same conditions prevailed, in general, in all the industries of the U.S.S.R. . . . The Bolsheviks for the second time were leading a rich and prosperous country into terrible poverty and dreadful famine."[71]

If one believed what Tchernavin wrote, and by this point Chambers did, there could be nothing left of the communist dream. Cruel necessity was something that Chambers could tolerate, as long as he didn't look at it too closely, but if Tchernavin was right, then there was nothing at all in the Soviet Union to justify any of the cruelty. The whole thing was a fraud. It was the corruption of the modern world distilled into a putrid essence. It didn't ennoble people; it debased them. It didn't dissolve alienation; it exacerbated it. Neither Tchernavin nor Chambers knew, at the time, how many millions of people had died of starvation and disease as a result of the economic policies and practices of the regime, or how many millions more would die in the prison system from which Tchernavin and his family managed to escape. Such possibilities were implicit, however, in what Tchernavin described: a system that had gone insane.

There were other blows to Chambers's faith in communism. An old friend of his, someone who'd helped recruit him into the underground, returned from a trip to Moscow terrified for his life. "I will not work one more hour for those murderers!"[72] he told Chambers. Another old acquaintance, a woman who'd been in the first party unit that Chambers had joined, was abducted and murdered by the Soviet secret police after she'd deserted the underground. People Chambers knew kept being sent to Moscow and then disappearing. Others whom he knew only by reputation were killed by the GPU as they tried to escape.

That his own underground story could end similarly was brought home to him, most directly, when he was assigned a new boss in the fall of 1936 (after his previous boss was recalled to Russia, never to be heard from again). Colonel Boris Bykov—"Peter," as Chambers knew him— was a petty, paranoid, vulgar Stalinoid type who distrusted Chambers from the first and who subjected him, for the next year and a half, to a running stream of accusation and interrogation. Bykov was the threat of the purge in person, always questioning Chambers about his loyalty, half-ordering him (daring him, really) to go to Russia to prove his commitment, and taunting him with snippets of information about the latest old Bolshevik who'd been forced to confess to treason before being shot.

"'Where is Bukharin?' Bykov asked me slyly some weeks after the Communist Party's leading theoretician had been sentenced to death for high treason.

"'Dead,' I answered rudely.

"'You are right,' said Bykov in a cooing voice, 'you are right. You can be absolutely sure that our Bukharin is dead.'"[73]

With the arrival of Colonel Bykov in America, the sleeper cell was activated. By early 1937, Chambers had set up a slick operation to transmit classified U.S. government information to the Soviet Union. He'd meet his sources at some unremarkable spot in or around D.C. (a park, an intersection, a diner). They'd hand off to him whatever documents they were able to procure since their last meeting. He'd take the documents back to a rented apartment in Baltimore, photograph them, return them to his contacts, and then, once or twice a week, deliver them to Bykov in New York. It was a simple process, made difficult largely by the fact that Chambers and Esther had recently succumbed to their country-lust and were living out in rural Pennsylvania, about a three-and-a-half-hour drive away from Washington and an hour and a half from New York.

As the apparatus got up to full speed, and the volume of information increased, Chambers moved his family back to Baltimore. He also brought in two party photographers to help handle the flow of documents, which were coming primarily from four people: Alger Hiss, who was then at the State Department; Harry Dexter White, a Harvard-trained economist who was at the Treasury Department; William Ward Pigman, a biochemist who was at the Bureau of Standards; and Julian Wadleigh, an economist at the State Department.

The information, which would later prove so spectacular as evidence in the espionage trials that made Chambers and Hiss household names, was on its own terms rather unspectacular. It consisted of the kinds of messages, memos, analyses, and statistics that were classified mostly because the government, as a matter of course, didn't think it was a great idea to expose its inner workings to the world. Once in a while Chambers glanced at what he was photographing to see if it was interesting, but it quickly became apparent that there was nothing in the documents that an intelligent observer of world politics couldn't extrapolate from reading the papers and knowing his history.

As the foreman of the operation, Chambers observed a few of the secrecy protocols that he'd learned when he was new to the underground, but he wasn't nearly as cautious as he'd once been. He'd long since realized that there was no organized counterintelligence program within the American government. If his cell were to be found out, it would happen because someone on the inside had chosen to inform on the party, not because a team of FBI agents had painstakingly surveilled and deconstructed the cell's movements and organizational structure. The topography of Washington, too, with its broad avenues and austere neoclassical buildings, wasn't nearly as conducive to the dramatic experience of underground life as was New York, with its shadows, alleys, canyons, and teeming masses of suspicious people.

What was stressful, for Chambers, was everything else. He was still cruising for sex with men, which was no less shameful to him than it had been when he began. He was still moving the family around frequently, and the effects of this were becoming evident in his daughter Ellen, who was visibly lonely. Colonel Bykov, like all bad bosses, was making it difficult for Chambers to take pleasure in his work. And the revelations about the horrors of Stalin's regime had pushed Chambers to the point of ideological collapse. He knew that communism was not what he'd thought it was. What he didn't know, and what he needed to know before he could take action, was what could replace it.

Chambers began praying, awkwardly at first, sometime in 1937. It was a new practice for him, but not exactly a novel experience. He'd always had his moments of wonderment, his experiences of communion with forces greater than himself. Usually such feelings had come to him in the presence of nature, or in the aftermath of a death. His conversion to communism had a spiritual quality to it. It was felt with far more intensity than could be explained by any rational evaluation of the state of the world and the various ideological approaches to it. And if *Witness* is to be believed, he'd had encounters even as a boy with a presence that he'd named "God," though he'd never managed to stitch together such encounters into a coherent and sustaining religious narrative. What was different, this time, was that he began praying, and he kept to it. And as the prayer became a habit, and a steady source of consolation, he began perceiving in his spiritual discoveries a possible answer to his crisis of political faith.

"In those days, I often moved about or performed tasks more or less blindly from habit, while my mind was occupied with its mortal debate," wrote Chambers. "One day as I came down the stairs in the Mount Royal Terrace house, the question of the impossible return [out of communism] struck me with sudden sharpness. I thought: 'You cannot do it. No one can go back.' As I stepped down into the dark hall, I found myself stopped, not by a constraint, but by the hush of my whole being. In this organic hush, a voice said with perfect distinctness: 'If you will fight for freedom, all will be well with you.' The words are nothing. Perhaps there were no words, only an uttered meaning to which my mind supplied the words. What was there was the sense that, like me, time and the world stood still, an awareness of God as an envelopment, holding me in silent assurance and untroubled peace. There was a sense that in that moment I gave my promise, not with the mind, but with my whole being, and that this was a covenant I might not break."[74]

In front of Chambers, from that point on, lay a complicated path. He'd have to find a way to keep his family safe while detaching himself from the party. He'd have to decide whether to go to the government and confess his sins. He'd have to find a way to pay the bills.

The paramount challenge, however, had been dissolved by his encounter with the ineffable. In God he'd found a replacement vision that seemed deep enough to sustain him emotionally and rich enough, in its explanatory power, to provide answers to the questions about modern life that still haunted him. The crisis of his time had not, in his opinion, gone away. The world, he believed, remained profoundly alienated from itself. Chambers still felt the calling to fight for the redemption of humanity. But that fight, now, was on behalf of what was godly in man, and against its nemesis: "the whole web of the materialist modern mind—the luminous shroud which it has spun about the spirit of man, paralyzing in the name of rationalism the instinct of his soul for God, denying in the name of knowledge the reality of the soul and its birthright in that mystery on which mere knowledge falters and shatters at every step."[75]

Some version of the materialist heresy had always been at the root of what tortured Chambers about the world. If this was all there was to life—dirt, blood, bureaucracy, power, money, lonely people reaching desperately for each other in a futile attempt to escape their loneliness—then his own misery not only had no salve, it had no meaning. As a boy, he'd mostly just struggled to survive, to find some consolation in nature and in books, and to separate himself as much as possible from his family. As a college student Chambers had decided, along with his friends, that in the face of the world's emptiness the only courageous response was to embrace it. As a communist he'd sought resolution in a politics of solidarity, sacrifice, and future harmony. The turn to God was his latest (and, it turned out, his final) answer to the question of what to do with a world that was manifestly unable to satisfy the yearnings or assuage the fears of the men and women to whom it played host. He would be devout. He would be faithful to his wife. He would tend to his children, and teach them to love God and dwell close to the earth. He would live in the countryside, among decent people of simple faith, away from the corruptions of the city and the blandishments of intellectuals. And, because he was who he was, unable to live without high purpose, addicted to politics, he would fight communism with all his heart and soul. Against this falsest of false idols, this nightmare vision of man worshipping himself, he would dedicate himself as a soldier of God, of freedom, and (with many qualifications) of the American way.

From the autumn of 1937, when he decided to break, until the spring of 1938, when he finally packed his family into a car and disappeared into the Baltimore night, Chambers devoted himself to three purposes: He planned his escape from the party; he began to translate his spiritual conviction into a workable political, philosophical, and personal program for how to live out his remaining time on earth; and he endeavored to carry on his espionage work, under the suspicious eye of Colonel Bykov, as if he were as staunch as ever. For Chambers it all merged into one grand crescendo of principled, performative defiance.

Over the subsequent months, Chambers laid the groundwork for his break. In order to protect himself, he bought a knife, which he began carrying around with him whenever he felt vulnerable, strapping the blade under his vest in such a way that he'd be able to draw it as quickly as possible if threatened. In order to have somewhere hidden to take his family when he made the break, he rented rooms in a house just outside the Baltimore city limits. With a loan from Alger Hiss, he was able to exchange his old clunker (which the party knew about and might be able to trace) for a more reliable and more anonymous car. He was even able to get himself a job with the federal government, under his real name, with the assistance of one of his assets, who was the research director of the Railroad Retirement Board. For a few months he worked for the National Research Project, in the process both establishing a public identity (which would make it harder, in theory, for the party to simply disappear him) and earning some money to support his family once he was in exile. Through Meyer Schapiro, his old friend from Columbia, he found some work as a translator that he could do after he went into hiding. And he began keeping for himself copies of various documents and memos he got from his sources, putting together a cache of material that included, most fatefully, documents typed on Alger Hiss's typewriter and notes scribbled by Hiss.

In April of 1938, Chambers had his last meeting as a Communist. He collected documents from one of his sources, kept some of them for his secret stash, and turned the rest over to one of his photographers. Then he disappeared. When he re-emerged, it would be as a mortal enemy of communism.

"I could, possibly, have had myself transferred, on one pretext or another, from the underground to the open Communist Party—such transfers are not uncommon," he wrote. "Once back in the open party, after a suitable period of shuffling, I could gradually have lapsed from it. It would have been unpleasant. There might have been some petty annoyances. It is unlikely that I would have been physically molested. But such a course would have meant some agreement, some kind of hobbling terms, between the Communist Party and me. I wanted no terms. I deliberately deserted from the Communist Party in a way that could leave no doubt in its mind, or anybody else's, that I was at war with it and everything it stood for."[76]

2

The Finest Brain: James Burnham

Jim is not essentially a poetic mind; he is a first-rate mind of another breed.[1]

—WHITTAKER CHAMBERS

Burnham does not recognize the dialectic, but the dialectic recognizes Burnham.[2]

—LEON TROTSKY

And now from that warmth, that youth, that careless confidence, to be plunged (and how soon) into this long frost of the human spirit! Abruptly, and for reasons there certainly was no professor to explain, everything we had been bred to and trained for, everything the College had polished us to attain—the easy good manners, the charm, the intelligence, the stations in life hereditary to the ruling caste whose blossoming generation we had been told we were—all this vanished under a mountainous rubble of avalanching quotations from a thousand chattering stocktickers; and suddenly nothing remained to us at all—our training and competence nothing, our prerogatives nothing, our intelligence with nothing to be applied to, our lives with nothing they could return to or think of as their own.[3]

—W. M. SPACKMAN (PRINCETON '27)

There's a moment in James Burnham's tenth book, *Suicide of the West* (1964), that captures something of the special quality of his voice. It comes at the start of the sixth chapter. Burnham, a senior editor of the conservative *National Review*, has spent the previous chapters laying down some technically accurate but rather provocative definitions of what American liberals believe. Before he pivots to the more aggressive parts of the book, where he'll argue that liberalism is steering the ship of Western civilization straight into the iceberg of decline, he pauses to make sure the reader is up to speed. He writes:

> *The preceding three chapters have put before us, lighted and focused under an analytic microscope, the ideology of liberalism exhibited as a set of nineteen primary ideas and beliefs—twenty-two, if we include the three corollaries. Just as in the case of the thirty-nine sentences listed in Chapter II, I think most Americans and Europeans will find that they agree with almost all of the nineteen, or disagree with many or most of them. That is to say, Americans and Europeans are either infected with the liberal ideology and therefore manifest many of the symptoms of the liberal syndrome; or they are not, and don't.*[4]

If this chapter were a study of James Burnham written by James Burnham, it would extract from the biographical data about its subject a unified theory of history, politics, and psychology. It would parcel up his life into discrete units of analysis, then run each unit through the filter of his analytic microscope, and fit it all back together again into a completely analyzed whole. It would chart out the deep grooves of history that were able to take a man like James Burnham and herd him, along with so many of his contemporaries, along such a specific itinerary, from modern literature to Marxism to nationalism to conservatism. It would be generous in its deployment of numbered lists. And it would get some important things right about what kind of person Burnham was.

What Burnham would miss, were he able to look at himself with the cold analytical gaze he cast on others, would have been something more existential. Leaking out past the margins of his numbered lists and through the seams of his many theses there was an excess. His "schematism," as his friend and fellow ex-leftist Whittaker Chambers once called it,[5] simply couldn't do what he needed it to do, which was contain and order not just the data of the external world but also the psychical energies he sublimated into intellectual activity. Thus, for all the surface control his writing exhibited, its most salient literary quality was a kind of unassigned, surplus emotionality. Also a persistent habit of making utterly confident, and consistently erroneous, predictions about the future of the world.[6]

For Burnham something essential was not in control. This was true in the late 1920s, when he immersed himself in the cultural activities that were in vogue among American intellectuals. It was true in the 1930s, when the stage for political heroism and struggle widened, and the politics and philosophy of Marxism offered the most compelling vehicles through which to intervene. And it was true after he rejected Marxism, and went on to devote a great deal of the remainder of his life's energies to fighting the Soviet Union's influence in the world and Marxism's and liberalism's influence among American and European intellectuals.

In each iteration Burnham couldn't close the gap between what his powerful but human mind could do and the excessive demands he placed upon it. And each ideological system in turn, until he settled into conservatism, fractured in no small part because it failed to process and interpret the data of the external and internal world adequately for Burnham. Marxism made the most possible sense to Burnham, intellectually, for most of an unusual decade, at a moment in his life when he was open to influence. But it would prove an ill fit for him in many other ways. Once it began to lose intellectual cohesion, the bonds of loyalty and community that tied him to the Left were too weak to sustain the political attachment. Set free from that unlikely commitment, in that age of extremity, he made his way to the political identity one might have prophesied for him from the start, if one had looked down on him in his cradle and had to guess which flag to lay upon it. And he stayed there for the rest of his life. Not because conservatism failed him intellectually any less often or less predictably than his left-wing theories had, but because it met more of his nonintellectual needs, and no man is the sum of his intellect. Even, or particularly, those like Burnham whose journey is fueled by the desire to achieve just such a synchrony.

James Burnham was born on November 22, 1905, into unusually fortunate circumstances. His nation was rising as a military and economic power. His city, Chicago, was becoming one of the signal metropolises of the industrial age. His family, propelled by the drive and intelligence of his father—the son of poor immigrants from rural England—was ascending rapidly toward the upper reaches of Chicago society. James and his younger brothers David and Philip would grow up in a world that seemed fitted to their advantage.[7]

In 1914 the Burnhams moved from Chicago to Kenilworth, a tiny suburb just north of the city that was part of the belt of wealthy communities along Lake Michigan known as the North Shore. Kenilworth had been the grand project of a retired industrialist with visions of suburban utopia, and it was designed, even more than its fellow North Shore suburbs, as a refuge from the disorder of the city. It was an enclave of 175 families of the highest character, and income, buffered from the disruptive emanations of the city by the lake on one side and the suburban principalities of Winnetka, Wilmette, and Evanston on the other three.[8]

In many ways the Burnhams were like their neighbors in Kenilworth. They had servants, nicely landscaped grounds, and a membership in the country club. They were white. They believed in America and its promise. What distinguished them was their Catholicism, which was understated but genuine; their intelligence, which was exceptionally high; and a fusion of those aspects into a sense of moralism and mission that would ultimately manifest, in each of the children, as a calling to write (about faith, for Philip; fiction, for David; on politics, for James).

In the fall of 1922 James and David were sent off to the Canterbury School, a small boarding school in rural Connecticut that had been founded, only a few years before, precisely for affluent Catholic parents like the Burnhams. Unusual for the time, it combined a religious education that was properly Catholic with a social preparation that was entirely pre–Ivy League.

At Canterbury, which he entered as a junior, James excelled. His grades were the best in his class for both of the two years he was there. He scored higher than any student had ever before scored on the college placement exams. He played a brisk game of tennis, and he wrote a lot, mostly for the school literary magazine.

His first published essay, "Riding a Morning Round-Up," was a precociously written report of the morning when he finally got permission from his parents to round up cattle with the cowboys at the dude ranch out West where the family vacationed. To the extent that the essay revealed anything about Burnham, it was that, aside from an unusually sophisticated way with language, he was a lot like other boys his age. He was very proud of being able to ride horses well. He admired cowboys, and bought into the mythos of the West, a place where men spoke little but did much. And he'd probably read more westerns than was entirely healthy for a budding young psyche.

"It was thrilling," he wrote, of the climax of the roundup, "the two hundred animals running all together, snapping and biting at each other, sending up clouds of dust which choked us—every muscle working to its utmost in the furious strain of the gallop—the roar of eight hundred iron shoes, pounding and clicking on rocks and stones—and, above all, the horse smell, the horse atmosphere, all seeming to put us into a very maelstrom of restless, rushing, turbulent horses. For a half mile it continued, and then headlong into the corral rushed the whole wild herd, and as after an angry storm at sea, they gradually subsided, milling, chafing, muttering, moving, more and more slowly, until at last they were still, quiet, peaceful, at rest."[9]

Subsequent pieces in the literary magazine would reveal the same blend of exceptional skill and fairly typical attitudes for a boy of his background. He was a bit racist, a bit snobbish, very patriotic, and profoundly romantic. In almost every one of Burnham's schoolboy pieces—fiction and essays alike—his hero was someone who had put aside the normal attachments of life in order to seek out a higher truth or serve a greater cause.

"He would be talking to you or listening to you, and you would suddenly realize that his eyes were no longer focused, but were gazing far, far off," wrote Burnham, describing the hero of one of his short stories. "They were not looking at any distant object or indistinct horizon; they seemed to be contemplating infinity itself. He never missed a word of what you were saying, but those eyes looked on towards bottomless depths and topless pinnacles."[10]

Burnham closed out his time at Canterbury by winning the Headmaster's Essay Contest, the topic of which was "Do Present Conditions in America Stimulate the Production of Literature?" His answer was a brash yes. World War I, he wrote, had so upended life in the Western world, had so "revivified existence," that America, which was the most dynamic of the Western countries, was poised to produce a tidal wave of literature that would transform the world's culture as surely as American industry and ingenuity were transforming the world's economy. It would be a literature, he argued, that would fuse the legacy of the past with the dynamism of the modern world. It would take from the factories and tenements of the East as much as from the broad blue skies and endless plains of the West. And it would be manifested in the world by a rising young generation of American writers for whom the literary life was the highest calling of them all. "They wish to write," he wrote, "and they will write."[11]

When Burnham arrived as a freshman at Princeton University in the fall of 1923, there were better Ivy League schools. Yale had its future senators, Harvard its medievalists-in-the-making, Columbia its budding literary critics. There was nowhere, however, that was more seductive than Princeton, nowhere more redolent with the scent of privilege and pleasure. It was where you went to learn, more enjoyably than anywhere else, the manners of the upper class. These were the jokes that could be told, and at whose expense. These were the drinks one drank, and the way that one handled oneself when too much had been drunk. These were the ways that one conducted an illicit affair, and the fashion in which one negotiated its consequences. These were the prejudices that were acceptable, and the vulnerabilities that weren't. This was how to climb without looking like you were breathing too hard.

Burnham was at home in this world. He improved his game of tennis, and picked up golf and boxing. He spent many a late night playing bridge with his friends, or drinking and jousting with his comrades in Tower, one of the university's exclusive eating clubs. He relaxed into the life that F. Scott Fitzgerald had described so languorously in his Princeton novel, *This Side of Paradise*, "lazy and good-looking and aristocratic—you know, like a spring day."

Burnham enjoyed this Princeton, but was animated as well by a sense of purpose that was more urgent than what was typical for his milieu. In the spaces between one bridge session and the next, he read Tolstoy and Proust and T. S. Eliot. He surrounded himself with other boys who cared more than was strictly necessary for books and culture and ideas. He became known among his classmates, and by the faculty, as an exceptional generalist, someone whose passion lay more in the exercise of his mind than in its application to any particular topic.

"Without any question the finest brain I have encountered in all my years at Princeton," one of Burnham's literature professors later said of him.[12]

Burnham also wrote, though not nearly as much as one might have predicted from his habit at Canterbury. He spent some time with the *Princeton Tiger*, the campus humor magazine, producing the kinds of glib pieces that the rest of the staff were doing. More interesting were the two stories he wrote for the campus literary magazine, both of which turned on how often men hide or look away from love, and on the consequences of such evasion.[13]

After the end of his junior year, when the second story was published, Burnham wouldn't write anything else while at Princeton. He spent his last year much as he had his first three, relaxing enough to keep pace with his classmates while working hard enough to surpass them. He graduated in May as the class's top scholar, and was honored at commencement for, among other accomplishments, best exam and best thesis on the topic of British philosophy.

Upon graduating, Burnham signed up for another two years of the frictionless life, transplanted to Balliol College, Oxford, one of the more storied of the ancient university's colleges, recognized as the place to go for young men possessed not just of good breeding but of exquisite taste and intellect as well. Over the course of his two years at Oxford, he played golf in Scotland, drank wine in Paris, admired the austere beauty of Florence, and traveled to Bayreuth, Germany, for the annual Wagner festival. He continued to impress his teachers— among others, J. R. R. Tolkien for medieval literature—and to refine the cool style he'd adopted at Princeton. His isolation, or insulation, from politics continued. The life of his mind was oriented around Aristotle and Eliot, Aquinas and Joyce, not yet Marx and Engels, Trotsky and Stalin.

"It's not a third so different from Princeton as the story books tell us, Oxford isn't," he wrote to an old friend from Kenilworth, "especially with ten of my own class here, and eighteen other Princeton men besides. Of course the town is bigger than Princeton, and the buildings are older, and it rains more, and there's no central heating, but people *do* just about the same things: drink and play cards and go to the movies (they're 'flicks' in England) and talk nonsense and study a little and drink."[14]

Not long after arriving at Oxford, Burnham began corresponding with a former professor of his from Princeton, Philip Wheelwright, about starting a journal of culture and philosophy when Burnham returned to the States. He also engaged Wheelwright, who had moved over from Princeton to Washington Square College, in New York City, to help him find a teaching job.

In June of 1928, about a year after Burnham arrived in England, his father died. It wasn't sudden, exactly. Claude Burnham had been laid up with a heart condition for six months before succumbing to pneumonia. But it was disruptive. The elder Burnham was only forty-seven when he died, and he left his sons little time to adapt to the idea of life without a father.

There's no direct record of what the death meant to Burnham. Just a few years later, however, Burnham's younger brother David would publish a novel, *This Our Exile*, about the sickness and death of a family patriarch and the devastating effect it has on his three very Burnhamlike sons. The attention it pays to Fred, who is clearly modeled on James, is in many ways the gravitational center of the book. He is the most forceful and charismatic of the novel's characters. The most loved, and resented, by his mother. He is given the smartest lines. And because he denies himself the consolation of any form of grieving that strikes him as sentimental or irrational, he ends up the most lost. The stoicism, and the emotion compressed into it, reach a crescendo in a confrontation he has with the middle brother, an alter ego of David Burnham, as they drive to church one Sunday not long after their father's death.

Fred [James] was driving. When he drove he always sat very stiffly at the wheel, leaning forward and never taking his eyes off the road. He said straight into the wheel, "I went to see some friends of mine in Paris the day after their only child, a fourteen-year-old boy, had died. When I got there I thought I must have made a mistake. They were having what looked exactly like a reception, and there wasn't a sign of mourning in the whole house. The boy's mother said to me, 'Why should we mourn? Will it help Richard?

Will it help us? Will it help anyone? We've had fourteen years of a pleasure we might not have expected: should we mourn because of that?'"

"That's abnormality in the other direction."

"It's sanity, not abnormality," said Fred. "Regret is beyond all question of a doubt the most worthless of human emotions. I do it too great an honor to call it an emotion; it's a sentimentalist's perversion."

"You won't deny, though," I said, "that you feel regret as a natural response. Or at least grief—you yourself feel as much grief over Dad's death, you must admit, as either Jackie or I."

"Feeling it," Fred said into the wheel, "only serves to remind me to fight it to the utmost of my endeavor."

". . . Emotions aren't run by logic."

"Then," Fred said, "it shall be my life's work to see that they are. I shall devote my life and my magazine to educating the public to a new emotional consciousness." [15]

When Burnham arrived in New York in the fall of 1929, after two years in England, it was in many respects another soft landing. Most of his friends from Princeton were living there, working in business or journalism or the law, continuing the lives of ease and dissipation they'd learned at Princeton. They were having the same kinds of parties they'd had back on campus, lubricated by the same potent Prohibition liquor and animated by the same cynical, sizzling, sexy conversation that had already been mythologized as the representative banter of the 1920s.

Burnham dipped into that world comfortably, but rarely at the expense of his work, which was and would remain the primary channel for his energies, particularly at moments of high emotional stress. Wheelwright had been able to secure for him an instructorship in the philosophy department at Washington Square, teaching introductory surveys and the occasional elective. It wasn't glamorous work, and it was outside Burnham's academic focus at Princeton and Oxford, which had been literature, but it was a good perch from which to establish himself in the city, and the teaching played to his strengths. He was a diligent worker, able to spend long hours preparing lectures so that they might appear effortless by the time they were delivered in class. He was also a natural explicator, able to untangle thorny concepts into the kinds of discrete threads that students could more easily grasp, and then to methodically weave the pieces back together into a clear narrative.

Whatever gaps there were in his knowledge, when he began teaching, were filled in quickly by his hard work, or obscured by his general sheen of sophistication. He benefited, as well, by the fact that the bar wasn't too high. The American academy hadn't yet been fully professionalized, or meritocratized, and the faculties of even the best schools were nearly as full of cranks and fossils as they were of serious scholars. At Washington Square College, which wasn't yet one of the finest schools, the median professor was underwhelming. Among Burnham's philosophy colleagues was one first-rate thinker—Sidney Hook, a brilliant young Jewish fellow from Brooklyn who'd studied with John Dewey at Columbia—and a few capable ones, but also plenty of dimmer lights.

It was the students, and the site, that hummed. Housed mostly in a converted factory building in Greenwich Village, the college was a satellite campus of New York University. It was a place for those students who couldn't afford, or weren't welcome at, the more socially exclusive NYU campus up in the Bronx. There were no living quarters down in the Village, no playing fields, no verdant lawns, not much in the way of jolly college life, and not much access to the resources of the main campus. Yet for all its shabbiness it was a more intellectually vibrant place than the campus up north, brimming over with the energies of the city and with the ambitions of its students, many of them children of Jewish immigrants from eastern Europe. The physical space of the college, too, was an emblematically modern American space, a factory for the production of students and knowledge, filled to bursting with aspiration and energy. And it was located in the Village, a place where artists, intellectuals, eccentrics, and political agitators had long gathered to attune themselves to the slightest emanations from the zeitgeist. It was no accident that the arguments the students were having with each other and with their teachers—about the causes of, and solutions to, the economic situation; about the great ideologies of the twentieth century; about the peculiar agonies and excitements of modern life— were the ones that would come to define the intellectual spirit of the decade.[16]

The figure that Burnham cut, in these surroundings, was a striking one. Young, urbane, reserved, elegantly turned out, he seemed to his students an emissary from the world they were in college either to join or to overthrow. On his colleagues he made a forceful impression as well. They were for the most part better credentialed than he was, and more senior at the college, but Burnham walked among them as if he were their natural superior. Wheelwright, his old teacher, seemed more than a little bit in love with him. The old guard were threatened by him. Even Hook, who was smarter and more subtle than Burnham, found him impressive.

For Burnham the air of absolute assurance was both a genuine expression of his sense of himself, and a defense. He'd been raised as though the things of the world were his entitlement. He'd been told, over and over again, that he was the smartest boy in the room, and had learned that the world would reward him for acting that way. But he was also still a young man, still uncertain who he was and what he was meant to be like in the world. And circumstances had conspired to inject a rougher kind of uncertainty into his life than was familiar. His father had just died. He was no longer embedded in the matrix of achievement and approval that had structured his identity as a student. And for the first time in his life he was expected (more or less) to earn his own way, a condition that was compounded, two months after starting his job at Washington Square, when the stock market crashed, setting off what would become an extraordinary period of economic uncertainty and hardship in the nation's life. The result of all this turmoil, evident in his writing if not in his manner, was an urgent, compensatory drive to prove himself.

In January of 1930, he and Wheelwright published the debut issue of their journal the *Symposium*. It was the result of almost two years spent assessing the optimal vector from which to make their arrival on the New York intellectual scene. They'd taken a sounding of their own expertise, the cultural mood, and the talents of their friends from Princeton (who contributed about half of the content). They'd called upon their dean at the college to fund the publication. And they'd solicited content from friends, mentors, colleagues, and luminaries.

The initial product was, if not exactly a success, then at least a start. It had some impressive names, including that of John Dewey, who was the pre-eminent American philosopher of the time. There was one really exceptional piece of criticism, a review by Lionel Trilling of new novels by Faulkner and Hemingway. And for filler there were many unembarrassing contributions from Princeton friends and from colleagues at Washington Square.

Burnham himself wrote two things. The first, cowritten with Wheelwright, was a short introductory comment at the front of the *Symposium*. It announced the mission of the journal, which was to "bring out more clearly the relations among contemporary ideas" in philosophy and the arts. The second was a long review of *Practical Criticism*, the pioneering work of literary criticism by Cambridge professor I. A. Richards. It was Burnham's real debut as a professional critic. And it was a mess. Far from bringing clarity either to Richards's work or to the realm in which he was a player—the coalescing field of modern literary criticism—Burnham wrote about *Practical Criticism* as though, underneath it all, he didn't really care very much about poetry or about literary criticism, as if they were merely the pretext for the hurricane of saying and observing that Burnham himself needed to unleash. He spent pages scoring trivial logical points. He digressed on psychology and etymology and communications theory. His sentences fell on top of each other in a nettle of clauses, qualifications, references, and interjections.[17]

Burnham's style would settle down a bit after that, but almost all of his essays and review in the *Symposium* over the next two years would manifest a similar anxiety. Sometimes he wrote as though he were still trying to impress the teachers and tutors who'd been his exclusive audience until only a few months before. Sometimes he seemed impatient, as if his subject were standing in the way of what he really needed to say. He seemed desperately, if unconsciously, in search of a system that would allow him to make sense of the disorderliness of the world. Whatever the topic—late-seventeenth-century English drama, the occult in literature, a novel by a good friend of his from Oxford—what was consistent was a pose of utter certainty betrayed, in its execution, by an inability to say anything simple and straightforward about what he believed or cared about.

Conspicuously absent from Burnham's product, and from the magazine as a whole, was reference to the political and economic situation into which the *Symposium* was born. In a limited way the magazine was impressive, in touch with the main currents of modernism and savvy about whom to solicit for contributions. And to the extent that it was created to establish Burnham as a player in the New York intellectual scene, it succeeded. Very quickly he became a name the right people knew and took seriously. But there was something off in the angle of the magazine's attention. For the *Symposium*, for too long, life went on as if it were still 1928, when Burnham and Wheelwright had concluded that the problems of modern existence were cultural and critical rather than political or economic.

In the spring 1931 issue of the *Symposium*, in an essay otherwise about the state of contemporary physics, Burnham finally allowed himself to refer to the economic troubles. He mentioned the Depression twice, and apparently offhandedly. Politics were present, however, in the anger that suffused the essay, which was wildly out of proportion to the topic that he appeared to be addressing. He was annoyed with Einstein and his fellow relativists for the "wretchedly bungled" terminology they'd devised for their theories. He was furious with another physicist for using his scientific reputation to sell half-baked Christian metaphysics to the masses. Burnham even seemed resentful of the discipline of physics itself, for the chasm between its power to uncover facts about the universe and its impotence in revealing to us what any of the facts mean.

"What difference does it make to anyone whether the world ends in a thousand or a million or a billion years?" he wrote. ". . . [W]hat could it mean for the whole universe to expand? What could size be when there is nothing to have it? What is a year when there is nothing to measure a year by? . . . Neither God nor the good life is to be found at the end of telescope or microscope, or lurking among the Lorentz transformations."[18]

At first glance the autumn 1931 issue of the *Symposium* wasn't too different from past issues. Most of the feature essays were once again absurdly broad attempts to lay a foundation for literary criticism in the twentieth century. The contributors were once again drawn from the familiar coterie of Ivy League–, Oxbridge-, and City College–educated men who would, in fact, lay much of the foundation for literary criticism in the twentieth century.

Amidst the usual poetry, criticism, and philosophy of the autumn issue, however, were two articles that struck a different note. One was a short review of two recent books on economics and the state of the American economy; it dismissed them, curtly, for their failure to analyze the Depression through a sufficiently socialistic lens. The other odd duck of the issue came from Sidney Hook, Burnham's colleague at Washington Square, and soon his guide in the ways and ideas of the Left.

"Toward the Understanding of Karl Marx" was the longest essay the *Symposium* had ever published, and a departure not just in its subject matter, but in its maturity. Unlike Burnham, Hook wasn't still questing for a system with which to order the world. He had a system—two, in fact. He'd been a Marxist since high school, and as an academic he'd been immersing himself for years in the study of pragmatist philosophy.

When he wrote of Marx and Marxism, it was with a fully formed voice, rooted in Marxist theory but also comfortable reinterpreting the canon in light of changed circumstances and a competing philosophical tradition.[19]

"The world today stands in the shadow of a man not yet dead fifty years," Hook began. "The doctrines of Karl Marx, comparatively unknown and ignored in his own lifetime, exercise a stronger influence upon the present age than the social theories of any of our contemporaries. History is being made in their name. A new philosophy of life, avowedly Marxist in inspiration, is slowly emerging to challenge the dominant attitudes and values of Western and Oriental culture. No one interested in the philosophy of civilizations can escape the necessity of coming to critical grips with it."[20]

Over the next forty pages, Hook succinctly laid out the basics of what he saw as the four major strands of contemporary Marxism, concluding with his own vision of how Marx should most authentically be interpreted. It was a bravura performance, not just a crash course on Marxist theory for his audience of discombobulated American intellectuals but also, it would turn out, a rather good forecast of the conflicting and overlapping tendencies that would characterize the Left in America and Europe over the coming decade.

There were the fuddy-duddy German Marxists, who used Marx, and his "scientific" assurances of a socialist future, as an excuse to rest easy with the bourgeois present. There were the social democratic revisionists, who were even happier to forgo the revolution but were at least intellectually honest about it. There were the syndicalists, embodied for Hook in the French thinker Georges Sorel, who had cut out from Marx almost everything that was practical, leaving behind a prophetic vision of revolutionary action that was beautiful in its fire but troubling in its lack of specificity. And there were the Bolsheviks, pragmatic and ruthless, who had concluded (correctly, in Hook's view) that the proper focus of a socialist movement in a not-yet-socialist society had to be, before all else, the seizure of power by the proletariat.

And, finally, there was what Hook thought Marxism truly was.* In many respects it aligned with the arguments of the Bolsheviks. Hook agreed with them that the proletariat would never attain power simply through the good grace of History, as the fantasies of the orthodox German Marxists would have it. True socialism would never evolve, gently, from the selective action of the legislature, as the social democrats would have it. It wouldn't arise magically from the ashes of a society disintegrated by the poetic violence of the syndicalists. It would occur only through the action of a dedicated and theoretically informed corps of professional revolutionists, who would both ride and shape the wave of militant proletarian consciousness that was the prime actor in the latest phase of economic history.

Yet for Hook, Marx was something more than a strategist of revolution. He was a philosopher—someone who had, more masterfully than anyone else in recent history, created a philosophical system that was subtle enough to reveal the world's inner structures, potent enough to alter them, and supple enough to reshape itself in response to the evidence of failed hypotheses.

The world, in this interpretation of Marx, was a vast experimental laboratory. A good revolutionist came to the lab bench with the best available facts, categories, and hypotheses, and with whatever degree of revolutionary commitment he could muster. Beyond that, however, nothing was predetermined—not the character of the revolutionary leadership, not the tactics appropriate to a particular historical moment, not even the necessary superiority of Marxism as a paradigm through which to understand the world. What was essential was to act, observe, reflect, and act again in light of reflection. And so on and so on, unto the revolution.

Characteristically, Hook concluded his essay not with a call to the

---

* Or "Sidney Hook's Day-dream of What Marx Might Have Said Had He Been a Pupil of John Dewey," as Max Eastman later described it.

barricades, but with a note of caution. Beware the tendency, he wrote, to place too much faith in Marx as a person, or in Marxism as a system. At its best, he argued, Marxism was a method—fueled by principle and belief, but constrained by evidence and reality. It was *dialectic*, in conversation not just with the world but with itself as well, and open to being revised or even superseded if reality so demanded.

"The interpretation of Marxism as an exact science . . . rather than as a realistic method of making history," wrote Hook, "makes of it a modern variant of the religion of absolute idealism; a religion which Marx bitterly fought from the time he attained critical self-consciousness to the last days of his life."[21]

The essay would mark a break for the *Symposium*. Literature and art and academic philosophy wouldn't disappear from the pages of the magazine, but there was now an implicit awareness, which grew more explicit with each successive issue, that to be a responsible intellectual in the context of the Great Depression meant reckoning with more than just fictional narratives. It meant reckoning with how the narrative integrity of the nation itself was under threat.

In this respect the intellectuals who oriented around the magazine were no different from any other group in America. People all over were seeking answers, or fleeing from them, with an intensity unimaginable just a few years before. Answers were sought in religious observance, prophetic ecstasy, mass entertainment, conspiracy theory, collective action. Families took to the road, traveling thousands of miles on the wispy promise of a handbill or a rumor, hoping for an answer to the question of how to feed themselves. Laborers banded together into unions in order to answer the question of how to match, or at least approach, the still considerable power of the industrial titans, who were proving even more exploitative in bad times than they'd been in good. Even among the affluent, the dread was palpable.

What was distinctive about the intellectual classes was the degree to which their answers were found in one or another emanation of

Marxism, which had, in the eighty years since Marx first published his manifesto, grown into something far more than a theory of historical analysis and revolutionary change. It had become a whole universe of theories, icons, stories, leaders, factions, parties, rituals, meanings, moralities, and—significantly—options. For every intellectual temperament there was a band of heroes to emulate, a school of theorists to assimilate, a network of journals and papers to read and publish within. There were Marxist aesthetics, Marxist diets, Marxist romances. There were book groups, youth groups, art exhibits, knitting circles, broadsheets, and barn raisings. In the Soviet Union, there was even a bona fide Marxist homeland. It was a rough place, still dredging itself up from the muck of its barbaric past, not yet the utopia of which everyone dreamed. But just the fact of its unlikely revolution, and the sheer world-shaking defiance of its continuing survival, were inspiring. It was a living, progressing, inexhaustibly *laboring* testament to the possibility that the workers, with the help of the intellectuals, might yet inherit the earth.

For many of Burnham's peers, one or another of these Marxisms came at them with a force they had no desire to resist. It was an opportunity, for the ambitious and inspired, to throw over the old hierarchies, to fashion themselves into artists and thinkers of the future. It was a relief, for the authority-seekers, from the burdens of the modern, neurotic, artistic consciousness.

For Burnham, it was complicated. He wanted to believe. His yearning for system and purpose had been acute even before the world plunged into the abyss, and it was no accident that after the crash he'd turned for consultation to his friend and colleague Hook, who was emerging as one of America's most influential interpreters of Marx. Hook had been guiding him in the basics of Marxist thought, pointing him in the direction of the key texts, arguing with him about the causes of the crisis, and introducing him, gradually, to the society of socialists and socialist sympathizers that seemed, more and more, to be bleeding into the broader world of arts and letters in which Burnham was at home. And that influence was telling.

In the spring 1932 issue of the *Symposium*, Burnham finally broke his political silence, declaring that he now accepted the basic Marxist identification of capitalism, and its intrinsic contradictions, as the cause of the crisis. He also accepted as its challenge that most basic of Leninist questions: What is to be done? How should one conduct oneself as an intellectual in the face of a situation that seemed to demand concrete action rather than philosophical reflection?[22]

What he wasn't yet willing to say, however, was that he was a Marxist. It was still too new to him, and too unintegrated with other commitments he'd made, for him to make that leap. There were, as well, so many evident problems with it. From what he'd seen it was not hospitable to the aesthetic positions he'd very recently assumed he would be explicating and defending for the rest of his life. There was such a vulgarity to actually existing Marxist political life in America—most evident in the rude machinations of the Communist Party U.S.A. He shared Hook's reservations about the ease with which the tenets of Marxism, in the eyes of its adherents, were treated as articles of faith rather than as propositions to be tested against empirical data.

Then there were all the unanswerable questions about what it would mean, in practice, for him to just hand over to radical politics the identity he'd been constructing for himself as a man of letters and philosophy. What of the *Symposium*, which had staked its reason for being on questions of culture, not politics? What of the influence he had accumulated as its editor, and the expertise he'd acquired through years of reading and thinking about literature and philosophy? Would he have to sacrifice it all, and start over as an apprentice in an unfamiliar craft? What about his job at Washington Square College? Would he have to quit? Would he have to indoctrinate his students? He had a template for what his life would look like as a professor and critic, and reason for confidence that he would succeed in that mold. As a revolutionist his future was much murkier.

The scale of the crisis, and the genuine attractions of Marxism, were too great for Burnham to rest easy in the role he once thought he'd play. But precisely because he took the demands of revolutionary politics so seriously, he wasn't willing to just throw himself into action without thinking through the implications. The thicket of identity, belief, ego, and commitment he'd brought to the moment was too dense to be cleared out so easily. And so the work before him, which he undertook with the same focus and energy he applied to all his work, was to write and think his way into a vision of the political and intellectual life that made sense in the context of who he was, what he was coming to believe, the kinds of influence he wanted to exert, and the radically changed and intensified political and economic circumstances in which he found himself.

From that first public declaration of partial Marxist allegiance, in the spring of 1932, to his joining of a Marxist political party in the fall of 1933, the journey would take about eighteen months, with a number of halts and reversals along the way.

What would prove the seminal encounter, however, occurred fairly quickly, when Burnham read and reviewed Volume I of Leon Trotsky's *The History of the Russian Revolution*. It would be through Trotsky, Lenin's former right-hand man and Stalin's defeated and exiled rival, that Burnham would be able to envision a Marxist life for himself that felt not just defensible, or objectively appropriate, but actually desirable.

"This book," he wrote in the July 1932 issue of the *Symposium*, "is . . . an organic whole, the unified work of a man who has done much more than adopt at second hand a convenient methodology for filing his ideas—who has, rather, lived through, in thought and action, an integrating philosophy that is as fully a part of him as his nervous system."[23]

Thanks to the course of Marxist study he'd undertaken, Burnham was familiar with the basics of communist theory. But what he'd failed to find in Marx or Lenin was an application of it that felt as intimate, or as dramatic, as what Trotsky offered in *The History of the Russian Revolution*. If Marx was the Creator, vast and unapproachable, and Lenin was the Sword, steely and inexorable, then Trotsky was the Maestro. In his hands, through the vessel of his dashing and theoretically correct prose, history was a kind of symphony. Roaring forward with the force of a tidal wave at one moment, slowing to a hush in the next—harmonized, beneath the surface, by the cadences of dialectical materialism and the subtlety of Trotsky's imagination.

Here, in Trotsky's history, was Czar Nicholas II, a man endowed by nature, and by the dialectical gears of Russian history, with a character so spectacularly ill-suited to confronting the revolution that after a while his stupid, stubborn complacency came to seem almost a virtue. Here you were, suddenly, on the streets of St. Petersburg during the February Revolution, as the workers realized themselves with such majesty that in a matter of days they brought an empire tumbling down. Here was Lenin, arriving in the city three weeks later, armed with a will of such iron that he was able to take hold of the world-historical forces unleashed and bend them to his own purposes.

What Burnham found in Trotsky wasn't just a system for ordering, understanding, and predicting the world, but one that left room in it for individuals—heroes, really, and villains—to alter the course of its history. Trotsky spoke to Burnham not just as one intellectual to another, but as one romantic to another.

"We thus find that the nature of Trotsky's style cannot be separated from his view of history," wrote Burnham. ". . . The wink of the Cossack to the worker was the mark of the drawing together of the army and the proletariat, by which alone the revolution could succeed. The bouquet handed to Lenin was the gesture of the Compromisers, who thought that the harvest of the workers' and soldiers' revolution could best be gathered by turning over the power to the liberal bourgeoisie; and Lenin's awkward appearance was the sign of his rejection of the compromise, his insistence that the revolution must be carried through, that the work of February would be finished only by October."[24]

In characterizing Trotsky, in distilling his arguments and describing his methods, Burnham was suddenly lucid in a way that he'd never been when writing about literature or philosophy. He wasn't transformed into Trotsky. He wasn't a storyteller. And he was never able to achieve the pitch of intellectual excitement—the sense that everything depended upon the outcome of a paragraph—that seemed to arise so naturally from Trotsky's writing. But in his engagement with the man's work he'd hit upon his own approach, which was fundamentally expository, and he'd found the evidence he needed that the committed Marxist life could also be a life of intellectual and artistic integrity.

Finding Trotsky wasn't the end of the story for Burnham. For one thing, he had no connection to the Communist League of America (CLA), which was the main Trotskyist party in America, and he had little sense of what it would mean, pragmatically, to be a Trotskyist. For another, he wasn't ready yet. He'd only just begun imagining life as a revolutionary intellectual, and there were still quite a few philosophical kinks to work out, the most troublesome of which was Marxism's treatment of the arts, which promised a great deal more than it had yet been able to deliver.

For the fall issue of the magazine he and Wheelwright decided to alter their editorial policy—which had excluded poetry and fiction—in order to publish *Red Decision*, an explicitly Marxist sequence of poems by a young writer who'd recently graduated from Columbia. They weren't endorsing the poems, Burnham and Wheelwright insisted in their introduction, nor their crudely propagandistic conclusions. What seemed clear to them, however, was that the old ways of creating and consuming literature were no longer apposite. The new approach hadn't yet proved itself, by bringing forth a work of great originality and style, but it seemed a possible way forward—the only one on offer, so far as they could tell.

The next issue Burnham continued down this path with "Marxism and Esthetics," a much more direct exploration of whether the two systems he held most dear could be reconciled.

"Action follows being," he wrote. "Dante did not have to be

prodded to bring his poem to a Catholic conclusion, for he was in all ways a Catholic; nor Eisenstein to make his movies marxian; . . . the first task on the marxian esthetic program should be to make the artist a good Marxist, or rather to join artist and marxist as one unified person. Then there will be no difficulty about a revolutionary conclusion. The artist will know a revolutionary reality."[25]

So far so good, in theory. In practice, however, Burnham couldn't help noticing that when actual Marxists did actual analysis of actual works of art, or tried to create Marxist art of their own, they seemed to go screwy. They fell into the most sordid ranking of works according to their ideological content, or they would contort themselves into theoretical pretzels in order to find allegedly proletarian criteria to redeem the works that their bourgeois or modernist selves secretly treasured. As artists, they made propaganda, or used political veneers to disguise sentimentality and spirituality. Even Trotsky lost his good sense when trying to think about what Marxism meant for the future of art.[26]

By the end of the essay, despite acknowledging all that was "good and true" in Marxism, and bending over backward to imagine what an integrated approach might look like, Burnham had to admit failure. Marxism fell short, he wrote, not just as a set of prescriptions for making art and writing criticism, but as a value system rich enough to sustain the kind of life that made great art possible.

"There are some beliefs and systems of belief," he wrote, "that seem to be more adequate for art than others: Dante's religion more than Milton's; Keats' humanism more than Shelley's Rousseau-Godwin-paganism; Mann's balance more than Gide's perversions. They are more adequate not simply because they are logically more consistent or metaphysically more harmonious, but because they are more human in the full sense, they offer sets of values to which human beings can more profoundly respond. For art is part of life, of human life. And because I believe that marxism is, in the last analysis, false, false in this sense—inhuman and offering an order of values not acceptable to man nor in keeping with man's nature—I do not rest my hopes for art in any esthetics it can give birth to."[27]

It was an off-ramp for Burnham if he wanted one. Marxism was the fashion among American intellectuals and artists in the 1930s, but it was not imposed upon them. There was room for dissent or uninterest, and it was precisely on this matter of culture and the arts—this suspicion that there was something insufficiently humane about Marxism—that many of Burnham's fellow intellectuals had found themselves too troubled to go any further. Burnham had made no commitments or promises. His personal friends weren't radicals. His family was rather dumbfounded by his flirtation with revolution. He wasn't secure in his position at Washington Square College, and he would be inviting trouble by entering the fray as a Marxist.

What kept him moving left, at that moment, wasn't a desire to be current with the fashion. It was a more visceral desire. He wanted to be in the game. He wouldn't surrender his humanistic convictions about art, or coerce a synthesis between art and Marxism when one wasn't emergent. But nor would he pretend to keep caring deeply about the future of literature and philosophy when it was the future of politics that now inflamed him. And he wouldn't pretend that the romance and explanatory power of revolutionary Marxism didn't excite him. It did.

In April of 1933, Burnham and Wheelwright led off the *Symposium* with "Thirteen Propositions," their programmatic attempt to assess what was happening in the world, and to determine with whom a critically minded intellectual should align himself in anticipation of the coming shake-up.

"We may feel the moral coarseness of both the revolutionary and the counter-revolutionary positions," they wrote, "and may make a thousand modifications for our private position; but when the revolution itself begins there is certainly, if we are to be socially effective at all, an intelligible sense in which we must be on one side or the other."[28]

Forced to such a choice, Burnham and Wheelwright chose communism. What remained unresolved, however, was precisely what kind of communism to adopt, and how many small sacrifices of their private position were acceptable to make before the sum of the sacrifice was too much. So violence, for instance, was probably going to be necessary, but shouldn't be celebrated. A revolutionary movement had to be for the masses, but if the movement were to be effective it had to be steered by an elite and theoretically sophisticated leadership. And though the Soviet-led international communist movement had so far made the best arguments for what the revolution should aim toward—a workers' state, with the means of production collectivized—and seemed the only group around organized and powerful enough to bring such a society into being, no party could be the measure of all things.

The American Communist Party, in particular, couldn't be the measure of much at all. Its attitude toward art and culture, wrote Burnham and Wheelwright, was barbaric. Its grasp and application of Marxist theory was crude. Its factional intrigue was always frittering away whatever small gains were made in organizing the American working classes. And its slavish devotion to the Soviet Union was, frankly, embarrassing.

"I remember reading an editorial some time ago in *The Daily Worker*," wrote Burnham, "ending with a cry for the workers [of America] to go into the streets to defend the Soviet Union, and I remember stopping for some minutes to wonder what possible meaning this could have—what possibly were the workers meant actually to do."[29]

The only hope for the American party, they wrote, was to stop listening so much to Moscow, start listening more to people like them, and begin addressing the American people with a stripped-down program that adhered to the essence of Marxism but was flexible on most everything else.

Burnham and Wheelwright were significant enough as figures, by that point, for the party to take notice, which it did in two ways. Offense was taken publicly, in the *New Masses*, to the tone of Burnham's criticisms, and to his presumption. How dare a professor like him, with his posh background, arrogate to himself the right to lecture to real workers about the workers' revolution? Behind the scenes, however, Burnham was targeted as a potential recruit. His criticism of the party, it was apparent to the more sensitive of his readers, was as much a product of disappointment as it was opposition. He wanted to join up, to ally his theoretical work to practical political activity. If only the party could get its act together enough to meet him halfway, it seemed, Burnham would be willing to travel the other half.

Over the next few months Burnham would move toward the party, and further down the road of political commitment. As a teacher at Washington Square, he kept his cool gaze fixed on topics like "Aquinas and Dante" and "Thought and Literature of the Renaissance," and to the degree that he touched on politics inside the classroom, he did so with an even hand. Outside the classroom, however, in the free hours he'd once given over to fiction, poetry, and criticism, he devoured politics. He would publish one more literary-minded review, in the *Symposium*, but it was a desk-clearing effort, without even the restless energy that had characterized his earlier work.

His Communist students, encouraged by his general acceptance of Marxist theory, and not too deterred by his quibbles, began working on him to think more openly about joining. Sidney Hook remained, for the moment, an uneasy fellow traveler of the party, still open to arguments that one should tamp down one's intellectual reservations for the greater good. Even the inauguration of Franklin D. Roosevelt, which came as a relief to many left-leaning intellectuals, was received by Burnham as more evidence of the need for revolutionary change. The new president, for all his fine words about the plight of the common man, seemed to Burnham to be fighting primarily to save capitalism for the capitalists.

Over the summer Burnham took a driving trip through the Midwest that exposed him for the first time "to the class struggle, the starvation and terror in act."[30] Although he didn't leave a detailed record of what he'd seen, that summer was the most brutal of the

Depression, and the region he visited was among the most afflicted. Detroit, which was rolling out fewer than a fifth of the cars it had been making at its peak a few years before, was devastated. In Pittsburgh, which depended on the auto industry to buy its steel, almost half of the workforce was unemployed, and even the men and women who held on to their jobs saw their wages cut, in some cases, by more than half. The roads leading into Chicago were clotted with refugees from the boarded-up coal-mining towns of northern Illinois, and Chicago itself, that churning, smoking dynamo of American vigor and pride, had been reduced to a wheezing ember of its former self. Its factories were closed, its banks broken, its neighborhoods bleeding, its churches and relief organizations and city agencies overwhelmed by the needs of suffering men, women, and children.

Manhattan, where Burnham was coming from, had by no means escaped the Depression. The homeless and aimless, the hungry and desperate, had become a part of the city's topography, massing and grouping and sliding like silt into every cavern, alley, closet, pool, and crevice. Every imaginable symptom of social dysfunction was manifest—increased suicide, crime, infant mortality, divorce, disease— and every reached-for remedy was proving embarrassingly inadequate to the scale of the crisis. Yet through it all there was, in the battered-but-still-wealthy metropolis of New York, a certain minimal degree of continuity, of life as usual, that had been obliterated in many of the cities and towns of the Midwest. Or perhaps it just seemed that way to Burnham, who by 1933 was accustomed to many of the city's adaptations to the Depression, and for whom life in New York had, in fact, gone on much as before.

He was, in any case, shocked by what he saw on his trip, and he returned to New York convinced that the center wasn't likely to hold for much longer. By the fall he was ready to commit to the Marxist cause. The means of doing so, for Burnham, quickly narrowed to two. He could join the Communist Party U.S.A. (CPUSA). Or he could join the American Workers Party (AWP), a new, independent revolutionary

Marxist group that Hook, having finally abandoned his own attempts to finesse his differences with the party, was helping organize.

Burnham spent the fall semester feeling out what life might be like in the party. He made his debut in the *New Masses*, writing a review of a biography of Lenin. He agreed to act as faculty advisor to the campus branch of the Young Communist League, and he even took a meeting with Earl Browder, the leader of the American party (and an old hand at dealing with wary intellectuals). Browder allayed many of Burnham's specific concerns, and reassured him, more broadly, that the party was committed to Americanizing itself, even hinting that Burnham might have a significant role to play in such a process.

Burnham wasn't quite persuaded, but he was impressed. Not just by Browder, but by what he saw as the facts of the matter. The Communist Party, for all its flaws, was the real thing. It led strikes, published journals, crafted propaganda, infiltrated unions, conducted espionage, assembled coalitions, coordinated actions, and even occasionally ran candidates for electoral office. It had a voice not just in the Comintern, the official body of the international communist movement, but in the homeland itself—Soviet Russia. And if there was something unsightly about the way American communists were so easily awed by Soviet glamour, and so willingly obedient to Soviet authority, there was also something persuasive about the devil's bargain they'd struck. If the revolution came to America—when it came—who else would be better positioned to take control of it? Maybe, thought Burnham, it was a bargain worth striking.[31]

For his part Hook did what he could to exacerbate Burnham's fears about everything that was still wrong with the Communists. For the first time he also had an alternative to offer. The AWP, whose statement of principles Hook was crafting, wasn't even an actual organization yet, and promised to launch as a small one at best, with a small core of anti-Stalinist Marxist intellectuals in New York City and some affiliated unions and unemployed leagues in other parts of the country. Yet it had the potential, argued Hook, to become what Burnham had been wishing the Communist Party would become—a truly American group, informed by a truly dialectical attitude, led by an alliance of real workers and genuine intellectuals. The American Workers Party also offered Burnham an opportunity, precisely because it was so new and so small, to be formative in a way that simply wouldn't be possible for him in the Communist Party of the United States of America, which not only had its own institutional and ideological history but was freighted down with all the Soviet Bolshevik baggage as well. Among the Communists, Burnham could be a leader, but not a maker. In the AWP, anything was possible.

In retrospect, Burnham's decision to join the American Workers Party seems fated. By the time he came into the fold, the party was already in negotiations to merge with the main Trotskyist party in America, and there was the prospect that Burnham would soon have a direct conduit to Trotsky himself. In the Communist Party, by contrast, Trotsky was anathema, and membership would have meant for Burnham not only forswearing Trotsky, but regularly and vigorously denouncing him and anyone else (Hook, for instance) whom the party suspected of harboring Trotskyist sympathies.

The AWP was also just a much better temperamental fit for Burnham. Led by A. J. Muste, an idiosyncratic labor leader and ex-minister with a history of dramatic ideological zigzags, it was from the start a natural home for people who were passionate about changing the world but were, like Burnham, simply too ideologically complicated, and proud, to flourish within political organizations that demanded more uniformity and subordination.[32]

There was Hook, for instance, who was so committed to his autonomy that, despite helping create the American Workers Party, he would never actually join it. Other early members included James Rorty, a poet and journalist who'd been recently purged from the Communist Party for trying to slip the poetry of Robinson Jeffers into the *New Masses*, and George Schuyler, a black journalist for the *Pittsburgh Courier* who would end up, by the 1940s, repudiating all of his left-wing beliefs and committing himself to the conservative cause. V. F. Calverton, a literary critic and editor who'd made a name for himself as a champion of modernist literature and sexual libertinism, was an associate of the AWP, as was Edmund Wilson, perhaps the most sophisticated American critic of his generation. Of particular significance, in Burnham's case, was Germinal "Gerry" Allard, a young mineworker, writer, union organizer, and former Communist Party member who was on the organizing committee of the new party, and whom Burnham met during the crucial autumn months of 1933.

As a real person, Allard wouldn't go on to matter much in Burnham's development. Allard wasn't based in New York, and wasn't formidable as a theorist or political strategist. Other members of the AWP, and of the Trotskyist party with which the AWP would soon merge, would spend the decade sparring and engaging with Burnham in ways that would leave an imprint on his thinking long after he'd turned his back on the politics of the Left. As a fulcrum, however, Allard was decisive. At that moment of decision, when Burnham was looking for a sign, he found in Allard everything he'd been seeking to see embodied in a Marxist party. Allard was like a hero from one of Burnham's schoolboy fictions—his face scarred by work in the mines, his rakish sense of humor undimmed by years of struggle. Allard's birth, according to legend, had even been blessed by the local syndicalist leaders in the French mining town where the boy was born. Upon the newborn Allard's cradle they had laid a red flag, which had been sewn by his mother to honor workers who'd been killed in a mine explosion two years before.[33]

For Burnham, Allard was the proof he needed that the American Workers Party could make an authentic connection to the American working classes, and could do so by embracing rather than suppressing its romantic spirit. It was also the last piece of evidence he needed against the Communists, who had expelled Allard when he'd refused to turn on a friend of his who'd fallen out of party favor. If the Communists couldn't find a place for a man like this, who'd repeatedly put his life on the line for his fellow workers-in-arms, then perhaps the Communists didn't deserve the support of a man like Burnham.

By the end of 1933, Burnham had decided. He would join the American Workers Party, and turn against the Communists.

He would also wrap up things with the *Symposium*, quietly allowing it to expire after publication of the autumn 1933 issue. Burnham's last contribution, a review of a book on economics by two soon-to-be New Deal brain trusters, bore a strong stylistic resemblance to the writing he'd done when he launched the magazine four years before. There remained the tendency to show off his learning, the fondness for numbered lists, the arrogance, the subtle hiss and poppings of anxiety, the occasional flashes of dark humor. The material concerns of this last piece, however, were worlds away from where he'd been in late 1929. No more I. A. Richards, no more poetry, Faulkner, Restoration drama, or Kantian idealism. He was done with all that, and done, too, putting Marxism on trial. The Marxism upon which Burnham finally settled— Marx, filtered through Hook, inflamed by Trotsky—wasn't exactly orthodox, but it was coherent enough at its center, and fluid enough at its margins, for him to move forward at last (albeit with reservations) with the project of revolution.

Burnham, his mind finally made up, was instantly welcomed into the leading clique of the American Workers Party. At the founding convention of the party, in November 1933, he was given responsibility for formulating its foreign affairs position. Within months he had a regular column in the party's newspaper, *Labor Action,* and when a merger was soon proposed, between the AWP and the main Trotskyist group in America, the Communist League of America (CLA), it was Burnham and Hook who were given the responsibility for negotiating with the Trotskyists, and Burnham's advocacy for the merger that helped drive it forward.

In December 1934, after months of negotiation, the AWP and

the CLA became the Workers Party of the U.S. (WPUS), and for a little while the future looked promisingly revolutionary. The organizing breadth of Muste and his AWP, which had members and allies in unions and unemployed leagues around the country, was being joined to the theoretical depth of the CLA, which brought to the marriage not just Max Shachtman, the outstanding American Trotskyist of the moment, but Trotsky himself, who paid special, almost paternal attention to the American outpost of his global empire of dissent.

Both groups, too, were coming off stunning real-world triumphs. In Toledo, Ohio, in the spring of 1934, the AWP had resurrected from the near-dead a strike of workers at the Electric Auto-Lite plant, transforming what had begun as a local struggle over wage increases and contract stipulations into a bona fide class-consciousness-raising moment, replete with National Guardsmen, tear gas, martyred workers, emergency envoys from the American president, the threat of a general strike, and a small army of scabs forced to take refuge inside the factory under a volley of bricks and stones from righteous workers. In Minneapolis, at almost the same moment, Shachtman and his fellow CLA leader James Cannon were taking to the field personally to captain striking Teamsters and their comrades through a months-long campaign of picketing, politicking, and violence. Both strikes ended not only with contracts for the unions, but with entire cities turned, as if by revolutionary alchemy, into strongholds of labor consciousness.

If the merger of these two organizations, fresh from victory, was announced in excessively grandiose terms—as, inevitably, it was[34]—there was more than enough evidence on the ground to justify optimism, even exhilaration. Not just the victories, which would prove to be historic, but the extremity of the defeats—the violence their efforts called up in the souls of the bourgeoisie—seemed to announce that the nation was moving toward a climax of some kind, a tectonic clash of forces that would leave in its wake a landscape transformed.

Such a climax, for most of the leaders and members of the new Workers Party of the U.S., could only be the revolution that Marx had (maybe) predicted. Burnham, who shared Hook's belief that Marxism was a method rather than a crystal ball, remained agnostic on the question: Maybe communism was coming, but maybe History would tip the other way, toward an American version of the fascism that was reshaping Italy and Germany. Or perhaps neither mold would take, and modern society would simply disintegrate, devolving backward to God knows what preindustrial stage of economic development. But what wasn't in the cards, clearly, was that things would go on as they had, spasmodically limping forward. Nor were they going to revert to the capitalist equilibrium of the 1920s.

The task that Burnham set for himself, in this context, was to do whatever he could to tilt the odds in favor of a communist outcome. With Muste, Shachtman, Cannon, and the other chosen leaders of the new party, he would deploy the matériel at hand—people, organizations, events, publications, campaigns, emergent crises—to the optimal revolutionary ends. For Burnham that meant, among other things, taking responsibility for chores as mundane as keeping in touch with organizers in the field, making sure that rent was paid on the party offices, and scheduling the order of speakers at party events. It meant consulting with Trotsky about how to calibrate the party's foreign policy positions in response to the shifting allegiances of Stalin. It meant coaxing his fellow AWP alums, who'd come into the merger wary of being swallowed up by the Trotskyists, into a unified, disciplined Trotskyist whole. It meant, often, sacrificing Burnham's own opinions in the name of party discipline and unity. It even meant, at the more clandestine end of things, helping plan and execute a scheme to join the Socialist Party of America—Norman Thomas's more reformist-minded group—with the intention of either taking it over or, if that failed, poaching its more radical members on the way out. Above all it meant for Burnham an enormous, ceaseless expenditure of energy in service to the overthrow of the American government.

"It is the business of the revolutionary party," he wrote, "not to foster but to smash parliamentary illusions; not to suggest the possibility of reforming the bourgeois state, but to make clear, in the living experience of the masses, the necessity of destroying that state and of setting up in its place a new state, the workers' state. . . . Our attack must be against capitalism; Our struggle must be for socialism. And for this attack and this struggle there is one, and only one, political weapon: the revolutionary party. Our task is to forge this weapon. There is no other that will serve."[35]

Yet throughout the decade, Burnham held a major part of himself apart. Even as he worked, often to the point of exhaustion and ill health, to hold the party together through the procession of mergers, breakups, factional struggles, and petty power plays that seemed to be endemic to so many of the political sects of the 1930s, he stayed on at Washington Square College, continuing to educate the bourgeoisie and soon-to-be-bourgeoisie in the life of the mind. He kept up his friendships with the old Princeton crowd, none of whom had followed him into the farther reaches of the Left. He took frequent trips abroad with the Burnham clan, to the spas and beaches of Europe. And in the spring of 1934, he married Marcia Lightner, a well-bred Presbyterian gal from the Midwest who was the cousin of a Princeton classmate.

In December of that year, at almost exactly the moment that Burnham and Hook were being denounced in the pages of the *New York American*, a local Hearst paper, for their subversive influence on the youth of Washington Square College, the newlyweds relocated from the Village to an apartment in Sutton Place, one of Manhattan's most exclusive enclaves. When their first child, a daughter, was born soon after, it was into a home not so different in its comforts and rhythms from the one in which Burnham was raised.

Where most of his comrades in the party had concluded that the world was in the balance, and therefore everything—family, friendships, romances, professional ethics, criteria of taste—had to be reassessed in light of whether it made the revolution more or less likely, Burnham had concluded that the world was in the balance, but he should serve the revolution only in the hours remaining between a full day's work and a domestic and social life that was almost entirely distinct from those of his socialist comrades.

"And try as we would—directly, by indirection, by pressure, by suggestion, by cajolery, by every device we could think of—we could never induce him to come to work in the party office," remembered Shachtman. "And I won't say that he thought he was above that. It was obvious—and as I became increasingly more intimate with him, increasingly obvious—that he was torn. There were clearly times when he was on the very verge of throwing it all up—namely, his job at the University—and perhaps other personal involvements and coming to work for the party, and that he felt this urge very strongly and very sincerely. It was not an act on his part. Indeed, he was not given to acting or pretending."[36]

This ambivalence was not unnoticed by his fellows, but it was tolerated because his upper classness had its uses. He lent a sheen of respectability to the group, which had its shabbier aspects, and he seemed to have an intuitive access to the thought patterns of the American elite that simply wasn't available to men like Shachtman and Cannon, whose radical roots went deep but whose social reach had a ceiling. Burnham was also accepted because many of his Marxist comrades, despite themselves and their egalitarian principles, were as impressed by his cool and his class as his students at Washington Square were. And his value as a leader was acknowledged, even by those who didn't like him (Cannon, for one, who came to loathe him), because he was so committed to the party in most respects. And because he was good. He was organized, reliable, smart, fair, honest, and capable of inspiring respect and admiration (if not quite affection) from workers and intellectuals alike.

It was in the role of revolutionary intellectual, unsurprisingly, that Burnham most distinguished himself. Immediately upon the merger, he joined Shachtman as editor of the *New International*, the group's monthly theoretical journal, and would, with a brief interregnum, use it as his intellectual home base during his career as a Trotskyist. Over the course of the decade he would also write essays, reviews, and opinion pieces for the *Nation, Socialist Appeal*, the *New Militant*, the *American Socialist Monthly*, and *Partisan Review*. He would help Sidney Hook edit the short-lived *Marxist Quarterly*, whose quixotic mission was to foster civil debate between rival theorists of the Left. When the Trotsky-ists merged with the Socialists, in 1936, and had to shut down their publications as a precondition of joining, Burnham was part of the team that quickly, quietly took over one of the Socialists' more obscure committees, conniving to use it as a rhetorical base from which to wage their factional battle. And when the Trotskyists smashed their way out of the Socialist Party the following year, and reconstituted themselves as the Socialist Workers Party (SWP), Burnham was once again named editor of the *New International*.

The range of topics he addressed during this time was broad. He wrote about fascism in Europe, and the war that seemed to be coming. He wrote about Stalin's betrayal of the ideals of Lenin, as well as the parallel sins of the American Communist Party. Franklin Roosevelt in particular seemed to fascinate him, and Burnham spent many thou-sands of words, over many years, trying to impose some kind of Marxist order on the improvisatory genius of the president.

"Roosevelt came into office," wrote Burnham, "in a sense as a sav-ior: precisely as the savior of the capitalist order in the United States, as a stop-gap to tide over U.S. capitalism in a dark hour, as a channel to turn aside mass discontent from any development toward genuine social change. But, naturally, to accomplish these ends, Roosevelt could not *appear* in his actual economic role. The psychological and political requirements had also to be met. And to meet them, his program had to embody the half-formed dreams especially of the middle classes, and even, though to a lesser extent, of labor. This, then, was the material of the New Deal: in economic substance, a series of mostly temporary measures designed to help pull the business cycle out of the hole; in psychological and political form, a group of vague but enspiriting gen-eralities constructed to rally behind the Administration all who were bewildered, confused, and resentful."

Although Burnham wasn't interested in breaking new ground as a theorist of Marxism, he was relentless in applying his preferred synthesis to the events of the day, to the internal sectarian battles of the party, to pretty much anything that presented itself. It was from this angle that Burnham was even able to intervene, on occasion, as a literary critic, assessing the revolutionary merits of writers like Hemingway (not great, but showing signs of improvement), Auden (not bad at all), and at the top of the heap the Frenchman Andre Malraux and the Italian Ignazio Silone.

Silone, even more than Malraux, became for Burnham the model of the integrated revolutionary artist, someone whose fiction had resolved the tension between art and Marxism that had continued to occasionally worry at Burnham. Silone understood, as very few other so-called socialist writers did, that "classes are concrete only in the form of specific individual human beings."

Silone's work also revealed, at least in Burnham's interpretation, the vanguardist truth that although the workers were the raw fuel of history, they needed to be refined by an enlightened leadership lest their crude energy be wasted.

"His treatment of his peasants," wrote Burnham, reviewing a collection of Silone's stories in the *Nation*, ". . . reveals them simply as they are: stupid, often brutal, ignorant of the meaning of their lives, chained in the mesh of their prejudices, coarsely humorous. And being what they are, they are also something more than this: . . . They are the birth pangs of history. His peasants in their blind movement are waiting and preparing—waiting for consciousness, for leadership; even demanding leadership."[37]

If there was an elitism in passages like this, a sense that Burnham wasn't so much disappointed in the lower classes for their confusion as he was grateful for the opportunity to clarify them, then it was an elitism that afflicted not just Burnham but the basic weft of the party. The nimble and brilliant Shachtman, a City College dropout whose family emigrated to New York from Warsaw when he was an infant, saw himself as among the chosen, as did the charismatic, hard-drinking Cannon, an Irish-Catholic man from Kansas who'd cut his activist teeth with the Wobblies in the years before World War I. Particularly after 1934, when the party gave up any last hopes that it might someday reunify with the Communist Party, the members' political identities coalesced around the conviction that they were the lonely few who kept alive the flame of Bolshevik purity, and that without them revolutionary hope would die in the world.

It was, of course, basic doctrine of nearly every post-1917 Marxist party that Lenin had been right, that every revolution needed a vanguard of disciplined and trained leaders in order to succeed. But in the Soviet Union the revolution had already been won. To tease out the correct facts about the nature of revolutionary leadership was no longer so important. What was important was to secure the power of the leadership. Behind closed doors the Soviet party was rigidly hierarchical, and in its dealings with the working classes was ruthlessly, murderously cynical. When speaking to the world about the working classes, however, the voice of the party spoke in egalitarian tones. It was the workers who called the shots; the workers—thick-sinewed, heroically indomitable, possessed of an almost biological intuition for right Marxist action—who were responsible for every twist and turn, every purge and trial, in the life of the party; and the workers whose voices were being silenced by the elites of every other nation and party.

The Trotskyists were willing to play at this game, too, when they had to, but it went against the grain for most of them—for the intellectuals of the New York contingent more than most, and for Trotsky more than anyone.

The calling of the revolutionary Marxist leader, in Trotsky's eyes, was to live correct vanguardist theory, not to stroke the egos of the workers for the sake of short-term gain. Even during the meanest years of the revolution, and the wars that followed, he'd been a man who at every point had relied on what he saw as the precise application of Marxist theory to the moment. And he'd been vindicated in this course. He'd rallied the sagging spirits of entire cities, transformed the Red Army into a lever of history, helped usher a new form of government into the world, and stood down the massed armies of great nations—always by trusting to "the creative possibilities of the word."[38]

Even so, a different man than Trotsky might have spent a few moments in exile reflecting on the limits of words. His theory, after all, hadn't predicted his fall from such heights, nor saved the Soviet Union from the ascent of Stalin. It hadn't kept his old Soviet allies from facing the hangman, nor yet resolved for any of his new American and European allies the enigma of how to obtain power. A more reflective Trotsky might have moved forward just a bit less certain of the perfection of his theory. The actual Trotsky, however, was a man of extraordinary but tragically narrow intellect and imagination. So what he did instead, in his exile, was to reimagine not just his triumphs but his failures as evidence of the consistent and continued rightness of his own course.

He told a story—a brilliant, beautiful, absurd story—that bound together the heroic past and beleaguered present into the only kind of narrative structure that his ego could bear to carry. In the past lay his own glory, and the glory of Lenin. They strode like giants through the faltering last years of the czar's empire, sowing as they went the seeds of revolution, reaping in their wake the force and rage and joy of millions.

"In every factory, in each guild, in each company, in each tavern, in the military hospital, at the transfer stations, even in the depopulated villages, the molecular work of revolutionary thought was in progress," wrote Trotsky in his epic *History of the Russian Revolution*. ". . . Elements of experience, criticism, initiative, self-sacrifice, seeped down through the mass and created, invisibly to a superficial glance but no less decisively, an inner mechanics of the revolutionary movement."[39]

In the present, and the future, was the continuation of this struggle. There were new maps and new superstructures, new betrayers and new comrades, but so long as the theory remained sound, the way forward was clear. Fight on. Theorize on. Continue to trust in the logic of Marxist dialectics, which for Trotsky was the highest logic that mankind had yet evolved. Assign the failures of the Soviet state to Stalin's betrayal of proper theory. Relocate the pure heart of the revolution away from the Soviet Union over to the "permanent revolution" that Trotsky and his cadre of brothers were actively taking to the rest of the world. When apparent conflicts arose within the party, look to the lessons of the October Revolution to resolve them (where once was Bukharin, now is Burnham). When the immensity of the world's problems made Trotsky's threadbare movement seem embarrassingly inadequate, furiously refer back to the early years of the Bolshevik movement, when Lenin himself was dismissed as the leader of a tiny sect, with a few hundred loyalists at his back, grandiosely pitting his will against an empire.[40] They had triumphed then through the proper application of revolutionary theory. So they would again.

Burnham was more skeptical than most Trotskyists toward the Old Man (as Trotsky was known). And it was a point of pride, for Burnham the philosophy professor, to dissent from some of the more circular aspects of Trotsky's thinking. Yet he was as seduced as anyone by the romance of the party that emerged from Trotsky's vision. He thrilled to the idea of himself as one of an elite corps of technologists who saw so deeply into the machinery of history that they would be able to re-engineer the world with the right tightening of the screws here, the right heightening of the contradictions there.

The virtue of this construction, aside from its romance, was that it allowed the Trotskyists to cloak weakness in a rhetoric of strength. Internal factional fights weren't a waste of energy; they were a ridding of the party of reactionary toxins. Trotsky, Burnham, Shachtman, Cannon, Abern, Oehler, Hook, and the rest fought with each other so fiercely over the minutiae of party platforms, the precise angle from which to criticize Soviet manipulations in Spain, and the ideal interpretation of the eleventh of Marx's theses on Feuerbach, not because they were compensating, neurotically, for the power they'd failed to acquire. They did it because that was how one prepared for the acquisition of power. The party that hoped to seize the moment of revolutionary opportunity would serve itself best by purifying its theory and annealing its will, not by fretting about the length of its membership rolls or the number of rubles in the party piggy bank.[41]

"Corruption does not set in in an instant," wrote Burnham in 1935. "It is the result of a developing decay, manifested first in little things, in isolated spots and tissues, and finally, unchecked, taking possession of the entire body. So, likewise, is strength built up—by a long process of vigorous exercise, healthy diet, discipline and control. Thus, it was the generation-long fight of Lenin against the incursions of opportunism, reformism, sectarianism, that brought the Bolsheviks intact and ready through to 1918. . . . It was the Bolshevik party alone—even more narrowly, the Leninist wing of the Bolshevik party—that stood unshaken before the October insurrection."[42]

The more chaotic things got on the outside, the easier it became for Burnham and his fellow Trotskyists to imagine themselves as latter-day Lenins. When the conflagration came, as it surely would soon, it would be just such men as they, afire with Marxist comprehension and hardened by Marxist practice, who would know what to do and have the strength to do it.

They were affirmed in this taut vision of themselves, ironically, by Stalin himself, who had refused to let Trotsky recede into irrelevance. He had chosen instead to make use of his old rival as a scapegoat for all seasons. In Stalin's propaganda (and possibly in his paranoid imagination), Trotsky lurked behind every one of the regime's failures, and every real and imaginary plot against the Soviet state. Trotsky caused the famines. Trotsky was conspiring with the Nazis, or, depending on the year and the shifting geopolitical alliances, conspiring with the enemies of the Nazis. His agents assassinated Kirov. He suborned generals and sabotaged factories. The show trials of 1936–38, through which Stalin humiliated and then murdered most of the remaining old guard of Bolshevik leaders, were largely premised on the existence of a grand Trotskyist conspiracy, and there were years when one could barely get through a page of Communist Party propaganda anywhere in the world without encountering the demon figure of Trotsky, whose influence was everywhere and behind everything, moving always to thwart the destiny of the proletariat.

Actual Trotskyists, of course, knew that most of this was pure fabrication. There were only a few thousand of them, scattered around the world, strapped for cash, challenged for influence. But even as the slander infuriated them, it couldn't help but inflate their sense of importance. If Stalin felt it necessary to cleanse the Soviet Union of anyone who had ever shown even a trace of Trotskyist sympathy, and to so feverishly warn against the global influence of Trotskyism, then he must genuinely be afraid of the power that Trotsky possessed. That power, therefore, must be immense. And that power, as it happened, consisted of them. Trotsky had no shadow council but the counsel of men like Burnham, Shachtman, and Cannon. He had no weapons but his reputation and his words. He had no army but his people.

There were many reasons why men and women (mostly men) in the 1930s were willing to follow Trotsky, and to commit their lives to the revolutionary course he charted. For one, the Old Man was one of the Great Men of his time—cracklingly brilliant, courageous, decisive, shepherd to one of the epochal events of the twentieth century. To join the movement was to become an heir to the Russian Revolution and a father, perhaps, to the revolutions that were coming. It was to join in a kind of communion with history, channeled through Trotsky. One received affectionate notes from him, as well as stern rebukes. One's actions were praised or rejected by him with reference to what Lenin or Bukharin, or Kamenev, or Zinoviev had done in similar situations. The lucky few were brought down to Mexico to play chess and argue theory. He seemed always on call to settle a thorny theoretical question or to mediate between rival factions, the very fact of his attention conferring a sense of historic weight on what his people were doing.

For some of Trotsky's followers, this was enough. Trotsky was enough. He was everything. For others, many of whom were excommunicants from the Communist Party, it was the movement that coalesced around Trotsky that was the thing. It sheltered them as they continued the struggle for revolution outside the party they'd left, which by the 1930s was entirely the creature of Stalin, deformed and craven and simply too brutal to be endured.

The Trotskyist movement was also, more humbly, a vehicle for participating in the struggles of working people, one of the ways of doing something at a time when it felt like something had to be done. After 1934 the group would never again, in any of its incarnations, reach the heights of those strikes in Minneapolis and Columbus. After Muste's religious conversion in 1936 and his consequent withdrawal, the party would drift further and further away from a base in the working and used-to-be-working classes. But it still had its moments, and even at its most neurotic was more than just a debating club.

"Serving on the political committee of the American Workers Party was a rewarding and humbling experience for me," wrote Sidney Hook, decades later, trying to come to terms with what was meaningful in his experience of a political organization whose ideology he had come to reject. "I got to realize how little I knew about the nature of the country whose system I was trying to revolutionize. I acquired a sense of the nature of the difficulties of the men and women in the field. . . . Without making too much of a thing about it, almost all of them had sacrificed opportunities that would have resulted in comfortable and well-thought-of careers for lives heavy with the risk of violent injury and imprisonment. Whatever their motives—unclear and complex as they may have been—it would be jejune to reduce those motives to the desire for power. These people were dedicated to their task and accepted hardships without a murmur."[43]

Burnham was influenced by every one of these aspects of the movement. He was, in his burnished way, an ally of the working classes, and an enemy of the system that exploited them. He enjoyed the intraparty arguing, the fellowship, the maneuvering. Trotsky became a mentor, and even a friend (in the over-cerebrated way in which both men tended to make friends). Shachtman became a good friend. Most of the party held Burnham in high esteem. His counsel was valued. His orders were followed. His essays were read closely. Even his oratory, which often came across as pedantic, was good-naturedly tolerated by his comrades.[44]

On the outside, too, thanks to the calculus of that desperate decade, Burnham saw his social stock rise. Few of his old friends were willing to travel nearly as far to the left as he was, but at a time when so many were so shaken it became easy to admire Burnham for his air of certainty, his hardness, his apparent readiness to fight to the end for his vision of a new world. In intellectual circles in particular Burnham's radicalism was admired, and his passage into the inner sanctums of New York intellectual life was actually sped up by his association with Trotsky, who in his pristine exile ended up serving as a useful totem for those Marxist-minded writers who wanted to register their support for the cause, broadly speaking, without quite signing up for the program.

What kept Burnham going, however, wasn't primarily the status, or the community, or even the conduit to Trotsky. It was the intellectual work itself. He remained enthralled by that spirit he'd first glimpsed when he read Trotsky's *History of the Russian Revolution*, that astoundingly bold presumption that one could bring all of history, politics, economics, and culture into focus and then, like a sculptor circumnavigating a block of marble, discern within it a future that could be chiseled out if one was able to strike at just the right points with just the right degree of force.

Burnham's greatest intellectual arias of the 1930s were delivered from this space. Given a discrete political question—to support or not the creation of a third party, to adopt or not a particular slogan, to defend or not the actions of the Soviet Union—he would map out the contending classes, the charismatic personalities, the pending legislation, the clashing ideologies. Then he'd lay each interpretive frame on top of the other, like a set of transparencies, revealing hot spots and fault lines, gathering storms and hidden fragilities. It wasn't quite a determinist universe in which Burnham's intellect ranged in these essays. Choices mattered. Different outcomes were possible. It was, however, a highly ordered, highly transparent universe. Given the right set of intellectual concepts and a brain capable of applying them, its inner machinery could be perceived.

At his best Burnham was able to make use of the tools of Marxist analysis to illuminate the world as it was. Franklin Roosevelt may or may not have been, as Burnham believed, the enemy of the proletariat. But one could differ with Burnham's ideological predicates and still benefit from his running analysis of the president. One could even reject as meaningless such categories as "the proletariat" or "the bourgeoisie" and still find in Burnham's writing a great deal that was true about how adroitly Roosevelt played to the anger of the masses while protecting the structural interests of industry. Similarly, Burnham deconstructing the cynicism of the Communist Party revealed an intellectual and moral integrity that transcended whatever Marxist categories Burnham had deployed to reach his conclusions.

Where Burnham fell short, as he would throughout his life, was less in a dogmatic adherence to ideology than in an almost dogmatic faith in his own faculty for prediction. Not content to plumb the world as it was, he would, like a grand master sitting before a half-played board, chart out the futures that were most likely to emerge from the interplay of all the game pieces, each wending across the board according to its own inner dictates. Except he wasn't a grand master. And the world wasn't as much of a chessboard as he wished. He would, again and again, seize on one tendency of the historical moment and project it schematically forward into the future, selecting his set of data points with a particular preference for those that had the scent of brimstone about them. What had been is what would be, except more so—with lots of death and destruction. Fascism was on the rise in Germany ➔ fascism was likely to rule large swaths of the planet for decades. Capitalism was in crisis ➔ it was moving inexorably toward extinction. The masses were frightened, desperate and angry; in the past this stew had bubbled over into revolution ➜ so it would again.[45]

For much of the 1930s Burnham's commitments, his blind spots, and the apparent direction of events reinforced each other. Things kept getting worse. The center wasn't holding. Burnham concluded that the center would continue to spin apart, and used the tools of revolutionary Marxism to explain and predict the coming collapse.

The problem arose for Burnham, incrementally at first, and then with increasing urgency as the decade neared its end, when the center kept showing worrisome signs of holding, even of reconstituting itself. He was confronted with the question of what exactly tethered him to the cause if the bet he'd been making, that as a Trotskyist he'd be in the mix when the revolution came, was a losing one. Not even a losing bet, actually, but a ghost bet, on a game that wasn't going to be played.

There was no watershed moment when Burnham's loyalty to Trotsky, or his faith in Marxism, began to erode. His enthusiasm probably peaked in 1936 or 1937, during the year when the Trotskyists were embedded in the Socialist Party, when Burnham was writing for a much larger membership and also scheming—to seduce that membership—on a much grander scale than he'd ever schemed before. He was in that moment a major player in a conspiracy that went all the way up to Trotsky and all the way down to party organizers in the field, with whom Burnham would exchange long, elaborate strategy letters about how to push the Trotskyist agenda with just the right degree of subtlety to draw potential sympathizers closer without provoking the old guard socialists to outright opposition.

It was at that time as well that Burnham played a role in organizing the American Committee for the Defense of Leon Trotsky, which was set up, after the first of the show trials in Moscow, as a means of clearing the Old Man of the accusations that were coming at him from Stalin and his agents. It proved, for Burnham and his comrades, a publicity coup of a high order. They were able to persuade an august group of liberal and left-wing cultural figures to join the committee, and when the time came to put Trotsky to the question, it was the unimpeachable John Dewey himself, then seventy-eight and just retired from his teaching post at Columbia, who went to Mexico to chair the commission of inquiry.

The tableau of Dewey and his fellow notables sitting across from Trotsky, in Diego Rivera's house in Coyoacán, sifting through the grim record of Stalinist lies and betrayals, with photographers and reporters from throughout Europe and America on hand to play witness, was enormously embarrassing for the Soviet Union and its sympathizers and subsidiaries in the West. It had the effect not only of exacerbating the doubts of many on the Left who'd been discomfited by the hard-to-believe confessions coming out of the Moscow trials, but of elevating Trotsky in the process. For a brief moment it was Trotsky who commanded the world's attention as prosecutor for the cause of international socialism, and Stalin who stood accused.

When the commission issued its conclusions in December of 1937 with an unalloyed exoneration of Trotsky—"We therefore find the Moscow Trials to be frame-ups," they wrote[46]—it was, arguably, the high point of his reputation in the West.

Also his last gasp.

By the end of 1937, the world was moving past the brief phase of history that seemed to have had space in it for a stateless Trotsky to maneuver. In the Soviet Union, Stalin's ruthless extermination of anyone who might pose a threat to him wasn't, as Trotsky had hoped, generating its own dialectical antithesis. It was achieving its purpose of eliminating threats to the regime. In Germany, which had been one of the strongholds of Trotskyism, the Nazis had crushed the entire spectrum of Left opposition. In Spain, the non-Stalinist Left (which had a complicated but still resonant relationship with Trotsky) was rapidly losing a civil war on two fronts, against both their Communist "partners" in the Republican government and the Nationalist rebels led by General Franco.

And in America, Trotskyism's greatest enemy—stability—was continuing to reassert itself against the entropy that had been unleashed in 1929. The economy had bottomed out in 1933, and had then, under FDR's canny guidance, begun a slow but increasingly undeniable process of recovery. Things were still awful. Unemployment remained at near-historic highs. Migrants still crowded the roads, in search of somewhere to settle. Labor battles continued to be violent. Crucially, however, things were getting better. Fewer people every year were without jobs, and many of those who weren't working were getting unemployment benefits. Fewer kids and old folk were going hungry, thanks to relief programs and the newly created Social Security system. Workers were winning contracts. The political system was adapting, with the prime adapter himself, Franklin Roosevelt, winning re-election in 1936 in a landslide so decisive it could only be interpreted by honest revolutionaries as a sign not of crisis but of restoration. Perhaps most fatally for the Marxists' hopes, the American people—as individuals, families, communities, and polities—were beginning to adapt. They were learning to make do with less, and to lower their expectations. And they were discovering that so long as these lowered expectations could be met by their leaders (which, often enough, they were) then forbearance, if not quite trust, could once again be extended to the system.

For Burnham, this return of equilibrium wore away at one of the foundational premises of his Marxist commitment, which was that history had winnowed the world's options down to three: fascism, communism, and barbarism. When the choice had seemed to him to lie between communism and alternatives that were nothing but darkness, he'd been able to set aside his doubts. But what if the alternatives weren't so obviously awful? What if there was time yet to reflect on the nature of the system he'd chosen as it compared, say, to the surprisingly resilient one Roosevelt was helping to hold together?

Deprived of the security of the either-or model he'd constructed for himself, Burnham found himself worrying again at some of the basic questions he'd set aside when he joined up with the movement.

He wondered again at how easily Marxist commitment, in practice, seemed to take on religious-seeming undertones, and whether it was sufficient to simply hold oneself apart, as a skeptic, when so many of one's colleagues were true believers. He delved again into the history of the Revolution, and looked with a more suspicious eye at those episodes that seemed to reveal even in the early Bolshevik period a certain dictatorial habit of mind, among its leaders, that would bloom so vengefully in Stalin. He began looking ever more critically at Trotsky— at his personal flaws, at his tortured loyalty to the Soviet Union, at the wisdom of the particular choices he was making as leader of their small group. And he began asking himself, as he had at the beginning of his left-wing journey, whether Marxism was a structure that could bear the weight of reality.

In the fall of 1937, Burnham engaged his comrades on two fronts. Disturbed, despite what he already thought he knew about the Soviet Union, by the show trials and what they revealed about the sickness of Stalin's regime, he challenged his comrades about the degree to which decision-making in their own party was centralized. If even the Russian Revolution, the source of it all, could descend to such depths, how could their party be sure that its own desired revolution wouldn't follow the same course down? Perhaps it was the right moment to institute more democratic processes so that the party wouldn't be vulnerable, organizationally, to the kind of centralization of power that Stalin had achieved in the Soviet Union?

Burnham proposed some specific reforms, but backed off after a personal appeal from Trotsky, who promised to give his concerns due attention after the necessary work of founding the new party was complete. He pushed forward, however, on the far more provocative matter of "the Russian question."[47]

The issue of whether dissident Marxists should defend the Soviet Union—intellectually, and if it came to it militarily—had been haunting Trotsky and his people since Trotsky was exiled from Russia and excommunicated from the Communist Party. What to do about a place that was both the enemy and the homeland, the site of the Revolution's greatest betrayals and the wellspring of its great legends and heroes? To condemn how Stalin had tainted the dream was necessary—and it was the Trotskyists, more than anyone, who were doing that work—but it would be a leap far beyond that to give up entirely on the Soviet state.

Trotsky hadn't been able to do it. He'd written thousands of pages about the betrayal of the vision of Lenin, the entrenchment of the Soviet bureaucracy, and the shameful disempowerment of the workers. But his revolutionary soul couldn't bear the thought of what a dark place the world would seem if, indeed, his world historical accomplishment—and the single most awesome deed that revolutionary Marxism had achieved—was done for. So his answer to the Russian question was to split the difference. One should assail the Soviet leadership, and work for the internal overthrow of the regime, but one should keep in mind as one attacked that the Soviet Union remained a state in which certain basic steps had been taken toward achieving a just Marxist society.

Property had been nationalized. The power of the capitalist elite had been broken. The Soviet people had a cultural memory of what it was like to take their own destinies in hand. And if dialectical materialism was to be trusted, then the internal contradictions of Stalin's state would continue to swell until, in proper dialectical fashion, they would split the state open and a new, more authentically socialist synthesis would emerge from the husk. Yes, the current regime had become an enemy of its own people, a disgrace to the revolution, a charnel house. But it remained in its fundamentals a workers' state, and therefore closer to the promised land than anywhere else, if only by a few inches. And because the stakes were so high, those few inches were worth defending against all who would see them erased.

For Burnham, by the end of 1937, this logic was wearing thin. He wasn't ready to break completely with the Soviet Union, but it was excruciating to keep defending a state that was dedicated to the expunging of his own group from the face of the earth. It was a serious drag on the party's efforts to recruit sympathetic intellectuals, many of whom had become so disgusted by Stalin that they were appalled by anyone who would mount any kind of defense of his state. And, as it happened, all these sacrifices, compromises, and public relations headaches were unnecessary. Trotsky's answer to the Russian question, Burnham concluded, was wrong on the merits. The Soviet Union wasn't a workers' state anymore. It was at best a "semi-bourgeois" state that had some progressive features but functioned primarily to serve the interests of the party leadership, the bureaucracy, the upper ranks of the army, the secret police, and a few other privileged groups.

Burnham had argued many times before with Trotsky and his comrades on matters of strategy and tactics, over whom to ally with and whom to conspire against, when to fight and when to flee. And the concrete reforms he ended up proposing, with regards to the Russian question, weren't that radical. What was radical, however, was his willingness to challenge the Old Man on sacred semantic ground. He was confronting him, for the first time, on questions of *language*. And he was rather tart about it.

"What is the argument of the Committee majority, reduced to its simplest and essential form?" Burnham wrote. "We ask them, what kind of state is the Soviet Union? They answer, it is a workers' state. We ask, why is it a workers' state? They answer, *because* there is nationalized property. We ask, why does nationalized property make it a workers' state? And they answer, *because* a workers' state is one where there is nationalized property.

"This is, in form, exactly the same argument used by those who tell us that the bible is the Word of God. We ask them, how do you know it is the Word of God? They answer, *because* the Bible itself says that it is the Word of God. We ask, but how does that prove it to be true? And they answer, *because* nothing that God said could be a lie."[48]

In December 1937, at the inaugural convention of the new Socialist Workers Party, Burnham offered a proposal that his language on the

Russian question be adopted. It was defeated 89–4 in favor of hewing to Trotsky's most recent formulation of the Soviet Union as a "degenerated workers' state." He accepted the loss graciously. He was shaken, though. Not just by the lopsidedness of the defeat or the stubbornness of Trotsky's loyalty to the Soviet Union, but by the criticisms that came at him during the course of the debate. Cannon, in particular, was quite frank about his belief that Burnham was having a tantrum, that his bourgeois true colors were showing.

"Now, I must tell you, dear friend, that I think he is suffering from the intellectual soul sickness," Cannon wrote to Trotsky, toward the end of 1937. "Who can cure that? If he were completely identified with a group of worker Bolsheviks, and could be brought under the influence of their spirit in day to day struggle, one could have more hope. But there's the rub. He does not really feel himself to be one of us. Party work, for him, is not a vocation but an avocation. He is not in a position to travel the country, to take part in the action of our comrades in the field, to live with them, and learn from them, and come under their influence in his personal life. . . . In such a time as this, when we must take arms against the world of enemies and disintegrating factors, Comrade B. is greatly handicapped by his background, his environment, and his training."[49]

After the convention, with the launch of the new party, Burnham was again confronted by Cannon and Shachtman about his continued refusal to commit fully to the cause. Troubled, he took a short break from his leadership responsibilities to contemplate whether Cannon was, in fact, right about him, whether he needed to go all in or get out altogether. When he returned to the job, however, it was from the same half-in/half-out position as before, only intensified. He abstained for the next year or so from picking fights with his comrades, but privately his doubts festered. Were these really the kind of men, he wondered, whom one could trust with power over millions? Was Trotsky quite the theorist he claimed to be, or was he, instead, a master stylist who

covered over his philosophical weaknesses with beautiful prose? Burnham even began indulging his more subversive doubts about Marx,
and about those tendencies in Marx's theories that had the feel of the
metaphysical about them.

As he agonized, he acted the good party leader. He corresponded
regularly with Trotsky, and transmitted his desires to the American
contingent. He served on both the National Secretariat and the Political Committee (PolComm) of the new party. He edited the *New
International*, and wrote a column in the weekly *Socialist Appeal*. He
taught a class with Shachtman and Cannon, at party headquarters in
the Village, on "The Bridge to Revolutionary Action." And he counter-
programmed against the last and most egregious of the show trials in
Moscow, this one eliciting confessions from, among others, Nikolai
Bukharin, who made the fantastical admission that since 1918 he and
a "Bloc of Rightists and Trotskyites" had been conspiring to undermine
the Revolution.[50]

As a writer, Burnham took loyally to the task of gaming out the
war in Europe that seemed to be coming, and of crafting a position for
the Trotskyists that would distinguish them from competing factions
and tendencies on the American Left. On the surface it was the kind
of challenge on which Burnham thrived. Take the messiness of the
world, the agora of competing voices and interests, the blur of change
and upheaval, and sift it all through the clarifying filter of rigorous
philosophical analysis. And it wasn't difficult for him, in the specifics,
to sincerely make many of the arguments he was called upon to make,
particularly when they involved critiquing others. Yet even as he laid
into the inadequacies of rival movements and philosophies, he found
himself underwhelmed by the answer that his own movement gave
to the multiplying questions of war and peace. No matter the details
of the situation, the lay of the battlefield, the identity of the aggressors, or the grievances of the victims, the Trotskyist logic was always
the same: It was capitalism, and its self-devouring need for profit,
that was the cause of war. The only answer to war was to overthrow

capitalism and replace it with socialism. And the only source of true socialism left in the world was the Socialist Workers Party.[51] Or, as the recruiting posters put it:

> IF you are against the wholesale slaughter of the workers of the world;
>
> IF you are against the world-wide tyranny of fascism:
>
> IF you are against the criminal destruction of the results of centuries of labor in creating the wealth and culture of the world

> THEN YOU ARE AGAINST CAPITALIST WAR!

> SOCIALISM ALONE CAN END WAR!

> JOIN THE SOCIALIST WORKERS PARTY

Burnham's articulation of the case was more detailed, and made more references to Marxist theory, but in the end wasn't much more nuanced or adequate than the poster. And he knew it. Or almost knew it.

In the spring of 1938, Max Eastman published "Russia and the Socialist Ideal," a long polemic in *Harper's* arguing for a socialism that was stripped of what he saw as the worst of Marxism's historical, metaphysical, and dialectical baggage. It was one of the last of a series of breakup letters that Eastman, the fair-haired colonel of the American Left, had been writing to Marx, Lenin, and Trotsky almost since the moment he'd first visited Moscow more than fifteen years before. Within two years he would sever his ties for good, but in 1938 he was still holding on to the last tendrils of his socialist hopes. The essay was a final plea of sorts, to his old friend Trotsky, to admit to a few difficult truths about the Marxist project. One was that the Soviet Union, which Eastman had once seen as the hope of the world, was an abject failure, "a crude and bloody personal despotism resting on a privileged bureaucracy which exploits the wage worker much as he is exploited elsewhere." Another was that that failure couldn't be cordoned off from one's evaluation of Marxism in general. Honest Marxists should reflect on whether their theory bore some responsibility for the disaster of Soviet socialism. The most urgent of Eastman's arguments, however, left Russia behind for the molten core of Marxism.

"Marx inherited his philosophical belief from Hegel," Eastman wrote. "It is a belief that the world is evolving of its own necessary motion, and by a 'dialectic' procedure, 'from the lower to the higher.'. . . But it is not sensible to take utopian aspirations out of your own head and attribute them to the external world. And no matter how much you disguise the process by calling the world 'material,' and by invoking the word scientific, it is not science to do this. It is just the opposite— religion. It is primitive, unverified, and unverifiable belief in what you want to have come true."[52]

If Trotsky, whom Eastman had once described as "the most universally gifted man in the world today,"[53] could acknowledge such a defect at the core of Marxism, and set himself to the task of reformulating his philosophy accordingly, then Eastman might have reason to hang in there with the socialist experiment. If not, then the intransigence of the world's most gifted socialist would be yet another datum, for Eastman, suggesting that Marxism simply wasn't compatible with the clear and coherent exercise of political intelligence.

Trotsky, predictably, would have none of it. He banged out a few disdainful paragraphs on Eastman in the middle of a long, bitter survey of what was wrong with all of his many detractors on the Left,[54] and then delegated the frontal assault to Burnham, whose response was published in the June 1938 issue of the *New International*. The rebuttal, "Max Eastman As Scientist," was an interesting piece of work. On its surface it was Burnham at his most haughty, rapping Eastman's knuckles for his fuzzy use of terminology, schooling him on recent trends in contemporary philosophy. Yet when it came time to respond to Eastman's primary thesis, that Marx's philosophy was infected by a faith that the universe was trending toward justice, Burnham did something unexpected. He pretty much conceded it.

"We all know . . . that Marx made a number of false statements," wrote Burnham. "None of us, if we take historical method seriously, is surprised that Marx was limited by the stage which scientific knowledge had reached in his day, or that his terminology was influenced by the social context in which he lived. I, for one, agree with Eastman that it is desirable to change, in part, this terminology, in order to bring it more closely into accord with contemporary scientific method and practice. However, these problems of scholarly research and linguistic reform are comparatively leisurely, impersonal and postponable. The Marxism which is of decisive moment to revolutionists is not the dried letter of Marx's books but the theory and strategy of the living revolutionary movement."[55]

It was a rather odd way to wage a critique, to concede Eastman's argument and then act as if that concession didn't matter. It was also a rather disingenuous attitude, for a Trotskyist of all people, to take toward theory. But Burnham was hamstrung. He couldn't bring himself to argue in defense of dialectical materialism, nor could he admit what was really the case, which was that the meaningful divide between Max Eastman and James Burnham, by 1938, wasn't philosophical. It was emotional. Eastman was done with socialism at a gut level, and Burnham wasn't yet. They could go to the mat over the subtleties of leftist theory, but the fight wasn't about that. It was about loyalty, friendship, tribe, identity. Eastman couldn't own up to the real stakes because he wasn't ready to accept that his passion for socialism, which had given his life meaning for so long, was completely dried up, or that his friendship with Trotsky, which had run so deep and cost him so much, was dead. Burnham couldn't fess up because he couldn't admit, in principle, that there were such things as emotions, or at least that they had any role to play in the conduct of his intellect. The feelings were there on all sides, though, embedded in the subtexts and silences. Eastman's choice to publish his essay in the bourgeois *Harper's*, rather than in the *New International* or the Trotsky-friendly *Partisan Review*, was a statement of eroded loyalty. Trotsky's handing off to Burnham the job of responding to Eastman was a statement of contempt for Eastman as well as a challenge to Burnham (Are you willing to defend the family honor?). Between the lines of Burnham's vehement answer (yes!) lurked a counterpoint of self-doubt.

"It is not the kind of article a man writes who really wishes to grapple with a problem," Eastman noted, perceptively, in a response to Burnham that was published in the August issue of the *New International*. "Burnham either agrees or does not agree with my criticism of dialectic materialism as a disguised metaphysical idealism. I suspect that he agrees more than he disagrees with it. But he is careful not to let anybody, perhaps not even himself, perceive this, for the very simple reason that he is politically a Trotskyist, and he knows that if he renounces dialectic materialism, or even questions it, Trotsky will renounce him—and probably call him a coward besides."[56]

At the end of his response to Burnham, Eastman made one concession. He allowed that Burnham was justified when he demanded of Eastman that he offer "another . . . program" in the place of the socialist one he seemed to be in the process of junking. And Eastman promised to give it a try, to see if he could follow his doubts all the way down to a reformed socialism or all the way through to a nonsocialist vision for a just society.

"If I live I will complete my thesis," he wrote. "If the profession of struggling against dialectics were a little more lucrative, I would complete it sooner. But even so I would not hurry. I know it cannot seem so to party militants, and they have always my humble respect, but to me it seems just now in America a period for deliberation. It is so at any rate in my own life."

It was an oddly gentle note on which to conclude his attack. It was also, in its way, one of the more threatening things that Eastman was to say in his exchange with Burnham. To counsel deliberation rather than forward-marching action. To speak of one's own life in the same breath, and with the same degree of consideration, as one's political goals. Even to use words like "humble" and "respect," and to worry about so humble a thing as making a living or so wistful a thing as whether one will live long enough to see one's ambitions realized. These weren't attacks, from Eastman, on the planks of the Trotskyist platform. They were a retreat from the whole worldview, as well as evidence of the return to vigor of a competing worldview, liberalism, which the Trotskyists had been certain was croaking out its last gasps.

It was disappointing to the Trotskyists that Eastman would backslide, but not terribly surprising. He was the product of another age, the "lyrical left" of the pre–World War I years, and had never been entirely at home with the totalizing habits of Marxism or the feverish tempo of the 1930s. What was more upsetting was that Eastman, who'd spent the previous decade irritating almost everyone on the Left with his idiosyncratic critiques of Marxism, was no longer the odd man out. He was, it was fast becoming apparent, one of a wave of intellectuals and artists who were giving a second chance to good old-fashioned liberalism and bourgeois moralism. In January of 1939, Burnham and Shachtman addressed this worrying trend in "Intellectuals in Retreat," a four-part essay on the shift in manners and morals as it was playing out in the work of sixteen representative intellectuals.

The purpose of the piece, ostensibly, was not just to characterize this trend but to try to persuade these writers, and others who were on the same trajectory, to return to the Trotskyist bosom, and there were some halfhearted efforts at fairness and flattery. But fairness wasn't really the Trotskyist way, and Shachtman and Burnham, in any case, were feeling too besieged and abandoned to keep their aggression under wraps. The best they could manage was steely analysis mixed with heavy dollops of condescension and occasional sprinkles of empathy.

"Out of the troubled conflicts of our subjects," they wrote, "an ideal, a dream emerges. In a world pressing tumultuously, imperiously against every one of its inhabitants, grinding and battering them from every direction, they seek a little peace, quiet, a chance to cultivate and bring to harvest their talents. . . . They ask to be able to do and write what they wish without having to accept the consequences when what they do and write affects others; they ask not to be pushed around by others who are sure of their ideas and intend to fight for them; they ask to be released from responsibility."[57]

Eastman, naturally, was lambasted from this angle. Edmund Wilson was chided for an overheard remark that "Writers should not sign anything; they should merely write." Philip Rahv and William Phillips, whose *Partisan Review* had been friendly to the Trotskyists, were put on warning. James T. Farrell and James Rorty, among others, were knocked for contributing articles to the house paper of the Social Democrats. John Dewey, alone among the targets of the essay, was afforded some genuine respect, as "a man of outstanding intellectual probity," but his theories were given no quarter.

The most sustained of the essay's critiques was directed at Sidney Hook, who had over the previous few months taken two dramatic steps away from revolutionary Marxism. He'd published an essay in the *Southern Review*, "Reflections on the Russian Revolution," that went down many of the same heretical paths that Eastman's essay had traveled. And he'd begun organizing his fellow backsliding intellectuals into a "League Against Totalitarianism," which discarded the old Marxist categories in favor of drawing what Hook now saw as a much more important distinction, between those nations that were totalitarian in their essence—Germany, Italy, Russia, Japan, and Spain—and those nations, the United States among them, that allowed a space for "the thinker and the artist to function independently of political, religious, or racial dogmas."[58]

For Burnham, Hook's apostasy was particularly painful. It had been Hook, after all, who had been Burnham's guide into the mysteries of Marxism, Hook who had brought him into contact with the American

Workers Party, Hook who had labored with Burnham to negotiate the AWP's merger with the Trotskyists, and Hook who had been the most forceful of Marxist theorists in America. The two men had never felt it necessary, as friends and comrades, to keep in alignment with each other on every last point of Marxist strategy and theory. But Hook's *Southern Review* essay, and his founding of the league, were more than just friendly quibbles; they were declarations of divorce from revolutionary politics.

So Burnham and Shachtman responded as the partisans they still were. They tore into Hook as though he were just another bourgeois dilettante who'd flirted with revolution when it was fashionable but now, as war approached and revolutionary ardor faded, was reverting to his base class self-interest.

Hook's essay, they wrote, was "presumptuous," rife with "disingenuous sophistry" and "facile generalizations." Hook was thin on his Bolshevik history, confused on his theory, willfully ignorant in his use of quotations, and above all unwilling to own up to the real nature of his break from the movement, which had far less to do with the theory or practice of revolutionary Marxism than it did with a realignment of Hook's loyalties at the more visceral level. He was losing his revolutionary nerve, and taking comfort in all the flimsy old notions he'd once had the vision to see through.

The essay was a remarkable act of fraternal aggression, or filial loyalty, depending on whether you were looking in the direction of Hook or Trotsky. From neither angle did it sit easy with Burnham. In March of 1939 he pushed back in the other direction, publishing a short piece in *Partisan Review* that expressed, more clearly than ever before, his rejection of the philosophy of dialectical materialism. It was ostensibly a book review, but the book was an excuse. Burnham was taking up Eastman's dare: Could he be frank about dialectical materialism without, as a consequence, starting an intellectual slide down a slope that would end with him tumbled in a bourgeois heap with Eastman and Hook? And was the party flexible enough for him to be honest about his dissent without incurring a backlash?

What he synthesized was a version of the kind of argument that Eastman had been making for some time, but one made with a great deal more generosity, and pragmatism, than Eastman was able to muster up by the late 1930s. Yes, dialectical materialism was a series of fuzzy metaphysical conjectures that made sense (though not really) only to Germans. And yes, it had to be excised from the movement, because it was toxic to clear thinking and strategic action. But to argue, as Eastman was now arguing, that it had always been so toxic was to misunderstand how ideas function in history. It was to fail to appreciate that dialectical materialism, in its time, had enabled Marx and Engels and many of their successors to express other ideas that needed expressing.

"The principles can best be understood as *metaphors*," wrote Burnham. "Through them Marx and Engels seem to have expressed . . . above all their rejection of gradualist methods in politics; their insistence on the irreconcilability of the major class conflict in modern society, and their contention that the social revolution could be brought about only through political revolution."

From this pragmatic perspective, dialectical materialism was not the original sin of Marxism, dooming all that issued forth from its taint to corrupt and die. It was an early adaptation in the history of the evolution of revolutionary Marxism, one that had served its purpose in a different time and place but was now, like the appendix in the human body, "vestigial." One didn't look at an appendix that had become infected and leap to the conclusion that the whole body was corrupt and needed to be destroyed, or that there was some essential flaw in the design of the body that meant that it never should have been born in the first place. One cut out the appendix.

"Let us, then, perform the necessary operation, and remove this appendix from the *corpus* of Marxism," wrote Burnham. "And let us take our clear point of departure from Marxism understood first and most profoundly as the science and art of the social revolution."[59]

On August 23, 1939, the Soviet Union and Germany formally signed a treaty of nonaggression. It was one of the bigger geopolitical surprises of the twentieth century. All the signs had pointed to an alliance in the coming war between the Soviet Union, Great Britain, France, and, if it got involved, the United States. The Soviet Union had been conciliatory toward the big bourgeois liberal democracies for the past few years. Public negotiations had occurred almost exclusively between these countries, and just six months past the Soviet Union and Germany had been arming opposite sides in the civil war in Spain and demonizing each other in their state propaganda. It was only two decades before that, as well, that millions of Russians and Germans were brutalizing each other on the eastern front of World War I. The two nations were ideological nemeses. They were historic enemies. They were even archetypal enemies, rival bands of wild men roaming the steppes of Europe's id.

So when the treaty was announced, and the pictures wired out to the world of German foreign minister Joachim von Ribbentrop standing by a smiling Stalin, it was a shock. To the Communists outside the Soviet Union, in particular, it was a betrayal from which many would never recover. It was one thing for Communists to talk as though capitalists and the fascists were cut from the same cloth. That was rhetorically useful, and maybe theoretically defensible. But for Stalin to actually act upon the world stage as though the Nazis and the Allies were morally equivalent, as though it didn't matter which one you danced with so long as it served the interests of the Soviet state—that was more cynicism than even many red-blooded Communists could bear. For Jewish Communists, in particular, it was a soul-breaking thing to have to watch their chosen leaders break bread with a regime so viciously anti-Semitic it made the czar look hospitable in retrospect.

For the Trotskyists, the treaty was cause for less surprise, but not much less confusion. They'd seen Stalin clearly enough to know him capable of such amorality, and had been warning for years of the possibility of just such an accommodation with Hitler. There was also, in theory at least, a golden opportunity for the Trotskyists to peel off some of the Communists who were in the process of withdrawing from the party. Yet most Trotskyists, when it came to it, didn't feel vindicated when they heard the news. They felt dread, at the thought of world war that seemed now irrevocably in motion. Or they felt shame, at the Soviet baggage their own party still insisted on carrying. Or they felt disgust, at Stalin and the Soviet Union. Or they felt some combination of all these emotions, along with a sense of betrayal that wasn't all that different from what their Communist Party rivals were experiencing. Many of the Trotskyists, after all, had been carrying Soviet baggage not just out of loyalty to Trotsky and his theories, but because their own dreams of a socialist future were so deeply rooted in the soil of the Soviet past. Every time Stalin did something to tarnish the legacy of Lenin, that attachment became a heavier burden to bear, and the fine distinctions on which the Trotskyists prided themselves became harder to maintain.

On September 1, 1939, one week after the nonaggression treaty was signed, Germany declared war on Poland and invaded. In response, France and Great Britain declared war on Germany. Two weeks later the Soviets invaded Poland from the east, and within a few weeks the Second Polish Republic had been conquered and sliced in half, with the Germans and the Soviet Union meeting in the middle and amicably respecting each other's new borders. Although the major powers wouldn't engage with each other for another eight months, it was the beginning of World War II. It was also evidence, on the ground, of how deep the collusion between the Soviets and the Germans had gone. They were in the process of parceling up eastern Europe between them.

Burnham had had enough. He'd been struggling to suppress his rebellious impulses for more than a year. He'd been loyally, and neurotically, channeling his aggression outward, with a special degree of venom reserved for friends and former allies who were saying forcefully the things he was only muttering under his breath. He'd also, quietly, been cogitating upon a new theory of the Soviet Union, as a "bureaucratic collectivist" state, that seemed to him to fit the facts of the matter much better than Trotsky's construction.

With the Soviet invasion of Poland he saw an opportunity to take a stand. He called for an emergency meeting of the National Committee and once again raised the Russian question, this time upping the stakes. He asked for a condemnation of the Soviet "war of imperial conquest" in Poland and, more fundamentally, for a redefinition of the Soviet Union as no longer a workers' state of any kind. He was again voted down, but by a razor-thin margin, and by the end of the month he'd won Shachtman over to his side.[60]

At that moment Trotsky could have backed down. Burnham and Shachtman were two of his three top men in America, and they were making it clear they would keep forcing the issue. The potential costs of battling it out with them were high: At best, there would be a short but bitter intra-party fight; at worst, the party would break in half. The costs of letting Burnham and Shachtman have their way, by contrast, seemed much lower. Trotsky's pride would have taken a blow, and he would have had to either revise or place in escrow for a while his theory of the Soviet state, but otherwise his authority within the party would have remained largely intact. And the Soviet albatross, which had been dragging down the party for years, would have been cut loose at just the right moment, when everyone's energies would be far more strategically spent on seizing the opportunities that were likely to coalesce from the chaos of war.

But Trotsky, being Trotsky, didn't suffer blows to his pride willingly. And Trotsky, being Trotsky, didn't believe that practical gain could be achieved by sacrificing theoretical principle. False theory led to foolish action, while true theory led to right action and the optimal revolutionary ends.[61] For Trotsky, any price was worth paying if the alternative was adopting false theory (or admitting he was wrong). So he didn't back down. He fired back with a long essay in the *New International*, "The USSR in War," that not only didn't make any concessions but extended the basic logic he'd already applied to the Soviet Union to the territory of Poland that was in the process of being gobbled up by the Soviet army. Nothing had changed, for Trotsky, except for the quantity of square mileage under consideration: "Our program retains, consequently, all its validity."[62]

The essay was typical Trotsky. It was pigheadedly stubborn in its assumptions, brilliantly flexible within them, and callous with respect to any goal or values exterior to those of revolution. There was one new chord struck, however, and it was one that would reverberate through the series of essays, letters, votes, proposal, counterproposals, catfights, and shouting matches between Trotsky (and his crew) and Burnham (and his crew) over the next half year.

Trotsky was in danger of losing his faith in the world. He remained cocksure of himself and that his course was the only one that could plausibly bring about a socialist future. But the years of exile and failure had worn away at him to the point where he was beginning to entertain the possibility that his dreamt-of future wouldn't come to be at all, or that if it did emerge it might be centuries later than he'd anticipated.[63]

Burnham, too, was dwelling on the prospect of socialism's failure— on what it meant for the future of the world, on what it demanded of men who would take responsibility for engineering that future. But whereas Trotsky couldn't imagine a meaningful life for himself in a world in which socialism was gone, Burnham wasn't quite so constrained. There was room for him to crane his neck around. He had a life outside the movement, a marriage that wasn't premised on it, a network of friends whose pleasure in his company had nothing to do with his fidelity to revolutionary praxis, and a steady job that would grow only more secure if he chose to distance himself from radical politics. It was excruciating for him to contemplate breaking with the party, and painful to attack Trotsky, who was a hero and fatherfigure. But it was possible for him to have such thoughts, and take such actions, without shivering to the ground his whole identity, livelihood, reputation, and philosophical edifice. The balance, in fact, had begun to tilt the other way. It was now easier for Burnham to bear the psychic costs of dissent than it was to hew to a party line that seemed so rank with hypocrisy and incoherence. As Trotsky entrenched, then, Burnham began to strain at the bonds, and the fight between the two men and their factions blew up like a marriage gone bad, with all the hurts, betrayals, and suspicions that had been suppressed for the sake of family comity rising up, and seeping out, to suffuse the whole relationship.

From Mexico, Trotsky began firing out essays and letters at a rapid clip, marshaling his forces to oppose Burnham and the group that rallied around him on the Russian question. In the States, Cannon began stacking committees with his loyalists, spreading gossip about the Burnham/Shachtman faction, working the bureaucracy to keep oppositional resolutions from being heard, and stoking the class resentment of workers and non-intellectuals in the party against the "petty bourgeois intellectuals" of the minority, who were losing their nerve, he argued, as such people almost always did when the rough choices of the revolutionary struggle proved too much for their delicate sensibilities.[64]

The minority held fiercely to its position on the Soviet Union, rapidly adding supplementary exhibits to the indictment as the Soviets, following their conquest of Poland, forced themselves on Latvia, Lithuania, and Estonia, and then, at the end of November, invaded Finland with half a million soldiers after the small nation stubbornly refused to become a vassal state. Burnham also began locating his stance on the Russian question within a broader critique of the party status quo, once again raising questions about internal party democracy that he'd let drop two years before, this time citing Cannon, by name, as the primary source of tyranny within the party.

By December, the fissure in the party had cracked wide open. At a meeting of the New York City chapter, where the minority had its base, Burnham and Cannon went directly at each other in a debate on the war on Finland.

"The debate had all the tension of a battle," wrote Cannon, in a letter to an ally. "We didn't discuss with each other, we fought each other. We couldn't 'discuss' because we didn't proceed from the same premise and couldn't talk on the same plane. . . . Two sides. Two camps. Burnham laid aside the professorial urbanity which he never entirely loses in polemics against the class enemy and attacked the National Committee with truculence and even impudence, as though it were indeed the main enemy. He challenged me, with the brutal arrogance of a man who has his opponent in a corner, to go out and face the popular clamour at a public mass meeting on the Soviet invasion of Finland. To all of us he seemed to speak with an unwonted self-assurance and self-confidence, like a man who feels powerful forces behind him."[65]

A week later, Trotsky published "A Petty-Bourgeois Opposition in the Socialist Workers Party" in the *New International*.[66] His past critiques had been angry, but they had kept the grounds of the theoretical disputes circumscribed enough that either side could have backed down afterward without entirely losing face. The new essay left far less room for retreat. It took each of the individual points of conflict—the nature of the Soviet state, the invasions of Poland and Finland, the internal structure of the Socialist Workers Party, the personal animosities between Burnham and Cannon—and recast them as symptoms of a far more fundamental clash.

On one side, wrote Trotsky, there was the Trotsky/Cannon majority. It was at one with the proletariat. Because of that, it moved organically according to the rhythms of dialectical materialism; its theorists theorized on a firm foundation of dialectical materialist reasoning; and it was able to shift in response to dramatic events without losing its anchor in principle. On the other side was the Burnhamite petty-bourgeois minority. They just didn't feel dialectical materialism in their brains or in their bones, and as a consequence they careened all over the place. One minute they were attacking "intellectuals in retreat"; the next minute they were running along with them. They raised the

Russian question one day only to drop it the next only to raise it again the day after that.

There were some distinctions in Trotsky's typology of the minority. Burnham was under the influence of the bankrupt tradition of pragmatist philosophy. Shachtman was a little too malleable to resist the influence of Burnham, and too "eclectic" in his thinking to hold firm to theoretical principle when confronted with such dizzying world events. Abern was still acting out the same personal dramas he'd brought with him from the Communist Party so many years before. These distinctions, however, were really just gloss on a singular truth, which was that the kind of incoherence the minority was now exhibiting was the kind that always arose when petty-bourgeois intellectuals were unable to transcend their class roots sufficiently to get in tune with the contradiction-resolving wavelengths of dialectical materialism.

As a polemic, "A Petty-Bourgeois Opposition" was masterful. Trotsky was ruthless with the minority's record of ambivalence. He turned their past words against their present selves; traced their shifting allegiances back through years of mergers, faction fights, and rivalries; and discerned, with a gift for reading between the lines of political documents that few of his era could match, the incriminating distance between where the minority's intellects claimed they were and where their hearts had already taken them. Then he asked, simply and devastatingly, whether the trajectory that he'd charted was one that was more characteristic of hardened revolutionaries or of the ex-movement intellectuals whom Burnham and Shachtman had so recently pinioned to the table and dissected.

On the matter of Burnham, in particular, Trotsky turned to his tactical advantage an undeniable truth. It was indeed different for Burnham, with his affluent background, bourgeois profession, and ties to the world outside revolutionary politics. Burnham was different. He didn't feel the rhythms as organically as many of his comrades did. He was more prone to doubt, and felt more entitled to dissent, because of where he came from and who he was. So there was a truth in what

Trotsky was saying, but also a dangerous omission. Burnham's difference was a big part of precisely why he was so valuable, and why his recruitment had been such a coup in the first place.

In calling him out on these fronts, then, Trotsky succeeded polemically while failing miserably to move Burnham and his allies toward the only political objective his essay ostensibly sought, which was to stave off a split. After Trotsky was done there was no room left for his opponents to do anything but submit or separate. The essay also staked far too much of its credibility on an elaborate and not very persuasive defense of the Hegelian guts of dialectical materialism. Hegelianism was a mode of thinking that Trotsky, for all his firepower as a historian and essayist, wasn't so well suited to inhabiting, and it was one that he seemed drawn to, at that moment, out of pique more than anything else. He seemed incredibly irritated that these Americans, who were so untested and so unvindicated by any demonstrable revolutionary successes, could be so dismissive of a system of thought that had been more than good enough for the leaders of the Bolshevik revolution. He seemed incensed, in particular, by Burnham's treatment of the subject. So he decided to put the professor in his place. The deeper he dug into the subject, however, and the more enraged he became by Burnham, the more he fell into precisely the kind of quasi-mystical hopscotching that had always made German idealism such a hard sell in America.

"The fundamental flaw of vulgar thought," wrote Trotsky, "lies in the fact that it wishes to content itself with motionless imprints of a reality which consists of eternal motion. Dialectical thinking gives to concepts, by means of closer approximations, corrections, concretisation, a richness of content and flexibility; I would even say 'a succulence' which to a certain extent brings them closer to living phenomena. . . . Dialectical thinking is related to vulgar in the same way that a motion picture is related to a still photograph. The motion picture does not outlaw the still photograph but combines a series of them according to the laws of motion. Dialectics does not deny the syllogism, but teaches us to combine syllogisms in such a way as to bring our understanding closer to the eternally changing reality."

Burnham, confronted with pages and pages of this, was underwhelmed.

"I stopped arguing about religion long ago,"[67] Burnham said to one of his comrades, when asked whether he was going to respond to Trotsky's defense of dialectical materialism. The remark rippled quickly through the revolutionary grapevine to Trotsky, who was so infuriated by it that he fired off another long essay, "An Open Letter to Comrade Burnham," almost before he'd come down from the last. And with that the last pretenses of comradeship fell away.

With "An Open Letter to Comrade Burnham," which was published in the *New International* in early January of 1940, the war between the two factions, and the two men, went public, and even further downhill.

The ostensible issues were the same ones that had been dividing the party since the Hitler-Stalin treaty, but the tone was personal in a way it hadn't been before, as the insecurities and animosities that Trotsky and Burnham usually kept so well camouflaged were given rein. They began firing letters and essays at each other, in public view, at an extraordinary pace, each man pouring out so many words of attack, rebuttal, riposte, and insult over the course of the first few months of 1940 it was a wonder either had time to do anything else.

Trotsky was furious at being belittled. He was wounded by the political abandonment of a friend and colleague. He was terrified of losing the nearly half of the party that Burnham and Shachtman had thus far managed to win over to their position. He was afraid of dwindling even further into an irrelevance that, though he wouldn't admit it to himself, he knew he was already circling around. And he was really steamed that after everything he'd been through, after all the jailings, redemptions, revolutions, and exiles, after clasping hands with giants and crossing swords with tyrants, he was reduced to having to wrestle for control of his own political party with a second-rate philosophy professor who'd grown weary of dabbling in revolution and was now angling to recover favor with his bourgeois intellectual buddies.

As Trotsky vented his anger, Burnham lashed out in response. Faction fights were faction fights, and dialectics were dialectics, but Trotsky had begun talking down to him as if he were just another political enemy, reducing his ideas to the sum of his class origins and treating his years of party service and personal friendship as though they meant next to nothing now that Burnham had dared question the Great Leader on hallowed doctrine. He was doing to Burnham, in fact, what Burnham had very recently done to Hook, and Burnham felt betrayed—all the more so for the intellectual violence he'd only recently committed against his friend in Trotsky's name.[68] So he struck back. If Trotsky was going to go dirty, then Burnham would do the same to Trotsky.

What was destroying the Socialist Workers Party, Burnham wrote, wasn't the minority's defection from proper theory, or the infiltration of petty-bourgeois sentiments. It was Trotsky's judgment, and his character. It was a flaw in Trotsky's makeup that had been present from the beginning, a fatal weakness for style and metaphor at the expense of logic and empiricism, exacerbated by a pride that was immune to the uncooperative facts of the world. Trotsky's style drew people to him, and could be a magnificent tool when put to the right ends, but it wasn't the extension of a character or intellect that was solid enough to anchor a movement caught up in events as cataclysmic as those the world was experiencing. Rather than acknowledge error, or adjust his theory in light of new evidence, Trotsky retreated ever further into the consolations of style and abstraction. With each new cycle of pride and error, his responses to his critics became more crabbed and defensive until the party was on the verge of expiring from the burden of carrying around his monstrous ego.

It would be another three months before Burnham would formally abandon revolutionary Marxism, but the essay he addressed to Trotsky in February of 1940, in response to Trotsky's "Open Letter," was the decisive emotional break. With it, he separated himself not just from

Trotsky, but from the iteration of James Burnham who'd been seduced into Marxism by Trotsky's voice eight years before. He wasn't that man anymore, Burnham made clear, and he would no longer tamp down all the other voices in his head out of deference to his admiration for Trotsky.

"Comrade Trotsky, while reading and thinking about this Letter, I recalled also the first time that I had ever given really serious attention to your work: in a lengthy review of the first volume of your *History*, published in the July 1932 issue of *The Symposium*. I re-read that review, which I had not done for many years. There, too, I found that I had been compelled to discuss first of all your style, your wonderful style, which in fact I analysed at considerable length. And I saw more clearly than ever before what is, in my eyes, an important truth: that you have a too literary conception of proof, of evidence; that you deceive yourself into treating persuasive rhetoric as logical demonstration, a brilliant metaphor as argument. Here, I believe, is the heart of the mystery of the dialectic, as it appears in your books and articles: the dialectic, for you, is a device of style—the contrasting epithets, the flowing rhythms, the verbal paradoxes which characterise your way of writing.

"Comrade Trotsky, I will not match metaphors with you. In such a verbal tournament, I concede you the ribbon in advance. Evidence, argument, proof: these only are my weapons."[69]

In February of 1940, Burnham, Shachtman, and their allies held a national meeting in Cleveland to plot strategy, while Trotsky and Cannon called for an emergency meeting of the whole party, to be convened in April, for the purpose of resolving the disputes once and for all.

Both factions claimed to want to avoid a split, but neither was inclined to submit to the other on any of the major issues. The minority wanted more democracy within the party. They wanted a newspaper of their own, which would have official party sanction but total editorial freedom. And they wanted to be able to fight it out—on the Soviet

Union, on dialectical materialism, on internal party organization—in full view of the membership, for as long as they felt like it.

The majority was done with the yammering. They were a revolutionary Marxist party in the Bolshevik tradition, not a debating society. If the minority wanted to repent and rejoin, wrote Trotsky, then they could, but they would have to do so on his terms. They would have to stop complaining about the party's theoretically correct position on the Soviet Union every time Stalin behaved like a Stalinist and did something awful. They would have to stop whinging about democracy every time the appropriately centralized decision-making processes generated a conclusion with which they disagreed. They would have to stop questioning basic Marxist doctrine in the party's publications. And they would have to commit to some serious re-education.

To no one's surprise, neither faction gave way at the emergency convention in April. A series of resolutions were put forth by Cannon and his people that demanded an up-or-down vote on many of the divisive issues. The minority was defeated on each of the resolutions, and then, a week later, its leaders were given the choice of either committing to the newly codified positions or giving up their leadership posts within the party. They walked away, taking a sizable chunk of the membership with them.

A month later, Burnham announced that he was done with Marxism for good. He'd briefly joined with the rest of his fellow exiles in the process of organizing a new revolutionary Marxist party, which would be called the Workers Party (WP), and he'd spoken at their first organizational meeting as though he planned to serve in the leadership. But as the founding convention approached, and Shachtman and the others scrambled to figure out just what it was that would differentiate the WP from the SWP, Burnham realized the nuances didn't matter to him anymore.

To the degree that he still shared any strong convictions with the new party, they were almost exclusively negative convictions. The Soviet Union wasn't a workers' state anymore. The world war was an imperialist war, fought by all sides in the pursuit of profits and territories. The era of bourgeois liberalism was over. Cannon was a bully. Trotsky had gone tragically astray.

As for the positive goals of Marxism, and the insights into history and society that Marxian analysis was supposed to offer, Burnham no longer bought much of it. He still found the Marxist vision of the good society beautiful, but he'd concluded that it was beautiful like a fantasy was beautiful, corrosive to clear thinking and right acting in the ways that fantasies almost always were when people mistook them for possible realities. He'd been able to hide this life-altering conclusion from himself for a while, by focusing on the ideological debates with Trotsky and the factional fights with Cannon. Now that those struggles were spent, though, and the challenge confronting him was a generative one, to participate in the building of a new party, all the un-Marxist critiques, revisions, and revulsions that he'd carefully kept partitioned away from one another, so as to protect the structure of his Marxist commitment, were let loose. They were given the freedom to inform each other, to fall into position with respect to each other, in whatever kind of philosophical structure hosted them most organically. And with that, the old scaffolding crumbled to dust and a new truth suddenly snapped into place. Burnham wasn't a Marxist anymore.

On May 21, 1940, Burnham gave his letter of resignation to the Workers Party. It was a much softer document than anything he'd written in a long time. There was a sadness in it, at the friendships he was surely ending and the life he would be leaving behind, as well as a touch of embarrassment over abandoning his comrades so soon after the brutal split that he'd done so much to provoke. The letter was decisive, though, in its intentions. He would be willing to phase himself out slowly, even write for the party publications for a few months if it would help ease the transition, but he saw no future for himself as a Marxist.

"When I say that I reject Marxism," he wrote, "I do not at all mean that I am scornful of or consider myself 'superior to' Marxists. Not at all. I am humble, believe me, before the loyalty, sacrifice and heroism of so many Marxists—qualities found so widely within the ranks of the Workers Party. But I cannot act otherwise than I do."

Shachtman, in whom Burnham had long confided his doubts, wasn't terribly surprised by Burnham's decision to quit. Nor were some of the other leaders, who'd been close enough to the center of things to have had a sense of Burnham's unhappiness. For most of the members, however, and for many within the leadership, Burnham's letter was shocking. Not so much that he was leaving—abandonment, after all, was part of the existential condition of being a Trotskyist—as that he was leaving with a political perspective that seemed so radically different from what he'd been articulating so forcefully so recently. In February, he'd been arguing that he was a better Marxist than Trotsky. In April he'd been helping draft a constitution for the new party. By May he was no longer a Marxist of any kind.

Burnham was sensitive to how dramatic this shift appeared, and half-apologetic, but he insisted in the letter that what had happened to him was not any kind of radical conversion or de-conversion. For years he'd held, and could document holding, many of the critiques of Marxism he was now citing to explain his departure. And he'd always been honest about those Marxist claims that he was willing to endorse only provisionally, so long as they made sense of what was going on in the world. What had changed between then and now was that his critiques had remained constant while almost all of his Marxist hypotheses had been refuted by the data of events. And, too, he'd been forced by the actions of Cannon and Trotsky and their gang to conclude that Marxism wasn't so alluring, to many of its adherents, despite its worst flaws but because of them. The authoritarianism, the deterministic faith in the ultimate triumph of the movement, the hubristic claims to having perfect understanding of all realms of knowledge, the irrational loyalty to the Soviet Union, and, particularly, the mysticism and disguised eschatology of dialectical materialism—these weren't infected appendixes one could simply cut away from the body of Marxism. They were its heart, its lungs, its liver, its spleen.

Trotsky was right, Burnham concluded. There was no Marxism without dialectical materialism, no Marxism without the Soviet Union, no Marxism without a Bolshevik-style command structure, and no Marxism without a ruthless will to power that would sacrifice anyone and anything—even entire nations—to the cause of its own realization. And if that was the case, Burnham could be no kind of Marxist.[70]

3

When the Team's Up Against It: Ronald Reagan

I had become a Democrat, by birth, I suppose, and a few months after my twenty-first birthday, I cast my first vote for Roosevelt and the full Democratic ticket. And, like Jack—and millions of other Americans—I soon idolized FDR.[1]

—RONALD REAGAN

It is not new. It is, in fact, man's second oldest faith. Its promise was whispered in the first days of the Creation under the tree of the Knowledge of Good and Evil: "Ye shall be as gods."[2]

—WHITTAKER CHAMBERS

There's a story that Ronald Reagan tells, in the first of his two autobiographies, of his father, Jack. It's set in Dixon, Illinois, the town that Reagan would always consider his home.

Whether Reagan wrote the salient pages himself is impossible to say. He had a co-writer for the book, which he published in 1965 to till the soil for his run for governor of California the following year, and there are passages in the text that don't sound much like him. The morality tale sounds like Reagan, though. It has that efficiency that would have so much to do with the long arc of his success as a politician.

As the story begins, in the depth of the Great Depression, Reagan's hard-drinking, charismatic, bon vivant father, Jack, has finally seen some reward from his years of loyalty to the local Democratic Party. He's been rescued from his own unemployment and hired by the Federal Emergency Relief Administration to take responsibility for distributing food and food vouchers to the town of ten thousand.

"Dixon was really hard hit," wrote Reagan. ". . . Every week the line would form—not bums or strangers but friends, fathers of kids I'd gone to school with. Most of them were first names to Jack and he was Jack to them."[3]

The charge invigorates Jack, and he takes upon himself not just the relief duties for which he's being paid but the much more noble task of finding work for the men he's helping. What Jack understands about these men, as Reagan tells it, is what President Roosevelt himself would express so elegantly in his second inaugural address, that "To dole out relief is to administer a narcotic, a subtle destroyer of the human spirit."[4] Without the opportunity to work, though their bellies might be fed, the souls of Jack's fellow citizens would go hungry. So he got them work, as best he could, by hook and by crook.

"It took him only a few weeks to start rounding up every odd job, every put-off chore from raking yards to thinning the woods at Lowell Park for the Park Board. He worked nights arranging a round-robin schedule so that every week a number of the men in the line got jobs for a few days or a week—and when they did, they skipped coming in that week for the handout."

And so it might have gone on, with pride, fellowship, and discipline building upon each other, lifting Dixon out of the Depression, if the efforts had been left in the hands of men like Jack Reagan. Doers, not paper pushers. Men, not bureaucrats. But they were betrayed.

"One day," wrote Reagan, "the welfare workers arrived with loads of furniture and, of course, the card files—enough to require a whole floor of offices in a downtown building. . . . people became cases. 'Get me the file on the Smith case.'—'Let me see the card on the Jones case.' The day came when Jack, who'd kept right on in his regular routine, told a group he had a week's work for them and they said, 'Jack, we can't take it.' To his stunned surprise, he was told that the last time they took his jobs the new welfare staff had cut them off relief. Then their cases had to be reopened with interviews, applications, and new cards. The process took three weeks and in the meantime their families went hungry—all because they'd done a few days' honest work."

In Reagan's telling Jack kept fighting the good fight, and over the course of his government employ he'd accomplish amazing things in Dixon. He would put men to work building parks and bridges. He would mastermind the tearing up of the streetcar rails on Main Street to use for the skeleton of a hangar at the new airport. But what had begun for him as redemptive, restorative work had turned into a soul-sapping plod, a losing tussle with the blob of the federal bureaucracy. He got dead drunk the night after he first ran up against the welfare workers and their card files, a temptation he'd been able to resist, Reagan implies, so long as he was empowered to do good according to his instincts and initiative.

"That night Jack didn't spit in the eye of the curse. He arrived home on foot, with a severe list to port. Knowing that he had the car, I backtracked him and found it right where it had proved too much for him—sitting in the middle of the street with the door open and the motor running."[5]

The whole sequence is classic Reagan: personal, moral, and political all centrifuged together into a tight parable of conservative wisdom. This is what you get, it says, when the state inserts itself between work and the wealth it's meant to produce, between decent folk and their responsibilities to their families, neighbors, and communities. You get men whose internal compasses are knocked out of balance, who list severely to port even as they desperately struggle to stay on the straight and narrow. You get a society left in the middle of the road, its engine turning over but no foot on the gas or hands at the wheel.

That the story is rooted in a profound distortion also goes to the core of who Reagan was, and to the nature of his influence.

For Reagan didn't tell the tale he could have, of his father's unflagging loyalty to the policies of the New Deal and his visceral hostility toward Big Business. He didn't delve into the full-blooded liberalism he inherited from his dad, which remained strong in him well into the 1940s, nor explain why it eventually gave way to conservatism. He passed up the ready-made dramatic structures and archetypal scenes that so many of his fellow travelers from the Left to the Right employed to tell their stories. Not for Reagan a descent into utopian delusion, followed by a long dark night of the soul, culminating in a baptismal emergence into the light of God, truth, and conservatism. No traumatic breaks with comrades or father figures. No moment of soul-testing when he was pressed up against an essential aspect of the Left that he simply couldn't endure.

In Reagan's conversion story there was no conversion at all. There was, instead, a creep of beliefs, friendships, history, and circumstance that happened so slowly that not only was Reagan able to convince himself, in hindsight, that he hadn't changed much at all, he was able to carry with him into his new ideological residence much of the emotional and symbolic furniture of his liberal past. In this alternate history, he, his father, and FDR were states' rights and small government men from the start. It was the Democratic Party that changed, not them, and it was the modern Republican Party that was the natural inheritor of the legacy of, among others, FDR, Woodrow Wilson, and Thomas Jefferson.

"I didn't desert my party. . . . It deserted me," he would say not long after being elected president. ". . . I looked up FDR's old platform, and I discovered that it called for a restoration of states' rights and a reduction in the national budget. You know what? I'm still for that."[6]

Reagan's genius as a politician lay in his talent for telling stories that made common sense of conservative ideology and policy. He understood, intuitively but also as a consequence of decades of thoughtful practice, that most people aren't moved to vote, march, donate, call their congressmen, or change their minds if they aren't given stories that locate political ideas and plans in their own lives.

His own backstory, as he told it, contained serious factual and historical flaws. That's demonstrable, and important on its own terms. As important, and more interesting, is what is true within it. That for Reagan, and for tens of millions of Americans who would travel with him to the Right, political transformation wasn't marked by catharsis and epiphany. It didn't involve the conscious rejection of political heroes, the dissolution of close friendships, or the dismantling of dearly held beliefs. It rarely even revealed itself as a transformation. It was life, lived year to year, decade to decade, with the disruptions and involutions massaged into a narrative of political and personal constancy that gave more comfort and was less anxious to bear than a story of discontinuity and change would have been.

Dramatic political transformation, of the kind that Reagan experienced, is painful even when it emerges incrementally and subtly. In his case it entailed a rejection of the beliefs and commitments of his father, as well as an active struggle to roll back the political accomplishments of his idol Franklin Roosevelt. It also involved an implicit judgment of his younger self, who believed in policies and ideas that his older self would condemn as socialistic and un-American.

People do different things with that kind of trauma, and it's possible to imagine a parallel-universe Ronald Reagan who did the psychological work of understanding his evolution to the point where he was at peace with his past, where he could evolve into a conservative without losing the capacity to return, imaginatively, to the beliefs of his younger self. That alternate Reagan would have been able to do certain things better, speak to certain kinds of people more effectively. He probably would have been a better actor.

It's also possible to imagine a Ronald Reagan who never had to undergo such a transformation in the first place, because he was the person whom Reagan claimed in retrospect to have been—a conservative from the get-go. That Reagan, too, would have had a lot going for him. Good looks. A beautiful speaking voice. An exceptional talent for connecting with an audience and telling stories that moved them. He might have been governor, senator, perhaps even president.

Neither alternate Reagan, however, would have been transformative in the way the actual Reagan was. For he wouldn't have been compelled to tell a story that so many millions of Americans wanted to hear to help them change their political loyalties. They wanted to be told that a vote for Reagan, for the Republican Party, for conservative ideas, didn't mean that they'd changed, that their past selves had been wrong, or that their past allegiances had been misguided. What came from Reagan putting his genius to work finessing his own incongruities was an arsenal of stories, lessons, evasions, and stratagems that enabled others to change in the way he had, by detaching politically from past loyalties without taking an axe to the emotional ties—of family, workplace, ethnicity, religion, history, and geography—with which those loyalties had been bound up.

It was said of Reagan, mostly by his critics, that his political success depended on his experience as an actor. That he learned in Hollywood how to play a role, play to the camera, follow directions, and manipulate emotions through the artful deployment of voice, body language, and lines of dialogue that had been written for him by someone else. Implied, too, in the charge, is that as a politician he was a vessel for other people's interests in the way that an actor, even a great one, is a vessel of other people's narratives. And there's some truth to this. Reagan's acting experience aided him enormously in his performance as a politician. And he could be used by others, when what they wanted from him didn't run contrary to any of his core instincts. But to perceive Reagan as simply an actor who switched studios from Warner Brothers to the Republican Party is to see only half, or less, of what he absorbed from his years in Hollywood, not just the lessons of the actor but those of the marketing department, the editing room, the producer's chair, and the screenwriter as well.

It's also to miss his ambition—what his younger son would call the "cold but steady flame" that burned within him.[7] What drove Reagan to Hollywood, to the governor's mansion in Sacramento, and ultimately to the White House wasn't just the typical actor's narcissistic desire to be seen, affirmed, and celebrated, but also, crucially, a fundamentally political instinct to bend the world to suit his internal narrative of how it should be.

Reagan offered himself to the nation in the performative role of president, but he also was able to provide, to the voting public, much more than that. Not just the hero, but the hero situated within larger stories of unity, uplift, continuity, comfort, redemption, and shared meaning. It was only within the frame of those myths, which he distilled from the raw material of his life before, during, and after Hollywood, that his performance moved people, and a nation.

On October 5, 1940, *Knute Rockne—All American* premiered in South Bend, Indiana, on the campus of the University of Notre Dame, where Rockne had built his legend as football coach. Thanks to savvy marketing from Warner Brothers, and a South Bend that loved its Fighting Irishmen, it was a spectacle, the focal point of a weekend full of speeches, red carpet parades, pep rallies, and photo ops that was bracketed by the arrival and departure of the Super Chief, the luxury train that carried the stars and their entourages from Hollywood and back again.

For Ronald Reagan, who starred in the movie as the beautiful and doomed halfback George "the Gipper" Gipp, it was a moment.

Reagan had already been in more than twenty films since he'd arrived in Hollywood in 1937. They were mostly low-budget B-list productions, however, and his few spots in top-tier productions had been brief and nonessential. *Knute Rockne* was the first A-list movie in which Reagan was really a star. He was up there on the marquee, and his casting in the role was a signal from the higher-ups at Warner Brothers that he was being considered for bigger things. His parents, Jack and Nelle, were even able to be there in South Bend with him—had in fact been sent there in style, in the same luxurious train cars as the cast, as a favor from the studio to its star.

More than anything, the role of Gipp was one Reagan felt suited him. From a young age Reagan had been drawn to the movies in part because they told the kinds of stories that spoke to his own fantasies of what he might become. He had grown up on stories of Gipp and Notre Dame's heroics. He'd played football (enthusiastically, if not all that well) in high school and college. He'd even arrived in Hollywood with the specific ambition to play Gipp in a movie about Rockne.[8] When he'd heard that the film was being made he'd fought more aggressively for the part than he'd ever fought for a part before, or would after. And his scenes in the movie proved as resonant as he'd hoped they might be. His jaunty stroll onto the practice field early in the film, and the dropkick he launches over the top of the distant bleachers, is the moment of destiny when the great coach finds the vessel into whom he can channel his genius. His death scene, and his dying plea to Rockne to use his memory to someday rally the boys' spirits "when the team's up against it," is the fulcrum of the movie's final act.[9]

Gipp's whole relationship with Rockne, though it ends with Gipp's death not too long into the movie, is the purest expression of the movie's prime philosophical commitment, which is to a vision of America as a place where small-town fathers and sons, through sports and the rituals of male camaraderie, keep vitality coursing through the national veins. It was a vision Reagan could compellingly inhabit in no small part because it was one he shared.[10]

"He's given us something they don't teach in schools, something clean and strong inside," said Reagan as Gipp. "Not just courage but a right way of living none of us'll ever forget."[11]

Knute Rockne—All American proved to be a moderate success for Warner Brothers. That was good enough, along with the excellent reviews of Reagan's performance, to establish Reagan in what he would later call "the shaky-A's." He was up there, but not so high up that he couldn't still be called down to the B-list if he was needed to fill out a cast.

Over the next year, until the war interrupted his film career, Reagan solidified his status in the Hollywood ecosystem, generally distinguishing himself in roles that drew on his natural, insouciant charm, while fading competently into the background in those movies where he was asked to emote more thoroughly or to match the screen presence of a truly luminous star.

At that moment, just before the war diverted him, Reagan seemed golden. He was a rising star. He was married to Jane Wyman, another rising star, whom he'd met on the set of a movie. Their daughter Maureen had been born in January of 1941, and together the family made such a picture of domestic bliss that they were featured in Warner Brothers promotional material as evidence of Hollywood's commitment to the values of the heartland.[12]

Even Jack Reagan's death in May of 1941, following a series of heart attacks, was good timing for Reagan. He'd already made his father proud. He'd supplanted him as the patriarch of the family—buying a house in L.A. for Jack and Nelle, even hiring Dad to answer his fan mail. And though Reagan missed his father, it was liberating to be free from him and from the fear that Jack might at any moment bring embarrassment, disorder, or shame into his son's life.

The war crept up on Ronald Reagan. It wasn't that he was ignorant of the rising conflict. He had the knowledge to see it coming. He read the newspapers, would talk politics with his friends and his wife until they begged him to stop, and was an officer in the cavalry reserves, having enlisted back when he was doing radio in Iowa in order to be able to ride the horses on the local base. A number of his films in 1940 and 1941 were war films, greenlit very consciously by the Warners as a means of helping the Roosevelt administration rouse the American people into a war-making mood.

If one had asked Reagan during this time about the lineup of combatant nations in Europe and Asia, or the shifting tides of the campaigns being waged, he would have been able to answer in much greater detail than most Americans. He certainly would have had something contemptuous to say about fascism and the anti-Semitism of the Nazis.

Emotionally, though, Reagan was almost entirely focused on his film career. Even after his first call to active duty, which was deferred thanks to an intervention from Jack Warner, Reagan didn't redirect his gaze. When the war finally came to Reagan, after two more deferments, he was almost surprised.

Reagan reported for active duty a few months later, on April 19, 1942, at Fort Mason in San Francisco. In theory, it was possible that he would be sent overseas to fight, or at least to support those who were fighting. Other entertainers, including a few celebrities, ended up in combat zones, and Reagan was a physically courageous man, who when younger had saved dozens of lives while lifeguarding on a nasty stretch of the Rock River in Illinois. He was also fervently patriotic, and devoted to the leadership of Franklin Roosevelt. If asked, he would have gone.

He wasn't so exceptionally keen to fight, however, that he rejected the help that Warner Brothers and his influential agent, Lew Wasserman, could offer in arranging an alternative. Nor did he go out of his way to obscure the very good reasons to keep him stateside. Reagan was thirty by this point, with a wife and child. He was a well-known actor with a wholesome image and a lot of team spirit, all traits that would be more useful to the army's propaganda effort than to its military one. And his eyesight, serendipitously, was just awful.

When he'd first enlisted in the cavalry he'd had to sneak in and memorize the eye chart in order to game the physical. This time around Reagan didn't dissemble. Before he even arrived at base, Warner Brothers had put out the word to its friends in the Hollywood press corps that his eyesight was bad ("Ronnie can't see clearly over five feet from him," as it was duly reported).[13] When the time came for another physical, on his first day at Fort Mason, Reagan played it straight.

"I went through the same old business with the eyes," he wrote, "and one of the examining doctors said, 'If we sent you overseas, you'd shoot a general.'

"The other doctor looked up and said, 'Yes, and you'd miss him.' "[14]

Reagan spent five weeks as a low-responsibility bureaucrat and on-base celebrity at Fort Mason before he was transferred back to Los Angeles, to serve in the newly established First Motion Picture Unit (FMPU).

For the next three years, until the war ended, Reagan would exist in an alternate, semi-militarized version of the life he'd been living for the previous few years. Every day he would report for duty at the Hal Roach Studios in Culver City, a sprawling feature film studio complex the FMPU had taken over in 1942. One of his commanding officers was the recently commissioned lieutenant colonel Jack Warner, whose brainchild the unit had been. His thirteen hundred or so fellow soldiers/ coworkers were the same kind of people, and in many cases literally the same people, with whom he'd been making movies for Warner Brothers—not just actors but producers, writers, directors, artists, wardrobe managers, cameramen, and technicians. Even his domestic life was a slightly surreal version of its previous incarnation. He had a bunk on base, and would sleep there often, but military discipline in the First Motion Picture Unit evaporated almost before it was established. It wasn't too long after his billeting that Reagan was free to go home at the end of the day, to see his wife and daughter and fraternize with his off-base friends, so long as he kept the rather pleasant terms of his wartime service beneath the radar of the gossip and society pages.[15]

While in the service the most visible work Reagan did was as a poster boy. Patriotic portraits of him in uniform, usually with an American flag waving in the clear blue sky behind, appeared regularly in government posters, in Warner Brothers marketing material, in magazines and newspapers. This image—of the handsome and virtuous soldier, proud to be in uniform, eager to take it to the enemy—served double duty. For the government it was a kind of ideogram, one of the key visual signifiers out of which America wove its tapestry of rhetorical war, meant to intimidate the enemy abroad and keep the citizenry unified and stalwart at home. For Warner Brothers it served to keep Reagan in the public eye, and in a role that might maintain or even enhance his commercial stock for when the war was over and he could go back to making money for the studio.

In the articles and captions that ran with these pictures it was never quite said that the handsome young lieutenant was on a particular front in Europe or Asia, battling a specific enemy, but it seemed he was somewhere far away, doing something of a martial nature. Periodically he would be dispatched to a Hollywood event or premiere, where he would show up in uniform, as if just back from the front, to pose with his dutiful, loving wife. Wyman always expressed proper gratitude at having her man back home for what few moments the U.S. government could spare him.[16]

In truth it didn't matter what the dry facts of his service were any more than it mattered whether his marriage to Jane Wyman was the storybook affair the press made it out to be (which by the end of the war it wasn't). For Reagan, as for the constituencies he served, it was the Narrative that mattered, and the Narrative was served by what he was doing in the military.

Many decades later, when he was president, Reagan would occasionally be observed mixing up what he *did* in the military with the roles he *played* while in the military. At other moments he would recount scenes from war movies he'd seen as though they were true war moments he'd witnessed or read about. Such confusion was evidence, mostly, of the rather fluid boundaries between fantasy and reality that were characteristic of Reagan's psyche from at least as far back as there is documentary evidence of Reagan's psyche. It was also the case, however, that his wartime service as an officer of the First Motion Picture Unit was precisely an exercise in blurring those boundaries. He acted the part of the furloughed combat soldier on the red carpet at film premieres in Hollywood. He was the voiceover of the briefing officer in training films shown to soldiers as part of their actual briefing before being sent off to fight. He spent hundreds of hours watching combat footage—including incredibly grisly scenes of soldiers dying in battle—in order to help excerpt the footage for newsreels, propaganda pieces, and training films that he might then narrate or star in.

When he was tasked by a general with putting together a morale-boosting blooper reel—consisting of outtakes from FMPU productions—he and his fellow soldiers, like characters in a war buddy comedy, decided to fake it rather than tell the general that they hadn't been saving any outtakes. They scripted and staged original outtake-like scenes.[17]

In 1943, he was temporarily detailed back to Warner Brothers to star in *This Is the Army*, an adaptation of an Irving Berlin musical that was so committed to blending truth and make-believe, and was such a pastiche of styles and cultural winks, that if it hadn't been done in utter patriotic earnestness it might later have been classified as an early instance of postmodernism in film.[18]

Perhaps most extreme, in its fusion of reality and fiction, was the period in 1944 that Reagan spent on a top-secret mission to help Allied pilots prepare for bombing runs of Tokyo. In order to do this, the set builders and special-effects technicians erected a scale model of Tokyo so big it covered an entire soundstage and so precisely detailed the crew could accurately depict the shadow cast by a ridge as the sun came over the horizon. They then simulated a pilot's approach to the city so believably that veterans of the war in the Pacific couldn't tell the difference between the footage of the model, shot from a crane inside the studio in Los Angeles, and footage from actual flights over Japan that alternated screen time with the simulations. Reagan was the voice of the virtual briefing officer, who would take the viewers through their run.

"Bombing crews in the Pacific," Reagan wrote, "would sit in a theater and view a motion picture apparently taken from a plane traveling at, say, thirty thousand feet. Beneath them would be the Pacific, in the distance the hazy coastline. My voice, as briefing officer, would be heard above the sound of the plane motors. I would usually open with lines such as, 'Gentlemen, you are approaching the coast of Honshu on a course of three hundred degrees. You are now twenty miles offshore. To your left, if you are on course, you should be able to see a narrow inlet. To your right—' Then I would mention some other visible landmark. In this way we would take the bombing crew right into the point where my voice said, 'Bombs away.'"[19]

Such fakery, of course, was what Reagan had been doing as an actor before the war. But in the FMPU there was a unique tension to the illusion-making. It was in service to a much grander cause than that of generating box office revenue. Reagan and his fellow soldiers were helping train soldiers. They were keeping spirits up at home. They were assisting with sensitive intelligence projects. Toward the end of the war Reagan was part of a team that processed and screened film footage shot at recently liberated concentration camps. The memories so horrified him that he actually cadged a reel when he left the service "to show doubters and skeptics in the future."[20]

Reagan was grateful, at the time and later, for the chance to wear the uniform of the army that helped end such atrocities. But he was also uneasy with the relative safety and frivolity of the circumstances in which he wore it. He was playing dress-up, and often having a helluva good time of it, while others were dying overseas. He got his uniform from the wardrobe department. If there was blood, it was fake blood. And when people died, they came quickly back to life after the director yelled "Cut!"

Later in his life this tension manifested as a notable inconsistency in how he remembered his wartime service. Depending on the context, he could be proud or defensive, basically truthful or utterly confabulatory, or sometimes so conflicted that one could almost hear the rival voices fighting for dominance in his head.

At the time he was actually living through such dissonance, the effects on Reagan were more subtle. On the surface he was his normal affable self, content with his military existence and also looking forward to returning to civilian life, with the hope of building on the success he'd had before the war. But beneath the surface, something was shifting in Reagan. He began to feel as though he needed to do more in the world, or for the world, than act. He began to search, stumblingly at first, for a cause that was epic enough to do justice to his desire to *be* rather than play the hero. And as a consequence of this search, and the political experiences that followed from it, Reagan began to struggle for really the first time with whether the liberal commitments he'd inherited from his father genuinely cohered with those elements of his character, and his worldview, that were the fundamental stuff of which authentic politics needed to be made.

Toward the end of 1943, when Reagan was looking around for some kind of political organization to join, he was targeted for recruitment by two groups. Sam Wood, who'd been director on one of his better films, approached him about joining the Motion Picture Alliance for the Preservation of American Ideals (MPA), a small group of powerful Hollywood conservatives who were organizing to counter what they saw as the dangerous influence of communism in the industry. At roughly the same time the writer-director Bernard Vorhaus, Reagan's closest buddy in the FMPU, began trying to sell him on the Hollywood Democratic Committee (HDC), another recently formed group that sought to bring left-wingers and liberals into coalition around the common goal of re-electing Franklin Roosevelt for a fourth term.

There may have been a few other Hollywood figures who were wooed by two groups as allergic to each other as the MPA and HDC, but there couldn't have been many. The founding manifesto of the MPA stated that its purpose was to counter "the growing impression that this industry is made of, and dominated by, Communists, radicals, and crackpots."[21] The HDC was not (yet) a Communist front, but it was an organization that was pretty hospitable to its sizable contingents of Communists, radicals, and crackpots. Vorhaus himself would later be blacklisted for alleged Communist ties.[22]

That Reagan ultimately joined the HDC and not the MPA was evidence that he was a liberal, perhaps even with some vaguely left-wing impulses. That he was nonetheless considered by Sam Wood a possible recruit to the MPA, and that he contemplated joining, were evidence of the visible seams in his liberal identity. He struck not just Wood but many who'd known him over the years as someone who had a well of latent conservatism in him (as early as 1941 conservative friends of Reagan had tried to persuade him to run for Congress as a Republican). And his liberal convictions, though fiercely articulated, had an evident shallowness to them. They'd never been tested by the kinds of concrete political struggles that might bring his superstructure of political beliefs into conflict with his base of core characterological drives. He'd never fought it out with Communists for control of an organization, as many leftists and liberals had been doing throughout the 1930s. He'd joined the Screen Actors Guild in a period of relative labor comity and had never had to make hard decisions, as either a member or leader of the union, about whether to strike, whether to honor the strike of another union, or how and when to deploy or deplore more militant tactics. He'd never had to do much, in truth, other than vote for Franklin Roosevelt and take the liberal side in arguments with his conservative friends.

That detachment began to erode during the war. He became an active recruiter for the Hollywood Democratic Committee. Even more significantly, he began to feel at a gut level that his politics, in a time of such catastrophe, had to grow into something more than rhetorical.

When Reagan was discharged in the summer of 1945, he stepped into something of a void. He was once again earning the salary of a star. The multiyear, million-dollar contract that Lew Wasserman had negotiated for him before the war had resumed paying out the day he took off his uniform. But when the actual roles opened up for casting in the studio offices, the executives didn't find themselves turning to Reagan to fill them. The game had moved on without him. Some of the unique talents whose careers had been interrupted by the war would prove able to resume where they left off. Reagan was too fungible a commodity. When the lead roles came up it was more natural to cast the stars who'd been making bank for the studios while Reagan was making propaganda for the government. It would be a good six months before he was cast in a film, and though he'd make movies steadily for another seven years, he'd never regain the heat he'd had before the war.

His marriage, too, had cooled. It had in truth never been a pairing destined for ease. There was too much ambition and self-absorption on both sides of the dyad. Though the war hadn't literally put an ocean between husband and wife, it had changed the dynamic between them sufficiently for the exceptionally talented, and romantically rather fickle, Wyman to drift away. She began to do what she likely would have done sooner or later anyway, which was to seek out greater things and newer men. When the war had begun she was typed as a competent, second-tier actress, good for disposable roles in fluffy romantic comedies. The differential between her status and Reagan's in the Hollywood hierarchy had been mirrored by their roles in the marriage. By the time Reagan got out of uniform, she had already surpassed him as an actor and was on the verge of surpassing him as a star. First thing upon being mustered out he drove to see her at the place she'd rented at Lake Arrowhead, in the San Bernardino Mountains, where she was shooting her new film *The Yearling*. His intention was to use the next few months, while his agent looked for some good parts for him, to reconnect with Wyman and with the kids (they'd adopted a baby boy, Michael, in March). But she was so immersed in her role, which would eventually earn her an Oscar nomination for Best Actress, and so uninterested in spending time with him, that he ended up feeling more distant from her than he had when the army was keeping him away.

In the absence of anything else to do, he spent most of the remaining months of 1945 working on two projects: He built model boats, and he set out to save the world. The boats were a one-time thing. He assembled a tiny shipping freighter and a tiny ocean liner, set them in a nice spot in his house, and moved on. The world-saving, however, was just the start.[23]

Reagan had become active in politics toward the end of the war, but it had been a fairly low-impact commitment, and one that didn't involve him in any real fights. After he got out, Reagan joined the United World Federalists. He upped his commitment to the Hollywood Democratic Committee, which after Roosevelt's re-election had reconfigured itself as the Hollywood Independent Citizens Committee of Arts, Sciences and Professions (HICCASP). He joined the board of the Hollywood chapter of the American Veterans Committee (AVC), one of the few politically active veterans groups that drew left-wing rather than right-wing conclusions from the brute data of the war.

For the last few months of 1945, and the first few months of 1946, Reagan believed, with these organizations, that there were two main tasks for postwar America. One was to forge a lasting peace with the other nations of the world. That meant, for instance, supporting the establishment of the United Nations, and abolishing or instituting international control over nuclear weapons.

Reagan's other mission in that immediate postwar moment was to continue striving toward the vision of America that Roosevelt, who had died in April of 1945, had sung. Expand on the economic foundations of the New Deal. Distribute more equally the wealth that was sure to come now that the nation's decade-and-a-half-long state of emergency was finally over. Invest the state with the power to meet the needs of its people and balance the interests of management and labor.

What really stirred Reagan's blood, however, was less any specific program or legislation than it was the bedrock of fellowfeeling he saw as the necessary foundation to all of it. Beneath the programs of the New Deal lay what Reagan saw as the deeper ethos of Rooseveltism, which was a patriotism based on the idea that to be an American was to recognize, in people of all classes, races, religions, and ethnicities, fellow citizens of the United States and fellow participants in the project of building a better future. Later in his life Reagan would prove fairly thickheaded, and often quite cowardly, on matters of race, and there were seeds of those tendencies in his earlier self. But he'd been raised by his parents to believe in racial and religious equality, and his feelings on the subject had been inflamed by the war. America's triumph over the "venom of Fascist bigotry," as he called it, had been won by the shared sacrifice of all creeds and colors of Americans.[24] That the end of the war was met by, among other things, an upsurge in racism and anti-Semitism infuriated him to the point of righteousness.

In December of 1945, he volunteered to speak at a rally organized to protest some recent attacks on returning Japanese-American veterans. Reagan had been willing, a few times in the past, to lend his name to a cause or a candidate. In the run-up to Roosevelt's final campaign, for instance, he had been one of a chorus of big-name stars who'd contributed to a radio broadcast endorsing the president. He'd been willing to make personal calls to other actors to recruit them to his organizations. But this was one of the first times Reagan had stepped out in public as an individuated political figure, one willing to speak in something like his own voice, articulating values that were deeply personal to him. He began by thanking the parents of Kazuo Masuda, a staff sergeant whose heroic death in the war, while leading a patrol against a German-held position, was the focal symbol of the event. Then he gave his short, heartfelt speech:

"The blood that has soaked into the sands of the beaches is all one color. America stands unique in the world—a country not founded on race, but on a way and an ideal. Not in spite of, but because of our polyglot background, we have had all the strength in the world. That is the American way."[25]

In this first blush of political activism, Reagan spoke out not just against anti-Japanese prejudice, but for the equal treatment of blacks and Jews as well, and he did so in a fairly courageous fashion. He named by name those groups, including veterans groups, from whom he thought he caught the stench of fascism.

For a brief moment, Reagan seemed poised to evolve into a deeper version of his younger liberal self. Still a bit too in love with the sound of his own voice saying noble things, perhaps, and still enough of a careerist to back off when taking a stand might endanger his standing with the studio,[26] but also able to be genuinely courageous on occasion, and committed enough to a better world to involve himself in concrete struggles that had the potential, as all such struggles do, to change his life in unforeseen ways. And for a few more years, on some issues, that was how Reagan was. Well into the 1950s, he persisted as an advocate of racial equality, using his position as president of the Screen Actors Guild to lend (rhetorical, but still meaningful) support to the calls from black actors for more and better roles for blacks in the movies. And his hopes for world peace, though they'd soon be transmuted by the crucible of the Cold War, would never go away, and would retain some of their liberal cast to the end.

But the purity of Reagan's commitment to these causes, and with it the unity of his liberal identity, began to erode almost as soon as he was forced by events to confront the complexity of being on the liberal Left after the war ended and the Cold War began.

It was after one of his anti-neofascism speeches, delivered to the men's club at the Disciples of Christ church where he was a congregant, that Reagan would get the first intimation of the conflict that would, more than any other, separate him from his liberalism.

He'd just finished his speech when the minister came up to him and said that, though he agreed about the dangers of neofascism, he thought Reagan should mention that he'd oppose communism, too, if it seemed that it represented a threat to America.

At that point Reagan's orientation toward communism was basically emotional. He was politically sophisticated enough to know that communism in its starker forms was incompatible with the blended system of free enterprise and benevolent government management that he favored. This incompatibility, however, mattered less to him than his friendship with various party members and sympathizers. None of them seemed to him, in their souls, any different from the rest of his friends. And the undemocratic aspects of the Soviet Union mattered less to him than the credit the empire had earned by sending its soldiers to fight and die along with American soldiers to keep the world free from fascism.

He'd heard the whispers that the Soviets were no longer our friends in the world, that, indeed, they were trying to infiltrate America with their agents, but in the immediate aftermath of the war he wasn't inclined to worry about it. He had more important battles to fight. His gut told him that most American Communists were decent people, "liberals who were temporarily off track."[27] He also didn't trust the motives of the people who were most energetically banging the drum about the dangers of communism. It seemed to Reagan, and he wasn't alone in this suspicion, that it was the New Deal, and the electoral coalition that Roosevelt had assembled around it, that was the real target of the anticommunist campaigns beginning to pick up steam around the country. The aim of anticommunist conservatives, he suspected, was to use accusations of Communist influence to delegitimize the whole root and branch of the liberal establishment.

When confronted by his minister about the dangers of communism, though, some instinct in Reagan responded. Perhaps he wanted to put an end to the rumors he'd overheard that he was looking a bit Red himself. Perhaps it was the moral authority of his minister, who'd been an influence on his thinking in other political realms, and who was reinforcing what Reagan was getting from his brother Neil, who'd been an early and ardent convert to anticommunism and who was getting tip-offs from the FBI that some of the groups Reagan was joining were infiltrated by Communists.

Almost certainly Reagan wasn't satisfied with the causes he'd picked. It felt wholesome to thunder against neofascism, and to stand up for world peace, but there was an epic quality absent from these fights. Worthy nemeses and opportunities for heroism kept failing to materialize. The really scary fascists, after all, were all dead. Reagan may have sensed that he was going to have to bait some more hooks if he hoped to land the great cause for which he was searching. In any case, the next time he gave his antifascism speech, he kept its focus the same, but at the end he tacked on a few lines about communism.

"I've talked about the continuing threat of fascism in the postwar world," he said, "but there's another '-ism,' Communism, and if I ever find evidence that Communism represents a threat to all that we believe in and stand for, I'll speak out just as harshly against Communism as I have fascism."[28]

Not long after, in a column he wrote for the *Bulletin* of the American Veterans Committee, he went a bit further. The prime threat remained domestic fascism, and the skill the hatemongers had shown in exploiting the public's uncertainty and anxiety. But the Left had to answer for its extremists, too.

"They, too, want to force something unwanted on the American people, and the fact that many of them go along with those of us who are liberal means nothing because they are only hitching a ride as far as we go, hoping they can use us as a vehicle for their own program."[29]

Soon Reagan would encounter this manipulative dynamic on his own turf. At the state convention of the American Veterans Committee, held in April of 1946 in Los Angeles, the Communists in the organization began to play their hand, deploying the kinds of factional tactics that the party had been evolving since its earliest years in Russia. They exploited the rules of order, using quorums and calls to order as weapons. They took over small committees in order to establish organizational beachheads. They kept the discussions going so long, and key votes delayed so interminably, that they were able to have their way simply by waiting until everyone else had given up and gone to bed. Most potently, they were organized, strategic, and unified in their actions where most of the rest of the membership showed up to the convention as individuals. As a result they exerted influence vastly out of proportion to their numbers, and within months had taken control of the Los Angeles chapter of the AVC.

None of this was new to Left and liberal activists who'd been in the thick of things during the Depression, when it was a given that the Communists were ruthless. It was the cost of doing business on the Left, and you had to play rough yourself if you intended to hold them off. Indeed by the national convention in June the more seasoned liberals in the AVC's leadership had gathered their forces sufficiently to fight off the Communists, permanently banning them from membership in the organization. But the Communist tactics were a shock to Reagan, who knew little to nothing about the kinds of intra-Left fights that during the 1930s had played out at every level, from brawls between rival unions on the docks to bureaucratic knife fights in the various houses of the Roosevelt administration. Disorienting, too, was his realization that the Communists meant what they said about abolishing private property and establishing the dictatorship of the proletariat. They weren't just overzealous liberals, who obsessed a bit too much about the failings of their country. They wanted to tear the whole thing down.

"They even succeeded in having the words 'Private Enterprise' struck from the paragraph reaffirming our support of the Statement of Principles!" Reagan wrote to one of the leaders of the national organization, reporting on the state convention.[30]

Over the next few months, Reagan would run into the Communists again and again, both in the AVC and in HICCASP. By July, when he attended his first meeting as part of the executive council of HICCASP, the issue of Communist influence had reached a sufficient pitch that many liberal groups had begun actively, publicly, repudiating any association with communism. At the HICCASP meeting it was James Roosevelt himself, the oldest son of FDR and one of the charter members of the group, who raised the issue, asking the leadership to issue a declaration of principles that affirmed the American system of free enterprise and democracy and repudiated communism.

"It sounded good to me, sort of like that last paragraph I had inserted in my speech," wrote Reagan. "I was amazed at the reaction. A well-known musician sprang to his feet. He offered to recite the USSR constitution from memory, yelling that it was a lot more democratic than that of the United States. A prominent movie writer leaped upward. He said that if there was ever a war between the United States and Russia, he would volunteer for Russia."[31]

Reagan would learn by the end of the night that Roosevelt and his fellow liberals, including actress Olivia de Havilland and MGM studio head Dore Schary, had been hoping to provoke a reaction in order to "smoke out" the Communists. But while Roosevelt was up in front of the group, taking fire from the radical members, apparently alone in his willingness to state a preference for the United States over the Soviet Union, Reagan felt that he had to intervene.

"Here was a HICCASP that I had admired and honored," recalled Reagan. "Suddenly it was broken up into a Kilkenny brawl by a simple statement which I thought any American would be proud to subscribe to. . . . I decided that an Irishman couldn't stay out. I thought besides that Jimmy [Roosevelt] needed someone to stand up for him. I took the floor and endorsed what he said. Well, sir, I found myself waist-high in epithets such as 'Fascist' and 'capitalist scum' and 'enemy of the proletariat' and 'witch-hunter' and 'Red-baiter' before I could say boo."[32]

It was a seminal encounter for Reagan, and one that would in many respects become the template for his encounters, over the remainder of his life, with the ideas and movements of the Left. It was dramatic. It was about rhetoric, about the words that would represent the values for which he believed America stood. It turned on a stark moral principle— indeed, for Reagan, the starkest of moral-political principles. Were you for or against America? And because his opponents were (or had been manipulated to appear as) the aggressors, the dynamic afforded Reagan the chance to heroically stand down the bad guys without feeling as if he was being a jerk.

After the meeting, Reagan would be invited over to de Havilland's apartment, where the liberal conspirators had gathered to congratulate themselves on the success of their ploy, and he would participate for a little while longer in the doings of HICCASP. But his taste, it soon became apparent, wasn't for this kind of behind-the-scenes organizational work. Nor for organizations like the AVC and HICCASP that had to be willing, at a minimum, to reach some kind of workable détente with radically minded members.

By the end of the summer of 1946, Reagan had left the AVC, despite its expulsion of its Communist contingent. He stayed on a bit longer with HICCASP, which came increasingly under Communist control, but only in order to report on its doings to the FBI, which had approached him after hearing from various sources (his brother likely among them) that he might be willing to help. By October he had resigned from that organization as well.

What exhilarated Reagan, he was discovering, wasn't the backroom stuff. It was the moment when he could stand up for his values, for America, for his industry, for his friends, in the face of angry crowds, insults, rumor campaigns, even physical threats.

In September of 1946, as Reagan was winding down his involvement with the AVC and HICCASP, he fell into what seemed at first a very different kind of conflict, this one between two rival Hollywood unions marking up each other's territory. His involvement in the labor conflict would constitute his first truly substantive political experience, and it would be a formative one. By the time it was over he had in many respects matured into the political actor he would remain.

It had begun the year before, in the final months of World War II, when the members of the Society of Motion Picture Interior Decorators went on strike against the studios. They were joined on the picket lines by thousands of their fellow members in the Conference of Studio Unions (CSU), one of the two coalitions of craft unions in town. At issue was a simple question of recognition and legitimacy: Were these workers entitled to detach themselves from the International Alliance of Theatrical Stage Employees (IATSE, or IA), which was the older and larger of the coalitions, and affiliate instead with the CSU? An independent arbitrator had declared that they were indeed entitled to join the CSU, but the studios—which preferred dealing with the IA—had refused to recognize their new affiliation or to bargain on those terms.

At issue, too, were broader matters of labor temperament, strategy, and history. The CSU was a militant group, confrontational in its tactics, relatively democratic in its organization, and mathematical in its conviction that labor would get the pay, power, working conditions, and respect it deserved only by wresting it, through strikes and other forms of open conflict, from capital. Its militancy had to that point reaped considerable benefits. Its numbers were growing. It was winning better wages and conditions for its members than what the IA seemed interested in extracting from the studios. And it had the gestalt of a cause, nurturing within its members a sense of solidarity and empowerment that felt redemptive and even, for some, revolutionary. For many of the same reasons it also brought a dangerous edge to its campaigns, creating enemies as it went, provoking potential allies, and courting not just defeats but extinction.

The IA was cut from a different mold, one that bore the imprint both of the union's very recent entanglement with the Chicago mafia and of its pre-mafia roots as an old-style trade union. Power in the union was concentrated at the top. That leadership saw its interests as aligned, broadly, with those of the studios, and felt that as long as money was coming in and was distributed adequately there was no reason to fight. In the event that a fight seemed imminent, it preferred to get its way not by striking or seeking common cause with allies on the Left but by quiet intimidation, backed by the occasional demonstration of force. It was a fairly mercenary arrangement, a unionism without much sense of common purpose or idealism, but it was stable, had its payoffs, and lent to the union a different, more ominous aura of power than what emanated from the CSU.

Then, too, there were the rumors of secret affiliations and loyalties. It was alleged that Herb Sorrell, the CSU's charismatic leader, was an agent of the Communist Party, part of a grand conspiracy to infiltrate

Hollywood and use its films to subtly propagandize the masses. The IA, for its part, had been purged of its visible mob ties in a series of investigations and prosecutions before the war, culminating in the 1941 imprisonment on racketeering charges of its two chief leaders. Many in town suspected, however, that the mob remained the unseen power behind the union.

It was, in other words, incredibly complex. In play were towering egos, geopolitical machinations, hidden alliances, mountains of money, long-standing philosophical divisions within the labor movement, the broader struggle between labor and management, and, for those like Reagan and the actors he would soon come to represent, excruciating moral dilemmas about how far to sacrifice one's own economic interests in the interests of solidarity. If the actors were to side with the striking CSU workers, it might mean not just a temporary loss of wages but a fundamental shift toward militancy in the orientation of Hollywood workers toward management.[33]

The first strike, which was over before Reagan got involved, lasted weeks and became the bloodiest labor conflict the entertainment industry had ever seen. It ended with a modest victory for the CSU. The studios agreed to acknowledge the CSU as the representatives of the set decorators, and negotiations on a contract began. In the hopes of preventing future such conflicts the American Federation of Labor, to which both unions belonged, appointed a committee to once and for all divide the on-set responsibilities between CSU and IA workers, and for a little while there was peace.

It was an unstable peace, though. The studios continued to stall on signing a contract. Sorrell continued to look for more locals he could detach from the IA. The IA began to look for ways to end the CSU threat permanently.

In early September 1946, in studios throughout Hollywood, members of CSU-affiliated carpenters' and painters' unions were ordered to do some finishing work on sets that had been built, in defiance of the

AFL-brokered agreement, by IA workers. The carpenters and painters refused to do the finishing work, and they were given an ultimatum: Do the work as ordered or you'll be locked out.

From the outside, where Reagan was at that moment, it seemed a rather legalistic dispute, over which group of skilled craftsmen was responsible for constructing sets. And the CSU refusal to finish sets—which were needed, after all, to make the movies—seemed rather childish. From the inside, however, things were different. The AFL's brokers had decreed that the construction work went to the CSU-affiliated carpenters. All the involved parties knew that. So when the studios had the sets built by the IA workers, and then gave those orders to the carpenters and painters to finish them off, they were deliberately insulting the workers to see if they would take it, or if they would push back.

They hoped for the latter. Because in addition to it being an insult, it was the first move in a meticulously planned conspiracy. The studios and the IA leadership had been holding a series of secret meetings in which they plotted out how to use the ambiguity of that single job designation to provoke a confrontation and then progressively amplify it by replacing striking or locked-out CSU workers with IA workers. The material goal was to destroy the CSU. The political goal, for many of those involved, was to root out what they saw as a major beachhead of communism in Hollywood.

The plans included sample scripts for what managers were to say to CSU workers in order to maintain the pretense that the studios were acting in good faith. There were discussions of how to navigate the actors past the picket lines in a fashion that was least likely to inflame their sympathies for the locked-out workers. Security was coordinated in advance with local police departments, and arrangements were made with the leaders of the local Teamsters union to have heavies on hand to physically break through the picket lines. Essential to the conspiracy were members of the leadership of the Screen Actors Guild, who would work to ensure that the actors crossed the picket lines.[34]

Reagan, by this point, was in the thick of things, but not as a wit-ting member of the conspiracy. He'd become active in the Screen Actors Guild not long after the dust cleared from the first strike, and he was up for election as third vice president when the troubles began again. This time around he made a point of getting involved, joining the emer-gency committee responsible for recommending to SAG's membership how they should respond to the conflict.

First thing after his appointment to the committee, Reagan orga-nized a meeting between the producers and the rival union leaders. His charge was to head off a strike, and if that proved impossible, to get enough of a sense of the right and wrong of it to advise the SAG board on whether the actors should honor the CSU picket lines that were set to go up.

"The actors were in a key position," Reagan later wrote. "If we re-fused to cross the CSU picket lines, the industry would be shut down. If we crossed the lines, it could stay open and make movies."[35]

According to his own later accounts, Reagan went into that meet-ing as a neutral party, hopeful that he could succeed in brokering peace, inclined to believe that every side was acting with good intentions. It's likely that this is true, as far as it goes. What it doesn't capture, how-ever, is how stacked the deck was in almost every respect other than Reagan's personal conviction that he intended to be fair. Reagan didn't know that his superiors in SAG were conspiring to break the CSU, but he knew what outcome they wanted. He knew what most of the actors wanted, which was to keep working. He hadn't yet come to the conclusion that the CSU was Communist-controlled, but he had a lot of friends who were telling him that Sorrell was compromised, and he was primed by his own recent brushes with Communists to take such warnings seriously. And in his bones Reagan was just more in sync with the IA and the producers. He wasn't militant. He didn't see conflict as inevitable or desirable when contemplating labor and management any more than he did when he was making the case for international control of nuclear power. And he didn't feel like a laborer, in the way carpenters and painters were laborers, nor did he see the producers as natural enemies, bent on exploiting labor. The producers were his friends and benefactors. They were the people who'd raised him to stardom.

It was fairly predictable which way Reagan would go. What was less predictable was how far he would go. Had Reagan been a different kind of person, more cynical, less in need of an undiluted right and wrong, more *political*, there would have been no problem. He would have found a formulation that gave the actors enough cover to cross the picket lines without explicitly lining up against the CSU. But precisely because he wasn't that person, he was faced with a problem. His gut told him where he wanted to be. The people whose affirmation and respect he sought were pushing him in the same direction. But he'd told himself that his task was to be fair, and the facts of the matter remained profoundly unclear.

So Reagan, faced with a degree of political complexity he wasn't willing to disentangle and a degree of emotional contradiction he wasn't constitutionally capable of maintaining, did what people often do in such situations. He made it all line up. He sanded, shaved, and refitted the elements so that what he wanted to be the case converged with what, in his mind, ought to be the case.

Reagan emerged from the meeting with an intense dislike of Sorrell, who had come on very strong, and had probably been very open in his contempt for Reagan's naiveté about the underlying politics of the conflict. Reagan was also persuaded of the justice of the IA case, and of the perfidy of the CSU, to a degree far beyond what was necessary to recommend neutrality. He believed in these things, indeed, beyond anything that was believed by the IA leaders and the producers themselves, who after all were well aware of how they'd manipulated events.

"When we held the meeting it was obvious that the CSU strike was a phony," wrote Reagan. "It wasn't meant to improve the wages and working conditions of its members, but to grab something from another union that was rightfully theirs."[36]

Later that month Reagan was elected third vice president of the Screen Actors Guild. More significantly, he became the guild's most public advocate for "neutrality," which in practice meant taking the side of the producers and the IA.

On September 19, just a few days before the picket lines were set to go up, the SAG board sent a letter to its membership advising them to cross the picket lines and "live up to their contracts."

The actors listened, and when the strike/lockout began the following week, with violent clashes at the gates to Warner Brothers' studios, the show went on. IA workers replaced CSU workers. Actors (including Reagan) made it through the picket lines, often protected by the fire hoses of local police and the burly arms of Teamster escorts. Movies kept being made.

There was enough protest from solidarity-minded SAG members, however, that a general meeting was called to hold a formal vote on the matter. Reagan was designated to represent the board at the meeting and to make the case for continued neutrality. His growing role in the process, and his potential for influencing others, didn't go unnoticed by the CSU and its allies.

A few days before the big meeting, he got a phone call. On the other end was a voice warning him to step back, or else.

"The caller wouldn't identify himself," wrote Reagan, "but said that if I made the speech, a squad of people would be waiting for me."

" 'Your face will never be in pictures again,' the voice said."[37]

Reagan was worried enough to begin carrying a pistol, which he would keep with him until the conflict ended the following spring. But he wasn't deterred. Quite the opposite. The threat of violence, for merely speaking his mind, further confirmed for him that he'd picked the right side of the issue, and made him more intent than ever on making sure that his side won.

At the mass meeting of the SAG membership, Reagan was magnificent. He took the conflicting data, the competing philosophies, the contractual minutiae, and the rival claims on the actors' loyalty and distilled it all into a narrative that told the actors what most of them wanted to hear, which was that they could cross the picket lines in good conscience. He was persuasive, and the membership voted overwhelmingly to continue in their stance of neutrality, and to keep working.

It was a dynamic that would be repeated as the conflict wore on. Reagan would be presented with a set of circumstances that he was unable to absorb in its full complexity. He would, in what felt to him like good faith, discern the simple truth beneath the surface complexity and arrive at the morally pure course of action to take in response to it. And he would be accused, in some sense unfairly, of acting out of impure motives, of knowingly cooking the books. And with each (unfair and hurtful) attack it would become more obvious to him that the CSU and its allies must be the bad guys. With each slur (fascist, company man, Red-baiter) that was hurled at him it became easier, too, to ignore the rhetorical and physical violence that was being done by his own side. The lost jobs, the destroyed careers, the actual beatings—of Sorrell, for instance, who was at one point kidnapped, beaten severely, and left by the side of the road—Reagan either didn't see or was able to rationalize as the necessary response to the ugliness coming from the other side.

Helpful, too, in clearing Reagan's mind of doubt was the fact that many of the most vicious attacks on his reputation, as well as some brutally violent attacks on others, came from people who he knew or suspected were Communists. It wasn't clear (and remains to this day unclear) whether the Communists lined up behind Sorrell and the CSU because Sorrell was one of them, or because they did the math and felt that the CSU was a more likely vehicle for their future interests than the IA, but they were very clearly on the CSU side, and Sorrell was very clearly willing to accept their help. For Reagan that was sufficient. He saw his enemies lining up against him, and it was exhilarating. At last he'd found his great cause.

Reagan began seeking out opportunities to advocate for his side. He got a call one day, for instance, from the actor Bill Holden, a good friend he'd gotten to know primarily through their mutual involvement in the guild. Holden had gotten word of a meeting that suspected Communists had organized to try to influence some well-known actors to side with the CSU. Holden thought it was a "brainwash job," and asked Reagan if he wanted to come with him to crash the meeting.

Reagan agreed. He and Holden drove over to the gathering, which was presided over by the actor Sterling Hayden. They listened for a while as Hayden and his comrades presented their version of the events, which heavily favored the CSU and demonized the IA and the producers.

"I writhed in my seat," remembered Reagan, "but Bill held me back, like a jockey going into the stretch. At last, as the denunciations—in pretty familiar language by this time—had run down, Bill patted me. He said, 'Now!'"[38]

Reagan got up in front of the assembled actors and held forth for forty minutes, handling questions and attacks with great facility, turning what had been intended to be a rout for the pro-CSU forces into, at a minimum, a draw. He was putting to political use the improvisational skills he'd honed much earlier in his entertainment career, when he'd worked as a baseball play-by-play man for an Iowa radio station and his task had been to take the raw game data coming over the wire into the broadcast studio and narrativize it, embellish it, dramatize it, in close to real time, so that it evoked in his listeners a sense of actually being at the game.

In this case, as in the earlier one and many future ones, Reagan was very good at taking errant data and smoothing it into, or deflecting it around, the flow of the story. He had, too, a way of conveying an emotional truth about what was going on that mattered more to most of his listeners than isolated questions about what was, factually, going on.

In the first few months of his involvement in the conflict, the truth he conveyed was a fairly local one. The CSU was in the wrong, and if the actors sided with them, they were going to suffer. By the end of 1946, Reagan had begun fusing that truth with another, more global one. There was a fight brewing, in Hollywood and throughout the nation, about the influence of communism on and in our cultural and political institutions, and it was one that would force people to choose sides.

Reagan began making it clear that to side with the CSU meant more than standing up for what the CSU explicitly said it stood for—democracy within the labor movement, better wages and benefits for workers, respect from management, a refusal to accept the cozy business unionism of the IA. It meant picking the wrong side in the emerging civilizational struggle between communism and the forces of freedom and democracy.

By March of 1947, when Reagan was elected to the presidency of the Screen Actors Guild, it was clear to him that his task was to represent the interests of the actors in substantial part by working to purge Hollywood of the taint of communism. And when the CSU strike died out not long after, in no small part due to his efforts, it was in his eyes a victory not just for common sense, or for the cause of moviemaking (which Reagan had always held as sacred), but for democracy as well.

Reagan's political efflorescence coincided with, and ended up being reinforced by, a withering in the other major realms of his life. His career wasn't recovering from its wartime interruption. He was getting some leading roles, but they weren't in good movies, and the buzz about him he'd enjoyed before the war had evaporated. He was still a star, but not a rising one, possibly a fading one.

The nadir of this phase of his career came with the 1947 film *That Hagen Girl.* It was an adaptation of a lurid novel about an outcast teenager in a gossipy small town and her relationship with a returning veteran who was either her illegitimate father or her potential lover. In the part of the girl, in what was intended to be her breakout role as a romantic lead, was former child star Shirley Temple. Reagan was cast as the much older father-or-lover. He'd tried to turn down the part, which sounded like a bad idea to him on every level, but he was pressured into taking it by Jack Warner, whose suasion he was rarely able to resist.

The movie itself was quite mortifying. At a test screening the audience was so disturbed by a romantic moment between Reagan and Temple that the studio went back and recut the whole ending of the movie. Even more mortifying was the recognition, for Reagan, of how much he'd aged, in Hollywood years, since before the war. As a twenty-nine-year-old in 1940 he'd been persuasive as a college football player. Seven years later he was grossing out audiences when paired with the nineteen-year-old Temple. He couldn't get by anymore as the boyish charmer, and the less success he found in the roles he was playing, the less inclined the studio would be to support him as he sought out parts that better harmonized with his more mature affect.

Compounding the troubles in his film career were the troubles in his marriage, which had from the outset rested on the rather fragile foundation of Reagan and Wyman's shared love of the image of themselves in love. At some point, likely during the war, their narcissisms began to repel instead of attract each other.

After the war, nearly every element of their lives pushed them further apart. Wyman's acting, which Reagan had little interest in, consumed her. She fought hard for the parts she wanted, and when she got them she immersed herself completely in her roles, a devotion that led to recognition as well as a steady stream of roles that took her away, both geographically and emotionally, from her husband.

Reagan's career, which Wyman had once found attractive, stalled. His new passion for politics bored Wyman enormously. By the spring and summer of 1947 there had already been items in the gossip columns suggesting the couple was having troubles. The final breaking point, however, likely came in June of that year. While filming *That Hagen Girl*, Reagan got a nasty form of viral pneumonia, and for days he teetered close to death. While he was sick, Wyman, who was six months pregnant, went into premature labor, possibly after contracting the same virus, or in response to the stress of Reagan's illness. She delivered, and the baby girl died nine hours later.

It was a brutal succession of shocks that would have put a strain even on the best of marriages. For Reagan and Wyman it was unprocessable. Reagan, who lost seventeen pounds during his sickness, went back to work within days of his release from the hospital and the loss of the baby. He gave what little remainder of time he had to SAG, which was in the process both of renegotiating the actors' contract with the studios and of determining how to respond to the news that the House Un-American Activities Committee (HUAC) was scheduling hearings on the infiltration of Hollywood by Communists.

Wyman was back to work the following month, preparing for her role as a deaf-mute in *Johnny Belinda*. She studied sign language, hired a local deaf woman to come to the Reagan home a few days a week to practice with her, and spent evenings studying film of the woman in order to try to master how her deafness inflected her body language. Wyman ultimately became so obsessed with the role that she spent much of her time silent, with wax in her ears, to better understand what it would feel like to be deaf and mute.

After shooting began in September, Wyman fell in love with her costar Lew Ayres, who played the sympathetic doctor who taught her character sign language.

The closeness between Wyman and Ayres, which may or may not have been consummated on set, further alienated her from her husband, and within two months of the completion of the shoot, Reagan moved out. There were a few attempts at reconciliation, but they failed. In June of 1948 Wyman and Reagan were divorced.

The last few years of the 1940s were the darkest of Reagan's life. He lost a child and a marriage, and saw his career suffer a series of blows from which it would never recover. Into that abyss he poured politics.

Most formatively, he became further involved in the anticommunist movement, which had gradually begun to revive itself after the war, once the Soviet Union was no longer fighting with the United States against the Axis powers.

In Hollywood the CSU strike was over, and with it specific worries that the Communists would take over the craft unions. But until there could be a reckoning with the moviemakers themselves—the actors, directors, and screenwriters—the greater fear of the anticommunists in Hollywood and Washington remained unassuaged: Were radicals using the movies themselves to subtly propagate their ideology?

The Motion Picture Alliance for the Preservation of American Ideals (MPA), which had tried to recruit Reagan during the war, continued to warn about the dangers of Communist infiltration of the industry, and more or less invited HUAC to investigate, which it did in the fall of 1947, holding hearings in Washington and calling a host of actors, directors, and screenwriters to testify.

When it came time for Reagan to testify, in October of 1947, he played a subtle game. He was clear in his denunciation of the party, its ideology, and its tactics. But he named no names, and when asked by one of the committee members whether he thought party membership should be criminalized, he drew a distinction between criminalizing the expression of communistic ideology and criminalizing the activities of the Communist Party.

"As a citizen," he said, "I would hesitate to see any political party outlawed on the basis of its political ideology. We have spent a hundred and seventy years in this country on the basis that democracy is strong enough to stand up and fight against the inroads of any ideology. However, if it is proven that an organization is an agent of a foreign power, or in any way not a legitimate political party—and I think the Government is capable of proving that—then that is another matter."[39]

It was a testament to Reagan's performance that the first half of that formulation, the defense of free expression and association, was what left the most striking impression on many watching. As an indicator of where Reagan himself stood, however, the second half was more salient. He already believed that the party was, in fact, an adjunct of the Soviet Union. And since the spring he'd been talking to the FBI, apprising the Bureau of those actors he believed were Communists or Communist-sympathizers.

He'd carefully coordinated his testimony in advance with the members of HUAC. And his goal in the hearings was to maintain his own credibility within Hollywood, as a man with the actors' interests in mind, while saying to the government, quietly, that he was someone with whom they could work to solve the communism problem.[40]

There was a degree of deception in Reagan's performance. He wasn't honest about his cooperation with the government, and he benefited from the perception that he was more of a civil libertarian than in fact he was. But give or take a few degrees, Reagan was sincere. He didn't believe it was in the best interests of anyone for the government to take upon itself the task of rooting out every single Communist in Hollywood. Not because the government wasn't entitled to do so, but because it wasn't yet necessary. It would be taking up the sledgehammer when a fine chisel was sufficient.

What should happen, he believed, was that the government should set the broad policy and legislate once and for all that the Communist Party was a "foreign inspired conspiracy."[41] Then the task of purging Communists in Hollywood could be delegated to the unions, the studios, the agencies, and the various other private associations and institutions that existed or might come into existence. These groups would be more discreet, less likely to identify false positives, less likely to cause friction in the great engine of movie production, and fully capable of bringing the government into the process if, but only if, it proved necessary.

When ten of the unfriendly witnesses from the hearings were cited by the House of Representatives for contempt for refusing to answer questions about communist beliefs or associations, Reagan supported the vote. But he thought the more significant action was what followed shortly after. The studios announced they would fire the "Hollywood Ten" (as they became known), and would "not re-employ any of the 10 until such time as he is acquitted or has purged himself of contempt and declares under oath that he is not a Communist."[42]

It was an early salvo in the barrage of domestic anticommunist actions that would come to be known as McCarthyism, and though it didn't yet have the full aroma of thuggishness that McCarthy would lend to it, Reagan was sensitive enough to the smell of what was happening that he carefully navigated his way around the charge that he "named names" or was complicit in a "purge" or "the blacklist."

He wasn't ambivalent about the mission, though, and was willing to put himself out there in service to it. He stayed in touch with the FBI, and connected with the newly established Central Intelligence Agency. He actively sought to purge the Screen Actors Guild of Communists. He was a prime mover in positioning the guild as a supporter of the studios' right to fire or refuse to hire anyone who wouldn't publicly dissociate him- or herself from communism.

In 1948 he joined with the president of the MPA to found the Labor League of Hollywood Voters, a group that sought to promote Democratic candidates who were both pro-labor and anticommunist. The following year he joined forces with the studios and the anticommunist unions to create the Motion Picture Industrial Council (MPIC), the mission of which was twofold: to convince the public and concerned politicians that the industry was winning the fight against communism, and to do the work of winning that fight.

Reagan became personally involved, through his work with MPIC, in vetting people who were suspected of being Communists. He'd study their files, talk to their friends, and ultimately confront the suspects themselves, offering to facilitate a meeting with the FBI or HUAC so they could clear themselves of the suspicion or, if there was fire beneath the smoke, confess and recant. His attitude toward his subjects, during this process, was a blend of compassion and ruthlessness, a product of his belief that communism was less an ideology than a kind of prison. Abroad, it was literally a prison, an iron cage the Soviet regime had dropped down around its citizens and its satellite nations, with tanks and men with guns guarding the walls. In America, it was a psychological prison, a system of integrated loyalty, ideology, secrecy, and hierarchy that was impossible for anyone to escape without suffering a massive disruption of his or her life. And though an initial grant of sympathy was due to American Communists, many of whom had chosen to join the party with good intentions, the fact remained that they didn't literally have guns pointed at their heads. The cost of breaking out of their prison was high, but it wasn't paid in blood, and if they were willing to make their break for freedom there were friends on the outside ready to help.[43]

Toward those who were willing to accept this offer, to go to the FBI or HUAC and confess their communistic sins, and ideally name a few other Communists in the process, Reagan was magnanimous. He was also genuinely worried about making mistakes, and was glad when he could help clear innocents of suspicion. But toward those who weren't willing to bare all to the government, either about their own sins or the sins of their friends, he was coldly dismissive.

"The system allowed people to clear themselves and it worked, it really worked," he wrote. "The industry and the public accepted our recommendations of innocence. If on the other hand, someone said, 'I won't do that,' we simply said: 'We can't help you.'"[44]

All of this, for Reagan, was entirely what it meant for a democracy to be "strong enough to stand up and fight against the inroads of any ideology." It meant that as a private citizen you should be free to advocate for your beliefs, and to associate with others who shared them, so long as you weren't acting as an agent of a foreign power. But the community had rights, too. It had the right to define its own norms and to establish mechanisms for enforcing them. If you trespassed on those norms, or refused to participate in the enforcement of them, the community was within its rights to choose not to associate with you.

None of this was in opposition to any specific politics Reagan had held before. In many ways it was a continuation of the faith he'd always had in the virtue and good sense of the community. The essential change in Reagan's orientation, as the decade progressed, was more subtle. During the Depression, and in particular during the war, it had been inclusion that defined American community for Reagan. Everyone was in it together, no matter their color or creed or politics, against the threats of global economic crisis and fascism. It was Staff Sergeant Kazuo Masuda who represented the best of what America was. It was Rosie the Riveter. It was the rough-edged working man, with a rolled-up magazine in his pocket, standing up to speak his mind in Norman Rockwell's "Freedom of Speech" print. It was the Tuskegee Airmen, the pioneering group of black air force aviators who were featured in a government short Reagan had narrated. It was those who tried to draw invidious distinctions who were the enemies of what made America the ragtag, scrappy nation it was. As his commitment to anticommunism deepened, Reagan didn't turn against this idea of an inclusive society, but inclusion was no longer the means through which his ideal community defined and differentiated itself. It did so, instead, through a winnowing out of those ideas, and people, that threatened to destabilize the norm.

This philosophical shift, over the nature and purpose of community, led to and was reinforced by a shift in the actual communities of which Reagan was part. He was dropped by friends who wanted nothing to do with his anticommunist crusade and were somewhat horrified by his indifference to the careers it was destroying. He lost enthusiasm for friends who seemed bothered no end by the supposed existence of a blacklist but couldn't be persuaded to care in the least about the millions of victims of Stalin's regime, the final loss of China to Mao in 1949, or the revelations coming out of the increasingly aggressive HUAC hearings, where ex-Communists like Whittaker Chambers and Elizabeth Bentley were telling sensational stories of Soviet espionage in America.

His anticommunist friends, most of whom were conservative Republicans—they got it. As the years passed they occupied more and more of Reagan's social calendar. Through them he was exposed to new books, new magazines, even the occasional expatriate ex-Communist, who would report back to Reagan and his friends on the exotic nature of life behind the Iron Curtain.

He began to connect with the people in Washington who were busy building the (transpartisan, but conservative-ish) intelligence infrastructure that would fight the clandestine side of the Cold War over the next few decades. He joined and raised money for the Crusade for Freedom, a CIA-founded and -funded group that helped build the broadcast towers that beamed Radio Free Europe into the satellite nations of the Soviet Union. Over cozy dinners and lunches with men like Allen Dulles, future director of the CIA, Reagan would bat around ideas about how the mass media, and movies in particular, had a role to play as offensive weapons in the fight against communism and the Soviet Union.

Through all this Reagan became closer, socially and politically, to the producers, who in the fight against communism worked side by side with him as peers. That identification was compounded by the bread-and-butter work he was doing as SAG president, a post to which he was elected every year from 1947 to 1952. As he sat on the other side of the bargaining table from the studio executives, hashing out how the money and power would be distributed, he saw the conflicts between the two sides as insignificant relative to the larger goal they shared, which was to make sure that the American film-going public got the movies it deserved and the world was able to see, through these movies, the awesome bounty of the American system.

The most significant social contact Reagan made during these years was with Nancy Davis, a young actress he met and began dating in the fall of 1949. In the three years between their meeting and their marriage, he would date many other women, but it was Davis who was the steadiest, and it was her influence on him that was the greatest. The nature of that influence wasn't political, exactly. Davis came from a very conservative family, which over time had some influence on Reagan, but she herself didn't care much about politics, and didn't believe it was her role, in any case, to influence the men in her life in that fashion.

What was of the most political consequence was the adoration and unconditional support she gave to Reagan as he evolved toward something different from what he had been.

In 1948 Reagan had campaigned for Truman. In 1950 he publicly supported Helen Gahagan Douglas, a personal friend and liberal Democrat, in her race against Richard Nixon for a Senate seat from California. As the 1952 presidential election approached, Reagan's priorities had shifted to the point where he was willing to consider, for the first time, voting and campaigning for a Republican. Part of it was his personal admiration for Dwight Eisenhower, whom he'd tried to recruit to run as a Democrat before it was known which party Ike would pick, along with a lack of enthusiasm for Illinois governor Adlai Stevenson, a solid anticommunist Democrat in the Truman mold. Part of it was the continued attenuation of his liberal economic beliefs. The biggest part of it, however, was the degree to which the fight against communism had become, for Reagan, a crusade, a fight not just for the national interests of the country he loved, or for the cause of freedom throughout the world, but for no less than the spark of the divine in Man.

Such a fusion of political, philosophical, and spiritual beliefs was probably inevitable for Reagan. For years he had been working to stitch together the experience of the local fights he was fighting in Hollywood with both the global perspective that the Cold War had imprinted on everyone and the Christian beliefs that he had long kept compartmentalized from his politics.

The fusion was hastened, however, by his encounter that year with Whittaker Chambers's autobiography, *Witness*, which the *Saturday Evening Post* began serializing in February and which was published in full in May.

Reagan had read and admired many of the major anticommunist works of the time, but what he'd found in them had been primarily secular investigations of communism, written by intellectuals and intended to engage and persuade other intellectuals. They had dramatized the diabolical brilliance of dialectical reasoning. They'd explored the psychological and social mechanisms the party used to seduce and entrap members, the geopolitical ambitions of the Soviet Union, the checkered past of the Bolshevik party, and the ways in which the Communist Party in the West had tried to infiltrate and influence the institutions of its capitalist nemeses. When they dealt with spiritual and existential themes, which many of them did with great subtlety, the perspective was psychological, and the tone was elegiac. They might have mourned the universal faith in God that once held Christendom together, but God, alas, was dead, and the fight now was to prevent communism—*The God That Failed*, in the formulation of one of the texts Reagan read—from becoming a substitute faith.

Whittaker Chambers didn't stint in his psychological and historical analyses of communism, but when it came to his discussion of the spiritual dimensions of the fight against communism, he didn't write with any ironic or intellectual distance. God, to Chambers, wasn't at all dead. He was a living force in the world, in fact the source of all life and being. It was ignorance of His love from which Chambers had unknowingly suffered as a boy. It was God who raised Chambers up into the light after he fell into the false faith of communism. And it was God's antithesis—Evil—that was really on trial in the public confrontations between Chambers and his old friend and comrade Alger Hiss. For communism was the locus of Evil at that moment in history, the modern expression of "man's second-oldest faith," that we could be as God, that we had the power and knowledge to alter the world for the better.

"It is the great alternative faith of mankind," Chambers wrote. "Like all great faiths, its force derives from a simple vision. Other ages have had great visions. They have always been different versions of the same vision: the vision of God and man's relationship to God. The Communist vision is the vision of Man without God."[45]

Such hubris, believed Chambers, could lead only to barbarism, for we are not God. We have neither the power nor the wisdom to act appropriately to remold the world to our liking. And if we try, we will fail, and then in our pride and guilt and fear we will act again, to correct for that failure, to run away from the evidence of our frailty and smallness and inadequacy. The failures will compound and the actions that seem necessary to remedy them will grow in scale and force, amplifying, until there is nothing left but blood and screaming.[46]

Reagan didn't need Chambers in order to support Eisenhower in 1952. Eisenhower was advocating a far more aggressive set of policies toward communism than Stevenson was, and that was sufficient for Reagan's vote.

What Reagan found in Chambers, however, was a moral and spiritual language that was of a different order than the language he'd been using or hearing. It had the power not just to persuade people but to convert them, to move them, to hook into and tug at their deepest ethical and spiritual commitments. And it was a language that Reagan would forever after use—reading and rereading *Witness* until its cadences were native to him, memorizing entire passages, quoting and paraphrasing them at length in political speeches—to articulate to the world his own set of beliefs about what America stood for in its fight against communism.

"[T]he great ideological struggle that we find ourselves engaged in today is not a new struggle," Reagan said in June of 1952, in a commencement speech to the graduates of William Woods College in Missouri. "It's the same old battle. We met it under the name of Hitlerism; we met it under the name of Kaiserism; and we have met it back through the ages in the name of every conqueror that has ever set upon a course of establishing his rule over mankind. It is simply the idea, the basis of this country and of our religion, the idea of the dignity of man, the idea that deep within the heart of each one of us is something so God-like and precious that no individual or group has a right to impose his or its will upon the people."[47]

In August of 1952 Reagan stepped down as president of the Screen Actors Guild, staying on as a member of the board. He didn't fully explain why he no longer wanted to run the show, but it was likely the convergence of a few factors.

He and Nancy had been married in March of that year, and she was due with their first child in October.

In July he'd been involved in, and may have wanted to distance himself from, what was coming to look like a very shady arrangement between the SAG board and MCA, the behemoth talent agency that represented Reagan as well as a number of other board members. The board had agreed to suspend SAG bylaws to allow MCA, but no other agency, to produce television shows on which its talent was working, an exemption that proved so significant it ultimately led to the meta-morphosis of MCA from a talent agency to a film and television studio. Reagan would later offer some rationalizations for the deal, but to most observers it seemed like simple cronyism.

Perhaps most significant in the decision to step down as president, however, was Reagan's desire to free up more time to focus on his acting career, which he had long worried was being compromised by his guild work.

"There's no question in my mind that Ronnie's political involve-ment had begun to hurt his prospects for work," Nancy Reagan later wrote. ". . . In a small community like Hollywood, an actor's reputation has a lot to do with his off-screen image, and the men who made pic-tures had come to see Ronnie primarily as a negotiator. He used to say that it had reached the point that if they were shooting a western, they'd probably cast him as the lawyer from the East."[48]

So long as his career was even halfway above water, Reagan had been able to push away these concerns, because the SAG work was so rewarding to him—far more rewarding than any film work had ever been. By 1952, however, things were dire. He hadn't starred in a stand-out movie in a few years, and hadn't distinguished himself in any of the mediocre ones. His contract with Warner Brothers, which had been his home since 1937, had ended in January of that year, and was not re-newed. Another contract with Universal, which he'd signed a few years before, was suspended after only two of the planned five films were made. The stated reason for the suspension was that Reagan had turned down some scripts. In truth the scripts were a pretext, and everyone knew it. He was dropped because he wasn't worth the per-film fee that his agent had negotiated for him at the start of the contract, when he was a hotter property.

Reagan soldiered on for another two years, turning down most of the bad scripts he was offered, making a few of the least bad, paying the bills with occasional guest spots on TV shows and some cigarette advertisements for Chesterfields, and hoping that if he held on long enough something better would come through.

Nothing did, though, and by the end of 1953 he was desperate enough that he didn't immediately say no when he was approached with the idea of hosting a nightclub act in Las Vegas. The Vegas pitch went through a few evolutions, including one in which the headliner would have been a stripper, and another in which he would have had to work during Christmas. Reagan eventually agreed to emcee a music and comedy revue—with showgirls with pasties, but no strippers—at the Last Frontier Hotel in Las Vegas, to run for two weeks in February of 1954.

It wasn't the disaster it might have been, in large part because Reagan was such a pro. He spent time with a comedy writer polishing his opening monologue. He took rehearsals seriously. He charmed the four guys in the quartet that was headlining the show. And he did what he was called upon to do—including a Three Stooges–style bit in which he and the guys in the band ran around the stage hitting each other on the head with rolled-up newspapers—in good humor, and with genuine comic skill.

The show was entertaining enough, and the audiences were big enough, that Reagan was invited to do another run, but he declined. There were only so many Vegas shows he could do before he became one of those washed-up former film stars who now did the nightclub circuit.

In the spring of 1954, MCA came to him with the idea of hosting a new television show that the production arm of the agency was putting together as an advertising vehicle for General Electric. It would run once a week, on Sunday nights, with each week featuring a different short drama, starring different guest stars. The host, in addition to performing in some of the weekly stories, would act as the show's first line of interpretation. At the start of each show he would speak directly to the audience, explaining what the week's story was about, identifying its morals, telling a few jokes when appropriate, and generally putting out the kind of friendly, upstanding, trustworthy vibe that GE wanted associated with its products and productions.

To that point Reagan had been resisting committing more deeply to television, fearing it would reduce his stature so much that he'd never get it back up. But in light of his ever-dwindling options, the terms of the deal he was offered to do *General Electric Theater* were too good to turn down. The money was excellent, with a high base salary for hosting plus more money every time he performed in one of the weekly dramas, and more again when Nancy did a guest spot, as she did occasionally. The format of the show alleviated one of his most acute fears, which was that he'd come to be overly identified with a single character. The idea of being under contract again—for a full five years, no less— was immensely appealing to him after his two anxious years as a free-lancer. As host he'd be able to scratch at least part of the political itch he'd been cultivating for most of the previous decade. GE didn't want him picking fights on air about communism, but he would be able to speak on a weekly basis to millions of viewers, as himself, on behalf of the homespun values that communism was so bent on destroying. And, perhaps the most unusual part of the job, he'd be able to take his spiel on the road.

"The real extra, however, and the one that had drawn me into the picture," wrote Reagan, "was MCA's idea to hang the package on some personal appearance tours, in which for a number of weeks each year I'd visit GE plants, meeting employees and taking part in their extensive 'Employees and Community Relations Program.' "[49]

In August of 1954, Reagan embarked on his first tour as GE's good-will ambassador, beginning with the company's factory in Schenectady, New York. The first half-hour episode of *General Electric Theater* aired the following month, on Sunday, September 26, just after the *Ed Sullivan Show*.

On both fronts—the show and the speaking tour—it was an immediate success. The show was rated first in its time slot within a few months, thanks in substantial part to the parade of genuine Hollywood stars MCA was able to persuade to guest star in the different stories. Reagan enjoyed the mix of hosting, occasional acting, and regular socializing on set with precisely the people from whose company he had feared he would be excluded. And if he cast a smaller shadow from within the television set than he had at his grandest moments on the big screen, it was still quite good to be a star again.

The speaking tours, which would have been excruciating to most actors, were invigorating for Reagan. He liked the long train rides from plant to plant, crisscrossing the country, during which he'd read and rest and have a good time arguing politics with the executives GE had assigned to shepherd him.

On-site he was exceptionally good at chatting up the assembly line workers, showing them that the fact that he was a famous actor didn't mean he wasn't also just regular folks like them, capable of talking sports with the fellas and flirting affectionately with the ladies. He excelled, too, at flattering the executives, talking shop with the foremen, and enthusiastically receiving facts and statistics from the scientists and engineers.

In between the informal encounters Reagan would give a speech, usually a version of the one he'd been giving for years as a thought leader in the entertainment industry. He would defend Hollywood, arguing that its image as a den of hedonism was undeserved, that its values were the values of the heartland. He would talk about the success he and his allies had had in keeping Communists out of the movies. He would tell funny stories about famous people. He gave good patter. It wasn't new for him, but the GE audiences weren't accustomed to being entertained on the job by celebrities, and they received him rapturously. A pathologically private man in many respects, Reagan thrived on the kind of quick, limited intimacy that was available in great quantities in these situations. He also thrived on the feeling, which he hadn't felt with such intensity in quite a while, that he was liked and wanted.

"The VP in charge escorted me down the iron stairs to the factory floor, and the pattern was established at that point," he wrote of that first visit to Schenectady. "Probably the VP and his fellow executives had never witnessed a movie premiere, so they were unprepared for what happened. Machines went untended or ground to a halt; the aisles filled with men and women bearing their children's autograph books. I walked, signing, answering questions, asking a few of my own, and generally having a hell of a good time getting acquainted. About four hours later, back in the upstairs office, the reception was equally heart-warming—the execs were ecstatic. . . . I was very well aware that anyone from Hollywood would have been given the same reception, but I wasn't about to volunteer that information. It was too good after the downbeat year and a half to bask in a little glory."[50]

Within a year or two of starting the plant tours, Reagan also began giving speeches to local civic groups and charities, from whom he got a similarly warm reception.

In all of the venues he played for the first few years of his GE tenure, Reagan's charge was nonideological. This wasn't because General Electric was an apolitical company. In fact GE had distinguished itself since the end of the war for the overtness of its hostility toward organized labor, and its willingness to attack the redistributive policies of the New Deal, at a time when most corporations, and indeed most conservatives, had resigned themselves to the power of unions and to the idea of the economy of America as a blended one.

Reagan's job, however, wasn't to sell conservative ideas. On-screen he was expected to help create a top-rated show and to make people feel good about him and about themselves, so that when the show cut to commercial, the positivity would transfer to the GE products that were being advertised.

In the plant Reagan's job was to tell the employees of General Electric that what the company was doing, on a foundation laid by their hard work, represented the best of what America was. It was to make the workers and executives feel seen and appreciated, and to help knit together the vast diaspora of GE operations—hundreds of thousands of employees at more than a hundred facilities in forty states—into one harmonious organ of industrial production and prosperity.

Out in the world, in his community relations work, he was given freer rein. He didn't have to say anything about the company at all if it didn't fit the moment. He could talk about education, charitable giving, the threat of communism, any one of a range of other topics about which he had something to say. The structural goal was the same, however. He was there to convey to the world, through the example of his excellence and charm, that General Electric was a force for progress and prosperity.

To the extent that there was a degree of political content intrinsic to any such work for any corporation, it was of a sort that didn't require adjustment from Reagan. Up through at least 1954 he was still, just barely, capable of saying words about the pernicious influence of big business, but those words had never attached to anything truly fundamental in him. He had never felt the anger or alienation as his father had. And even when his attacks on business had been more heartfelt, they'd routinely lost out when set against his much stronger instinct to identify with the people he was around and the group of which he was a part. He'd always been a team player. Now his team was General Electric, and that was the most important thing.

Plus, GE impressed the hell out him. He had spoken often, in his SAG and anticommunist work, of how the entertainment industry could help win the Cold War of ideas by simply showing the world how awesomely productive the nation was. Now he was seeing that abundance pouring forth, at the source, from the forges and factories of General Electric. It was a whirring, pumping, electrifying symbol of America ascendant.

"I drove a locomotive, revved up a jet engine, watched a plastic bottle receive a million volts of X-ray, and fired a 20-mm. cannon so top secret I couldn't even tell Nancy about it," wrote Reagan. "The trips were murderously difficult. I could lose ten pounds in three weeks and eat anything I wanted. The schedules were dovetailed on a split-second basis, and the demand on energy so great when you had to meet the fourteenth group with the same zip you'd shown ten hours earlier that I didn't really sleep until a trip was over. *But I enjoyed every whizzing minute of it.* . . . Sometimes I had an awesome, shivering feeling that America was making a personal appearance for me, and it made me the biggest fan in the world."[51]

As the tours went on, year after year, his politics *were* changed by the work, but the process was slow. He'd never been a radical, but for his entire adult life he'd believed in the capacity of government to help the common man. For years, as SAG president, he'd been obligated to see matters from the workers' side. And as an actor, in his relationship with the studios, he'd gotten his fair share of reminders that he wasn't the one who signed the checks.

By GE, though, he was being paid to see the world through management's eyes, and he was treated like upper management. When he and Nancy decided to build a new house, in 1955, GE engineers helped design it, build it, and equip it with the latest technological innovations. Workers and managers asked him to clarify company policies. GE executives were expected to brief him on plant operations and product lines. He went on company junkets ("Salmon fishing on a yacht off Seattle, deep-sea fishing under the same luxurious conditions in the Gulf of Mexico, riding an Irish hunter over stone walls in Connecticut").[52] As the years went on, he was invited more and more often to speak to outside groups not just as a Hollywood actor but as someone who had wisdom about the worlds of industry and politics.

Unsurprisingly, Reagan began to see the world in a different light. The double vision he'd had to maintain as an actor and a SAG activist gave way to the single unified vision of the GE spokesman: What was good for General Electric was good for its employees was good for America.

Reagan often had to step quickly, during his tours of the plants, to keep that equation clean. He might be asked to commiserate in the morning, with workers, about how the boss was always demanding more work for no more pay, while later that afternoon, in meetings with executives, he'd have to be impressed by the means with which they'd extracted greater productivity from the workers. But he'd always been good at that kind of dance, and it helped enormously that times were good. GE was growing. The economy was growing. The union contracts, thanks in substantial part to past militancy, were quite good, and in general the workers were part of that extraordinary expansion of the middle class that would have so much to do with defining what it felt like, for so many of the people who would one day vote for Ronald Reagan, to be alive and American in the 1950s.

It helped, too, that the conversation Reagan was having with the workers and executives at GE was shaped to an extraordinary extent by the very "Employees and Community Relations Program" of which he was the face.

Ever since GE had been brought to its knees by a strike of the United Electrical Workers, in the early months of 1946, the company had been waging a permanent campaign to tip the balance not just against the specific unions that represented its workers, but against what GE's visionary vice president of labor and community relations, Lemuel Boulware, saw as the "misconceptions" that had enabled labor and the policies of the New Deal to achieve such broad support in the first place.[53]

For every difficult question the workers had, there was a manual that had an answer that had been carefully composed to address their concern. For every executive who wanted to know how to change the behavior of his workers without provoking a reaction from the union, there was a five-point plan. There was a steady stream of surveys given to the workers to assess their state of mind, and more handouts produced in response to what the surveys found. There was a company-wide newspaper, plant-specific papers, an executive-only newsletter, a monthly glossy magazine, and a quarterly journal on issues of foreign policy and defense. There were three thousand specially trained employee relations managers (ERMs) who roamed the plants, solving workers' problems and reassuring them that the company was on their side. There was even a company college, with its own campus, that enrolled thousands of employees in its courses every year.

Underlying it all, knitting it all together in subtle and not-so-subtle ways, was Boulware's astoundingly pure belief in the virtue and decency of private enterprise. Also in the corruption of anything—unions, progressive taxation, social welfare programs—that would violate the sanctity of the body corporate.

"One of the top marvels of all the world's history," Boulware would write, "is the way we interdependent citizens have come together in business voluntarily, have so largely done for each other what each wants done in return for what he provides, and have in the process maintained our education and morals at a level that permits almost everybody to go around doing practically as he pleases without intruding on the free-choice and other rights, dignity, usefulness, economic progress, and spiritual well-being of his fellow citizens."[54]

This truth was so self-evident to Boulware that it led him, interestingly, not to demonize those who would contest it, but to assume that everyone who thought otherwise, with the exception of a few sick souls, must be misguided. They simply weren't in possession yet of the Truth. And if that were the case, then they could be enlightened.

Boulware's vision, which was religious in its intensity, didn't perfectly disseminate out into the bloodstream of GE. Workers didn't suddenly roll over and decertify their unions. Executives didn't immediately adopt as their own the far-right-wing precepts of the books that

Boulware's office would assign them to read. The corporate culture at GE, which until the war had actually been relatively progressive, didn't change utterly overnight, or even over the decade. The New Deal didn't wither away under the blinding light of the truth of unfettered free market capitalism.

But Boulware's system, which had the absolute support of GE's president, Ralph Cordiner, was enormously influential. It lent to the endless stream of paper and rhetoric that rained down on its employees an urgency and sincerity that could be very persuasive, particularly to management but often to workers as well. It meant that GE was committed, in genuine ways, to understanding its employees better and making their working lives better. It gave a missionary energy to Boulware and his corps of ERMs, who truly believed they knew their workers better than the union did, and were acting more in their interests than the union was. Plant closings and relocations, worker indoctrinations, hardball negotiation tactics with the unions—all of it could be earnestly described as a kind of holy sacrifice for the greater good of General Electric. Even when it wasn't effective in persuading it could be effective in demoralizing, disillusioning, or simply sowing confusion of the sort that worked to GE's advantage in its tussles with the unions.

For Reagan, what it all meant, at first, was two things. One was that he was an agent of the system, even if his ideology during his first few years on the job wasn't the same as Boulware's. He was the spoonful of sugar who made the medicine of newsletters, magazines, surveys, factory floor meetings, book clubs, and antiunion counterprogramming go down.

The other thing it meant followed from that dynamic: He had a lot of reading to do. It was possible, in theory, for Reagan to go about his business, year after year, dancing around the tough questions. He certainly had the skill to do it. But he was too politically minded to be satisfied with that. All the time, all across the country, he got questions and comments from the workers and managers he was meeting, sparked by the things they were reading and hearing, and he felt obligated to figure out what his responses should be. He read the newsletters, newspapers, magazines, books, and bulletins that were coming from Boulware's office. On his long train rides he relaxed with his GE handlers. He got to know Boulware and Cordiner, and heard from them the gospel directly. He began thinking about the world as it was described by Boulware, and wondering whether the descriptions made sense in light of his own experience. Gradually, he began to conclude that they did.

"From hundreds of people in every part of the country, I heard complaints about how the ever-expanding federal government was encroaching on liberties we'd always taken for granted," he wrote. "I heard it so often that after a while I became convinced that some of our fundamental freedoms were in jeopardy because of the emergence of a *permanent government* never envisioned by the framers of the Constitution."[55]

That Reagan went out among the people and heard this message, and not others, was the consequence of a few things. One was that Boulware's program was effective. He was shaping the terms of the conversation, and he was also, in Reagan's case, choosing the people with whom Reagan was having it. Another was that the broader political culture, and not just the slice of it that GE controlled, had changed. In the everyday business of domestic legislating in Washington, the New Deal consensus still held. Outside the Beltway, however, there was a great deal more space for conservative ideas than there had been for a long time. There was more money being poured into purveying them. (Boulware and GE were exemplary, but they weren't alone.) And there was, more broadly, a kind of reversion to the mean. The Great Depression had genuinely, and permanently, altered the beliefs of many Americans regarding the role of the government in the economic life of the country. But it had also, for many, involved only a temporary and contingent change. The return of sustained prosperity brought a renewed vitality to the deep-flowing currents of American conservatism that had taken such a hit during the deprivations of the 1930s.

Among the most potent instantiations of these converging trends was the launching in 1955 of a new conservative opinion magazine, *National Review*. Founded by William F. Buckley, a precocious young conservative from a wealthy oil family, the stars of its masthead were ex-Communists like Whittaker Chambers and James Burnham, and its product, week after week, was a conservatism informed by a deep knowledge of, and antipathy toward, the Left. Reagan, who was an early subscriber, almost immediately began incorporating ideas and information he found in the magazine into his speeches to civic and business groups.

Reagan wasn't required by GE to be part of this shift back to the right, however immersed in it he might have been. He wanted to be, however. Nearly everything was pushing him in that direction. His social world had become almost exclusively conservative, made up of GE executives, conservative anticommunist comrades, and the kinds of fancy folks Nancy preferred. His work world was an incredibly potent brew of affirmation, satisfaction, money, respect, camaraderie, and conservatism, each spirit in the mix reinforcing the others. He was tired, personally, of paying such high taxes. And in his heart he just didn't believe anymore that the government should be playing the role, in the economic lives of its citizens, that he'd once thought it should.

He'd been a liberal because it was his inheritance. Because the Great Depression was an exceptional period, which seemed to call for an exceptional response. Because the charisma of Roosevelt had spoken to him. And because the liberalism of Roosevelt, and of the nation during the Depression and war years, had contained within it certain qualities that authentically resonated with him. It was patriotic. It was vigorous. It told the story of America in a more forward-looking and expansive way than the conservatism of the 1930s and '40s could manage. But the fit had never been completely comfortable. And as the reasons to keep bargaining with the old liberalism fell away, one by one, he began to accept that there was another mantle that might drape more comfortably.

In the spring of 1957, Reagan was asked to give the commencement speech at his alma mater, Eureka College. It was in many respects a masterfully composed speech. He wove together the fight against communism, his own days of Eureka, the founding of the nation, and the ideals of democracy and freedom for which it stood. He was funny, flattering, stern, exhortatory.

He was also still clearly putting the finishing touches on a new political identity. Five years before, when he'd spoken at William Woods College, his great warning had been about communism, and his confidence in the righteousness of the cause was absolute. At Eureka College, it was the growth of government that threatened, and while the individual elements of the solution were clear in his mind—government should be smaller, taxes should be lower, regulations should be fewer—he was ambivalent about what the scale of the problem was, and to what degree the people who were perpetuating it were true enemies, or simply well-meaning people who were showing poor judgment.

"Now today as you prepare to leave your Alma Mater," he said, "you go into a world in which, due to our carelessness and apathy, a great many of our freedoms have been lost. It isn't that an outside enemy has taken them. It's just that there is something inherent in government which makes it, when it isn't controlled, continue to grow."[56]

It was a cautious speech. By the following year, Reagan was ready to be less cautious. In the fall of 1958, Boulware and Cordiner asked Reagan if he would be the face and voice of a much more directly ideological campaign they'd decided to launch, in anticipation of the 1958 congressional elections. He agreed, and with that agreement seemed to be set free. No more arguing with himself. No more qualifying his criticisms. The fight was on. And the enemy was clear.

"If I had to choose one word to describe the salient characteristic of the revolution of our times," he said in November of 1958, "the word would be *collectivism*—the tendency to center the power of all initiative in one central government. One central authority and its organs. And the weapon, the revolutionary agent that had brought this about, has been the tax machine."[57]

He was at last the conservative he'd been becoming for so long. His conservatism wasn't Boulware's conservatism, with its idolatry of productivity and private enterprise, and its hostility to labor unions. Nor was it the apocalypticism of Whittaker Chambers, the schematism of James Burnham, or the philosophical libertarianism of Arizona senator Barry Goldwater, whose presidential run in 1964 would end up being the platform that launched Reagan as a national political figure.

He shared principles with these men, and admired the clarity of their systems, but what grounded his politics, it became clear, wasn't a system. It was a narrative. It was a story about the fundamental decency, virtue, and productivity of the American people, and about what was needed, at each given historical moment, to make sure that they could live their lives in peace and prosperity, with as much freedom as possible. During the Depression, confronted with economic catastrophe, Roosevelt's government had had to step in to help. In the absence of such an existential threat to the normal functioning of American society, however, the government's responsibility was to recede, to leave the citizens of the United States as much breathing room as possible to make their own fortunes. Being Americans, they would do so splendidly.

That's what FDR would have done. What Jefferson would have done. What the Democratic Party that Reagan had once loved would have done.

"But then came the newfangled 'liberals' who rejected these beliefs," wrote Reagan. "They claimed government had greater wisdom than individuals to determine what was best for the individual and it should engineer our economic and business life according to its goals and values; dictate to states, cities, and towns what their rights and responsibilities were; and take an increasing bite out of the earnings of productive workers and distribute it to those who are not productive. To them, government was the fount of all wisdom—the bigger government was, the better—and they rejected the principles of Democrats who had gone before them."[58]

From 1958 on, this was the story that Reagan told, to enthusiastic audiences around the country. At the core of the speeches he gave was one big story, about liberalism as the stalking horse of socialism. What sold it, though, and sold him as the messenger of it, was the urgency and skill with which it was told. He took the work he had done on himself over the past few years, struggling his way out of his liberalism, and turned it outward. He took the kinds of facts and statistics that he had sought for his own needs to lend empirical weight to the gut feelings he had, and offered them back to his audiences to give substance to their intuitions. He took the resonant quotations and lyrical phrases that had reassured him that he was remaining true to himself, and he gave them to his listeners, many of whom had doubts about their own motives.

It's not you who have changed, he said, *but the world around you. It's not surprising that you haven't been able to put words to this change. It's been a subtle thing, like a haze in the air, thickening everything, provoking frustrations one can't quite name and anger for which one can't find a target. But let me tell you what the target is, let me give you evidence of its existence, let me reassure you that your anger is rooted not in resentment but in the best things about you and me and about America. And let me call you to arms, for you're needed, now, before it's too late.*

This wasn't the slowly simmering drama that infused many of Reagan's greatest presidential speeches, delivered when he knew, by virtue of his own election, that the crisis had been averted and America was itself again. In the final years of the 1950s, and the early years of the '60s, things were far more urgent than that. The crisis was here. Something had to be done. The facts and statistics needed to be known. The anecdotes, which in a few sentences encapsulated a deep truth, needed to be assimilated. The praises of freedom, and the warnings about tyranny, needed to be heard.

"We can lose our freedom all at once by succumbing to Russia," he said to an audience in Oregon, "or we can lose it gradually by installments—the end result is slavery."[59]

In Phoenix he described the strategy of the enemy: "Get any part of a proposed program accepted, then with the principle of government participation in the field established, work for expansion, always aiming at the ultimate goal—a government that will someday be a big brother to us all."

In 1961, in a speech about the legislation that would ultimately become Medicare, he warned in apocalyptic terms of what would happen if the good people in America didn't rise to stop socialized medicine.

"If you don't," he said, "this program, I promise you, will pass just as surely as the sun will come up tomorrow and behind it will come other federal programs that will invade every area of freedom as we have known it in this country until one day . . . we will wake to find that we have socialism, and if you don't do this and I don't do this, one of these days we are going to spend our sunset years telling our children and our children's children, what it once was like in America when men were free."[60]

In this conservatism, which was basically what Reagan would stick to for the rest of his life, there was a genuine continuity of belief from his days as a New Dealer. It was true that he'd always believed the government's role was to heed the voice of the American people. During the Depression and the war, the people were calling for an energetic federal response, and it made sense to listen. Now times had changed. Things were better. Many people were looking for the welfare state to shrink back down. But it was also true that Reagan was hearing that message with particular clarity because he was listening differently, his ears attuned to a different wavelength than it used to be. And he was surrounded by a different chorus of voices.

4

Mr. Yes, Mr. No: Norman Podhoretz

The trouble is that Podhoretz has a great ridiculous fat-bellied mind which he pats too often.[1]

—ALLEN GINSBERG

By three o'clock in the morning—the hour Scott Fitzgerald said it always was in the deep, dark night of the soul—I had decided to say No to the dying fifties and Yes to the coming sixties, to whose more adventurous and youthful spirit my first act of dedication would be accepting the editorship of *Commentary*, and my second, the effort to transform *Commentary* into its evangelical voice.[2]

—NORMAN PODHORETZ

In the spring of 1957 Norman Podhoretz, a twenty-seven-year-old editor at *Commentary* magazine, published an essay titled "The Young Generation of U.S. Intellectuals." It began by posing a question that was already, only a few years into his young career, recognizably Podhoretzian. *Who was this newest generation of intellectuals?* he asked, as though everything depended upon it. What did they believe? How were they different from those who preceded them?

"What makes it especially difficult to characterize the younger generation of intellectuals in this country is that they have not been articulate about themselves," wrote Podhoretz. "They have found no

spokesman to voice their protests or to proclaim their aspirations; nor
have they produced a *This Side of Paradise* or a *Farewell to Arms* in which
they might imagine themselves defined for all time, in which they could
see themselves dramatized, and from which they could derive a sense of
their own significance, of their peculiar mission in history."[3]

The cause of this formlessness, in the literary intellectual identity
of his generation, wasn't that the culture was alienating, as it had been
for Chambers and his fellow *ernste menschen* in the 1920s, or that it was
falling apart, as it had been in the 1930s. It arose, rather, from a lack
of resistance. In this sense, though from a very different perspective,
Podhoretz was responding to the same phenomenon Ronald Reagan
was: The liberals had won. They had won in matters of governance and
policy most obviously, but even more profound was the victory they'd
achieved in the realm of ideas. By the 1950s there was a liberal consensus in America that seemed so broad and settled it was hard to imagine
it ever unraveling.

For Reagan this was a crisis of civilizational proportions. If the tide
didn't turn soon, if people didn't rise up to take charge of their destinies, then the future would be, if not necessarily Orwell's nightmare
vision of a boot stamping on the human face forever, then something
almost as horrifying for its lack of drama. Half-men and half-women,
well compensated and cared-for by the social engineers of the state,
the union, and the corporation, going about their lives of earning and
eating and reproducing, slowly forgetting what it means to be fully
human. At stake, too, was the nation's ability to respond forcefully and
strategically to the threat of communism. Half-men would not be up
to the task.

For Podhoretz, a ravenously ambitious intellectual of the liberal
Left, the consensus was terrifying for entirely different reasons. He didn't
fear that the political order was trending toward tyranny. He feared
that within a political order as humane as the one America seemed to
be achieving, there would be nothing interesting left for young guns
like him to say. In this he was coming from his own rather narcissistic

perspective, but he was also part of a shift in how Americans, particularly young Americans, were coming to inhabit their politics.

For Reagan the obvious political question had been: What do the people want? His special destiny, as he saw it, was to channel and embody their wisdom. For Podhoretz the politics were much more interior: What did it all mean for him? What was his role in what was coming? What stance were he and his fellow young American intellectuals called to take toward this nation they had inherited? What kind of language were they to speak? Blocking their way, on the path to answering these questions, weren't the social engineers, liberals, communists, conservatives, or anyone so collective and faceless. It was their fathers and mothers. It was the voices of conformity inside their own heads.

The voices in Podhoretz's own head were legion. They came from his rather conventional immigrant parents, and the values of adherence, assimilation, and tribe they instilled. It was the masculine code of the streets of Brownsville, Brooklyn, and the banter of swagger and vulgarity he'd shared with his friends from the neighborhood. At Columbia University, where he'd been a scholarship boy, he'd learned from men like Lionel Trilling that his intellect could be the repository of all the learning of Western civilization. At the Jewish Theological Seminary, where he'd earned a simultaneous undergraduate degree, he'd supped on the ancient wisdom of Jerusalem. Then followed a fellowship at Cambridge, a few years in the service in West Germany, and finally the job at *Commentary*—a political and cultural journal published by the American Jewish Committee—where he found himself in the rarefied world of the "New York intellectuals," the influential group of left-wing political writers and literary and cultural critics that had coalesced in the 1930s and 1940s and now orbited around New York–based journals like *Partisan Review*, *Dissent*, and *Commentary*.[4]

It was these New York intellectuals, above all, whose voices haunted Podhoretz. They were the ones who had shaped his critical intellect with their essays, books, and classes. And not only had they already said so much of what needed to be said, before he'd even come on the scene, most of them were still alive and filling the pages of the journals and magazines that mattered with their diamond-sharp insight and their tragic-toned wisdom, crowding around him as colleagues, friends, and editors. There was Edmund Wilson on modernist literature, Clement Greenberg on avant-garde art, Robert Warshow on the movies, and Lionel Trilling on the failures of the liberal imagination. There was Hannah Arendt on totalitarianism, and James Burnham, Sidney Hook, and Max Eastman on Trotskyism. The evils of Stalinism and the Soviet Union had been so dissected by the New York intellectuals that it was a wonder the empire still stood.

Throw in the affiliated members of this society (the "cousins," as Podhoretz would later call them) and it seemed as if the whole universe was covered. Ask a big question about modernity, America, communism, the atomic age, literature, liberalism, Jewishness in an age of mass tolerance, culture in an age of mass education, or anything in an age of mass anything, and surely *Partisan Review* or *Commentary* had held or would soon be holding a symposium on it, featuring the most brilliant minds of America and Europe.

These men and women had been having the conversations that counted for decades. They hadn't arrived at all the answers, but they had evolved a perspective and voice that seemed so right to the times it was hard for Podhoretz to imagine alternatives. The perspective was left-liberal, but disdainful of the pieties and illusions of liberals and leftists. It was secular, but respectful of those religious insights and parables that cautioned against man in his pride. It was for a generous social welfare state, without any illusions that the government could legislate human suffering out of existence. It was inflected by the fact that a very high percentage of its articulators were Jewish. It was for racial equality, but prudence when it came to enforcing it. It was steeped in Freud, and took as its gospel his conviction that reason was but a skiff floating atop the sea of terror, confusion, and need that filled up most of the human psyche. It had a past with Marxism, but was now deeply skeptical of Marx and bitterly opposed to actually existing communism. And if its

memories of its youthful revolutionary past were still too fond for it
to fully embrace America quite yet, it was cautiously respectful of its
imperfect but functioning democracy, secretly thrilled by its hulking
tanks and planes and bombs that held Soviet expansionism in check,
impressed by its economy that had brought into being such broadly
shared affluence, and grateful for its intellectual and literary life that
had room for all comers, including people with names like Greenberg,
Schapiro, and Podhoretz. Above all, these intellectuals were for maturity, seriousness, and complexity.

The New York intellectual style of prose was the correlate of this
perspective. In its sentences of many clauses it enacted how heroically
the human intellect had to struggle to come even tangentially close to
the truth about the world.[5]

For Podhoretz it was the only game in town. To be a player in it
was the only worthy ambition to pursue. His was a parochial view,
very much the product of his particular education, but his sense of the
stature of his new family wasn't wrong. He was running with at least
a few of the greatest critical intellects of the twentieth century, and
the people who filled out the middle and lower ranks weren't exactly
chopped liver. The conversation they were having was inscribing itself
upon the world.

Podhoretz's first goal when he'd begun publishing, in 1953, had
been to make a space for himself in the conversation, to become the
next eminent New York intellectual. And he'd succeeded beyond even
his own immodest hopes. From the moment he'd arrived on the scene
he'd inhabited the voice and perspective so well, with such brio, and
with such a good nose for the zeitgeist that within months of first appearing in *Commentary* he was the toast of the scene, or at least a prime
locus of its gossip, scandalizing and delighting with his tough reviews
of, among others, Bernard Malamud and Saul Bellow.[6] So dramatic was
his ascent that in a single week, as a result of his stylish pan of Bellow's
The Adventures of Augie March, he received personal invitations to write
for both *Partisan Review* and the *New Yorker*. Less than a year into the

life he was offered a job as assistant editor at *Commentary*, and promised that it would be held open for him for the two years he was about
to spend in the army. He was more than in. He was anointed.

At first Podhoretz had thought he craved nothing more than acceptance. But it became manifest almost immediately, upon his assumption of his duties at *Commentary*, that he wanted more. He could write
in the style of his elders, and make the kinds of arguments for maturity
and complexity they made, but there was a difference. For intellectuals like Lionel Trilling, who'd been Podhoretz's professor and mentor
at Columbia, these arguments were organic. They were the product
of maturity, of the experience of youthful mistakes made and learned
from. They were the hard-won lessons, in particular, of the 1930s, when
so many left-wing intellectuals had been hoodwinked by the simplicity
and purity of Marxism.

For Podhoretz, though, it was hand-me-down wisdom. He accepted
its propositions. It had been revelatory when he'd first encountered it
as an undergraduate, just up from provincial Brooklyn. But now that
it was the mid-to-late 1950s, now that communism in America was
in disrepute even among intellectuals, now that once-heretical insights
and courageous stands of principle had settled into orthodoxies, now
that Podhoretz had come into ownership himself of the sacred wisdom,
it had lost its charge. So in Podhoretz's writing from the start there was
a restlessness. Again and again, in his early reviews and essays, he would
counsel caution and complexity and modesty, in the traditional style,
but he wouldn't like it.

The late novels of William Faulkner, for instance, were to be condemned for Faulkner's refusal to engage artistically with the growing
complexity of the world, but it was clear in the way Podhoretz went
about his condemnation that there was a part of him that could empa-
thize with why a great writer might fear that taking the world as it was,
in such gray times, would mean graying down his own imagination.

"He is saying to us," wrote Podhoretz, "'I am tired and bored and

bewildered by the way you go about things; I am sick of your conferences and your bickerings. They don't matter, they are little childish
games. What matters is Love and Faith and Hope.' Love of what? Faith
in what? Faulkner never tells us. How could he, when he cannot realize
that today as perhaps never before the question of man-and-his-des-
tiny is inseparable from the hard, dull, wearisome details of EDC's and
NATO's and Austrian Peace Treaties?"[7]

Television, in another early essay, was to be praised precisely for
its honest treatment of life as it actually was, and yet it was depressing
to watch what came out when artists chose to depict life in the 1950s
realistically: small stories, small morals, small men.

Podhoretz was far from alone in being depressed by the 1950s and
its cadence of conformity. It was "The Age of Conformity," in Irving
Howe's formulation, full of the "other-directed" souls of David Riesman's best-selling sociological study *The Lonely Crowd.* The young were
the silent generation, the men in gray flannel suits, the organization
men, all going about their business of producing the affluent society,
a new form of cultural-political-economic existence in which things
seemed to be going smashingly well but no one was happy.

If conformity-masquerading-as-maturity was the defining trait of
the decade and its people, then dissatisfaction with that mode was its
critical antithesis. What was unique about Podhoretz's version of it,
more than anything, was how personal it was. He wasn't classifying it
as a sociologist, as Riesman was, or despairing over it as a socialist, like
Howe. He was a writer, on his way to becoming a personal essayist and
memoirist, driven to deploy his own experience as the lens through
which to discover something big and necessary about the world in
which he lived. For him it was personal all the way down.[8] It was an
Oedipal struggle with his teachers and mentors, whose vast intelligence
and authority threatened to leave him no room to individuate. It was a
disappointment with his contemporaries, that they weren't Fitzgerald or
Hemingway, hadn't written his generation into eternity. Most acutely,
it was an interrogation of himself: Had he failed to struggle manfully

enough toward a new synthesis? Was he, for all his sound and fury, just
as guilty as the rest of his contemporaries of embracing the call to maturity with a passivity unbecoming someone of his unadvanced years?

"The Young Generation of U.S. Intellectuals" didn't say anything
radically new on these topics from what Podhoretz had said before.
But it was him saying it all in one place, with a decisiveness he hadn't
exhibited before. Podhoretz wasn't yet prepared to stake his claim as
the prophetic or novelistic voice of his generation, but at a minimum
he would be the man who would give it some borders so that such a
voice, when it was ready to manifest, would know where to begin. It
was a brash enough move, of the kind Podhoretz had been making
since he arrived on the scene, but it was also uncharacteristically vulnerable. Until that moment he had submerged his generation-defining
urges almost exclusively into the identification of how other people,
novelists mostly, had failed in one way or the other to get the job done.
In this essay he was at last owning up to his own desire to answer
the question he'd been dancing with ever since he began publishing
reviews and essays in the elite intellectual magazines and journals of
New York. He was also, and this would be a key dynamic in his political evolution over the next decade and a half, putting an enormous
amount of pressure on the answers he came up with. His essayistic
commitments weren't just empirical observations, or statements of abstract philosophical conviction. They were enactments of his identity.
If they seemed right, when tested against reality, they would point the
way toward what kind of man he should become next. If they proved
wrong, he might be utterly lost.

In this case his most salient argument was this: His generation had
been born too late. They hadn't been old enough during the Depression and the war, the two great character-forging catastrophes of the
age. As a consequence they'd been deprived, like seedlings with insuf-
ficient light, of the energy they needed to flourish. How they had developed under these conditions was understandable, almost admirable
in its way. They had listened attentively to their parents, studied hard

in school, gone to college, served their time in the military (some had seen combat in Korea; others had passed the time in West Germany, as Podhoretz had). They had read a great deal. They'd gotten good, solid, responsible jobs. They'd married young and seriously (Podhoretz in 1956, to Midge Decter, who had two young daughters from her first marriage). They'd stayed away from radical actions and utopian delusions, and had tried instead to find some grace, some quiet beauty, in "man's struggle to achieve freedom *through* submission to conditions."

If all this seemed rather pale when compared to the lives that their parents and grandparents had lived, then who, demanded Podhoretz, was anyone else to judge?

No one but themselves, was the answer he was finally ready to give by 1957. It was reasonable to play it safe when you were living, as he and his generation-mates were, in the aftermath of total war, under the shadow of nuclear annihilation. But a reasonable life was not the same thing as a life worth living, and in the gap between the two lay their challenge.

"It would be a mistake to accept the sobriety and composure of the young generation at face value," he wrote. "The truth is that this is a restless generation, and as it grows older it gets more and more restless; it is beginning to feel cheated of its youth. . . . Since this is a generation that willed itself from childhood directly into adulthood, it still has its adolescence to go through—for a man can never skip adolescence, he can only postpone it. And something very wonderful may come about when a whole generation in its late thirties breaks loose and decides to take a swim in the Plaza fountain in the middle of the night."[9]

From then on, his self-appointed quest as a writer and editor would be to understand what this something wonderful would be, and most of all who the writers would be who would give it voice. Who would have the audacity to look the Bomb in the eye and say, yes, I have to reckon with you, but not from my knees? How would they see clearly the civilizational threat of communism while refusing to always and in every case reduce all matters of global politics to *which side are you on*? How would they absorb the lessons of the 1930s, navigate around the seductions of utopian thinking, but nonetheless stride forward with the conviction that there was grand thinking yet to be done, that Americans could fight to wrest more from the world than a long, cold peace and the shallow compensations of material prosperity?

Podhoretz's imperative, too, was to figure out what his particular role would be in this return of the repressed adolescence of his generation. He had to be bold in pushing past some of the orthodoxies of his elders, but without losing the real wisdom embedded in them, or alienating the people to whom he owed debts of loyalty. He had to go out and grab the world by its lapels—experience things, not just read about them in books—but still care for his wife and daughters, honor the oaths he'd made to them, and pay the rent on their rather sizable apartment on the Upper West Side of Manhattan. He had to figure out exactly what kind of writer he was supposed to be.

He also, and this was no small thing, had to figure out what role *Commentary* would play in the quest upon which he was embarking. By 1957 it was no longer the place it had been when Elliot Cohen, its founder, editor, and guiding star, had first laid hands upon Podhoretz in 1953 and promised him a job. Robert Warshow, who'd been Podhoretz's best friend at the magazine, was gone, the victim of a heart attack. Cohen was in a psychiatric institution, victim of a depression so severe he was willing to submit to electroconvulsive therapy in the hopes of recovery. The brothers Clement and Martin Greenberg were in temporary charge, but were showing neither the vision nor the sense of entitlement to lead *Commentary* in a bold new direction. They also didn't like Podhoretz much, and were inclined to thwart most efforts he made to use the magazine as the vehicle of his own editorial desire to innovate or provoke.[10]

So Podhoretz was in a complicated position. He had a Grail for which to quest. But he didn't know where it was, what precisely it would look like if he found it, or whether he would possess the purity of purpose to turn it to his ends if ever he found it. And he had a lot of bills. And some enemies. So he wrote, edited, and struggled, hoping that through some combination of the three he would find what he was looking for.

Podhoretz was at home one evening, in the fall of 1958, when he got a phone call. On the other end of the line was a woman who said she was Jack Kerouac's girlfriend.

"I'm here with Allen and Jack who would like you to come see them tonight," she said.[11]

For a brief moment Podhoretz thought (hoped) it was a practical joke. Over the past year he had written three essays on the Beats, each one arriving at more certainty than the last that they weren't the Grail he was looking for. His culminating piece, published in the spring issue of *Partisan Review*, had been brutal. Not only were Kerouac, Allen Ginsberg, and the rest mostly bad writers, who'd written bad stories and books and poems, they were bad people, champions of dangerous impulses.

"The spirit of hipsterism and the Beat Generation strikes me," he'd written, "as the same spirit which animates the young savages in leather jackets who have been running amok in the last few years with their switchblades and zip guns. . . . Even the relatively mild ethos of Kerouac's books can spill over easily into brutality, for there is a suppressed cry in those books: Kill the intellectuals who can talk coherently, kill the people who can sit still for five minutes at a time, kill those incomprehensible characters who are capable of getting seriously involved with a woman, a job, a cause."

A powwow with Ginsberg, with whom he'd been friendly back in college, and Kerouac, whom he'd abused in print, was such a perfectly awful thing to contemplate that it seemed to Podhoretz it almost had to have been cooked up by a friend.

"But then Ginsberg got on the line, and the minute I recognized his voice and realized that this was no joke, practical or otherwise, I caught myself desperately fishing for some graceful way to avoid what was sure to be a very unpleasant encounter."

He was unwilling to be the coward, however, and Ginsberg was insistent. So he agreed. He'd make the trip down from his place on the Upper West Side to the Village, and hear them out. Before he went, though, he had to contemplate the state of his person. He needed a shave, and his clothes were all rumpled and ratty. No good. He couldn't show up to the battlefield kitted out like the enemy.

So he shaved, looked around at what else was available to wear, and remembered one of the lines from Ginsberg's "Howl,"[12] a poem Podhoretz had actually found quite impressive when he'd first encountered it back in 1956. Ginsberg had written, of the best minds of his generation, that they were:

> *burned alive in their innocent flannel suits on Madison Avenue amid blasts of leaden verse & the tanked-up clatter of the iron regiments of fashion & the nitroglycerine shrieks of the fairies of advertising & the mustard gas of sinister intelligent editors, or were run down by the drunken taxicabs of Absolute Reality.*

Podhoretz wasn't certain that Ginsberg had been thinking of him, in speaking of those *sinister intelligent editors*, but he thought he might have been an inspiration. And the poem wasn't quite saying that such editors would be wearing flannel suits. But it didn't have to be precise if you already had a taste for self-dramatization, not to mention the necessary suit. So he suited up, three-piece Brooks Brothers suit, tie, and everything, and headed downtown.

From the moment Podhoretz got to the apartment, the two men went at each other. First they argued over whether Podhoretz would smoke pot with Ginsberg. Podhoretz had smoked it a few times before, but he wasn't into it, and in any case he wanted his wits about him. So he refused. Then they got to the meat of the matter.

"All night long he hectored and harangued me for my stupid

failure to recognize both Kerouac's genius and his," remembered Podhoretz, "and the more I fought back, the harder he tried to make me see how insensitive I was being. It was I, he kept railing, who was the know-nothing, not they."

The argument they had—for four hours, by Podhoretz's later reckoning—was a multileveled one. It was literary: Podhoretz had no time for the style of the Beats. He thought they'd fallen victim to a spurious notion that the way to evoke the feeling of spontaneity and vitality on the page was to write spontaneously, from the gut, without care or precision.[13]

Ginsberg thought Podhoretz had shit for ears—had no feel for language himself so naturally was unable to perceive that Kerouac, in particular, was using spontaneous-seeming language to achieve subtle lyrical effects.[14]

The argument was also sociological. Podhoretz granted that the Beats had perceived, correctly, the torpor of 1950s America, but rather than rigorously applying their literary imaginations to the project of generating new sources of vitality, they had simply rejected it all, thrown in with "primitivism, instinct, energy, 'blood.'" At its worst, by Podhoretz's lights, this was a kind of proto-fascism, the glorification of violence for the sake of its dynamism and clarifying force. At its least bad it was a celebration of the infantile and adolescent in American culture.

Ginsberg saw in Podhoretz just another defender of the bourgeois status quo, afraid of the liberatory id of the American psyche. He was also a herd-minded member of a literally intellectual establishment that had been too stodgy to give Ginsberg his due as a poet.

The argument was also very personal. Podhoretz's first piece of published work, a long undergraduate poem, had been edited and published by Ginsberg when they were both at Columbia. Podhoretz had been Ginsberg's successor in the role of favored student of Lionel Trilling. After college they'd run in many of the same literary and intellectual circles, and had remained aware of each other. More than anything they were both vastly ambitious, rather narcissistic, moderately insecure Jewish-American young men of the same generation bent on using words not just as a vehicle with which to understand themselves but, if at all possible, as the hammer and chisel with which to carve out spaces in the culture that corresponded rather precisely to their particular projects. And those projects, because they began from such similar origins before going off in such different directions, couldn't help but bring the two men into a kind of intimate conflict with each other.

And so they went back and forth, back and forth, for hours. Ginsberg was for homosexuality; Podhoretz was against. Ginsberg said that middle-class values should be exploded once and for all. Podhoretz thought they were in need of moderate revision. Ginsberg was a drug experimenter; Podhoretz liked to drink (too much, as he would later realize), but was suspicious of drugs. Ginsberg was a literary rebel who craved acceptance from the establishment. Podhoretz had been anointed by the establishment but feared that its approval was more of a curse than a blessing. Ginsberg was a poet, Podhoretz a literary critic. Ginsberg, though he was older by a few years, was spiritually at home on the far side of the radical cultural break that was coming. Podhoretz, it would turn out, was born both too late and too early. He heard the call of the sixties, but he would never be at home there. In his heart he was a child of the 1950s. At his most adventurous he would be a creature of the early sixties, whose vision of the good life was some kind of fusion of New York intellectual–style depth, moderate Left politics, and Rat Pack insouciance.

"Inevitably, then, and along with everything else, it was myself I was defending," remembered Podhoretz. ". . . As against the law-abiding life I had chosen of a steady job and marriage and children, he conjured up a world of complete freedom from the limits imposed by such grim responsibilities. It was a world that promised endless erotic possibility together with the excitements of an expanded consciousness constantly open to new dimensions of being: more adventure, more sex, more intensity, more *life*. God knows that as a young man full of energy and curiosity, and not altogether averse to taking risks, I was tempted by all this. God knows too that there were moments of resentment at the burdens I had seen fit to shoulder, moments when I felt cheated and when I dreamed of breaking out of limits I had imposed upon myself. Yet at the same time I was repelled by Ginsberg's world."[15]

With the stakes so high, no quarter could be given, and on they went, past midnight, until they ran out of things to throw at each other. As Podhoretz left, Ginsberg threw out one last sally: "We'll get you through your children!"

A decade later that threat would prove one of the fulcrums around which Podhoretz would execute his hard pivot to the right. At that moment, though, in the fall of 1958, Ginsberg just sounded grandiose to Podhoretz's ears. The Beats, after all, weren't the problem. They were an overreaction to it, a symptom of it. They didn't want to just take a swim in the Plaza fountain at midnight; they were so consumed by emptiness they felt they had to have sex in it, with other men, while high, in order to approximate the feeling of being alive.

Podhoretz's encounter with Ginsberg and Kerouac did nothing to change his mind about the basic absence at the center of American culture and society, which was of an authentic vitality and passion, tempered by intellect. If anything the encounter highlighted just how challenging an equation he was trying to solve. The Beats were too hot. The New York intellectuals were too cold. But what was just right?

He searched and searched, occasionally identifying regions of interesting geological activity, but what the search revealed more than anything was how strained, by this point, Podhoretz's project was. He'd done yeoman's work as a writer articulating the impasse at which the culture now found itself: aware that maturity alone was a hollow thing in the absence of a passionate commitment for which it was the tempering agent, but lacking in any obvious such commitments to make, and thus adrift.[16] Now, however, instead of throwing himself into the world in search of his own material, in the hopes that perhaps he would be the one to bring back the fire, Podhoretz reacted not with the instinct of a writer but of an editor. He wanted to be the guy who found the guy.

Unfortunately he had no outlet in which to do that. After three increasingly miserable years at *Commentary* he'd finally quit, in the fall of 1958, when Elliot Cohen's long-awaited return to the magazine hadn't led to a restoration of direction and authority but instead to a further exacerbation of the tensions. After quitting he'd been hired by an old Columbia classmate, Jason Epstein, to be an editor at Anchor Books, but within weeks Epstein had left Anchor, and Podhoretz went with him. Other semi-jobs followed, including a joint venture in children's publishing with Epstein, but nothing that really scratched the itch Podhoretz was feeling.

So he did what he could, which was write, with complications. He got a contract to do a Big Book on twentieth-century American nonfiction, but gave up after only one chapter (on Edmund Wilson).[17] He persuaded his publisher that a big book on postwar fiction would be just as good, and the publisher agreed, but Podhoretz struggled with that one as well. Meanwhile, he kept on with the kind of writing he'd been doing from the beginning, essays and reviews, but with the ambivalence turned up an additional notch or two. The result was a period of well-written, intermittently penetrating, but fundamentally conflicted writing that was only half about the actual work he was assessing. The other half seemed to be an effort to reverse engineer, from what he thought his subjects had failed to do, some aspect of that new thing yet waiting to be born, which tended to sound in practice a great deal like the sprawling literatures of the eighteenth and nineteenth centuries that Podhoretz had revered as a student. So history, politics, and culture had to breathe holistically through the story, the setting, and the characters. At the core of the work there had to be a commitment to some vision of life that was religious in its intensity but not religious in its content. It had to be conditioned by intellect, but not stifled by it. There should be a searing darkness locked in struggle with a triumphant joy and light. There should be equanimity and grace. And there should be a recognition of the excruciating, overflowing tensions of American life and culture, the dialectical struggles between abundance and loneliness, optimism and anxiety, idealism and violence.

Toward the end of the decade, at one of the high-octane dinner parties that constituted the main circuit of the New York intellectual scene, Podhoretz finally met the writer who would, more than anyone or anything else, lead him into the 1960s.

"Mailer eyed me," he later recalled, "with a leer that mixed menace with irony when we encountered each other in Lillian Hellman's living room, and he immediately assumed the boxer's crouch that I was to learn he loved to affect whenever an argument of any kind threatened to erupt."[18]

Podhoretz had seen Norman Mailer once before, from a distance, at a rally for Henry Wallace's presidential campaign in 1948. Podhoretz was then a college student and Mailer was fresh off the extraordinary success of his debut novel *The Naked and the Dead*. In the intervening years Podhoretz had remained aware of Mailer, but until very recently had felt no need to engage further with him or his work. Mailer's novels could be impressive, according to the New York intellectual consensus, but they were too middlebrow to really matter. And the one Mailer essay to which Podhoretz had paid any attention, "The White Negro," seemed to him like a rather ludicrous effort to lay some intellectual tracks beneath the so-called "ideas" the Beats were riding.

"A stench of fear has come out of every pore of American life," Mailer had written, "and we suffer from a collective failure of nerve. . . . [T]he only life-giving answer is to accept the terms of death, to live with death as immediate danger, to divorce oneself from society, to exist without roots, to set out on that uncharted journey into the rebellious imperatives of the self."[19]

To Podhoretz this was underwhelming, and he'd said so in print. When he decided to write a book on the American novel after the war, however, an obvious corollary followed. He'd have to reckon more seriously with Mailer. *The Naked and the Dead*, whatever one thought of it, was indisputably one of the major novels that had been written about the war, and in general Mailer, whatever one thought of his answers, was someone who fearlessly, compulsively asked the big questions. So Podhoretz had set to work, reading through all the Mailer he'd ignored before. What he'd found in there hadn't just surprised him in its quality. It had exhilarated him in what it suggested about Mailer's potential. Here was not just a very good, if uneven, writer, but potentially a great one, and maybe something of a prophet as well. That would be the gist of the piece that Podhoretz was in the process of writing when he met his subject at Hellman's dinner party.

"If I had not been armed with the secret of my forthcoming article, I would almost certainly have tried to steer clear of Mailer that evening," Podhoretz later wrote. ". . . Yet even if I had tried to avoid Mailer that night at Lillian's, it would have availed me naught. Having figured out who I was even before we were introduced, he accosted me—skipping the social pleasantries and getting right down to business—with the inevitable charge of having misunderstood and misrepresented ['The White Negro']. I have no clear memory of what I said in my own defense, but I do remember cutting the argument short by telling him that I was working on a long article about his whole body of work and that maybe he ought to hold his fire until he had had a chance to read it."[20]

Mailer shot back that he didn't need to wait. He knew already what Podhoretz was going to say.

"You wanna bet?" said Podhoretz.

Mailer accepted the bet, and with that the friendship was born. That friendship, Podhoretz's biographer would later write, "was the most important one of his life from the late fifties through the late sixties." The two men drank together. They made the rounds of dinner parties together. They argued endlessly with each other. They almost had a threesome with Mailer's girlfriend. They pushed each other to be more than they were.

Some of what attracted the men to each other was instrumental. In Podhoretz, Mailer saw an ally within the ranks of the literary establishment. In Mailer, Podhoretz saw the possibility of the writer/figure for whom he'd been waiting. More than that, though, each man found in the other the things that tend to make for genuine friendship under any circumstances. They were about the same age. They were bilingual in the same two languages: the *hochdeutsch* of the New York intellectuals and the brash Brooklynese of their youths. They shared the same ambition to fuse those two languages, and ways of being, into a new language and orientation that would redeem American literature and culture. They loved to argue. And each thought the other was full of shit in precisely the right ways.[21]

This was true, in particular, of how Podhoretz saw Mailer. Even before they met, and then all the more once they were friends, Podhoretz was coming to believe that Mailer himself was perhaps the single most important text to read if one wanted to make sense of the subterranean vibrations of American culture. So even, or especially, when Mailer's writing fell short, when he said stupid things, when he made a fool of himself, it wasn't the failure that was important, but what that failure pointed toward, which was the next phase in his evolution, which might prove to be the next phase in the evolution of the national soul.[22]

What was so exciting about Mailer was that rather than inherit the wisdom accumulated by the past few decades of life on the American Left, as Podhoretz had done so precociously, Mailer ran himself through the gauntlet of earning it, "as though it were up to him to create the world anew over and over again in his own experience."[23] So although in theory *The Naked and the Dead* was a novel about World War II, about life and existence and masculinity and death and all those things that war novels are supposed to be about, in Podhoretz's construction it became the arena in which Mailer pitted his politics at the tail end of the 1940s, which were a shallow liberalism that was naïvely sympathetic toward communism, against his intuitive, imaginative antennae for life, which were too sensitive to be taken in by the formulae of either liberals or communists.

From there Mailer moved on, in *Barbary Shore*, to wrestle with 1930s-style Trotskyism. Perhaps what was needed was the marriage of radical will to revolutionary politics? But no, that was a dead end, too. Which brought Mailer, finally, to where he was when he and Podhoretz became friends, at roughly the same awareness of the Great American Cultural Impasse that Podhoretz had been lamenting, but with a great deal more reckless willingness to propose, and act out, possible solutions. In his 1955 novel *Deer Park*, and his 1957 essay "The White Negro," his answer was that the man in the gray flannel suit had to invert the calculation he had made. It was probably true that, with the world so big and complicated, and with the Bomb so scary, the private self was the only domain left in which one could exert real agency. But one didn't achieve moral depth or freedom through the tragic acceptance of the limits of politics in the age of the atom bomb, argued Mailer. Instead you did it through an existentialist acceptance of the meaninglessness of all life under such conditions, and a consequent willingness to just fuck and be Hip.

"The only Hip morality . . . is to do what one feels whenever and wherever it is possible," wrote Mailer, ". . . to be engaged in one primal battle: to open the limits of the possible for oneself, for oneself alone because that is one's need."[24]

As philosophy, for Podhoretz, this was mostly just the bushwa the Beats were offering, with some highfalutin philosophizing as window dressing. But Mailer was a special case. It wasn't what he was saying that was so important; it was how he arrived there, and where he might be arriving next. He would surely work his way through the problems with this position, as he had the last few, and from there he'd move on to the next phase. At some point, if all that processing never got him anywhere worth going, if it turned out that he could discard bad paradigms but never develop a good one to put in their place, then Mailer would have to be held accountable for just being wrong, over and over again.

At least for the moment, though, when it seemed as though something big was lurking just around the corner, it was worth giving him the rope to possibly wrassle it into sight.

"Mailer was so ignorant in so many ways," remembered Podhoretz, "but I came to admire that he would take nothing on authority. He had to feel it in his own nervous system before he would accept it. His ignorance in that sense was a virtue."[25]

The imperative, for Podhoretz, was to keep his eyes on Mailer as he went about his greatness-seeking, and, if the opportunity presented itself, to seek out some of his own.

In May of 1959, Elliot Cohen committed suicide. He'd never fully recovered from the despair that had led him to institutionalize himself in the first place, and when he'd returned to the magazine in 1958 it had been as a shadow of his former self. By the end he was so consumed by feelings of inadequacy that he once jokingly asked a friend whether he might be interested in hiring him as an office boy. It was a shock but not a great surprise when Cohen was found dead by his wife in their apartment, having suffocated himself with a plastic bag.[26]

Immediately, the American Jewish Committee (AJC) began looking for a successor, ideally someone who could continue to do for the cause of Jews what Cohen in his prime had done so marvelously, which was to use the magazine as a vehicle both to assimilate its Jewish readership to the main currents in American culture and to weave Jewishness—or at least a very highbrow version of it—more deeply into the American genetic code.

It was a tall task, and the AJC included in its search different kinds of talents within the broader New York intellectual ecosystem. There were men who were primarily editors, like Martin Greenberg, who'd been handling the magazine during the final year of Cohen's life, and Irving Kristol, an ex-Trotskyist who'd been an editor at *Commentary* and had cofounded the British journal *Encounter*. There were the more flamboyant critics, like Clement Greenberg and Leslie Fiedler. There was Daniel Bell, a systemic thinker who was finishing up the sociology dissertation that would become his book *The End of Ideology: On the Exhaustion of Political Ideas in the Fifties*, and the elegant Alfred Kazin, who'd made his name both as a literary critic and as an autobiographer. And then there was Podhoretz, who was some of a bit of a lot of these things, as well as the youngest candidate by a good decade.[27]

When the word went out that the search was on, Podhoretz was ambivalent. His time at the magazine had ended rather miserably, and it didn't feel like a good idea to eagerly put himself out there as wanting the job, exposing himself to more rejection. But he knew he might be a contender. But he didn't think he wanted the job anyway, but in truth, he later realized, he wanted it so badly he couldn't bear the thought of trying and not getting it. He also didn't want his old nemesis, Martin Greenberg, to get it. So what he did, amidst this jumble of conflicted feelings, was to wait and keep his eye on things. He also spun out what he was sure was just a silly little revenge fantasy of how events might proceed, which was to have the job offered to him, over Greenberg, and then to turn it down to complete the humiliation.

Extraordinarily, events moved in precisely the direction Podhoretz had fantasized they would. Greenberg stayed in the picture as the default candidate if no one better could be found, but the AJC made it clear through their actions that they were hoping for someone better. Kazin, Bell, and Kristol declined to apply. The job was tentatively offered to Leslie Fiedler, who was receptive but withdrew from consideration after the process dragged on too long. Then Podhoretz was approached, and since he was sure he didn't want the job, he told them so. The search committee persisted. *Would he at least sit down with a few of them, informally, have a chat?*

"I would and I did, around a lunch table at a private club, where I held forth for over an hour about the history of *Commentary*, the role it had once played in American culture, and the role it could conceivably play again. I could sense as I talked that the three members of the committee who were present at that lunch were completely sold, but again

I coolly indicated—with a shrewdness of which I would have been utterly incapable had I been consciously insincere or making an effort to be shrewd—that the job did not interest me."

His interviewers were impressed, and asked if he'd be willing to meet with the rest of the search committee. Again he met, and again he dazzled with the depth and breadth of his thinking about *Commentary*, and again it became clear to him during the course of this conversation that the job, amazingly, was his for the asking. But once again he said he didn't want it.

"Was there any way of persuading me to reconsider? Not really. Not really? Well, I supposed I would be strongly tempted if the right terms were offered. What were the right terms? A completely free hand, an agreement to let me make the magazine more general and less Jewish in emphasis . . . and (this said shyly) a large salary—perhaps even as much as twenty thousand a year? But of course I was only speculating. Of course, but would I, nevertheless, be willing to meet with the executive director of the American Jewish Committee to discuss those terms with him?"[28]

And so it went, until Podhoretz had an offer before him that was vastly better than what he might have gotten had he realized, from the first, how badly he wanted the job. With the exception of the salary—he was offered a few thousand less than he'd asked, but it was still twice what he was making at the time—his demands were wholly met. The magazine would be his to mold. He just had to say yes.

Even still Podhoretz was ready to say no. Or he thought he was. His friends were all advising him to turn it down, and their arguments made sense: He *was* too young. He hadn't finished his book yet. *Commentary* had been great in its day but its day was past. It was too great a risk. And so on. There were a lot of reasons, it seemed, to turn down the job.

As the day to give his decision to the AJC approached, however, the part of him that wanted nothing more in the world than to edit *Commentary* rose up in rebellion. It was true that becoming editor would get in the way of finishing his book, but he wasn't finishing it anyway. It was true that he was young, but didn't that mean it was a particularly good time to take a risk? It was true that *Commentary* was down, but that didn't mean it couldn't get back up. And it was true that he hadn't been happy when he was at *Commentary*, but not because he didn't like editing. In fact he'd loved the actual work of editing; the problem had been the people he was working for. If he took the job, though, everyone would be working for him, and the people he didn't like he could fire. And he'd be making far more money than he ever had before. And he'd have a magazine at his disposal to do the fundamentally editorial work, of being the guy who found the guy, that he'd been trying to squeeze into the square hole of his writing for the last two years.

"Once again I went over the reasons for my decision to turn down the job, simultaneously recalling to mind everything my friends had said in support of that decision; and as I did so, the conviction that we were all stark, staring, raving mad began to grow in me, exploding finally into one of those furious revelations which seem to illuminate the whole universe in a single great clue. Why had I been treating myself, and being treated by everyone around me, as though I were a sickly, delicate child who would contract a mortal illness if he so much as exposed himself to the air? . . . What were we all afraid of? What terrible dangers were we protecting ourselves against? Were magazines thrown up for grabs every day of the week that so extraordinary an opportunity should be tossed away with such smug complacency?"[29]

To pass up the opportunity, he concluded, would be to act precisely the risk-averse 1950s man he'd been critiquing for years. Put in those terms, it seemed absurd. So instead of saying no, the next day, Podhoretz said yes. And suddenly he was the soon-to-be editor of *Commentary*. And he was thrilled.

In January of 1960 Martin Greenberg edited and put out the last issue of *Commentary* that would list Elliot Cohen as editor-in-chief. As had often been the case in the years of Cohen's absence and decline, the January issue was a good but not very exciting thing. It included a British foreign affairs man writing about the consequences of the spread of nuclear arms to nations beyond the two major powers. There was an excerpt from the novel-in-progress of a Canadian writer whose greatest contribution to the cause of world literature would prove to be his *shtupping* of Saul Bellow's wife Sondra, the discovery of which fueled Bellow in writing *Herzog*.[30] An associate professor of Rabbinics at Hebrew Union College investigated how it was, and what it portended, that Hannukah had risen from its modest scriptural roots to become a major Jewish-American holiday. And so on. Lots of good stuff. Some boring stuff. No urgency. It was a magazine with virtue and intelligence but no sense of mission anymore.

The February 1960 issue was something quite different. Gone were most of the associate professors and mid-tier critics who'd been filling the magazine's middle pages. Back in force, as a result of Podhoretz's aggressive recruitment efforts, were the old gang, who'd been quietly migrating away from the magazine over the last few years. Lionel Trilling, who'd last appeared in *Commentary* in 1956, was back with a moving tribute to his friend Elliot Cohen. Irving Kristol reviewed a book on Mark Twain and southern humor. Arthur Koestler wrote about an Indian holy man. Notably absent was Norman Mailer, whom Podhoretz couldn't quite bring himself to publish yet (it would be another two years). But Mailer's latest book was reviewed affectionately by F. W. Dupee, an old ex-Trotskyist who'd been laying it down in New York intellectual circles since the days of James Burnham's *Symposium*.

Most dramatic by far was "Youth in the Organized Society," a long essay by Paul Goodman, a polymath writer and radical who'd been bouncing around the margins of the scene for decades. It was culled from Goodman's soon-to-be-released book, which Podhoretz had first encountered in excerpt form a few months before, in *Dissent*, when he was hustling to find the right content for his first issue. Podhoretz hadn't been terribly impressed by the bit he'd seen in *Dissent*, but he was intrigued enough that he called Goodman and asked him to send over the manuscript.

"It was called *Growing Up Absurd* and had been rejected, he told me with no apparent bitterness, by nineteen different publishers. I could hardly believe my eyes when I started reading the book. It was everything I wanted for the new *Commentary*, and more: it was the very incarnation of the new spirit I had been hoping would be at work in the world, as it had been at work in me."

Podhoretz immediately called his friend Jason Epstein, who was an editor at Random House, and told him that he needed to read the book. That it was going to be huge.

" 'Goodman?' he said skeptically, 'that has-been?' But I insisted that he read the book immediately—which he did, that very night in my apartment. . . . Goodman had a contract the next day."[31]

Although it was the full book that would become a cultural touchstone, and a seminal text of the New Left, the grounds for its success were laid by *Commentary*, where big chunks of it ran in three installments in Podhoretz's first three issues as editor: "Youth in the Organized Society," "The Calling of American Youth," and "In Search of Community."[32]

In later years Podhoretz would use his publication of Goodman, and a few other radical or radical-ish writers, as evidence of how far he and the magazine had gone to the left in the first half or so of the decade. And Goodman was indeed a radical, as was his critique of what was wrong with America and his proposals for what was required to fix it.[33] But the truth about Podhoretz as an editor, which was apparent even in the issues in which Goodman appeared, was that he was left-liberal in what was becoming a radical moment, and he was vital and flexible enough in his politics to be open to many of the currents of utopian exuberance and radical critique that were gathering force during this period. And he was a true editor, interested more in sponsoring insistent, restless curiosity and intelligence than in enforcing a systematic ideology.[34]

The truth, too, was that Podhoretz just didn't feel most of his politics terribly deeply. He believed in the stuff that good left-liberals of the time tended to believe in, but absent was that sense of incompleteness in the world that smoldered in his more political friends. What he cared about passionately was having a magazine that was alive to the world, that found its way to where the action was, had interesting things to say, and the right writers to say them.

That passion *felt* radical to him, particularly when he let it lead him and the magazine out beyond the borders of the discourse he'd inherited. But in practice, for readers, what it meant was that on most of the great matters and movements of the day—civil rights, the student movement, the nuclear arms race, the early stirrings of American involvement in Vietnam, the early stirrings of the sexual revolution, the rise of youth culture and the counterculture, the emergence of the New Left and the New Right—*Commentary* was there. It was often there with a fetish for nuance and complexity that was only slightly dialed down from its Cohen-era settings, and thus could seem out of tune with the moral and cultural melodies of what it was covering. But just as often, and more important, the classically trained New York intellectuals whom Podhoretz set loose on the sixties did the kind of work they were better equipped than nearly anyone else to do, which was to bring their experience of political and intellectual life on the Left to bear on the latest round of dramatic social and political upheaval driven by, or in reaction to, the energies of the Left.

It was exhilarating for Podhoretz. He loved being an editor-in-chief, and was good at it. *Commentary* published many of the best writers, was read by the important people, was saying important things. Advertising dollars and subscriptions went up and up, as did his own shares on what he would later call "the stock market report on reputations" that was issued every morning in New York, after the data from the previous night's cocktail parties had been tallied.

"It is invisible, but those who have eyes to see can read it," he wrote. "Did so-and-so have dinner at Jacqueline Kennedy's apartment last night? Up five points. Was so-and-so *not* invited by the Lowells to meet the latest visiting Russian poet? Down one-eighth. Did so-and-so's book get nominated for the National Book Award? Up two and five-eighths. Did *Partisan Review* neglect to ask so-and-so to participate in a symposium? Down two."[35]

There was no doubt but that Podhoretz's stock was rising. He was profiled in important magazines. He was now one of those people reporters called when they needed a pithy quote on some issue or trend that lived at the intersection of culture and politics where his *Commentary* had set up shop so authoritatively. He was invited to conferences and symposia. He lunched with important writers, and was called to Washington to consult with White House staffers and liberal congressmen. He became gossip buddies for a while with Jackie Kennedy, who would trade him D.C. dirt in exchange for Manhattan dirt, and who asked him to assemble her guest list when she wanted to host a dinner party for the cream of New York literary society.

Podhoretz had even lucked into an unexpected shift in the cultural attitude toward Jews, and in particular toward the kind of brainy, edgy Jews he and his friends happened to be, with their promiscuous ability to do deep-drilling analyses of whatever aspect of American life and culture you put before them. The vogue for Jewish writers and intellectuals became so intense—their bylines in the major magazines and journals swarming so thick—that it even provoked occasional complaints from gentile writers that they were suffering exclusion by virtue of their non-Jewishness. To be the editor of *Commentary*, one of the command centers of the new "Jewish Establishment," was to be something indeed.

The apotheosis of all this good fortune came early in Podhoretz's tenure as editor when he was invited to an exclusive retreat at Paradise Island, a private island in the Caribbean owned by A&P supermarket heir Huntington Hartford. Podhoretz had recently been recruited to write a monthly books column for a glossy magazine funded by Hartford, and the trip was organized, ostensibly, to further the magazine's

mission by bringing together cultural, intellectual, and political luminaries from the United States and Latin America. In practice it was a
five-day ensconcement in luxury beyond anything Podhoretz had ever
experienced. It became an almost holy experience for him, a sanctifica-
tion of his status as one of the elect.

"Something snapped in me the minute I set foot on the island, and
for the next five days I felt as a man is supposed to have felt before being
expelled from the original Paradise called Eden. . . . What did it? I think
it was that Paradise Island represented a realization of the fantasy I had
always carried about in my soul but had never been daring enough to
picture in vividly concrete detail: *This* was what Success looked like, all
its various components brought together in one dazzling display, and
the look of it made me drunker than all the gallons of rum I consumed
that week. This was what it meant to be rich: to sleep in a huge bright
room with a terrace overlooking an incredibly translucent green sea, to
stretch one's arms out idly by the side of a swimming pool and have two
white-coated servants vie for the privilege of depositing a Bloody Mary
into one's hand, to sign checks (which we had to do, though of course
we would never have to pay them) without giving money a second
thought. All around me, too, was the evidence of what it meant to be
famous (for the North American delegation was mostly composed of
people whose fame far out-weighed my own meager measure of it): it
meant that a serene self-assurance had been injected into the spirit to
combat the uncertainties and anxieties which, to be sure, remained, but
no longer had the field to themselves."[36]

Podhoretz's demons didn't just float away with the gentle currents of
the Caribbean. He was gratified by his success, but nagged by the sense
that there were enemies out there, and friends, who resented it and
envied him. In his dark moments he feared they had a point, that he
hadn't yet done anything significant enough—that is, hadn't written
anything weighty enough—to justify the rewards he was reaping.

He had a rollicking social life, but there was a flicker at the edge of those pleasures as well. He boozed to excess. He dipped his toe in the drug scene, then pulled it out very quickly. With sexual fidelity he wavered, maybe succumbed.[37]

In general he struggled, as he so often had in the past, with finding the right balance between his own desires and his deep and rather tortured sense of indebtedness to his friends, family, and the political intellectual community in which he was nurtured. And since the channels at his disposal through which to play out these struggles had multiplied so dramatically, there were inevitably some eruptions, and blockages. His ability to produce his own stuff would suffer for a while, as he discovered he didn't quite know what to say now that he was no longer writing through the restlessness he'd felt in the 1950s. He published essays and promoted perspectives that he knew would provoke friends, but then felt terribly betrayed when they reacted with anger. He fought with himself over what faithfulness to Decter meant, and he would write, later, of the enormous relief he felt when his libido was no longer abetted by his intellectual fealty to the naughty sexual politics of writers like Mailer.

Yet even in this realm of conflicted loyalties, where Podhoretz had the capacity to torment himself so thoroughly, the early and mid-1960s were more fulsome than frustrating. He was struggling, but who wasn't? It was a moment when the whole culture was teetering on the edge of dramatic change. And as it happened, he was the editor of a magazine at a moment when his inner conflicts were symptomatic of larger structural tensions, and he exploited this consonance brilliantly, following his instincts to where the action was, deploying writers to the scene as the instruments of his sublimation. As for his own writing, it would be in this realm, too, where loyalties clashed, that he would discover something authentic and powerful to say.

In the fall of 1961, Podhoretz asked James Baldwin to write an essay for him for *Commentary*. The assigned topic was the Nation of Islam and its leader, Elijah Muhammad. The Nation of Islam had been around for decades, preaching its message of black separatism and white devilry, but for most of that time the white devils hadn't paid much mind. Then the culture caught up with the Nation, and vice versa. Blacks, through the vehicle of the civil rights movement, were wielding political power in a way they never had before, and whites, even many of those who supported the movement, were unsettled by the change. Within the civil rights movement itself there were hints of a turn toward more militancy. There was the rise of Malcolm X, Elijah Muhammad's brilliant and charismatic lieutenant. And there was a more widespread feeling of change in the air, a sense, which Podhoretz himself had been articulating for a few years, that something new was bubbling up.

Baldwin, one of the black writers who fit most comfortably within the New York intellectual orbit, had already written a number of important essays for *Commentary*, and he also, as it turned out, had a particular interest in the Nation of Islam.

"I discovered that he too had grown interested in the Muslims and especially in Malcolm X," wrote Podhoretz. "Of course he did not take their program seriously; it was silly to think that a separate nation could be founded on territory ceded to the blacks as back pay for all the labor which had been extorted from their ancestors under slavery. Nor did their theology—a weird semiliterate version of Islamic doctrine—appeal to him. And certainly, as an open and active homosexual with a taste for the dissolute life, he was not attracted to their stringently puritanical moral code which forbade promiscuity, drinking, and smoking, and insisted on discipline, hard work, thrift, and all the other 'middle-class' virtues that he himself was always excoriating in his work. Nevertheless he was intrigued by the Muslims, and when I proposed that he write an article about them for *Commentary*, he jumped enthusiastically at the idea."[38]

Over the next year Podhoretz checked in with Baldwin periodically to see how things were progressing, his editorial excitement mounting as time went by. Not long after his Paradise Island epiphany he checked in on Baldwin again. How was the essay going? he asked. Actually, it was done, Baldwin said. Then Baldwin got a bit squirrelly.

"It was very long, too long for *Commentary*," Podhoretz remembered Baldwin saying. Podhoretz dismissed the idea: "Nonsense, length was no problem at all; I was dying to read it, and I would send a messenger for it immediately. No, there was no use doing that, he had given his copy to his agent. Fine, I would send a messenger to his agent. Well, he didn't think his agent had the manuscript either. Who had it then? He wasn't sure, but he thought his agent had submitted it to William Shawn at the *New Yorker*—not that they would want it, of course, and as soon as they returned it, he would send it right to me."

Baldwin was dissembling. He'd owed the *New Yorker* an essay on a different topic, and when he'd finished his piece on the Nation of Islam, and realized how extraordinary it was, he'd run the math and sent it directly to Shawn. By the time Baldwin and Podhoretz spoke, Shawn had already accepted it, scheduled it for publication, and promised Baldwin a massive paycheck, almost twenty times as much as Podhoretz would have been able to pay. It was published on November 19, 1962, as "Down at the Cross: Letter from a Region in My Mind" (and would later be republished in book form, together with a shorter essay, as *The Fire Next Time*).[39]

Podhoretz was furious. You don't take an assignment from one editor and then give the piece to another. The sting really took, however, when he was finally able to read the piece in the *New Yorker*. He hadn't just lost an essay he'd been promised, he realized instantly, but a classic. It was better than anything he'd published in the magazine so far and probably better than anything he'd ever publish, a once-in-an-editor's-career gem. And it had been stolen from him. Podhoretz turned to his friends to validate his anger, only to watch them make excuses for Baldwin (Hannah Arendt assured him, infuriatingly, that he wouldn't have had the courage to publish it in *Commentary* anyway). By the time Baldwin finally sat down with him to have it out, Podhoretz discovered he was far angrier with the white liberals and leftists who refused to censure Baldwin than with Baldwin himself. His sense of personal affront quickly gave way to a critique of the liberal psyche. How can we hope to truly integrate, he raged, if we're so twisted up we can't even find it in ourselves to do something as simple as condemn a black man for selling out a friend?

It wasn't just the red-blooded racism of the South that stood in the way of progress, but also the tangled tapestry of feelings that "integrationist" whites held toward blacks, only the nobler strands of which they could acknowledge. But the bad stuff was there, and it would tell. He gave as an example to Baldwin, who was listening intently, his own experience of growing up in Brooklyn, in one of those neighborhoods where "integrated" meant that the various tribes of white ethnic kids bullied whichever groups were lower down on the totem pole, and at the top of the pole were the black boys, who bullied everyone else.

"I told him several stories about my childhood relations with Negroes and about the resentment and hatred with which my experience had left me, and as I talked, Baldwin's eyes blazed even more fiercely than usual. 'You ought,' he whispered when I had finished, 'to write all that down.'"[40]

Podhoretz had in fact been mulling over just such an essay for a while, but had never been able to wrestle his feelings into rhetorical shape. Now over one long, intense weekend he did. It was published in the February 1963 issue of *Commentary*, as "My Negro Problem—and Ours," and was very explicitly a companion to Baldwin's piece, an exploration of white rage and ambivalence, drawing on Podhoretz's childhood, where Baldwin had delved into the psychological roots of black rage and despair by way of his own youth.

"During the early years of the war, when my older sister joined a left-wing youth organization," Podhoretz wrote, "I remember my astonishment at hearing her passionately denounce my father for thinking that Jews were worse off than Negroes. To me, at the age of twelve, it seemed very clear that Negroes were better off than Jews—indeed, than *all* whites. A city boy's world is contained within three or four square blocks, and in my world it was the whites, the Italians and Jews, who feared the Negroes, not the other way around. The Negroes were tougher than we were, more ruthless, and on the whole they were better athletes. What could it mean, then, to say that they were badly off and that we were more fortunate? Yet my sister's opinions, like print, were sacred, and when she told me about exploitation and economic forces I believed her. I believed her, but I was still afraid of Negroes. And I still hated them with all my heart."[41]

Podhoretz was far from the first writer to go diving down into the troubled psyche of the white liberal. Two of the greatest writers *Commentary* would ever publish—Baldwin and Leslie Fiedler—had in substantial part made their names mining this particular vein of the souls of white folk. And in the broader sense the work of exploring this tension, between the enlightenment ideals and the medieval brains of modern man, was one of the core activities of the New York intellectual endeavor. But there was something raw about the way Podhoretz did it that felt fresh. It wasn't "white people" or "modern man" he was anatomizing, but his own damned white self, and although it was a given, because of who he was and where the essay appeared, that by the last page of the essay he would work his way through to a mature perspective on race in America, the piece didn't belong to his adult self. It belonged to that boy who'd walked the streets of Brooklyn, afraid and hating, and that boy had kept a ledger of all the beatings and bullyings, the tension and intimidation.

The theoretical lessons the adult Podhoretz distilled from these experiences were in most respects the lessons that other writers, most obviously Baldwin, had already drawn. White racism was so much more than just contempt for blacks, or the presumption of their inferiority. It was also an inverted expression of fear, confusion, envy, and pain. Black alienation, in every respect a legacy of slavery and segregation, had nonetheless acquired an existence independent of white racism. And so on. Even the essay's most central argument, that the ambivalence of the white liberal was going to be a much greater obstacle to integration than had previously been recognized, was not particularly new.

What was new was the flesh Podhoretz put on these ideas: Here was his hatred and fear, delineated mercilessly, along with the rather persuasive assertion that it was not just his experience but was representative of the feelings of many of those whites who held the right kinds of opinions on racial equality. And here was Norman Podhoretz now, decades later, in the dawn of the 1960s, an officer in excellent standing of the left-liberal cultural establishment, possessor of degrees from two of the greatest institutions of higher learning in the world, still suffering under the whip of these emotions.

"I scream at them through tears of rage and self-contempt," he wrote, remembering a beating he got, "'Keep your f—n' filthy lousy black hands offa me.'"

He still felt echoes of that old fear of being assaulted by blacks, particularly when he was out late at night and had to walk past "a group of Negroes standing in front of a bar or sauntering down the street." He was still envious of blacks, now for the grace and power with which it seemed to him they danced and played sports where once it had been for the grace with which it seemed to him they wielded violence. And he still hated.

As a writer Podhoretz didn't hit all his marks perfectly in "My Negro Problem—and Ours." There were moments when his courage in owning up to the darkness in his soul shaded over the line into prurience. He said a few stupid things about black people (some of which he would acknowledge later, when they were pointed out to him by Ralph Ellison). And when it came to the end of the essay, to the moment when the form required that he deliver grand conclusions about the future of race relations in America, he made the same kind of conceptual error Baldwin had made in his essay, underestimating the capacity of the country to muddle forward, haltingly, in clumsy defiance of both the hopes of racial utopians and the fears of racial Jeremiahs. On the charge that he say something authentic and fresh about the world, however, that he answer to the demands of his unique experience and talents, Podhoretz succeeded far better than he ever had before. And he knew it. It was, he later wrote, "the first piece I had ever written in a voice that belonged entirely to me."

The reaction to the piece, upon its publication in the February 1963 issue of the magazine, more or less bore this conviction out. There was a great deal of anger. He was called a racist. He was accused by racists of lusting to see white women and black men in congress. He was chastised, by Jews, for airing the tribe's dirty laundry too openly. But there was also a great deal of praise, from readers, friends, colleagues, blacks and whites—from Lionel Trilling!—commending him for his honesty and making clear that they understood what he was trying to do, which was to let show the poison in his own veins so that the body politic would learn to recognize it and therefore, perhaps, how to purge it. Even James Baldwin liked it. And, perhaps most affirming of all, there was just an enormous amount of attention. There were hundreds of letters to the editor, and a slew of magazine and newspaper commentaries on the piece and meta-commentaries on the controversy surrounding the piece.[42] Almost none of the reactions, even the most negatively valenced, questioned his capacity as a writer of prose, or his status as someone who had important things to say. Those were the points where he'd felt most vulnerable before stepping out with the essay. And on those points he was profoundly (and as it turned out, dangerously) reassured.

After "My Negro Problem," Podhoretz managed during 1963 to write one more essay of similar ambition, "Hannah Arendt on Eichmann: A Study in the Perversity of Brilliance," a scathing assessment of Arendt's *Eichmann in Jerusalem: A Report on the Banality of Evil*. It wasn't personal in the way that "My Negro Problem" had been, but it showed the same degree of assurance. Again Podhoretz spoke in a voice that seemed entirely his own, and again he spoke on topics—in this case the Holocaust, Jews, the nature of evil, the judgments of history—that actually mattered to him.

There was, too, a subtler linkage between his response to Baldwin and his response to Arendt. Podhoretz was beginning to articulate more clearly to himself the basic position, not a new one in the world but a complicated one for him to fully embrace, that one's personal interests and loyalties were entitled to play an important role in one's politics, that any politics that disregarded or denigrated such interests were not just inauthentic but, in a profound way, inhuman. Later this "politics of interest," as he came to call it, would move to the center of his philosophical worldview. In the early and mid-1960s it was a constraint on how far he would let his universalist liberal principles take him. More important, it was the critical vantage point from which he was discovering he had something meaningful to say. He was the guy who knew when and how to call bullshit on people who were advocating liberal and left-wing positions that just didn't make sense in light of basic human psychology.

The moral universe of Arendt's book, about the trial in Israel of Nazi bureaucrat Adolf Eichmann, struck Podhoretz as the *ad absurdum* of liberals' denial of human nature. Arendt had fashioned herself into a being of such pure disinterested intellect, such "sophisticated modern sensibility," that she wasn't able to respond to the trial of Eichmann, who was responsible for transporting millions of Jews to concentration camps, with the natural instincts of a human being. She wasn't able to respond as who she was, which was a Jewish woman, forced into exile from her native Germany, living in the aftermath of the deaths of millions of her fellow Jews at the hands of her former fellow Germans.

"Thus," he wrote, "in place of the monstrous Nazi, she gives us the 'banal' Nazi; in place of the Jew as virtuous martyr, she gives us the Jew as accomplice in evil; and in place of the confrontation between guilt and innocence, she gives us the 'collaboration' of criminal and victim. . . . The only aspect of the trial that pleases her is that the judges behaved with scrupulous regard for the interests of Justice."[43]

Podhoretz wasn't the only Jewish writer who was upset by Arendt's book. The book, which was expanded from a series of articles Arendt wrote for the *New Yorker*, was so controversial it led to what a scholar would later describe as a "civil war" among intellectuals, as well as the "excommunication" of Arendt by the American Jewish establishment.[44] Where Podhoretz stood out was in how blunt he was in offering his critique from a perspective of Jewish particularism. He was angry with Arendt not primarily because of factual inaccuracies in her account, though he mentioned some, or because of what he saw as a fundamental error in her understanding of Eichmann's character. What bothered him most was that Arendt seemed to him so much more irritated by Jews than by those who had transgressed against them. Thus she found the Israeli prosecutor so terribly crude in his attempts to paint Eichmann as a textbook anti-Semite, but Eichmann himself was fascinatingly banal. The Nazis were awful of course, but that was a given; what called for deeper explication, and more visceral contempt, was how the Jewish councils in Nazi-controlled territory cooperated with the *Reich*, thereby enabling, Arendt argued, far more death than there would have been otherwise.

Enough, said Podhoretz:

"This habit of judging the Jews by one standard and everyone else by another is a habit Miss Arendt shares with many of her fellow-Jews, emphatically including those who think that the main defect of the story is her failure to dwell on all the heroism and all the virtue that the six million displayed among them. But the truth is—*must* be—that the Jews under Hitler acted as men will act when they are set upon by murderers, no better and no worse: the Final Solution reveals nothing about the victims except that they were mortal brings and hopelessly vulnerable in their powerlessness. . . . The Nazis destroyed a third of the Jewish people. In the name of all that is humane, will the remnant never let up on itself?"[45]

Arendt wasn't amused by Podhoretz's essay. The two argued about it a great deal, and though their friendship didn't end, it suffered. But the piece was well received in general, and it lent Podhoretz further confidence in three related, and fateful, propositions: that he could trust his gut to lead him to the right material, that he should follow his intuition even if meant conflict with friends, and that he would ultimately be rewarded in the world for doing so.

It was around this time, at the end of 1963, that Podhoretz was finally forced to admit that his book on postwar fiction was never going to be finished. His publisher, tired of waiting, asked him to substitute a collection of his essays and reviews instead, and after some resistance Podhoretz agreed. *Doings and Undoings* was published the following year, to more or less good reviews. For Podhoretz it was an excruciating experience. He'd known, rationally, that a collection of disparate pieces wasn't likely to blow the doors off the scene, but he'd hoped anyway that the whole of the collection would somehow prove greater than the sum of parts that he very well knew were good but not, with a few possible exceptions, extraordinary. He fantasized the book might do for him something like what Trilling's 1950 collection, *The Liberal Imagination*, had done for Trilling, which was to elevate his status to that of Major American Critic. Or if not that, then at least maybe it would give off some sparks like Mailer's more recent, also rather messy collection *Advertisements for Myself.* When *Doings and Undoings* did neither, Podhoretz suffered.

"Only a few years earlier," he later wrote, ". . . I had been delighted to see my name mentioned in print, even if the reference was unflattering. Now, unless a reviewer went into raptures over me, I thought him my enemy."

After the reviews stopped coming in, and the rhythms of everyday life reasserted themselves, Podhoretz realized a few things. One was that he had overreacted. If anything just the mere fact of his having published a book, something he'd failed to do before, had enhanced his stature. Another was that he had overreacted because something important had been at stake for him. Then he realized what that something was.

He wanted to be great, and wanted to be seen as great, extraordinarily badly. More badly than he'd known, and more badly than was in remotely good taste in the circles in which he moved.

"The whole business of reputation, of fame, of success was coming to fascinate me in a new way," he wrote. "Everyone seemed to be caught up in it, and yet no one told the truth about it. People capable of the most brutal honesty in other areas would at the mention of the word success suddenly lift their eyes up to the heavens and begin chanting the most horrendous pieties imaginable."[46]

Podhoretz had always been more naked in his desire for success than was fashionable, but his practice had been to atone for that with an extra helping of guilt and self-consciousness. Now he began to wonder if he'd had it backward all along. Maybe the problem wasn't the ambition, or people's labors to realize it. After all, most of the people he really admired were pretty ambitious. The problem was the hangover of guilt and embarrassment everyone seemed to feel they owed the cosmos. What good did that do anyone? It didn't seem to change how anyone behaved. It just got in the way of their being honest about it. The more Podhoretz ruminated, the more the pattern of his thoughts began to remind him of the internal ferment he'd felt a few times before, before feeling compelled to write the essays and reviews of which he'd been most proud. There was some bullshit out there that needed to be called out, and maybe he was the person to do it.

Over the next three or so years, as Podhoretz put aside most other writing to craft the memoir that followed from his rather un-lefty epiphany, his left-liberal politics remained rock steady. In fact, the more he thought about it, the more Podhoretz became convinced that this dissonance was precisely the point. A system of politics could only be as strong as its capacity to deal with people as they were, not as they imagined themselves to be. A good social democratic country of the sort Podhoretz envisioned should be able to honor and harness these self-serving impulses in ways that served the greater good, or at least didn't compromise it. We could have a guaranteed minimum income, a withdrawal from Vietnam, and striving, self-promoting intellectuals all at the same time. He hoped his book would be, among other things, an exercise in demonstrating the truth of this. He hoped it would help cleanse some hypocrisy and contradiction from the conversation about success in America, as he believed "My Negro Problem" had helped cleanse the conversation about race. Then everyone could move forward toward the shared goal of achieving a more just and beautiful society.

To the extent that anything politically meaningful did shift for Podhoretz during this time, it was 1) his interest in being "radical," which had cooled in roughly inverse correlation to how effectual he felt, and 2) the actually existing radical movements, which had been mostly hypothetical when Podhoretz had begun his editorial reign with Paul Goodman's radical blast. Now they were real, and growing in influence.

Podhoretz didn't turn the magazine against the emergent radical groups like Students for a Democratic Society (SDS), or against the more militant turn in civil rights groups like the Student Non-Violent Coordinating Committee (SNCC). On many of the big policy issues, like the escalating war in Vietnam, civil rights, and the distribution of power and wealth, *Commentary* was mostly in alignment with the radicals. But almost from the first Podhoretz kept the magazine at a critical distance from the radicals themselves.

Tom Hayden, one of the leaders of SDS, had actually approached Podhoretz with the Port Huron Statement, the group's historic envisioning of what a "new left" should be. Podhoretz had declined to publish it. Not because he disagreed with the broad outlines of what it was saying; indeed he recognized that it owed a direct debt to some of the stuff he'd been publishing by Goodman and others in the magazine. The problem was that Hayden and his fellows were writing like activists rather than intellectuals. Their views were "stripped of all complexity, qualification, and nuance." That wasn't what his *Commentary* was for.

Podhoretz held to this stance as the decade progressed. *Commentary* would give a hearing to the New Left, and other militant or radical movements, but its bedrock perspective would remain its own, sympathetic to but apart from the New Left, and when it gave consideration to the radicals it would do so on its own terms. When in late 1964 student protests broke out on the Berkeley campus, Podhoretz turned for commentary not to any of the students involved in the Free Speech Movement, but to former *Commentary* editor Nathan Glazer, who was a newly appointed professor of sociology at Berkeley and one of the faculty who'd intervened to mediate between the students and the administration. For perspectives on civil rights he turned most consistently to veteran activist Bayard Rustin, organizer of the 1963 March on Washington, and never to any of the younger activists who were at the vanguard of developing new tactics and ideas for the movement. When the voices of SNCC activists Robert Moses and Stokely Carmichael did appear in *Commentary*, in April of 1965, reflecting on the lessons of their heroic labors registering black voters in Mississippi, it was by way of an excerpt from Robert Penn Warren's 1965 collection of interviews with civil rights leaders, *Who Speaks for the Negro?* In 1966 a point-counterpoint was published on whether the new idea of "black power" should take the lead in guiding the civil rights movement forward. Bayard Rustin said nay. For the yea perspective Podhoretz turned not to Carmichael or any of the other leaders of the nascent movement but to David Danzig, a Columbia University professor of social work and former official of the American Jewish Committee.[47]

By 1965–67, the years when Podhoretz was working on his book, *Commentary* and its three closest siblings—*Partisan Review*, *Dissent*, and the *New York Review of Books*—found themselves negotiating a dialectic that was remarkably evocative of the one that had produced the New York intellectual synthesis in the first place. On the left the radicals, who could seem dangerously simplistic but whose critiques of American society were not easy to dismiss. On the right a vigorously liberal administration, capable of incorporating (or was it co-opting?) left-wing critiques and programs. Further to the right . . . well, nothing very impressive, but some people and tendencies that should be monitored closely. And at the tiller of the nation's intellectual conscience, men like Podhoretz, trying to steer the wisest course toward the distant shore of the best possible America.

There were stark differences, of course, between the 1960s and the 1930s. Affluence and conformity were the problem now, not Depression and revolution. Neither Berkeley radicals nor black militants nor draft card burners had much to do with the Communist Party. Paul Goodman wasn't Trotsky. Tom Hayden wasn't Earl Browder. Vietnam presented a very different set of challenges than the looming threat of war in Europe had three decades earlier. But it was precisely this quality of the 1960s, how it was the same but different, that made it so exhilarating for Podhoretz. He was actually living out a version of his fantasy, to redo the 1930s, but because it really was a different time, with a different set of issues and actors, he didn't have to follow the same script. It was up to him to forge a synthesis now. He could oppose the Vietnam War, even though the hawks tried to frame it as a simple choice between communism and the West. He could keep his distance from the radicals, many of whom seemed not to have learned the lessons of the 1930s, while recognizing that they themselves were not communists. He could support civil rights while keeping a watchful eye on the antiwhite and anti-Semitic sentiments that seemed to be creeping into certain regions of the movement. And he could use his magazine to level a relentless critique of the policies of the Kennedy and Johnson administrations while, personally, becoming rather chummy with members of both.

As for the book he was writing . . . well, that was more complicated. He had tried twice, and failed twice, to write the kind of book that followed most obviously from the coordinates of who he was and what he did. Now he was trying to do something else, to be not of the moment but ahead of it, to reach not for excellence but greatness. So he didn't write a book-length version of the kind of wide-ranging literary-political-cultural essay that was the characteristic form of the New York intellectuals. He didn't weigh in on race in America, or the Vietnam War, or the demands of the students, or the diagnoses of the social critics. Instead he looked to the form of what he'd achieved most beautifully with "My Negro Problem," the personal essay, and the example of his friend Mailer, whose brazenness had animated *Advertisements for Myself*, and the epiphanies of Paradise Island, and the harsh lessons of *Doings and Undoings*, and the satisfaction he'd gained from saying Yes to the *Commentary* job, and he rolled it all together, held it up to the light, and said Yes again. He would write the story of his own success, and make the wager that if he did so bravely, shamelessly, charmingly, perceptively enough, he'd win people over. He would say, I Want! And the people would say, We Do Too! and would be grateful. And the act of declaring his desires would generate the very satiation of them, and there would be increase, exponentially.

That was the plan, anyway.

The book that Podhoretz finally produced, with the aid of a great deal of alcohol and an open door at Yaddo, the artists' colony in Saratoga Springs where Podhoretz would frequently retreat from his editing duties to write, was not the book he'd hoped he was writing. It was a pretty good book. Podhoretz had insightful things to say about class and status in America, and about the pretzels into which people twisted themselves to avoid acknowledging their pursuit of them. And he was a good storyteller about his life, if he had sufficient distance—ten years, give or take—from the autobiographical material he was narrativizing.

It was interesting to hear about his childhood as the adored son of his Jewish mother in Brooklyn, his tense but fruitful relationship with the high school teacher who made it her mission to civilize him, his salad days at Columbia and Cambridge, his comic turn in the army. There was something universal about the conflicts he experienced trying to reconcile his increasingly sophisticated self and the more parochial world of his family and old friends. And there was something sociologically right, and quite endearing, about the way he described the subtle and not-so-subtle competition between his young self—so nakedly, aggressively ambitious—and all the "snobs" who wanted it as badly as he did but were inhibited, by the unspoken rules of being a gentleman, from admitting to it.

For all that was charming and right about the book, however, there was something fundamentally off in the weft of it that betrayed him, more and more as the book progressed. The anecdotes got dramatically less interesting after he got out of the army. His descriptions of his ambition were less charming, more grating, when he was describing his adult self. His continual return to the matter of other people envying his success started to sound whiny. He wasn't able to strike the right balance when dramatizing the characters and institutions of New York intellectual society; they were too close for him to see clearly.

Perhaps most fatal was the humiliating gap between the conceptual check Podhoretz wrote and his book's ability to cash it. He'd pointed to the center-field bleachers, and then knocked a solid single over the shortstop's head.

He'd wanted to do something Big and New. He'd wanted to take this "dirty little secret of the well-educated American soul," and use the story of his own life to model how it could be processed into something open and clean and powerful. But he didn't have the chops to execute it. Or perhaps more to the point, he didn't have the insight. At the end of it all, having bet everything that the book was an enactment of a new way of being, a higher synthesis of wanting and having and believing and enjoying, proof that he had in himself solved the problem of success, he actually sounded as if he'd regressed. Gone was the man who'd gone toe-to-toe with James Baldwin and come out the other side still standing. Back was the good bad boy of his earlier years, daring/entreating the world to love his naughty self, but laid bare, without even the protective device of channeling his plea through consideration of other writers' work.

"For several years I toyed with the idea of doing a book about Mailer that would focus on the problem of success," he wrote at the end of *Making It*, "but in the end I decided that if I ever did work up the nerve to write about this problem, I would have to do it without hiding behind him or anyone else. Such a book, I thought, ought properly to be written in the first person, and it ought in itself to constitute a frank, Mailer-like bid for literary distinction, fame, and money all in one package: otherwise it would be unable to extricate itself from the toils of the dirty little secret. Writing a book like that would be a very dangerous thing to do, but some day, I told myself, I would like to try doing it.

"I just have."[48]

When Podhoretz finished the manuscript he felt scared but good. Then he began showing it around to friends and colleagues. His agent refused to represent it. Roger Straus, the chief of the publishing house that had given Podhoretz a rather large advance to write it, told him he could keep the advance and the manuscript; FSG wouldn't publish it. His buddy Jason Epstein told him not to publish it. William Phillips argued with him about it. Jackie Kennedy broke off relations after she read it. Diana Trilling told him it was "completely humorless and lacked any touch of saving irony."[49] Most upsetting of all was the reaction of Lionel Trilling.

"Do not publish this book," Trilling said. "It is a gigantic mistake. Put it away and do not let others see it."[50]

Trilling begged him, if he insisted on proceeding, to at least add a chapter at the end that would soften some of the more extravagant claims of the book.

"If it appeared in its present form, he warned . . . it would be ten years before I lived it down."

There were some warmer responses. Mailer said he liked it. Another agent liked it and agreed to shop it around, finally finding it a home at Random House. But Podhoretz knew these were the exceptions. There was a consensus forming about the book, at least within the world of insiders who had access to it (or to the gossip about it). And he knew there was a good chance that the public reception, after it came out in January of 1968, would be similarly harsh. But he went boldly forth anyway. One didn't write a book such as *Making It*, the whole point of which was to lance a taboo, and then retreat because people were uncomfortable. It was a dangerous book. That was the point.

Making It came out the first week of 1968, and it was brutalized. Not in every single instance. There were some pleasant reviews. A few were middling. But most of the reviews were harshly critical, a number extravagantly so. And if *Doings and Undoings* had fared better than the mean of its reviews, *Making It* suffered the opposite fate. Once the critical consensus on the book was formed, each successive review was factored in only for how it could add to the tally of Podhoretz's failures.

As the bad reviews of January gave way to the bad reviews of February, and to those of March and April, a story coalesced about what kind of cultural event the publication of *Making It* was. This was evident both in the reviews themselves, which had their fun with Podhoretz, and in those blunter elements—headlines and art—intended to signal to readers what genre of drama was being acted out, and in what roles the actors had been cast: Podhoretz was in a comedy, and he was the buffoon.[51]

"An apologist for fame ought to be a better judge of it," wrote Stanley Kauffmann in the *New Republic*. "This aspect of Podhoretz's book can be closed off with one (appropriately) Jewish joke. A man makes money, buys a yacht and a captain's outfit, and then presents himself to his aged mother. The old lady says, 'Boychick, to me, you're a captain. To you, you're a captain. But to *captains*, are you a captain?'"[52]

Esquire's headline wasn't the worst—"The Dirty Little Secret of Norman Podhoretz"—but the nasty little couplet[53] they ran beneath it got to the emasculating nub of it.

Actually, it's neither dirty nor a secret
It is little, however.

What came through even in many of the reviews that were most complimentary was that *Making It* generated an almost physiological cringe in its critics. It was such a spectacle, so vulnerable, so naked in its neediness. And because it lacked the rhetorical command to take the unease it provoked and transmute it into a higher form, that unease rebounded on Podhoretz.

By far the most personally devastating review came from Norman Mailer, in the spring 1968 issue of *Partisan Review*. Podhoretz had been hanging some hopes for critical redemption on the piece by Mailer, who back in the fall, after seeing the manuscript, had told him he liked the book. More recently Mailer had even told him he was writing the review precisely as a corrective to the attacks.

But at some point between Mailer's first reading—which was probably only a half-reading or skimming—and his more thorough reading of *Making It* for the review, his judgment changed. He still liked the first half of the book. It had "the quiet authority of good art." But then it seemed to Mailer as though something went sour in the execution. At just that point where the book should have really gotten juicy, when Podhoretz joined the ranks of the New York intellectuals, when his restless and penetrating intellect finally encountered a milieu worthy of its attention, the story lost its nerve. It became nice. The protagonist "Podhoretz," who'd been capable of such ruthless observation of people and institutions when he was on the make, suddenly found, upon having made it, that nearly everyone was rather charming and supportive.

"*Making It* ceases to be a novel," wrote Mailer, "just so soon as its protagonist enters the climax of his narrative; we are projected right out of that rare aesthetic vineyard where autobiography dares to become that special and most daring category of fiction which is its inner necessity, and instead we are now forced to jog along on the washboard road of memoir. Characters come in and out, observations are made, names file through, Podhoretz suffers, becomes an editor, thrives, we do not care—the novel has disappeared—the interplay between ambitious perception and society which has been the source of its value now gives ground to the aesthetic perplexity of the author who must flounder in the now novelistically alienated remains of his hypothesis—that success is the dirty little secret. Now he has no novel on which to work it, only sketchy anecdotes, abortive essays, isolated insights, and note of the drone—repetitions. A fine even potentially marvelous book gets lost in a muddle, finally finishes itself and is done. No joy in closing the back cover."[54]

Mailer's review had its own problems. He was working with a knot of private loyalties and literary principles so thick and tangled even a swordsman of his virtuosity couldn't cut through it cleanly, and the jagged edges were manifest in the text. Mailer exerted himself to be compassionate to Podhoretz in one paragraph only to be viciously, brilliantly bitchy in the next. He didn't like the book but wanted to make clear he liked his friend. He was angry on his friend's behalf at how petty the gossip about the book had been within "the Inner Clan." But then, as he would admit much later, he was also still angry at his friend for excluding him from the list of invitees to a dinner party with Jackie Kennedy. He knew on some level that he shouldn't have written the review once he realized he didn't like the book, but he'd accepted the assignment and, besides, he had some interesting things to say. And hadn't he and Norman always prided themselves on being blunt with each other?

A different person than Podhoretz might have been able to hear in the review at least a few of the many notes of conciliation it struck. Even Podhoretz himself, at an earlier stage in the process, might have heard them. But the man he was at the moment the review arrived, after so much public humiliation, heard only betrayal and more humiliation. One of his dearest friends had determined that his book was so bad that the necessity of publicly declaring its badness yet one more time was more important than their friendship. Podhoretz had been tormented when *Doings and Undoings*, a cautious book, had gotten decent reviews. Now he had put himself so far out there he could feel the abyss keening

beneath him, and the worst had happened, in full view of everyone he
cared about and everyone whose opinion of him he valued (too much,
obviously). He wasn't great. He wasn't even good. He was a failure, an
object lesson, an object of ridicule. And he was wrecked by it.

The next two years would be the worst of Podhoretz's life. He began
drinking more. He retreated from his social life. He grew depressed. He
brooded over the reaction to *Making It*. As had often been the case in
the past, he also began to perceive that what was happening inside him
was connected, in some profound way, to something larger happening
in American culture.

That something, it soon became clear, was a shift in the temperature
of the American Left. The root optimism that had animated the Movement throughout much of the decade—the sense that for America to
be great it had only to heed the call of its better angels—was giving way
to perceptions of a more intrinsically rotten society, in need of radical
surgery or perhaps even euthanasia. Signs of the shift were everywhere.
The civil rights movement of figures like Martin Luther King, Jr., and
Bayard Rustin had been superseded by the more revolutionary black
nationalism of leaders like Eldridge Cleaver and Huey Newton. Out of
the ashes of Students for a Democratic Society rose the violent Weather
Underground. The Communist Party U.S.A., which everyone had
thought dead and buried, seemed to be making a comeback.

One of the key events for Podhoretz was the student protest that
broke out on April 23, 1968, at his alma mater, Columbia University, which soon escalated into the dramatic occupation of five campus
buildings. Protesters broke through doors and windows, barricaded
themselves in, briefly held some administrators hostage, and began issuing demands for, among other things, greater student involvement in
the running of university affairs; the severing of ties between Columbia
and the Institute for Defense Analyses (IDA), a group connected to the
Department of Defense; and a wholesale reevaluation of plans to build
a massive gym facility on parkland that sat between the predominantly

white area around the university and the predominantly black neighborhood of West Harlem.

The occupations were ended a week later by force of tear gas and police batons, and proved, within the limits of the students' concrete demands, modestly successful. The gym was never built. Some students were suspended, but none expelled. The university cut its ties to the IDA. Grayson Kirk, the president of the university, resigned. Administrative measures were instituted to increase sensitivity to student needs and to open up channels for more student influence on university policies. Yet the significance of the confrontation was taken by almost everyone, almost immediately, to extend far beyond the realm of those actions. The protests had become another one of those emergent little poems of history that were issuing up, so rapidly in those years, from the deep tectonic divisions in the American soul.

For the intellectuals in Podhoretz's circle, it was the kind of material upon which they'd been feasting for decades. But in this case the intellectual was personal in a way many of them hadn't experienced since the 1930s, or had never experienced. They were themselves alumni or employees of Columbia University, or close to those who were. They lived in the neighborhood, or not too far away (Podhoretz and Decter were a few stops down on the West Side subway lines). They drank in the bars near there, spoke at symposia there, had constituted their identities in substantial part around the education they'd received there or at similar institutions. The students were—intellectually, spiritually, in some cases biologically—their children. It was part of their world. It was who they were. And it was under attack. They were under attack.

In an essay on the protests published in *Commentary* a few months later, Diana Trilling wrote of getting an angry phone call from a student radical just hours after he got out of jail. He wanted to know why her husband hadn't been there at the end to protect him from the brutality of the police. But really, she understood, he was putting them on notice: Their neutrality had been registered.

"This was revolutionary scorekeeping, make no mistake," she

wrote. "Its tone couldn't have been nastier and it spoke of guillotines or their later historical manifestation, the concentration camp, the knock on the door in the night—indeed, the writer-professor's wife, who in her husband's absence had taken the brunt of the student's charge, was herself soon well up on the list of those who, come the tribunals of the young, would never be missed."[55]

Podhoretz's friends and colleagues didn't all react to the Columbia "uprising" with the same perception of imminent threat that Diana Trilling did, but most of them recognized in the upheaval at Columbia stark evidence that their particular synthesis, which derived so much of its vitality from setting liberalism and radicalism into fruitful tension with each other, was under severe, perhaps terminal strain. It was one thing to argue over tactics and rhetoric, while recognizing a commonality of interests, but now it seemed the interests were at odds.

Something fundamental had changed. In 1962 Tom Hayden had hoped that *Commentary* would publish the Port Huron Statement. In 1965, at Berkeley, Nathan Glazer and his faculty colleagues had been recognized by the student protesters as, if not quite allies, then at least good-faith partners in the process of creating a more humane university. By 1968, at Columbia, when liberal faculty members tried to step into a similar role, they were met with disdain. They couldn't solve the problem; they were the problem. Allen Ginsberg had been right back in 1958. They got them through their children.

"I'll use the words of LeRoi Jones, whom I'm sure you don't like a whole lot," wrote campus SDS leader Mark Rudd, in his open letter to President Kirk, published the day before the uprising: "Up against the wall, motherfucker, this is a stick-up."[56]

For most of Podhoretz's friends this was an unpleasant, even traumatic message to receive. For Podhoretz, the primal trauma was what happened to *Making It*, and the process of reassembling his identity was fueled to an extraordinary degree by his need to reconstruct the recent past so that his book's rejection by the world, and by his friends, would be endurable. That meant coming to the conclusion that the book's critics had been dishonest and hypocritical. More radically it meant going back to the genesis of the book and reimagining what kind of act its creation had been. Not primarily a literary act, as everyone had thought, but instead a political one. And it was as the raw material in this act of reimagination that the radicalism of the Left, at the tail end of the decade, assumed its significance for him. Podhoretz hadn't realized it at the time he was writing, but *Making It* was an expression of his soul crying out in protest against the indictments the New Left and other militant groups were handing down with ever-increasing fury and frequency.

It was a Yes to success and ambition and glory, but more meaningfully it was a No. He would not join with the growing chorus of those who saw the flaws in the major institutions and practices of American life as evidence that it was rotten all the way down. And it was for that political refusal, that act of dissent, that he was being punished. By the radical leftists, of course. By all the organs of the middlebrow media state, which deferred, as they always did, to whatever notions were fashionable at the moment. But also—and this he hadn't fully anticipated—by those friends and allies of his who should have known better.

Podhoretz's analyses of why particular people failed him differed. Some of them had been genuinely radicalized by the spirit of the sixties; they were philosophically on the side of the radical Left against him. Others were just too tired from battles past to take up the cudgel once again, so they persuaded themselves that the fight was just about a book, which they persuaded themselves they didn't like. As for Mailer, pure cowardice was the explanation. Such pure cowardice, and so deeply characterological, that Podhoretz couldn't help but revise his judgment of what kind of person Mailer had always been and what kind of game he'd been playing. He wasn't a rebel, as he claimed. He was the fool, the court jester of the Left, who got away with his rebellious-seeming insults because he delivered them with a wink and because everyone understood that in the end he knew who was paying for the dance. Mailer had had no choice but to turn against *Making It* if he wanted to retain his position at court.

"The first time he read the book," Podhoretz later wrote, "Mailer had not realized how subversive it was of the radical party line both in its relatively benign view of middle-class American values and, even more seriously, in its denial that the intellectuals—and the educated class in general—represented a true or superior alternative. Then, having become convinced by a study of the reaction that *Making It* really had overstepped the line, and wishing to dissociate himself from so dangerous a connection without seeming to behave in a cowardly fashion in his own eyes (and mine), he attacked me for ruining a 'potentially marvelous book' not by having gone too far but by having failed to go far enough in exposing what he himself called the new Establishment of the Left."[57]

During this period of reconstruction Podhoretz didn't go so far as to persuade himself that the book he'd written was as spectacularly good as its (corrupt) critics were saying it was bad. But by reimagining *Making It* as a political rather than a literary object, he shifted the criteria according to which its worth should be measured. The question was no longer whether its literary construction was good but whether its political content was right. He also shifted the temporal frame. What he had done wasn't necessarily done yet, wasn't bounded by the back cover of the book. It was a beginning, perhaps only the first chapter in an unfolding story of political and intellectual resistance. He could be redeemed over time, depending on what happened next.

From that point forward, Podhoretz began to reorganize his very self around the fight to win the war he hadn't been aware he was launching when he wrote *Making It*—in defense of America against the barbarians of the Left. This didn't mean a sudden conversion to conservatism. He had no template for that. But his sense of where the nation was, and what it needed, had always been a projection of his own feeling of place in the world. When he felt stifled, the nation needed release.

When he felt empowered, the nation needed to stride forward exuberantly. Up until that moment, when the book came out and everything started to go wrong, Podhoretz had been a certain kind of man. His vision of what America would look like at its best was to a considerable degree a nation full of people like him. Loud, open, warm, boisterous, aggressive, hopeful, joyful, loyal, mischievous, vulgar in a knowing and cosmopolitan way, confident bordering on arrogant in some ways but also vulnerable in his affections and enthusiasms.

Then *Making It* was published, and the landscape of his political imagination transformed. He began retreating from those parts of himself that had been in tune with, or seduced by, the spirit of the decade and "the Movement." He stopped looking around the corner for some new, fresh thing that might be coming, and began instead to retrench.

In 1969 Podhoretz got a contract to write a book on where America was now, as the 1960s came to an end. It would have a section each on the blacks, the young, and the war. Unsurprisingly, he found himself unable to finish it. He was depressed and drinking heavily. He'd failed at this kind of book before. And he was so angry and hurt.

The task was to filter his anger through a coherent set of political principles and commitments, but he didn't know what his politics were anymore. More to the point, he didn't know who he was anymore. Still the editor of *Commentary* magazine, but at thirty-nine-almost-forty no longer the precocious young editor of *Commentary*. Author of two books, and recognized public intellectual, but conspicuous failure in his efforts to ascend to the Olympian heights where men like Mailer and Trilling seemed to dwell. Even as a father and husband he'd seen better days. Nowhere in his crumbled identity was there a base of equipoise solid enough to critique the Left without descending into crankiness and reaction. And he was smart enough to know it.

It led to a brutal cycle for Podhoretz. In New York there was too much going on for him to concentrate on his writing, so he would retreat to the writers' colony at Yaddo, where he would feel reproached by "all the other wonderfully productive, painters, composers, and writers."[58] Then he would retreat to the farmhouse he and Decter had bought with the advance from the book he wasn't finishing, where he could dwell on the possibility that he would fail to write the book, have to return the advance, and be forced to sell the house, which he had quickly come to love. At each location he drank too much and wrote too little. What passages he did finish he would show to Decter. She would let him know, lovingly, that they weren't good enough. He would agree.

The pressure built and built, until it finally came to a climax one day in early 1970, on the grounds of his new summer home. He'd actually had a decent day of writing, and was rewarding himself with a stroll.

"I was finished working and was carrying a martini with me. There I was, walking on this beautiful, chilly, early spring day and the sun hitting the snow. I was feeling very content, benign, the writing had gone well, I had an excellent drink, and all of a sudden I had a vision. . . . I saw physically, in the sky, though it was obviously in my head, a kind of diagram that resembled a family tree. And it was instantly clear to me that this diagram contained the secret of life and existence and knowledge: that you start with this, and you follow to that. It all had a logic of interconnectedness."[59]

The vision lasted about thirty seconds. He would never come to a final conclusion about whether it was a true vision from God, whatever that might mean. He was sure from the start, however, that the image of the family tree expressed a foundational truth for him, which was that the Judaism he had always rather taken for granted, as a happy substrate of his primarily secular worldview, was much more than that. It was an expression of the most fundamental truths of the universe, of the natural order from which all things flow. Podhoretz also found himself, in the aftermath of the vision, in a state of heightened being that would persist for months. When he returned to New York he haunted his friends and family with his perceptions of both the cosmic truths of the universe and the unspoken secrets of their souls, all of which were now visible to him with a sparkling, unnerving clarity.

"I was like a fortune-teller," Podhoretz later told his biographer. "I could talk to you, look at you, and tell what was bothering you and what you should do about it. . . . I was like some sort of magician."

It was the most countercultural experience Podhoretz would ever have, and when the active spiritual (manic? dissociative?) phase of the journey was over, a few months later, he ended up where so many of his fellow countercultural seekers found themselves on the other side of their visions. Not really with a theology that would do much work in clarifying how one should live, but cut loose from old commitments and beliefs, free to become someone different. In the standard sixties version of that story, the content that rushed in to fill the void was the call of the wild, the id, liberation, eros. The ties had been cut to whatever was bringing you down: family, nation, monogamy, hetero-sexuality, the market, traditional religion. For Podhoretz, born too late, laid low (he had decided) by the sixties itself, it was something like the opposite. He would shut down those receptors that had been respon-sive to the wild energies of the sixties, and that had been responsible, he'd come to believe, for leading him so far astray. In their place he would plant the family tree, and all the commitments he'd come to see as branching out from it: to duty, obligation, religion, authority, tradi-tional gender roles, Israel, America.

Intellectually, the liberation was also from the New York intellec-tuals' lionization of complexity, from the idea that truth was many-layered, nuanced, and difficult to elucidate adequately.

"What emerged for me was clarity," he said. "Clarity is courage. There were truths that had to be articulated and defended, and they weren't, to use Lionel's favorite word, complicated. Everything was sim-ple. That was what that vision told me. There was nothing esoteric. There was a simple truth behind everything. From then on I went look-ing for the simple truth."[60]

Podhoretz hadn't reverted to an older version of himself. His transformation was much more unusual than that, and different in a fundamental way, not just from how ex-leftists and liberals of earlier eras had been changed, but from the experience of many of the close friends and colleagues of his who were turning to the right at that very same moment. Most of these figures—predecessors like Chambers and Burnham, contemporaries like Irving Kristol and Nathan Glazer— were recognizably the same characters on the other side of their political journeys. With Podhoretz it was as though he'd been replaced by a version of himself from an adjacent timeline. The politics he arrived at, after his encounter with the ineffable, were the ones he had already been on the path to adopting. They were politics he would share with his fellow neoconservatives. What was different was the way he held them.

When in the late spring of 1970 he returned his full focus to *Commentary*, and began writing regularly for the magazine again after years of absence, it was as a different person, or at least a different writer. He didn't just sound as though he'd aged twenty years. He sounded as though he'd never even been young.

5

The Betrayed: David Horowitz

Without exactly realizing it was happening, I had begun to feel the walls of my own life closing in. Perhaps it was the approach of middle age: I would be 35 in a few months; I was no longer a young man with my future uncharted in front of me. Perhaps it was the collapse of the Movement. I had not been one of those who believed in the imminence of the revolution, but I could not escape the deflation that followed its defeats. We had been a vanguard, and now it was clear that none of our grandiose aspirations would be realized. The tide of history had run out, stranding us on ordinary shores.[1]

—DAVID HOROWITZ

One old comrade, after a tirade in which she had denounced us as reactionaries and crypto-fascists, finally sputtered, "And the worst thing is that you've turned your back on the Sixties!" That was exactly right.[2]

—DAVID HOROWITZ AND PETER COLLIER

In October of 1974, David Horowitz published an unusually personal essay in *Ramparts*, the freewheeling left-wing magazine from which he was just stepping down as editor. The piece, "The Passion of the Jews," was Horowitz's most significant effort in years to sum up his positive hopes for how the Movement could reimagine itself in the wake of its mostly self-inflicted defeats of the previous few years. It was also the first time he really tried to theoretically unify his identity as a Jew, Marxist, and supporter of civil rights.[3]

His particular target in the essay was what he saw as a turn by American Jews away from the black freedom struggle. Particularly troubling, he wrote, were people like *Commentary* editor Norman Podhoretz, who were exploiting genuine but unrepresentative examples of black anti-Semitism, and real but not existential conflicts between the collective interests of blacks and Jews, to argue for a transformation in how Jews defined their political interests and principles in America.

In Podhoretz's telling, there had been a brief postwar period in America, a "Golden Age of Jewish Security," when things were so good for the Jews that they could afford to be universalist, to see their own interests as indivisible from those of the polity. Anti-Semitism had gone missing from public life. The doors of the great universities were opening wide to anyone who could earn good grades and score well on standardized tests (i.e., Jews). In some cultural circles it even became chic to be Jewish.

"Under such circumstances," Podhoretz had written in *Commentary*, "why would anyone ask whether anything was good for the Jews? Surely *everything* was good for the Jews."[4]

Then things changed, somewhere around 1966 or 1967. After Israel's stunning victory over its Arab neighbors in the Six-Day War, and its occupation of Palestinian lands, the Left and the militant black Left turned against the Jewish homeland. Anti-discrimination policies, which had benefited both blacks and Jews, began to morph into affirmative action policies that threatened to privilege certain minorities while diminishing some of the gains Jews had achieved. Anti-Semitism was making a modest but ominous comeback, most overtly among blacks and in the WASPier regions of the literary world.

"Discussing some of these tendencies on another occasion," Podhoretz wrote, "I said that they warranted neither panic nor hysteria but 'a certain anxiety.' Indeed I think they do. But I also think they warrant something else by way of a healthy Jewish response. I think they warrant a revival among Jews of that ancient and prematurely laughed-off question, *Is it good for the Jews?*"[5]

For Horowitz, this was wrongheaded on every front. It was alarmist about the dangers facing Jews in America, which were not nearly so great they required a reversion to tribalist attitudes. It mistook the present distribution of wealth and power in America, shares of which Jews certainly had been very successful in acquiring, as a status quo worth protecting rather than dismantling. It threatened to sever a historic political alliance between blacks and Jews that had been a potent force for equality in America. It would hurt blacks, who were "the Jews of America, the obsessional victim of the white majority in much the same way that Jews have been the obsessional victims of Christian majorities in Europe."[6] And it would strike at the ethical core of Jewish existence, which for Horowitz was grounded not in the tradition of Jews looking out for their own but rather in the liberation story of Exodus, the sensitizing experiences of diaspora, and above all the insight of the prophets that because of their own legacy of suffering Jews should have unique empathy for, and solidarity with, the suffering and humanity of others. For Horowitz this empathy was at the heart of what it meant to be a Jew and also, as it happened, at the heart of what he believed socialism should be.

"Today there is black and Jew, American and Russian, Israeli and Arab," he wrote. "But within each nation—Russia, America, Israel, Egypt—there are the aliens, the persecuted, the unassimilated, the 'Jews' who know the heart of the stranger and struggle for human freedom. Today they are separated; tomorrow they will be joined. Today the light of their faith shines in many national colors, but it is also expressed in the service that commemorates the Exodus and looks toward a future turning: *This year we are slaves; next year we shall be free men and women. This year in the lands of our exile; next year in Jerusalem.*"[7]

The essay had a forward-looking tone to it, and some optimism. In many ways, however, it was the product of exhaustion. Horowitz was only thirty-five, but it felt as if he'd already lived four or five lives on the radical Left, and was uncertain he was up for another one.

As a boy in the 1940s and '50s, he'd lived a double life, playing at being a normal Jewish kid from Queens while gradually absorbing from his parents and their Communist Party friends that there was another, secret world where their true loyalties lay. As an adult he'd devoted himself, with a compulsive energy, to building a Marxist Left that would somehow avoid all the errors of allegiance and logic, strategy and rhetoric, that had betrayed his parents and their generation.[8] That mission had taken him to Berkeley in the early 1960s, when the New Left was being born. It had taken him across the ocean to Europe, where he'd worked with some of the luminaries of the international Left and made his first real mark as a Marxist intellectual. It had brought him back to the Bay Area at the end of the 1960s to *Ramparts*. And it had brought him, in the early 1970s, into a close but fraught partnership with Black Panther leader Huey Newton, who for a few years seemed to Horowitz to embody within him yet another, possibly redemptive vision of what the Left should be.

By 1974 the Panther hope, too, had expired. The Panthers had been past their revolutionary prime even when Horowitz had first met and been entranced by Newton, in 1971, but for a while the charisma of Newton, and the absence of viable alternatives, had kept Horowitz engaged. Now the Black Panther Party was a fragment of its former self, with nearly every one of its charismatic leaders dead, in jail, up on charges, on the run, or in exile abroad. Newton himself had fled to Cuba in August of 1974 to avoid trial for allegedly shooting a prostitute.

A final blow had come the same month "The Passion of the Jews" was published, when a teen dance held at a Panther-run school and community center ended in the shooting death of a young Panther. Violence was nothing new to the group, but it wasn't supposed to happen at the school, which was supposed to be a refuge for kids, and which Horowitz had helped raise the money to build. It was the site where his engagement with the party was most intimate, and it was a moment, after Newton's flight from the country, when he was particularly vulnerable. At the memorial service for the young man who was killed, he realized it was the end for him.

"When I went inside, the children and their parents were reassuringly assembled almost as though attending a normal Learning Center event. But in front of the stage, beside the open casket, was an honor guard of blue-shirted Panthers, berets aslant, shotguns held aloft, as in the old days before Huey went to jail. The juxtaposition—children and guns—was jarring, and caused me to shudder. I felt as if at the bottom of the abyss. Tears streamed down my cheeks, and a strident voice sounded in my brain: '*David, what are you doing here?*' When I left the service, I knew I was never going back."[9]

It was a bleak moment for Horowitz. Even so, he knew it wasn't objectively the darkest moment in the history of the Left. The New Left and its affiliate movements were dead or enfeebled now a few years, victims of a confluence of factors: their own pathologies, their own successes in ending legal segregation and the ground war in Vietnam, countervailing movements on the Right, and coordinated and not-so-coordinated campaigns from the police and FBI to subvert and destroy them. But the revolution had fallen low before, in other times and places, and it was never the end of the story. People would rise once again to pose a challenge to the cruelty, violence, and inequality of the modern imperialist capitalist system. Future triumph wasn't assured, but future conflict was certain, because the contradictions at the core of capitalism were genetic. Next time around perhaps the outcome would be different. Or it wouldn't, but the story wouldn't be over then either, couldn't be over, because it was driven forward by a yearning for equality and justice in the human soul that was intrinsic and ultimately unfinessable.

In truth the movement wasn't even in such a rough position. There had been killings—of Panthers in Oakland, protesters at Kent State, little girls in Birmingham—but no purges. There had been arrests in

Washington, Selma, New York, Chicago, Berkeley, everywhere, but there was no gulag. There was the FBI and its arsenal of dirty tricks, but no secret police disappearing people in the night. There wasn't even a blacklist anymore. Most of the people who'd populated the Movement at the peak of its 1960s vigor were still alive, at large, and able to go about their lives, political or otherwise, unterrorized. Many were participating in their communities, writing books, becoming teachers and social workers and editors, having children. Things were bad but not so bad, and not beyond redemption.

Yet the moment felt so bleak to Horowitz anyway, because it wasn't History he was living through. It was his life, and it was his own intimate, excruciating experience of having to watch as one by one the fundaments of that life were dissolving away.

Students for a Democratic Society (SDS), the New Left group with which he'd most closely associated during the 1960s, had destroyed itself through factionalization and radicalization far more thoroughly than J. Edgar Hoover ever could have managed on his own. *Ramparts* was on its last legs, likely wouldn't survive another year. The Panthers seemed done. Even Horowitz's private life, which for fifteen years had been the bourgeois rock of his radical existence, was in disequilibrium. He'd had a brief affair with Abby Rockefeller, a radical-minded member of the Rockefeller family who'd given some money to *Ramparts* and was serving as one of his main sources on a book that he and his fellow former co-editor, Peter Collier, were in the process of writing on the dynasty. Horowitz's wife, Elissa, to whom he'd quickly and abjectly confessed, wasn't going to force him to leave her and their four children, but she wasn't happy.

So it was bad, but perhaps survivable had the badness eased up or even just remained stable. Much of his political writing over the previous few years had been an effort to come to terms with the increasingly obvious fact that the revolution wasn't coming anytime soon, and to consider responses in light of that fact. "The Passion of the Jews" was such an effort. At that moment, he seemed set to do what so many of his friends and allies would go on to do, which was muddle forward, wrestling with what it meant that the revolution wasn't coming, for the rest of an engaged but less urgently conducted political life. After all, what else was there to do? Where else was there to go? To a degree rare even among his fellow radicals, Horowitz's whole identity had been forged on, by, and in the company of the Left. It was in his blood. And it was almost certainly where he would have stayed, had things improved or remained merely dispiriting. Instead they got much worse.

In December Abby Rockefeller insisted on flying out to Berkeley to see the manuscript of the Rockefeller book, which was nearly finished.

Horowitz had already broken off the affair, but he'd kept in touch with Rockefeller for the sake of the book, keeping the wound open. A visit from the other woman to his wife's turf seemed dangerously provocative.

It also didn't help that he had lied to Collier about his arrangement with Rockefeller. Without telling Collier, he'd promised Abby that she could see the book before it was published, and that she'd have veto power. If she wanted something taken out, he'd vowed, it would be done. Now all the bills were coming due at once.

"Abby and I were sitting across from each other at dinner in the Berkeley marina, and she was telling me she wanted everything that we had written about her excised from our book. . . . [H]ow could I face Peter with her demand? I had gone behind his back to keep my trust with her. How could I ask him to jeopardize nearly three years of effort to honor a promise that was a betrayal of *him*? I told her I could not. 'You prefer the truth of your book,' she said bitterly, 'to the truth of me.' The next day she flew back to Cambridge. Before leaving, she called Peter and told him that she had read the text, thus exposing my breach of faith, and she wanted to see the chapter about her removed. Before Peter had time to react, however, Elissa's jealousy erupted."[10]

Horowitz and Elissa began fighting. Then in the middle of the fight, the telephone rang. Betty Van Patter, a Bay Area leftist who'd worked for him at *Ramparts* and whom he'd recently recommended to the Panthers when they were looking for a bookkeeper, had disappeared.

Van Patter's body would wash up on the shore of the Bay about a month later, on January 17, 1975. The autopsy determined that she'd died by a blow to the head. The murder would never officially be solved, but Horowitz quickly would come to believe—and later evidence would support this belief—that the Panthers had done it.[11]

And if that were the case, Horowitz realized, then he was to blame as well, for putting Van Patter in harm's way.

"What had I seen, yet somehow forgotten?" he later wrote. "What should I have noticed before that might have saved Betty, but did not? As soon as I was able to focus my thoughts in this way, reading back from the event, images I had buried began to resurface."[12]

As he went back over his own choices, and discovered more about the events leading up to her death, he grew to feel even worse. Van Patter had called Horowitz a few weeks before her disappearance, sounding upset, wanting to know if Horowitz knew how to reach Elaine Brown, who'd taken over the party after Newton fled. Rather than try to engage her, Horowitz had stayed quiet, worried for his own sake that if he began venting his own concerns about the Panthers then Van Patter might report on him back to Brown. Now Van Patter was dead, and he believed he was substantially to blame.

In the weeks and months following her death, his interrogation of himself broadened to include the whole history of decisions and judgments that had led to his involvement with the Panthers. Had the original sin, he wondered, been committed much earlier? When Horowitz first met Newton, after all, the Panther leader was awaiting retrial for the killing of an Oakland police officer, an offense for which he'd been convicted the first time around. Horowitz had accepted what Newton said, that the police had been out for Panther blood and Newton had only defended himself. But what if the alternative version were true?

What if it was Newton who'd shot first, who'd been waiting for an opportunity to kill?

In his life with the Panthers, Horowitz had faced a steady drumbeat of such questions about which of two irreconcilable versions to believe when it came to violence done by or to party members. He had always accepted the Panther answer, because doing so was part of the existential condition of being a supporter of a group whose basic narrative was that the American regime was too racist to tolerate black folks arming and defending themselves. The Panthers, by definition, created a disruption in the system that the state couldn't help but try to iron out. Thus Panthers in jail were political prisoners. Dead Panthers were martyrs. Panthers who'd fled trial were exiles, and Panthers being harassed by the police were dissidents. If you didn't buy that paradigm, then you had no business being involved with the party. Horowitz had chosen to believe.

Now he wasn't involved with the party anymore. His obligation to believe had been brutally severed, and every alternative version he'd once chosen to disregard was open for consideration again. Had Newton killed a prostitute? Could it be true? What about rumors from earlier in the year that Newton had cruelly beaten a tailor, who was at his apartment measuring him for some suits, simply because the man had made an offhand remark that offended Newton? What about the rumors that he'd abused Bobby Seale before expelling him from the organization the two had founded together, or the ones that Newton had been involved in a shooting outside an after-hours nightclub in Oakland that had left one man dead? Could it all be true? Could Newton all along have been the paranoid, rage-filled cocaine addict that enemies of his had said he was?

The more Horowitz mulled over the past, the more he concluded that it wasn't so much that he'd made many individual errors of judgment as that he'd failed to perceive from the outset what the proper interpretive frame was. The Black Panther Party in Oakland, in the years he'd known it, wasn't a political and service organization that had some unfortunate gangsterish tendencies around the edges. It was a street gang that also did some politics and service. The revolutionary politics may have been sincerely held, and the service programs had surely helped many people, but they weren't what you needed to know to get what the Panthers were about. They weren't revolutionaries first, he concluded. They were thugs. Because of this, no matter his intentions, it was their violence he had served.

With this conclusion reached, everything shifted. Only a few years before he'd been willing to harbor a fugitive Panther on the run from the police. Now Horowitz went to the police and told them everything he knew and suspected about the Panthers' involvement in Van Patter's death. He stopped talking openly to most of his friends and colleagues in the Bay Area radical community, for fear that if he said too much about Van Patter's case—which he would have; it was all he could think about—word would filter back to the party that he was causing problems. Then his life might be in danger.

He realized, too, that even though he still shared the same broad political goals with his lefty friends, he no longer could take for granted that his calculations of interest and self-interest were being made with the same math. He was driven to know and expose the truth about Van Patter's death, but what would happen, safety considerations aside, if he went seeking allies on the Left in this matter? His radical colleagues knew as well as anyone that the Panthers were dangerous. That was central to the group's allure. And the savvier among them probably knew on some level that there was lawbreaking and head-busting going on that had no possible political justification or motivation. But no one wanted to hear about it, or talk about it. It was too uncomfortable, touched on too many points of anxiety, guilt, and shame in the collective left-wing unconscious. So people would cut a check for the school lunch program, sign a letter of protest on behalf of a jailed Panther, make sure to keep themselves at a moderately safe distance, and veer quickly away from any facts that might complicate the story line. The last thing anyone wanted was to help serve up the Panthers to the police for the killing of a white woman.

"If I were to tell *any* of them what I thought—that the Panthers had killed Betty—I would have been disbelieved at first, and then suspect," Horowitz wrote. "Why would I even suggest such an idea unless I regarded the Panthers as enemies, or intended them harm? And not only them, but the cause as well. And why would I do that unless I had been infected by racism, or joined the other side?"[13]

Horowitz hadn't joined the other side, but in the aftermath of Van Patter's death he did two things that would lay the foundation for his eventual departure. He withdrew somewhat from his community. And he fell apart. He was of course done with the Black Panther Party, which had been the main vehicle of his activist energies for the previous few years. And while he was still connected to *Ramparts* as a board member and occasional contributor, that tie was broken when the magazine published its last issue in August of 1975. And with that much of the regular political and intellectual intercourse he had with other leftists dissolved, though his friends were still all leftists.[14]

The Rockefellers: An American Dynasty finally came out in March of 1976, and was a success even beyond Horowitz and Collier's hopes—Book-of-the-Month Club selection, *New York Times* best seller, subject of rave reviews. But the success ended up isolating Horowitz even further. For the first time in his adult life he didn't have to hustle to support himself and his family. So instead of finding another job in left-wing journalism, embedding with another radical community, he stayed home and tried and mostly failed to make progress on the two radical books he had in motion, neither of which he cared about anymore. In the long hours left in the day, until his kids got home from school, he loathed himself. For what had happened to Betty, for how he'd betrayed his wife, for the horrible, inescapable irony of how he'd betrayed himself.

He had spent his adult life on the Left trying to rescue Marxism from the mistakes his Communist Party parents and their comrades had so disastrously made, perhaps the most damaging of which had been the eager rush to suspend critical judgment when it came to hard-faced exotic revolutionaries who seemed to have the ruthlessness and certainty to get things done. For his parents it had been the Soviets. That crew had been out of fashion at least since 1956, when Khrushchev's secret speech acknowledging some of the crimes of Stalin was smuggled out and published in the West. Now it was the Chinese, the North Vietnamese, or the Cubans who were the exotic flavor of the month. Or if you were looking closer to home it was groups like the Black Panthers.

The union between himself and the Panthers had never been as complete as his parents and their comrades' identification with the Communists. He hadn't taken orders from the Panthers, or been willing to commit espionage on their behalf. He hadn't bought most of their propaganda (though he'd published some). He hadn't apologized for or looked away from mass murder. Whatever the Panthers' crimes, they were on a small scale; the group didn't control a nation, or even a city. But still, it seemed to him that the nature of his mistake had been the same. He'd been seduced. He'd been drawn to the aura of power and danger and action, to the chance to be a doer of deeds rather than just a writer of words. And death had been the outcome.

"It was a terrible vision I had," he said. "I was basically repeating the mistakes of the previous generation of the Left. I had sworn that I would never do that."[15]

For fifteen years, from the moment he graduated from Columbia University and took up life as an adult activist to the moment Van Patter disappeared, David Horowitz had been furiously productive. In Berkeley in the early 1960s he'd helped organize the protests that first gave shape to the radical energies emanating forth there.[16] He'd written six books, including one that would inspire Mario Savio to head west to Berkeley, another that would serve as an important theoretical text for the New Left in its critique of American Cold War policy, and another (his master's thesis from Berkeley) on Shakespeare and existentialism. In London he'd helped the Bertrand Russell Peace Foundation organize an intellectually star-studded "war crimes tribunal" to publicly interrogate the United States for its actions in Vietnam. He'd had four children, edited four more books, hatched and executed the plan that brought *Ramparts* back from the brink of extinction, and extracted enough money from wealthy leftists and liberals to build the Oakland Community Learning Center for the Panthers. And he'd achieved all this without great personal charm or much in the way of native writing talent. His tools instead were extraordinary reserves of energy, a penetrating intellect, a capacity for focus so intense Collier once told him it was like a "kind of autism," and a need to redeem the radical hopes and actions of his parents so fierce it burned through all the distractions and doubts that inhibit most people from simply doing every single thing they would like to be able to do.[17] Now after all these years of moving forward with such speed and surety of purpose, he was adrift, with no obvious target for his ceaseless intellection other than down onto himself and his failures.

"Unhappiness settled over my life like an arctic snow," he wrote. "Nowhere I looked provided me comfort. In the privacy of my grief, I focused on the past. I seemed to gravitate toward the center of my own disorder, taking morbid pleasure in becoming my own prosecutor, testing to see how darkly I could depict myself and what I had done. I had come to the end of everything I had ever worked for in my life, and I had no idea how to disentangle myself from my fate."[18]

For most of the remainder of the decade, where once there had been a reliable torrent of writing, editing, connecting, and doing, there was now instead disorder, depression, self-destruction, self-flagellation, and introspection. With the exception of one short book, an analysis of America's character through the lens of its originating interactions with Indians,[19] he basically stopped writing. He began drinking in a way he never had before. He fell out with friends, including Collier. He bought a sports car and then wrecked it, nearly killing himself, when he failed to notice until almost too late that a train was approaching the crossing where he was idling. Many mornings he would give up trying to work almost immediately and simply "collapse on the sofa and plumb my sorrows, sinking into their murky, bottomless depths, weeping in silence."[20]

He also destroyed what remained of his marriage by falling into a more serious and sustained affair than his last, this one with Jackie Dennis, the wife of a left-wing acquaintance of his. The two got talking one day at the elementary school his kids attended, where Dennis was a teacher, and she mentioned, among other things, that she was separated from her husband and that she was now doing psychic energy healing. A few years earlier, "psychic" anything would have elicited instant disdain from Horowitz, who'd never had any interest in the more metaphysical manifestations of the counterculture, and who had regarded even conventional psychotherapy as a refuge of the weak-minded. But what disdain he now could muster was reserved for himself and for those involved with, or in denial about, what had happened to Van Patter. People who were just out there following their own loopy enthusiasms, not hurting anyone, weren't beneath him. They were above him, and besides, Dennis in particular seemed "radiant and happy," not to mention very attractive. So he scheduled a session, and then another, and then another.

"About the psychic realm she introduced me to, I suspended disbelief," he wrote. "I was too thirsty for the elixir she offered to do otherwise. Entering, if only imaginatively, a world in which history and politics were left behind was healing in itself. And why, in any case, should I feel metaphysically superior? I had schooled myself in Hegel and Marx, and where had they led me? I had worshipped the gods of reason, and they had delivered me into the company of killers."[21]

The affair didn't start immediately. For a while it was just much-needed therapy. She guided him through visualization exercises. She moved her hands over his body, almost but not quite touching him, to clear his aura. She listened. And it felt good to be cared for, whether or not his aura was in fact being cleared. Dennis was also familiar enough with the radical scene, and detached enough from it, to be able to listen to Horowitz talk about what he was going through with just the right quality of sympathetic attention.

Then they began sleeping together, and his sense of what kind of man he was, which was already coming apart at the seams, was stretched to the point of disintegration. Exhilaration and release warred with guilt and self-loathing. He even discovered within himself a pleasure in destruction and recklessness that he'd never imagined he could feel before.

"I enjoyed watching [Jackie] betray her principles. Here was company. Here was behavior in accord with my new appreciation of human possibility. Was there a rule to be broken? I wanted to break it myself."[22]

Eventually the strain was too great, and he ended the affair with Dennis and confessed and tried to work things out with Elissa. But it was too late. The damage had been done, less to the marriage itself than to the person he'd been within it. He and Elissa went to marriage counseling. He went to a therapist on his own. Elissa was willing to soldier on, but he couldn't. He knew little about who he was anymore, or what he wanted his life to be. But like so many other contemporaries of his who'd been raised in the 1940s and '50s and then had their lives upended by the 1960s and '70s, he was sure of one thing: There had to be change. Soldiering on in the old way wasn't an option, and that was all that Elissa, whose stolidity he'd relied on for so long, could offer him. Theirs would become a version of the sour loveless partnership his parents had had, with himself in the role of his father, blaming his spouse for all the opportunities he'd missed and all the men he hadn't become. His "entire being rebelled at the idea."[23] So in the fall of 1978 he moved out, and they divorced soon after.

Horowitz's political intellectual life during this period was in many ways as disordered as his personal life, but there was an important difference. Romantically he was willing to float out into the abyss without exerting too much control over the direction of his drift. Politically the need to get to wherever he was going as fast as possible, through his own exertions, was much more urgent. To do that he had to wrestle with the past.

The primal text in this process was his continued investigation of the Panthers. He began tracking down and interviewing ex-Panthers, uncovering deeper and more horrifying layers of the dysfunction that had consumed the group at least as far back as Newton's release from jail in 1970. Under Newton's increasingly unbalanced leadership they ran protection rackets, extorting money from local businesses and local criminals. They used their legitimate activities to obscure and scrub their criminal ends. They claimed territory and used violence to enforce its borders. Newton, in whom the balance of idealism, intelligence, and pathology had always existed in crackling tension, had by the time Horowitz met him crumpled and twisted under a load of burdens so heavy it would have bent all but the sturdiest of characters. He took women as he wanted them, by force or command. He had an awful addiction to cocaine. He held audiences captive for hours, under threat of pain or death, forcing them to receive his elaborate theories of the world. He saw enemies lurking in every shadow, and dealt out violence suddenly and arbitrarily in a vain effort to exert control over his paranoia. There was even evidence that it was Newton, from Cuba, who had ordered Van Patter's murder, because she'd discovered that the Panthers were embezzling money from their legitimate operations.[24]

"Who *was* this man I had served at such great cost?" Horowitz wondered.[25]

Horowitz marinated in the details to punish himself. How could he have *been* so blind? On another level he was toiling as he always had, sifting through the data in order to discern the schema that bound it all together. How exactly *could* he have been so blind? And from the anger and self-hatred a political intuition began to coalesce. Barely even an intuition at first—a shard of pain emanating from the suppurating wound in his psyche gesturing in the direction of an intuition. He was culpable, of course, but it was more than that. He'd been infected, perhaps from birth, by a disease afflicting how the Left dealt with black people. It romanticized them, apologized for them, primitivized them, saw them before anything else as either the victims or the potential beneficiaries of the agency of white people.

This perception dispersed out to color almost everything he did and thought. He became obsessed with the case of Ellen Sparer, a childhood friend of his who'd been raped and murdered by a young black man. There was nothing overtly political about the death. Sparer had been a high-school math teacher in Englewood, New Jersey, and had had the terrible luck to be the last in a series of women in her neighborhood who were brutalized by her killer. Yet the more Horowitz learned about it, the more convinced he became that in an important way her death was a result of the same deadly contagion that he and others on the Left had been spreading for years.

"Ellen wanted to be mother to the world," a mutual left-wing friend wrote to Horowitz, "mother to the revolution, and I think her strongest wish was to mother a black child. . . . It is also true she befriended and succored all the sad, lonely, dependent souls with whom she came in contact—black and white."[26]

By the time Sparer was murdered she wasn't as political as she'd once been, but she was still a rescuer, still a compulsive subordinator of her own interests to those of the less fortunate, more needy. Earlier in her life she'd opened her home to radical-minded militants and ex-cons, including Black Panthers, to the point where it became one of the causes of her divorce. In more recent years she had made herself radically available to her students, kids in the neighborhood, all the young and lost souls she met who seemed like they needed rescuing. She kept the door to her (and her children's) home open at almost all times. She made loans to students that would never be repaid. She'd even once tried to help the young man who later raped and killed her. It wasn't that her death was inevitable, Horowitz concluded, but that some form of blowback was. Such extreme naïveté and recklessness, enabled by fantasies of rescuing the damaged and oppressed, invited its own violent disabusal.

"Given who she was and how she approached the world, I felt she was fortunate to have avoided her fate as long as she had," he wrote. "A similar idea about myself had entered my mind: Given what I had done and with whom I had become involved, I was lucky to be alive. . . . It now seemed obvious to me that both Ellen and I were destined to some kind of grief. We hadn't understood the way in which our good intentions could be dangerous, either to us or to others. It was as if there was a flaw in our DNA that deprived us of sensors that would have provided warnings."[27]

For his whole political life, with the brief exception of a period in his teens when he fell under the influence of Tolstoy and fashioned himself a "Christian Romantic," Horowitz had been a Marxist.[28] Not a rigid one. He'd seen how orthodoxy had distorted his parents' lives, and from very early in his adult intellectual life had vowed to himself that he would not make an idol of Marx. He would take those parts of the theory that held up to the test of rigorous philosophical interrogation and discard the rest. He would look unflinchingly at the brutalities committed by self-described socialist states, operating under the aegis of Marxist language, and wrestle with what, if any, theory was implicated by the awful praxis. He told himself he would be willing to reject it all if that was where honesty and rigor pointed.

In truth, though, his independence had run along a narrow band. He'd rarely questioned the baseline position that within Marxism lay the analyses that most powerfully identified the flaws in capitalist society as well as the blueprints for a more humane and just society. He would test himself against all critics, as long as their criticisms remained tethered to a fundamental loyalty to Marxism, but not against those writers, texts, or discourses that posed the greatest threat to his worldview, not against Chambers and Orwell, Bakunin and Hayek, *The God That Failed* and *Darkness at Noon*, *Partisan Review* and *Commentary*.

To tussle with Marxism was who he was. To look beyond that, and risk disabusing himself of Marxism, was to risk becoming someone else.

Now he began looking. Not systematically, with any conscious sense of what he was looking for, but questingly. And as had been the case with so many soon-to-be ex-Marxist intellectuals before him, the books he needed to find seemed to coalesce before him. Some of them went after the figure of Marx himself—his unconscious motives, his uneasiness with his Jewishness, his personal flaws. Other works defamiliarized the theory. He read about Marxism in the context of other nineteenth-century intellectual and political movements that shared many of its eschatological qualities. He engaged with critiques of basic Marxist concepts and language that forced him to contemplate, as he never had before, whether some of what he'd accepted as objective and scientific thinking from one of the great minds of history wasn't instead the idiosyncratic product of a brilliant but all too human brain.

Perhaps the most important influence on him, during this period of re-evaluation, was the Polish exile Leszek Kolakowski, whose own dramatic trajectory, from Communist Party member to dissenting Marxist to doubter to ex-Marxist, provided Horowitz a kind of road map for how he might wrest his own thinking out of the grooves along which it had run for so long. Kolakowski's writing was also particularly amenable to Horowitz for its lawyerly style, which was tonic to Horowitz at a time when he felt so buffeted by emotion that he questioned his capacity to reason at all. If Kolakowski had been able to formulate the grounds of his dissent clearly, with all the risks that that entailed for a writer laboring in the shadow of the Soviet Union, then perhaps David Horowitz of Berkeley, California, could achieve some clarity as well.

He read Kolakowski on the danger, implicit in all utopian movements, that if the material of human nature proved too weak or brittle to withstand the stresses that the utopian architecture tried to impose upon it, then the architects might prefer to discard the humans rather than their precious blueprints. He read Kolakowski's caustic response to Marxist historian E. P. Thompson, who had written a fifty-thousand-word essay chastising the Pole for his turn away from the Marxist Left. Particularly meaningful for Horowitz were the published proceedings of a conference Kolakowski had organized in England, a few years before, on the subject of "Is there Anything Wrong with the Socialist Idea?"[29]

The whole volume was precisely the kind of thing Horowitz had avoided in his past life, a series of good-faith interrogations, from men and women who had been or who remained socialists, of the basic premises of Marxist theory. No cheap shots. No sentimental appeals to God or apple pie. No easy resort to the unpleasant history of socialist regimes to answer the question of whether Marxism has contributions to make to a more humane and democratic future. But also no mercy. Everything was up for question, including the bedrock decency and defensibility of the intellectual and political project to which most of the participants in the conference had devoted a good part of their lives.

Kolakowski's own essay in the volume was a particularly brutal exercise in deconstruction. He made the case, methodically and relentlessly, that state ownership of the means of production could persist over time only through coercion. He held up to bone-dry ridicule the Marxist preoccupation with class conflict to the exclusion of all other sources of conflict in human life and politics. He analyzed and then undermined what he saw as the "primordial hope" at the heart of Marx's vision, which was the idea that in the socialist future there would be an end to alienation, to the separation between man as a private being and man as a political actor. In its place "man returning to perfect unity, experiencing directly his personal life as a social force."[30]

For Horowitz the delineation of this "Rousseauist" hope, as Kolakowski named it, struck the most resonant chord. It was a version of what his allies in SDS had celebrated in their Port Huron Statement, when they'd spoken of what "participatory democracy" would look like.[31] The dream, of an end to alienation, was baked into the bricks of the Panther school he had helped build, where children would be fed, housed, and educated together, nurtured into a generation of politically integrated and effectual black men and women. It was there in the spirit of how Ellen Sparer had lived her life. It was there in his childhood as a young communist, in his foray into Christian Romanticism, in everything he'd done as a leftist and Marxist. He'd declared for it himself, in his first book, when describing the exhilaration of marching together with his fellow Berkeley students as they protested the hearings being held by the House Un-American Activities Committee (HUAC) in San Francisco in May of 1960.

"The truth is that man cannot live for himself alone," he'd written, "that sooner or later the emptiness of such life overcomes him and he seeks involvement with others. The community of men and their history has the power to complete us in a way in which we never would be otherwise completed; it involves us in a way in which we cannot escape being involved."[32]

Horowitz wasn't ready to renounce all, or even most, of what he and his friends and allies had fought for over the previous fifteen years. But the more he read and reflected the more he felt compelled to detach from some of the psychological bases—guilt, romanticism, utopianism, anti-Americanism, Marxism, envy, elitism—that he'd come to believe they had sallied forth from. He also began to connect the dots between these tendencies, the failures of the Left to achieve its goals in America, and the refusal of the Left to look at its culpability in those horrors abroad, where left-wing governments had succeeded in acquiring the power to execute their goals.

He began trying to engage his fellow radicals in conversations about these ideas. He taught a class, at a radical institute, on the topic of "Is Socialism a Viable Idea?" He participated in a small seminar at Berkeley, on the topic of "Marxism and Post-Marxism," with a number of his fellow New Left veterans. He brought his issues up at dinner parties and over lunches. None of it resulted in the reasoned dialogues he imagined he was trying to generate. His potential interlocutors were too defensive or uninterested. He was too angry. In practice his efforts to start conversations manifested as a tendency to pick fights.

Compulsively, he would home in on all the things the Bay Area Left of the mid-to-late 1970s didn't want to talk about, and he'd talk about them. All the failures, elisions, and veins of bad faith that riddled the Movement. And not just their movement, in their country, at that time. The whole history of the modern Left, around the whole world. The Panthers. Weatherman. The Symbionese Liberation Army. The anti-white and anti-Semitic turn in some segments of the black nationalist movement. The long black record of Communist crimes in the Soviet Union, China, Vietnam, Cambodia, Cuba. The bad faith and deceptions of the Communist Party in America.

In the abstract he knew that the story of the dark side of the Left wasn't the whole story. Every political movement the world had ever seen had had a dark side, and you needed to consider the whole before declaring the entire project rotten. What he felt, though, was that this counternarrative of the Left hadn't been explored sufficiently within the Movement for anyone to feel complacent about their overall goodness. When he got really worked up, the bad stuff was all that mattered. America's crimes in Vietnam, which he'd once inveighed against so passionately, faded away, as did the Left's efforts to end the war. What mattered were the people slaughtered by the Vietnamese Communists after America withdrew, and the general silence of the Left in the face of these atrocities. Israel's treatment of the Palestinians disappeared; the Left's hostility to Israel, which sometimes shaded into anti-Semitism, was what was salient. When he was in high dudgeon, the centuries-long history of racism and brutality against blacks in America, and the equally long and inspiringly heroic struggle against it, receded to the status of prologue. The real story was the collection of those instances, in the past decade or so, where blacks had turned against their former allies on the Left.

"I began to review events of the past to which I had paid little attention before," he wrote, "like the expulsion of the Jews from the civil-rights movement in 1966. Jews had funded the movement, devised its legal strategies, and provided support for its efforts in the media and in the universities—and wherever else they had power. More than half the freedom riders who had gone to the southern states were Jews, although Jews constituted only 3 percent of the population. It was an unprecedented show of solidarity from one people to another. Jews had put their resources and lives on the line to support the Black struggle for civil rights, and indeed two of their sons—Schwerner and Goodman—had been murdered for their efforts. But, even while these tragic events were still fresh, the Black leaders of the movement had unceremoniously expelled the Jews from their ranks. When Israel was attacked in 1967 by a coalition of Arab states calling for its annihilation, the same black leaders threw their support to the Arab aggressors, denouncing Zionism (the Jewish liberation movement) as racism. Rarely had a betrayal of one people by another been as total or as swift."[33]

His Jewishness, which had always played second or third fiddle to his socialist politics, began intruding into discussions and analyses where it never would have dared intrude before. He didn't yet accept the full tribalist conception of Jewishness that he had critiqued Podhoretz and others for promoting—that Jews should act first or only from their collective interests. But that there were such interests, and that the world divided along them in ways that transcended socialist theory, he now believed firmly. *Black vs. White. Arab vs. Jew. Black vs. Jew.* These were base realities. One could work to mitigate the harm that arose from them, but only a fool would deny them, and looking back it suddenly seemed to him as though the only fools had been he and his herd of benighted white (often Jewish) leftists. The blacks had seen things for what they were. Other Jews had. He now resolved to do the same.

When he was calm Horowitz was capable of some nuance, but it was easy to disturb his calm. And when he lost it, and often even when he didn't and was just raising issues that made people uneasy, he was met with anger, suspicion, and silence. These reactions, in turn, entrenched further his feeling that the Left was unable to look honestly at its own flaws.[34]

Around and around he went, provoking confrontation, receiving rejection in return, wrestling with despair and confusion and radical uncertainty about what his life could look like going forward. He was too disillusioned with the radical Left to imagine that he could reconstitute the sense of purpose and identity he'd once had as a man of the Left. But what then? What was on the other side? While browsing the shelves one night at Moe's Books in Berkeley, he had a kind of epiphany, or a bottoming out:

"Visiting Moe's, I would sometimes get a headache just trying to take in the multiplicity of works and put them into some order in my mind. There were so many titles competing for others' attention, so many competing with mine. That evening, my difficulties were unusually intense. I envisioned not only the universe of authors, but the universe of audiences as well. Audiences that did not know the others existed, or care. There were entire worlds of readers who devoured nothing but mysteries, or romances, or works on the occult, or science fiction—all of which were as foreign to me as the worlds of sociology and political economy were to them. Whole tiers of Moe's were occupied with these disparate universes, sufficient in themselves to exclude awareness of others. While I was thinking these thoughts, I had a sudden shock of recognition. Although my own books were confined to a tiny portion of a single shelf in this vast array of human learning, I had always found security in the belief that a hierarchy ordered it. I visualized a pyramid whose apex was Marxism, which was my life's work and which provided the key to all other knowledge. Marxism was the theory that would change everyone's world. And put mine at the center. But in that very moment a previously unthinkable possibility also entered my head: The Marxist idea, to which I had devoted my entire intellectual life and work, was false.

"All around me, the room went black. In the engulfing dark, the pyramid flattened and a desert appeared in its place, cold and infinite, and myself an invisible speck within it. *I am one of them*, I thought. *I am going to die and disappear like everyone else.* For the first time in my conscious life I was looking at myself in my human nakedness, without the support of revolutionary hopes, without the faith in a revolutionary future—without the sense of self-importance conferred by the role I would play in remaking the world. For the first time in my life I confronted myself as I really was in the endless march of human coming and going. *I was nothing.*"[35]

Horowitz had more epiphanies, and picked more gratuitous fights, before his anger and despair began to settle from their peak level of intensity, but at some point around the end of the decade he began to re-establish some equilibrium. His anger wasn't gone, but he was able to formulate his thoughts more clearly, start fights less compulsively, accept that he had lost something in his relationship to the Left that he would never recover.

In the summer of 1979 he happened to be having dinner with the novelist E. L. Doctorow, and the conversation came around to some of the topics that had been so much on Horowitz's mind. Doctorow listened to him attentively, and then suggested that he formulate his criticisms into an article for the *Nation*.

"I told him I was skeptical that *The Nation* would print them," Horowitz wrote. "But I knew he was on its editorial board, and decided to give it a try. I titled my article 'Left Illusions,' and *The Nation*'s editors printed it in their December 8, 1979 issue."[36]

The article was surprisingly temperate, more mournful than indignant, not so different in tone from a number of pieces he'd written for *Ramparts* earlier in the decade when he felt he had some complicated truths to air that his allies on the Left needed to hear. He didn't mention Betty Van Patter or the Black Panthers. There was nothing on Jewishness or race. It was assertive, but not gratuitously provocative. Most of the points he made were ones that he'd absorbed from his reading of Kolakowski and others. The Left was too attached to Marxism. Marxism was fatally undermined by romantic delusions. The Left was not only averse to acknowledging responsibility for crimes committed by left-wing revolutionaries, it tried to drown out its bad faith by turning up the volume on its critique of capitalism and America.

"Despite the disasters of twentieth-century revolutions, the viability of the revolutionary god remains largely unexamined and unquestioned," he wrote. "Even worse, radical commitments to justice and other social values continue to be dominated by a moral and political double standard. The left's indignation seems exclusively reserved for outrages that confirm the Marxist diagnosis of the sickness of capitalist society. Thus, there is protest against murder and repression in Nicaragua, but not Cambodia, Chile but not Tibet, South Africa but not Uganda, Israel but not Libya or Iraq."[37]

What was new in the essay was subtle. Horowitz didn't declare that he was done with the Left, but he wrote of his attachment to it from a distance, and in the past tense. At the end of the essay, when he posed his final challenge to the Left, to "fashion a new, more adequate vision of radical commitment and radical change," he didn't seem to be including himself as among those who might be expected to take up the challenge.[38]

The other novel aspect in the essay was the shift in his attitude toward America. No longer was he willing to take as a given that the nation's flaws, which he acknowledged were many, added up to a totality that was deserving only of condemnation, critique, and revolution. That attitude made sense, he wrote, when you were comparing it to a socialist utopia that existed only in the imagination. It also made sense if you thought American "freedom" and "democracy" were little more than camouflage for a reality that was nearly as brutal as what prevailed in the more overtly undemocratic nations.

But Horowitz, by December of 1979, didn't see it that way anymore. There was a profound difference, he believed, between American democracy and the so-called "democracy" of places like the Soviet Union. And the credit for that difference didn't just go, as certain sectors of the Left would have it, to the people throughout American history who'd defied the system. It went to the system as well, for its capacity to absorb dissent and respond to it constructively. America was more than he'd been able to admit in the past. And the best aspects of the Left, of himself, were more of America than he'd realized.

At that moment, Horowitz had become something he never imagined possible. He was a liberal of sorts—critical of America, but from a place more of allegiance than alienation, and operating from a philosophical perspective organized more by traditional Judeo-Christian categories of right and wrong than by Marxist ones. And indeed he unenthusiastically voted for Jimmy Carter in the 1980 election, which was what liberals unenthusiastically did in 1980.

In a number of ways a new vision was taking shape of what Horowitz's future might look like. He had a new house, close to where Elissa lived with the kids. He was dating a bit. After the divorce he'd reached out to Collier, who it turned out had been traveling along some parallel paths in his thinking about the Left. The two became friends again, and partners. They signed a contract to write a book on the Kennedy dynasty, in the hopes of emulating the success of their Rockefeller book.

So he would write big, best-selling books on American history and culture. Fill in the gaps with articles that often, though not always, would have a political aspect. Keep working to repair the wounds his kids had suffered from the divorce. Maybe find someone with whom to share his life. Be happy, more or less, as a liberal-minded writer who was mostly content to tend his own garden.[39] It wasn't a bad vision, and in many respects it was the life he would lead over the next few years.

But something nagged at Horowitz. He had changed as a result of his years-long existential crisis. He'd genuinely come to believe that it was okay not to be saving the world all the time, or at all. Better than okay. It was healthy. Take care of yourself and your family. Live well. Be a good citizen. Find what joy and contentment you can during the flicker of time you have on the planet. Then die. That was the good life, with its notes of tragedy and fragility, and it was the Left that sought to defy death and the appalling insignificance of a human life with its dreams of a utopian future.

That was what he believed. Whether he could be content living according to that belief was another question.

In May of 1980 Fay Stender, a left-wing criminal defense lawyer who had represented the Panthers and led the radical prison reform movement in the late 1960s and early 1970s, killed herself. She'd been shot the year before by a member of the Black Guerrilla Family, a prison gang that was founded by a former client, and the resulting paralysis, pain, and depression had ultimately been too much for her to bear. So she waited until a few months after the trial of her shooter, then traveled to Hong Kong, mailed off letters to her friends and family, and overdosed on sleeping pills. Her death triggered something in Horowitz, and he decided to go to her funeral service in San Francisco. By the end of the service, he'd decided to write an article.

"Speaker after speaker went up to the platform to remember Fay—lawyers who worked with her, comrades who had served with her, friends who loved her. They were political activists who would normally have made a political symbolism out of the most trivial occurrence. Yet, on the occasion of Fay's funeral, they had nothing to say about the sequence of events that had ended her life. One after the other, they rose to praise her in abstract terms as a woman who had dedicated herself to the cause of social justice. They lauded her lifelong service to the powerless and the persecuted. But not one of them could bring themselves to confront the terrible ironies that had brought them all together. She had been killed by a Black ex-prisoner who, in justifying his awful act, had invoked the memory of [Black Panther] George Jackson—the most resonant symbol of Fay's radical life and of her dedication to the cause of the oppressed. No one present referred to this irony. No one mentioned Fay's expulsion from the Jackson defense team, or the fact that she had stopped representing prisoners. No one reflected on what these events might mean to them, or to her. The truth was too threatening to the cause in which they still believed. So they suppressed it. In her last years, Fay herself had chosen to preserve the silence surrounding the events that had altered—and then ended—her life. Leaving the funeral, I knew I had to break that silence."[40]

Even before leaving the funeral home, he approached a former colleague of Stender and asked her if she'd be willing to meet and talk. She agreed. From there he expanded his investigation outward, speaking to family, friends, and colleagues. From Eve Pell, a former colleague and friend, he learned about the intensity of the erotic charge that had coalesced between the black prisoners and many of the white women who'd worked for the Prison Law Project, which was the prison reform group Stender had founded.[41] From Marvin Stender, Fay's ex-husband, he learned about the years after George Jackson had died trying to escape from San Quentin, when Stender had turned away from her prison work and toward more feminist-oriented activism. Their daughter Oriane talked about the very end of Stender's life, after she was shot. Her lover, for whom Fay had left Marvin, talked. Law partners, old friends, ex-friends, and new friends talked. Horowitz was able to interview at least someone from nearly every firm, organization, and activist group with which Stender had been connected, including the Prison Law Project and the Soledad Brothers Defense Committee, which Stender had organized specifically to frame public awareness about murder charges filed against Jackson and two fellow inmates.

In many ways it was a similar experience to the one Horowitz had had interviewing ex-Panthers. Most of his sources didn't share his global critique of the Movement, but he didn't force it on them, and if he listened long and sensitively enough his interviewees were usually willing to wrestle with the more discrete mistakes they had made, and to ponder the conflicted motives that might have led to them. The main difference between the postmortem he was doing on Stender and the private ones he'd done on Van Patter and Sparer was that he had more distance now. From the crimes, the community, the ideology, and the fear. The anger was still there, and a bit of the fear, but neither was as raw, and he felt as though he was master of them, able to chain them to his purpose.

"It was therapy," he remembered. "I was really talking about myself."[42]

For more than a year, while also researching the Kennedy book, Horowitz interviewed and interviewed and wrote and rewrote his story on Stender. Toward the end he gave a draft to Collier and asked him to help him finish it, which Collier did.

"Requiem for a Radical" came out in the March 1981 issue of *New West*, a California-based sister magazine to *New York*. It was an exemplary piece of new journalism, in which Stender's life, her politics, and the history through which she lived were woven together into a story that was engrossingly novelistic. There was sex. Stender had affairs with both Huey Newton and George Jackson ("authorities at Soledad once had to separate her physically from Jackson and drag her out of the visiting area with her clothes half off").[43] There was psychobiography, with trips back into Stender's past as the nerdy daughter of a mother so controlling she forced the young Fay to wear unnecessary orthopedic shoes so that her feet would be prettier, and "bound her hands at bedtime to keep her from destroying a possible concert career by sucking her thumbs."[44] There was intrigue, betrayal, and violence, climaxing in a Capote-esque, minute-by-minute dramatization of the night Stender was shot. Most impressively, it was all propelled forward by a genuinely moving narrative of Stender's struggle to reconcile the opposing elements of her psyche, to learn from the mistakes she'd made, and to craft for herself a life of meaning and dignity.

There were moments in the article when Horowitz and Collier intervened too crudely, shoehorning the data of Stender's life into an interpretation that didn't quite fit. But for the most part it worked. They used the material provided to them by Stender's family, friends, and political allies—by what remained of Stender herself—to construct a voice that felt as though it were the collective conscience of the Left itself speaking, like a Greek chorus, pronouncing the judgment of history. And precisely because her complexities and values were honored, the case they made was all the more persuasive. Not a crude polemical one, that all that she'd done and stood for was a waste, but almost a dramaturgical one, that the arc of her story was tragic. From her embrace of radicalism in the early 1960s, to her joy in the New Left's triumphs, her pain and confusion as it descended into craziness and nihilism, her turn in the 1970s to the politics of gender and sexuality, and then, finally, her death, the story contained within it so much of what it meant, for good and ill, to be alive and on the Left in America during that era. It was tragic, too, in the sense that Stender, and the movement of which she was representative, were in the end destroyed not by enemies external—racism, imperialism, capitalism, the FBI, the pigs, the corporations—but by flaws within.

The essay closed after her funeral, with Ezra Hendon, a friend and former colleague of Stender's, struggling to make sense of what the shooting and her suicide meant for him, his radical beliefs, and the certainty with which he and so many of his brothers- and sisters-in-arms had held them.

"Her funeral marked the end of an era in my life," he said, "and I think the end of an era, period. Her conviction that you could be committed to a political goal, work for it, and be brilliant in its service—in a clean way—that's over for me. I don't know about the others, but I can't have that belief anymore.

". . . I guess it would be easy to say that Fay played with fire, and people who play with fire get burned. But it should count for something that she wanted to be a force for good in the world, that she was a brilliant, remarkable woman who dedicated her life to others and to making the world a better place."

Horowitz and Collier added: "As he said the words, Hendon's eyes rimmed with tears. Like others who missed Fay, he was mourning not merely for a lost friend but for a lost cause as well."[45]

The article should have been a triumph for the two men. It was art-ful, entertaining, and an important documentation of the period. For anyone in the future who endeavored to write about Fay Stender, the prison reform movement, or George Jackson, "Requiem for a Radical" would be there waiting for them, on the record. The *New West* editor liked it, and promised Horowitz and Collier more assignments in the future. On a personal level it was evidence that Horowitz had some-thing to say about politics that was different from what he had said before. He'd made it to the other side.

There was some blowback, of course. Eve Pell felt that her interview had been mishandled, so she wrote a nasty letter to the editor, and fol-lowed that up with a nasty article in the newsletter of a Bay Area trade association of journalists. A few other area leftists got involved, there was a public forum, and for a little while it was the mini-scandal of the community. But it didn't add up to anything that a self-respecting new journalist shouldn't have been able to shake off in a few weeks.

It got under Horowitz's skin, though. And the more he ruminated, the angrier he got. He'd written the article with a few objectives. He wanted to tell a good story, explore some of his own critiques of the Left, and honor but also interrogate Stender's life and commitments. And it had done all that, successfully. But as time went on it was his sense of having been maligned that ramified. He'd acted in good faith, and was treated like rubbish in return. Called a liar, a McCarthyist, an enemy of the poor and imprisoned, an opportunist, a dupe of the Right, an abuser of a dead woman's legacy. Most unforgivably, Pell had brought up his history with the Panthers as a means of discrediting him, implying that he was too twisted up about his own past to be taken seriously on the topic of Stender's life.

After everything he'd been through. After the utter failure of the Bay Area Left to speak for the memory of Betty Van Patter or to tell the truth about the Panthers, now he was the betrayer for having had the courage to tell the truth about another victim of the dis-eased political imagination of the Left? He was the dupe? He was the opportunist? Didn't she know what he'd been through? How he'd struggled? That he might wrest some insight from the trauma of Van Patter's death was one of the core hopes he'd clung to when he was going through the process of reconstructing his identity, and now that was being used against him. It was unbearable. The worst of it was that he knew, he just knew, that it was Pell's self-serving version of events that would be more palatable to the small, self-justifying world in which he lived. That's what would be absorbed into the narrative.

He looked out at the Left, and at the world, and at how people on the Left and in the world talked about the history he'd lived through, and he began to doubt that simply having told his own story well was enough.

It wasn't the kind of doubt that would have haunted someone who was content to be a good writer and a good American. Or someone who had fully integrated the tragic sense of life. Or just someone with a thicker skin. But too much ambition remained in Horowitz, too much anger and pain. When pushed against it, he wasn't content to simply say his piece, to live his small life well, any more than he had been back when he was a revolutionary. The world had to change as a result of what he said and did.

A decade later Horowitz and Collier mused to a journalist, who was writing about their now-completed journey toward conservatism, that if only the response to the article had been positive, they might have stayed on the Left.[46] It was a surprising, and appealing, admission. Most ex-leftists, particularly those as committed in their anger as Horowitz, come to perceive a kind of structural inevitability in their transformation. The opposition between the Left's falseness and their own better nature is so fundamental, they conclude in retrospect, that once even a bit of doubt is allowed to complicate their leftist worldview, the whole edifice will crumble. And for some leftists, depending on their circumstance and temperament, there's an aspect of truth to this picture. Whittaker Chambers was so far down the Communist Party's rabbit hole, for instance, and so full-bodied in the way he believed, that it was almost inconceivable that he could have simply moderated or nuanced his commitment when he began to admit to some of the party's flaws.

For Horowitz, however, it wasn't so simple. He was furious at the Left, and driven to see his anger effect some change in how the Left operated, but if the Left had been able to absorb his critiques in a meaningful way, and find a place for him in its larger ecosystem, he might have stayed. And at other times and places there were Lefts that were secure enough, and interested enough in rough-and-tumble intellectual sparring, to respond to "Requiem for a Radical" in a way that might have kept Horowitz in the fold longer, maybe even long enough for him to process his anger and move on. As it happened, though, he and Collier weren't speaking to any of those Lefts, at any of those times. They were speaking to the beaten, battered, activist Left of the Bay Area, to the once–true believers who simply weren't the kind of people who responded to crises of faith by engaging in the trial of public self-interrogation that Horowitz wanted.

It wasn't going to happen. What happened instead was that Horowitz turned his ambition and anger on the Left. As a revolutionary the goal had been future-oriented. He had wanted to be an actor in the process of changing the course of the history to come. Now he wanted to be an author in the process of redrafting the history he'd just been through. And until his version of that history was the one that was entrenched in the collective consciousness of the American people, he would feel as though he were losing the war.

From this perspective "Requiem for a Radical" was a volley fired while under siege. Maybe it did some damage, but the enemy's army was large enough to absorb it, and the balance of forces and terrain favored them. At best the article was a successful sortie, by a ragtag guerrilla force, that might eventually prove to be the first step on the long march to victory.

He looked out on the landscape and saw a culture that in many respects remained in the thrall of narratives that had taken shape in the 1960s. The Vietnam War, he believed, was seen primarily through the lens of the antiwar movement's analysis of it. "The sixties" had already acquired a romantic glow in the national imagination, as a time of progress, optimism, and idealism. The Black Panthers themselves were barely existent—by one estimate they had about twenty-five members total—but their myth lived on in popular culture, among blacks, and on posters on dorm room walls.

He knew it sounded crazy to his friends and former allies on the Left. All they saw when they looked around was Reagan everywhere, his plastic visage smiling down over the wasteland of their hopes and dreams. And it was true that the Right was winning elections. Its policies were ascendant. But what his old comrades missed, in their despair and disillusionment, was how many of the cultural and historical stories Americans were telling themselves were those that had been authored by the Left.

Until that war was won, until that respect and admiration was withdrawn, there would be no cease-fire from Horowitz, no sense of completion or contentment.

Horowitz didn't just up and enlist in the war as a full-time soldier. His day job was still interviewing Kennedys, and the sense of balance and perspective he had fought so hard to achieve over the previous few years was real. But as he moved forward, working and writing and living, the critique that he'd drawn from Kolakowski began to give way to a much more cynical and comprehensive take on why people joined left-wing movements and advocated left-wing causes.

"In our ongoing discussions, Peter had always maintained that the element of malice played a larger role in the motives of the Left than I had been willing to accept," Horowitz later wrote. "I resisted his judgment because I could not readily locate such negative passions in myself. But now I was having second thoughts."[47]

For a 1982 piece for *Rolling Stone* on the rise and fall of the Weather Underground, he interviewed former leaders and members of the group, and the more he learned about what had gone down the more convinced he became that describing their vision as "romantic," as he once would have, gave them far too much credit. It was rage and need and the desire for power that was driving them.[48]

In the summer of 1983 he and Collier wrote about the growing AIDS crisis in San Francisco and the political struggles, mostly within the gay community, over how to represent the science and how to deal with the public health implications of the bath house scene. On the advice of Randy Shilts, the pioneering gay journalist, Horowitz took a trip to a bath house in San Francisco and saw revealed, in the glory holes he found there, the nihilistic core of free love. Then he met the doctors who were treating people dying of AIDS, and saw the deadly consequences of it.[49]

For a piece on the juvenile justice system in California, and another on the role gangs were playing in the black community in L.A., he spent time talking to families of crime victims, and to criminals themselves. His conclusion was that the Left was so deluded about the capacity of the poor and young and black to commit evil that it amounted to a kind of racism by indifference, since it was the decent black folks who suffered when criminals went free as a result of lenient policies.

These meta-analyses of the Left weren't always evident in the text of the articles, but they were taking shape in Horowitz internally. What sense he had of the Left as a complicated phenomenon, containing good and bad impulses, admirable and contemptible people, dwindled. The more he looked, the more darkness he saw.[50]

Although it would become evident only in retrospect, there was a pattern—almost certainly an unconscious one—emerging to his interactions with the Left: Find the pocket of bad faith or unease, frame it as provocatively as possible, demand a response, wait for overreaction, then posit the overreaction as evidence of a larger claim about the fundamental toxicity of the Left.

The dry runs had been in the late 1970s, with his friends and colleagues. The first public performance had been with the Stender piece.

Most recently, he'd taken the lonely, brave work that Shilts and a few other activists were doing to improve the public health response to AIDS, which had engendered hostility from within the gay community even when it was presented in its driest form, and upped the emotional and political ante. The result was a complicated piece of rhetoric that was both courageous, progressive journalism—people were dying, the message needed to be heard—and callously insensitive in how it handled the ways some gay men were dealing, or not dealing, with the impending catastrophe.

For Horowitz, it was like the Stender piece all over again. He and Collier had put themselves on the line to save lives. They had quoted extensively from sources within the community. They'd checked and double-checked their facts. And they'd told a story that was intended to help a community advance in its thinking about life, death, and responsibility. Not only weren't they rewarded for it (except with a cover story in a glossy magazine), they were punished. Protests outside the offices of the magazine. Denunciations by prominent gay leaders. A public debate, between Horowitz and one of the activists whom he'd criticized in the article, got so ugly he feared he might be attacked.

"'I feel compelled to denounce you' one man said as he stood up, his voice pinched into a whine. Then he rehearsed his personal pain as a homosexual, and the persecution he felt from people like me. Others joined the attack. Suddenly I had become a symbol rather than a person—an object of passion and fear. Nothing I said was being heard. Voices began to call out epithets like 'Nazi' and 'homophobe,' stoking the general hysteria until one man cried out 'I'd like to kill you.' Not one person spoke in my defense—not even to suggest that I might be owed some courtesy as a guest outnumbered a hundred to one. There was only the collective rage vented in my direction."[51]

Later on, as a conservative, Horowitz would be intentional about initiating these cycles, but in the early years of his semi-anti-Left activity it was intuitive, unconscious. It was also, depending on the goals, either brilliant or self-defeating. It didn't achieve what Horowitz believed in many cases he was hoping to achieve, which was to initiate a conversation within a community about its goals and principles. But it provoked to stupidity those he was criticizing. And it laid down some fairly potent counternarratives in realms where the Left had been controlling the dominant narrative for a while.

It did something else, too. It repelled Horowitz ever further from the Left, and the Left from Horowitz, which was probably on some level what he wanted.

"It was piecemeal," he said, "and every time I came up with a piece I would be attacked, and I would lose friends, and that really turned me off the Left. It got to the point where I had no friends. None."[52]

As the 1984 presidential election approached, Horowitz began to contemplate voting for Reagan. It wasn't an obvious choice at first. If you'd mapped Horowitz's policy preferences, they probably would have aligned better with Mondale than Reagan, particularly on domestic issues. But Horowitz had never really cared much about the middle ground of politics and policy where most Americans sorted themselves out along Democratic or Republican lines. Truth was, he'd never cared much about voting, period. He'd done it in 1980 because he had a lingering bad taste in his mouth back from when Governor Reagan had antagonized the Berkeley radicals, but before that the last time had been in 1964.

So in a way it was a novel experience for him, and a clarifying one. What side was he on? It used to be the radical Left, which meant the question wasn't Republican or Democrat but whether there was sufficient difference between the two to make it worth voting at all. For the five years after Van Patter's death he'd existed in internal exile on the Left, attached but alone. For the last few years he'd been a liberal, vaguely, but hadn't joined the team in any meaningful way. Now where was he? He didn't hate Reagan anymore; he even liked him a bit for how much he irritated the Left, and he believed that Reagan saw the Sandinista government in Nicaragua clearly, as yet another in the line of totalitarian-leaning socialist groups. The better question was: Where was the Left? And with the issue framed that way, his choice became clear. They were against Reagan. They were affiliated, if not always comfortably, with the Democratic Party. They were sympathetic to the Sandinistas.

It was enough. He didn't know if he was a Republican. Probably not. But he knew what he was against, which was the Left. And he was ready to make a gesture in that direction.

"On Election Day 1984, I walked into the voting booth and, without hesitation, punched the line marked 'Ronald Reagan.'"[53]

6

A Man Alone: Christopher Hitchens

Against the Hitch physical and intellectual opposition are equally
futile. . . . I went mano a mano with him among the sawdust and
fagsmoke and bumcrack of an infernal Irish pub in a basement
off Piccadilly Circus. I was in the unwonted position of attacking
Christopher from the left: for defection, for betrayal, for taking the
rich man's shilling. . . . Our wills, my will and the will of the Hitch,
became concentrated in the glass we were both holding with our
right hands. It was a wine glass, and it contained a single whisk.
We were squeezing it, while looking implacably into each other's
eyes, squeezing it till it began to creak . . . I desisted. I climbed
down. Because I suddenly knew that he would not desist, not in a
million years, and when we went off to Casualty together . . . the
Hitch would have no regrets, no regrets about that gashed palm,
that missing finger, lost in the sawdust: none.[1]

—MARTIN AMIS

In October of 1987, David Horowitz and Peter Collier hosted a
weekend conference in Washington, D.C., for former radicals who
had come to see the error of their left-wing ways. Their "Second
Thoughts Conference" wasn't exactly a coming-out for the two men.
They had done that in 1985, with a defiant essay in the *Washington
Post* explaining their decision to vote for Reagan.[2] But it was a coming

together. It was the first time they'd really tried to gather around themselves a group of people who shared their experience, and who might constitute a new community of which they could become part.

For left-wing journalist Christopher Hitchens, there to cover the conference for the *Nation*, it was a target-rich environment.

"David Horowitz and Peter Collier, former editors of *Ramparts*, have come all the way from pink Pampers through Black Panthers to one-dimensional Reaganism," Hitchens wrote. "With a bit of effort, they could succeed in their current modest ambition, which is to become quite nasty."[3]

It wasn't just Horowitz and Collier that enticed Hitchens, or neoconservative elder statesmen like Norman Podhoretz and Irving Kristol, "awash with pompous mutual esteem." It was the rhetorical challenge. It was the opportunity to do one of the things the thirty-eight-year-old Hitchens did best, which was steer past all the historical and ideological shoals to arrive at what usually seemed, after his masterful treatment, the only possible ethically clean left-wing perspective on the matter. In the case of the Second Thoughts Conference, that didn't entail arguing that everything Horowitz and his fellow "breast-beating recusants" were saying about the history of the Left was wrong. Hitchens's own left-wing identity had been premised, in substantial part, on the need to be candid about the checkered past of the Left. It was that there was something bizarre, and rather rancid, about all these ex-leftists getting together at this moment in history to kick the corpse of Marx one more time. In America the Left was dead. Abroad it was moribund. Not only wasn't the Soviet Union the expansionist threat it once had been, it seemed as though it might be on the verge of genuinely liberalizing. The anticommunist wars the United States had fought or funded in Latin America, which were one of the main topics of discussion at the conference, couldn't remotely be justified as necessary acts of containment or rollback. They were exercises in imperialism. It was difficult, but essential, to keep all of these complicated ideas in mind, and in the proper perspective, at the same time.

The most Hitchensian moment of the piece was his identification

with one of the conference participants, a Nicaraguan ex-radical who'd
turned against his old Sandinista comrades but in the process had neither forsworn his sympathies for the wretched of the earth nor allied
himself to American power.

"He was blooded early as a Sandinista," wrote Hitchens, "experienced a great disillusionment in Cuba and became, successively, an
ex-Communist, an ex-Trotskyist and an ex-Marxist. But he has stopped
short of the full James Burnham apostasy. He now lives in Costa Rica,
where he leads a grass-roots movement of the poor and not long ago
was arrested for heading a demonstration in memory of the murdered
Archbishop Romero of El Salvador. He is passionately opposed to the
Contras and will have nothing to do with any Nicaraguan who sup-
ports them: 'They have burned down the possibility of civic opposition
and become corrupted with American money. They are shit!' "[4]

Here, for Hitchens, was nearly everything it meant to be the right
kind of leftist—passionate in one's commitment, intolerant of bullshit,
courageous on behalf of the vulnerable, offended by tyranny, willing to
break with one's fellow leftists if that was what truth demanded, wise
in the choice of one's allies, and unflinching in the (rhetorical) fight
against one's enemies.

For Hitchens, it was the last of these qualities in particular that mattered. He'd discovered early on that one of the great boons of the left-
wing perspective was the license it granted to aggress when the enemy
was power. In the battle against power—and its allies sanctimony, hypocrisy, corruption, and brutality—you weren't just allowed to rough up
your enemies, you were rather compelled to do so. This was why, though
he could grant certain points that Horowitz and Collier and some of
their fellow second-thoughters might make, he couldn't really grasp the
defensibility of where their second thoughts had taken them. To the side
of power. What joy, or righteousness, could possibly be found there?

The heresy of Christopher Hitchens—a former socialist who became,
in the aftermath of September 11, 2001, a scourge of the American

Left and a fellow soldier of the Right in its rhetorical war to go to war in Iraq—provoked many explanations. From the Left it was said that his intellect, cured by decades of heavy drinking, was no longer capable of resisting the baubles of power, influence, and money held in escrow by the Right for any leftist willing to sell out his colleagues. It was said that he was bored by the peace and prosperity of the 1990s, and narcissistic enough to mistake his perpetual need for conflict as a perpetual opportunity for the display of moral courage. And he was, it was also said, unbalanced by September 11, and consumed in its wake by his adoration of George Orwell—the patron saint of clear-sightedness in the face of global ideological and military conflict, leftist groupthink, and the blandishments of neutrality.

From the Right it was said that he saw, at last, what conservatives had known all along, that the mantras and arguments invoked by the Left to further its cause are merely disguises for their deep misanthropy, hatred of America, and alienation from themselves and their fellow citizens.

In his own eyes Hitchens's journey away from the Left—which upended his life, destroyed many of his friendships, visibly aged him, and alienated the readership from which he once drew his energy—wasn't a metamorphosis but simply the consequence of the application of his principles against the unspooling of history.

The truth, and the tragedy, of Christopher Hitchens isn't as pure as either his enemies or Hitchens himself would have it. It exists, instead, somewhere inside the confluence of his family, his past, his radical yearning for truth, his charisma, his narcissism, his dangerous brilliance, his self-deception, and the zigzag of history, which cooperates with no one's expectations or fantasies.

A navy brat, Christopher Hitchens was born in 1949 in the small but nostalgia-burdened city of Portsmouth, England, home to a naval base since the fifteenth century and the dry-dock grave of the HMS *Victory*, the ship from which Admiral Lord Horatio Nelson led the British to victory over the Spanish and French fleets at the Battle of Trafalgar in 1805.

Hitchens and his younger brother, Peter, were raised in a series of port towns, most of them inside England proper and all of them within the borders of the British empire. Commander Eric Hitchens, their father, was an officer from a long line of enlisted men. He was a conservative man, a Tory, and a gin drinker. Their mother, Yvonne Hickman Hitchens, was younger, more beautiful, and more charming than her husband. The couple met when they were both serving in the Royal Navy during World War II, and married in April of 1945, a month before the German surrender to the Allies.

The Hitchenses were a typical British family of the 1950s, poised uneasily between classes and eras, alert to the new possibilities but bewildered by the rapid social change and the radical dissipation of British aura. They moved every year or two, hostage first to the currents of Eric Hitchens's naval postings and then, after he was let go by the service, to those of his postmilitary career. Eric and Yvonne clashed over taste and money. There was unacknowledged, and unacknowledgeable, tension over religion: Eric was born and raised a Baptist but gave it up so that his sons could be raised in the Church of England. Yvonne was of mostly Jewish ancestry but pretended, even to her husband and children, to be pureblood Anglican. Britishness was enormously important to the Hitchenses, but it was no longer very clear, in the years when they were raising their sons, what that notion entailed.

The empire, which had been so elemental to British identity for centuries, was in eclipse. After the war Great Britain retained the world's most global empire—dominating vast regions of Asia, Africa, the Indian subcontinent, and the Caribbean—but it was no longer its most virile. The war had tangled up not only its delicate, transcontinental economy but the cat's cradle of imperial ideology as well, and there wasn't enough money, pride, will, or weapons left over for Britain to continue to maintain, or to justify, its domination of foreign lands and foreign peoples. British honor was burnished by its stand against the Nazis, but British wealth, power, and confidence were exhausted.

By the time Hitchens was born, in 1949, the specter of decline was acknowledged by all but the most blinkered of patriots. Even Winston Churchill, by 1946, was admitting to an American confidante that "Britain has had its day. At one time we had dominions all over the world. . . . But England is gradually drying up. The leadership must be taken over by the United States. You have the country, you have the people; you have the democratic spirit, the natural resources which England has not. . . . If I were to be born again, I'd want to be born an American."[5]

The heart of the empire, India, was granted independence in 1947. When Burma and Ceylon (now Sri Lanka) declared their independence the following year, the British didn't protest. The Holy Land was first grudgingly, and then quite hastily, given over to the simmering conflict between Jews and Arabs, and in 1948 the state of Israel was established in what was formerly the British Mandate of Palestine.

Perhaps most humiliating was Great Britain's failed conspiracy with France and Israel in 1956 to wrest control of the Suez Canal back from Egyptian president Gamal Abdel Nasser, who had nationalized the Anglo-French corporation that had long profited from the canal. When the British and French troops were forced by American and Soviet pressure to withdraw from Egypt less than two months after they occupied the canal zone, it wasn't just the passage from the Mediterranean to the Red Sea that was lost. Great Britain was revealed as a lesser power—at best a supporting player in, and at worst a distraction from, the hyperpower contest between the United States and the Soviet Union. It took another few decades for the rest of the empire to fully spin loose, but by the end of the 1950s the era of British preeminence was known to be over.

Not all was bleak in Britain, though. There was peace at last, and the war, and the project of shared sacrifice that it demanded, had shaken up the class system enough so that in its aftermath the working and middle classes saw possibility where once they'd seen exclusion. They got their welfare state, and they got their modern European economy. The domestic prosperity and tranquility that followed went some way toward compensating for the loss of the empire that had been the nation's symbolic bread for too long. And the Hitchens family shared in both the blessings and the confusions of the postwar world.

"I am sitting on the stairs in my pajamas, monitoring a parental dispute," wrote Christopher Hitchens. "The subject is myself, the place is on the edge of Dartmoor, and the year must be 1956 or so, because the topic is my future education. My father is arguing reasonably that private schooling is too expensive. My mother, in tones that I can still recall, is saying that money can be found. 'If there is going to be an upper class in this country,' she says forcefully, 'then Christopher is going to be in it.' "[6]

The passage is from "On Not Knowing the Half of It: Homage to Telegraphist Jacobs," one of the essential documents, in its dance of revelation and withholding, for anyone seduced into deconstructing Hitchens's picaresque life. The "Telegraphist Jacobs" of the title is a Jewish character in a novel that includes another character loosely based on Christopher's father. The unknown "Half of It" was Hitchens's mother's Jewishness, which Christopher discovered only in his thirties, a decade after his mother died and only a few weeks before his father died.

"[Your mother] didn't much want to be a Jew, and I didn't think your father's family would have liked the idea, either. So we just decided to keep it to ourselves," said Hitchens's maternal grandmother when he finally sought her out for an explanation of the family secret.[7]

The half of it was also pretty much everything else in the Hitchens family romance, all the tragedies, deceptions, and silences that Hitchens described in the traditional English fashion—stoically, sentimentally. The father was an honorable man, who devoted himself to country and family, but he was also a drinker, and his postmilitary life was a sadly anticlimactic one, spent in a series of undistinguished bookkeeping jobs and adrift in the England that emerged from the ashes of World War II. "[T]he remark that most summed him up," Hitchens once wrote, "was the flat statement that the war of 1939 to 1945 had been 'the only time when I really felt I knew what I was doing.' "[8]

Hitchens's mother, Yvonne, had far more native vitality to her. She was, Hitchens later wrote, "the cream in the coffee, the gin in the Campari, the offer of wine or champagne instead of beer." It was a vitality, however, that drained away over the course of his childhood and young adulthood, as the cosmopolitan life she'd once dreamed of living was slowly blotted out by the dreary one she actually was living.

She killed herself in the fall of 1973, when Hitchens was twenty-four. It was a double suicide, committed in an Athens hotel room, by Yvonne and the married man—a defrocked vicar—for whom she'd left her husband. The hint of murder even made it into the first newspaper reports and was ruled out by the police only when enough blood was cleaned away from the scene to reveal her suicide note, which was addressed to her oldest son, Christopher. "So that was sort of the end of family life really," Hitchens later said of the suicide.[9]

Traditional family life had really come to an end for him much earlier, at eight, when he was sent off to boarding school to study his way into the upper classes. For five years he lived and studied at Mount House School, in the southwest of England, and then it was on to the Leys School, in Cambridge, from which Hitchens graduated in 1966. The Leys had been founded in the late nineteenth century so that the sons of prominent Methodists could be prepared for Oxford and Cambridge. By the time Hitchens got there, it was less a religious alternative to the older, wealthier schools like Eton and Harrow than simply a humbler access point to the British upper classes.[10]

Like its more prestigious peers, the Leys mixed austerity and pomp in roughly equal measure, the better to prepare its students to bear comfortably the burden of privilege they would someday take up. The food was notoriously bad. The boys' lives were ordered from sunup to sundown. The living conditions in the dormitories were spartan. North House B, where Hitchens lived, packed its forty students into two large rooms. For privacy each student had only a kind of stall, called a "horse-box," at the end of his bed.

Yet the beds were made every morning by servants, and the grounds of the campus, spread out over fifty grassy acres less than a mile from the University of Cambridge, were meticulously landscaped and gardened. The young masters went to class and to meals in coat and tie. And the classroom buildings were designed in emulation of the elegant Cambridge style, with light redbrick exteriors, dark wood interiors, and vaulted, often elaborately carved and beamed wooden ceilings.[11]

The working- and middle-class students at the Leys acquired the manners of the upper classes as their more pedigreed classmates already had from birth—through habituation, immersion, and boredom. Eccentric traditions and rituals that were daunting at first soon came to seem mundane. The grandeur of the campus faded into transparency as it was internalized as, simply, home. Life with servants (life with deference) was lived until it was expected.

It was at the Leys, which was protective of its upper-class credentials as only a school of the second rank can be, that Hitchens's political identity came into focus. He developed, he later wrote, "a dislike for the class system and for the attitudes that it instilled not in its victims but in the people who thought they benefited from it—a suspicion of those who felt entitled to inherited privilege, of whom I was not one."[12]

Hitchens's strategy for managing this distaste wasn't to reject the manners of the upper class, or to spurn the opportunity he'd been given to join it. His parents were paying too much for that. It was to excel as a student, doing what was needed to ascend to Cambridge or Oxford, while devoting much of his remaining energy to the exploration of unfamiliar and challenging ideas. In this latter pursuit he benefited from the school's proximity to the university, and to the notes of cosmopolitanism that wafted in. He befriended some of the students whose parents were professors or alumni at the university, "boys with names like Huxley and Keynes, who really were from those distinguished families." He attended lectures and readings at the university on history, literature, and political theory. Perhaps most formatively, he became an increasingly discerning borrower from the quite well-stocked library at the Leys.

From a very young age he'd been a voracious reader. Until that point, however, his pleasure reading had consisted almost entirely of adventure books, or of more serious works of literature and history that he consumed as adventure books. He'd taken for granted the colonial and conservative politics implicit in most such stories. At the Leys he became conscious of the existence of politics, as a thing in itself, and found himself drawn to works that were explicitly and often transgressively political.

He was struck by *Hanged by the Neck*, an anti–death penalty tract coauthored by Arthur Koestler. That led him to Koestler's great anticommunist novel *Darkness at Noon*, and to the notoriously seductive dialectics of the novel's interrogators. The conservative government of the United Kingdom lost his teenage support after it offered noble rhetoric, but no force or substantive aid, in support of the struggle of the black majority in its colony of Rhodesia (later Zimbabwe) for equality with the white minority. The antiheroic war poetry of Wilfred Owen, first encountered in class, led to an intensive self-guided study of the poetry, history, and geopolitics of World War I, and to a profound revolution in Hitchens's understanding not just of the war, but of the ways in which tradition, the state, and even literature can distort history.

"I could feel all the ballast in my hold turning over," he wrote, "as I came to view 'The Great War' not as an episode of imperishable valor, celebrated every year on 11 November with the jingoistic verse of Rupert Brooke and Laurence Binyon, but as an imperialist slaughter that had been ended on such bad terms by such stupid statesmen that it necessitated an even more horrible second round in 1939."[13]

His most fateful literary encounter, while at the Leys, was with the work of George Orwell. In class it was the antitotalitarian novels, *1984* and *Animal Farm*, but it was outside of class, through reading Orwell's nonfiction works and lesser-known novels about lower-middle-class British life, that Hitchens was most influenced. It turned out that one could write about the lower classes with both passionate political conviction and genuine artistry.

In many respects the patterns that would lend shape to his existence were already discernible: he was a contrarian, a romantic, a perpetually

disappointed idealist. He was against things—killing, cynicism, hypocrisy, betrayal, abandonment—and he was for a world in which there
were fewer of the things he was against.

In 1967 Hitchens matriculated to Balliol College at Oxford, the oldest of the university's colleges and one known both for its leftist politics and its "tranquil consciousness of effortless superiority."[14] It was
a nutrient-rich habitat for a young intellectual who was beginning to
craft for himself what an editor would later describe as "an upper-class
sensibility attached to a heart ostentatiously identified with the toiling
masses."[15] Not just Balliol but the whole Oxford society was, by the late
1960s, being quickened by new blood while remaining flavored by its
centuries of tradition and history. Its student body had been expanding
and diversifying steadily since after the war, when an assimilable number of returning veterans from the common classes were allowed inside
as a kind of reward for their service. Their success opened the door for
others, and with the aid of government subsidies a healthy flavoring of
middle-class boys (and a few from the working classes) soon enriched
the old Oxonian crust. The boys had their rooms cleaned and meals
served for them, and their lives benevolently overseen by the head por-
ter—a kind of concierge of the college—but the rest of the world was
seeping in through the cracks in the neogothic walls.

  For the first time in his life, Hitchens found that he was at near-
absolute liberty to do as he pleased. He enjoyed himself on campus,
most often through the activities of the Oxford Union debating society,
which was an active and enthusiastic social club as well as an extraordinary vessel through which clever young men were able to meet, drink,
and argue with some of Great Britain's most eminent intellectuals and
politicians. He continued to read aggressively, preferring "books on any
subject except the ones I was supposed to be studying." He chose to
study a bit, and graduated with a third-class honors degree—the British
version of the gentleman's C—in politics, philosophy, and economics.

  His primary immersion, however, was in the life of the Trotskyist

Left. "Neither Washington nor Moscow but International Socialism" was the slogan of the International Socialists, the small, heterodox Trotskyist group that launched Hitchens's career as a political man.[16] He sold their newspapers on the corner, took part in their protests, and waged dialectical battles with his comrades into the blue hours of the morning. He was arrested for, among other incidents, making a spectacle of himself at a cricket match that an English team was playing against an apartheid-white South African team.

It was through the International Socialists that the not quite twenty-year-old Hitchens imagined himself into the global exhilaration and terror of 1968, when students and workers briefly shut down de Gaulle's government in Paris, when the Prague Spring bloomed in Czechoslovakia before it was trampled over by Soviet tanks, and when America was so overwhelmed by war, antiwar, assassinations, uprisings, happenings, and backlashes that it frequently seemed on the verge of disintegrating. It was a good year to believe both in the possibility of revolution and in the terrifying force of reaction, and it was formative for Hitchens.

He became a '68er, in love with the new, but unlike many of his fellow enthusiasts he was also fascinated with the old. He went about locating himself, intellectually, in the tradition of free-spirited, usually doomed, socialistic or anarchistic resistance. He found heroes in people like Rosa Luxemburg, the German communist leader who was clear-eyed enough to publicly criticize the totalitarian tendency of the Bolsheviks in 1918, a year before her death, while the rest of the international communist movement was still enraptured by the Bolshevik triumph. His loyalty to Trotsky was doctrinal but it was also personal: He was attracted to the figure of the man, who was a military hero as well as a brilliant intellectual, and he was seduced by Trotsky's romantic story of exile and martyrdom, which cleansed his legacy of any taint of compromise.

Hitchens lived in the 1960s, but he often wrote as if he were in the 1930s, as if everything still depended upon working out the finer points of Marxist theory. His first semiprofessional articles, which were published in the quarterly journal of the International Socialists, revealed little of the flamboyant iconoclasm that would later define his writerly voice.[17]

In 1971, Hitchens first got himself into the bookstores (if not too many of them) with *Paris Commune, 1871*, an edited volume of Marx's writings on the revolutionary government that took control of Paris for two months in 1871 before being crushed by the forces of the old regime. Hitchens's main contribution to the book was its thirty-page introduction, a dry, academic piece of writing that was straitjacketed by its party-line Trotskyist-Luxemburgist interpretation of Marxist theory. There were hints in the essay, however—submerged in praise for Marx—not only of the uncompromising attitude that Hitchens would later adopt to the controversies of his era but even of the precise arguments he would end up using to justify his stubbornness.

"The essence of his philosophy was commitment," Hitchens wrote, explaining why Marx stood by the communards even after their defeat and even though he'd tried to warn them of where, strategically, they were going wrong. "There is no sign, in his correspondence of the time, of any idea of abandoning the Parisians, even after they had flouted all his advice. . . . It should not surprise us that Marx subordinated his misgivings and criticisms to support of the fight *on any terms*. He had, after all, written in 1851: 'Men make their own history, but they do not make it just as they please; they do not make it under circumstances chosen by themselves, but under circumstances directly encountered, given and transmitted from the past. . . . World history would indeed be very easy to make, if the struggle were taken up only on condition of infallibly favourable chances.' "[18]

In his early twenties—on the strength of his socialist writings, his freelance criticism for the *Times* of London, and his accession to the elite guild of publishing world Oxonians—Hitchens was hired by the *New Statesman*, a left-wing London weekly that gave its bright young writers license to jaunt around the world in pursuit of their fancies.

The global ennui of the 1970s, which was so dispiriting in general to the European and American Lefts, was liberating for Hitchens. He held on to some of his Marxist categories of thought, and reported sympathetically on working-class politics, but he stopped caucusing with the International Socialists, and in the absence of intrusive world-historical conflict or dynamic ideological combat there was little pressure on him to adhere to a Marxist line in his writing.

He found himself drawn, instead, to moments of crisis and transition around the world, and he wrote on the CIA's antidemocratic interventions in Latin America, on the end of Francoism in Spain, on the division of Cyprus into its Turkish and Greek fractions. He sent dispatches from Jerusalem, Geneva, Athens, Warsaw, Baghdad. Hitchens often ended up allying emotionally with the communists or socialists in these places, but just as often he sided with people and movements that were primarily nationalist, or even religious, in their loyalties. The underdog was his party, and his commitment was to a vision of authentic democracy and exemplary nationalism that was attainable, perhaps, only in the breach. In Spain it was the Catalan and Basque resistance to Franco's regime. In Jerusalem it was the Palestinians he championed, but never Arafat and never the nascent Islamic fundamentalist movement. In Cyprus he found a hero in Archbishop Makarios, the charismatic Greek Cypriot leader who became a symbol of resistance to the military governments in both Athens and Istanbul. In Warsaw Hitchens reported on the dissident labor movement that would soon evolve into Solidarity.[19]

Free to do what he was discovering he did best, which was write well and believe passionately, Hitchens cherry-picked his causes and themes, and he labored to emulate the literary swagger of his colleagues, princes of urbanity like Martin Amis, Julian Barnes, and James Fenton. "I realized these guys were better at that kind of writing than I was," he later wrote. "It was rather intimidating that they were so good. . . . They persuaded me that it wasn't enough just to make the point; that style was substance."[20]

Hitchens and his fellow young literary lords became the hub of a roundtable of journalists, editors, critics, novelists, poets, and scholars who dubbed themselves, ironically but also accurately, the Modish

London Literary World. The group, which convened every Friday for lunch for more than a decade, included novelist Ian McEwan, journalist and TV interviewer Clive James, political cartoonist Mark Boxer, poet Craig Raine, poet/historian Robert Conquest, and novelist Kingsley Amis (Martin's father).

An invitation to the "Friday lunch," as it became known, was one of the most sought-after and feared invitations in the London publishing world. The drinking, smoking, and eating were to excess. The flavor was macho, and young. The gossiping was sufficiently juicy for the tabloids to salt their people at nearby tables in hopes of catching a good dripping. The Carnaby Street–style clothes were baroque—"There were velvet jackets, flared trousers, zip-sided boots," wrote Clive James in his memoir of London in the seventies, ". . . the average young male was carrying a greater proportion of artificial fabrics than an airliner's interior."[21]

It was the talk, however, that was the glory of the lunch. The conversation was half performance and half contest, with insult and assault, rather than consideration or tact, regarded as the truest expression of brotherly affection and loyalty.

Hitchens and Martin Amis were the double helix twining through and lending structure to it all. Amis was the storyteller, and the star: he did voices, he embellished like the novelist he was. He was funny. "When he got going," wrote Clive James, "he was like one of those jazz stars, relaxing after hours, who are egged on by the other musicians into chorus after chorus." Hitchens was the kibitzer, the interpolator, the amplifier. And he was generous. "Thus, if someone was being straightforward he could make them funny, and if they were being funny he could make them funnier."[22]

The politics of the Friday lunchers were left-leaning, but the conversation was open to anyone who could hold his own. Hitchens found good friends in anticommunist historian Robert Conquest, who delighted in puncturing Hitchens's illusions about Lenin, and in Kingsley Amis, an ex-communist who had by then become an outspoken, and frequently offensive, reactionary.

Hitchens, who was already developing a reputation as a bit of a rogue, poached many of his romances of the time from the extended family of the London literary elite. He had a fling with Sally Amis, Martin's sister and Kingsley's daughter. And he dated up-and-coming fashion editor Anna Wintour, who was the sister of his *Statesman* colleague Patrick Wintour.

His first wife, however, he met in Cyprus, in 1977, while he was reporting for the *Statesman* on the continuing conflict between Greek and Turkish Cypriots and their respective mother countries. Like Hitchens, Eleni Meleagrou was a writer from a family of soldiers and nationalists. Meleagrou, however, was a Greek Cypriot, and thus heir to a nationalism that was still germinating, one that was unblemished by either the burden of success or the shadow of decline. She could speak unself-consciously of the stories that her grandfather, who'd been a soldier in the Greek army, had told her of heroic Greek resistance to the Turks. To Hitchens, such purity was irresistible. To Meleagrou, Hitchens was an emissary from civilization beyond the island, "a romantic figure, attractive, clever, he had everything. He was a scholar, and he was interested in my people."[23]

Meleagrou followed Hitchens back to London, and was with him when, in 1978, he gave up the shabby chic prestige of the *New Statesman* for the better money, but trashier manners, of the tabloid *Daily Express*.

The couple was married in 1981, and the following year Hitchens was invited by the *Nation*, the flagship magazine of the American Left, to come to Washington for a trial stint as a correspondent. He went for it, taking with him to America the arrogant, louche, quintessentially English persona he was just about done crafting—equal parts Falstaff, Tom Paine, Tom Jones, Trotsky, and Oscar Wilde—and finding in the new world the perfect stage on which to perform it.

"And then one day, around 5:00 p.m., a dimpled, five-o'clock-shadowed face peered through my half-open door surrounded by a haze of smoke," wrote Victor Navasky, the editor and publisher of the *Nation*, of his first meeting with his new writer. " 'Drink?' asked the deep, richly accented baritone voice that accompanied all of the above."[24]

Sensing that in Hitchens he had found something rather different to offer to his readers, Navasky hired the British expatriate for good, and let loose that whiskey-touched baritone to deflate the pretensions of both establishment Washington and the Pharisees of the Left. Hitchens soon settled into a weekly column, Minority Report, which he would write for almost twenty years.

America, for Hitchens, was liberating. He scanned very differently in the new world than he had in the old. No longer surrounded by others like him—radical, rakish, sparkling literary types with an Oxbridge education but an edge of working- or middle-class alienation—and no longer grounded in a comprehensible tradition of such men, he appeared sui generis. To his American readers and colleagues, his Oxford accent obscured all traces of his nuanced class background. His devil's advocacy, which was just good manners in England, often seemed perverse to the more earnest American Left. His internationalism, which was almost unavoidable for a European intellectual, made him glamorous. And his stylistic flamboyance, which was modest compared to that of many of his friends and rivals in Britain, distinguished him from the more ascetic political journalists who set the tone of the opinion journals in America. Free at last from the full burden of Englishness, and yet also uncompromised by the parochialism of American politics, Hitchens settled into a voice that blended reporting and first-person narrative, erudition and polemic, and British irony and American forthrightness into something that was distinct.

He was valued by the tastemakers of the American Left, if not always loved or trusted, because by the time Hitchens arrived at the *Nation* in 1982, the Movement—what was left of it—was frightened and weary enough that it was willing to endure his needling in exchange for his eloquence and confidence.

"Now a new chill is in the air," wrote Andrew Kopkind in the *Nation* in 1983. ". . . There's a retro look to the political landscape, the feel of the Dulles days. Rebellion, utopias and tender-mindedness are out; conformity, realism and hard-heartedness are in. . . . It is the first wave of an advancing cold war culture, propelled by the neoconservative and New Right tides of the recent past, which will touch all that we think and do in the period ahead."[25]

There were good grounds for the Left's dejected experience of the 1980s. Ronald Reagan's popularity, and the ease with which he'd tossed out the postwar consensus on issues like labor and taxation, and the post-Vietnam consensus on Cold War interventionism, suggested to the veterans of the old and new Lefts that they hadn't succeeded nearly as well as they'd hoped in vanquishing the old conservative bogeymen. Rather than the continuation of the march of progress—from labor rights to civil rights to feminism to environmentalism to gay rights to whatever was next—the Left was confronted with a popularly elected, proudly conservative leader who'd once worked as an antiunion propagandist for GE and who'd made his mark as the Republican governor of California by scapegoating the Left for what was wrong in the lives of the American masses.

More than anything, the Left was overwhelmed by the sense of having lost a series of arguments it didn't quite realize it was having. Reagan's election revealed not just the renewed potency of conservative narratives but the organizational power of the New Right, a suddenly manifest network of political operatives, think tanks, publications, and party faithful that had discovered itself in the Goldwater campaign of 1964 and had been honing its ruthless ways ever since. Reagan's administration was populated, also, by neoconservatives, refugees from the Left who'd brought with them to the Right a seductive moralism that helped Reagan and the Republican Party rehabilitate laissez-faire capitalism and Cold War militarism in the eyes of the American public and the Washington and New York media elite.

The symbolic struggles over the narratives and morals that would define the American consensus were suddenly being fought substantially on conservative terms, and the American Left could no longer convince itself that either history or the American people were inexorably on its side. Hitchens, refreshingly, didn't care. He took for granted that the cultural permissions to copulate, miscegenate, blaspheme, and abort that had been won in the 1960s and '70s were too appealing to take away once given. And though he recognized that certain battles, foreign and domestic, were being lost in the policy realm, it didn't depress him in the same way it did many of his fellow leftists. He didn't care that much about most of the mundane injustices of the first world, and on the politics of the world, which were his passion, he was used to being on the losing side. In many ways he was most comfortable there, pulling for the underdog and chewing at the heels of power.

As a result, on matters of war and peace, he was almost singularly unself-conscious in both his soft international socialism and his independence from leftist orthodoxy. He never worried that being a socialist put him beyond the pale, and he never felt the urge to apologize for—or stay silent in the presence of—leftist-tinged tyranny. His American colleagues, always glancing over their shoulders for fear of being associated too closely either with Reds or with Red-baiters, shared many of Hitchens's impulses but could rarely match his confidence.

"One of these days," Hitchens wrote in the kind of mischievous passage that irritated so many of his comrades, "I'm going to write a book called 'Guilty as Hell: A Short History of the American Left.' . . . Where are we now? Joe Hill probably guilty as charged . . . Sacco and Vanzetti darker horses than we thought. The Rosenbergs at least half-guilty. Most of the Black Panthers (always excepting those murdered by the FBI) amazingly guilty."[26]

His attachments and antipathies around the globe, in any case, were visceral and personal more than they were ideological. Through his wife, Eleni, he came to know and love Greece and Cyprus. He disliked Turkey—found its culture crude and evasive—and took an almost personal offense at its cynical maneuverings in Cyprus and its denial of the truth of the Armenian genocide. Pakistan, he wrote, was "an artificial nation, born out of manipulation and middleman tactics."[27]

On the Israeli-Palestinian matter, which came to define Hitchens's leftism perhaps more than any other issue in the 1980s, he took as his guiding light Edward Said, the literary scholar who was the Palestinians' most eloquent advocate in America throughout the 1980s and '90s. They became good friends and political allies, and when Hitchens wanted to dramatize the injustice of Israel's legal preference for Jews over Arabs, he used their friendship to make it personal. "Under the Law of Return," he wrote, "I can supposedly redeem myself by moving into the Jerusalem home from which my friend Edward Said has been evicted."[28]

The Kurds, whose cause he championed years before it was fashionable, struck a particularly resonant chord in his psyche. They were tragic and beautiful—nomadic, gracious, steeped in history—and they became a kind of surrogate nation for him. "The historical memory of the Kurds is one of endlessly cheated aspirations," Hitchens wrote. "Their past and their location have combined to make them the classic victims of geopolitics. An experienced Kurd can tell his grandchildren of betrayal by colonial Britain and France; of promises made by Iran, Iraq, and Turkey to sustain the Kurds only for as long as they were fighting on a rival's territory."[29]

He reported extensively on the civil war in Nicaragua, weighing in for neither the Sandinista government, whose autocratic tendencies he recognized, nor the American-backed Contra revolutionaries. He favored, as he always did, the authentic democrats he could find—the outspoken newspaper editors, dissident activists, and radical poets and nuns—and the enemy was, as usual, cynical and self-interested power politics.

Blessed with an editor with a light hand, and temperamentally predisposed to stubbornness, Hitchens rarely bothered to ask himself: What should the *Nation* say, or what does Marxism indicate, or what does the organized Left expect of me? Nor were his motives purely contrarian: How can I do what they don't expect me to do? His method was emulative. It was to ask, within the matrix laid down by his principles, loyalties, and intuitions: What would Churchill do? What would George Eliot say? Above all others, what would George Orwell say? And his roving, reportorial eye was guided to its topics by a kind of anthropological cosmopolitanism that was excited by what it perceived as the authentic essences of cultures, but felt betrayed whenever civilized national pride deteriorated into chauvinism, sectarianism, religious extremism, or partition.

A stray reference to Lenin, Marx, or Trotsky turned up in his writing every once in a while, but their primacy had long since given way. Hitchens had his library, his international fraternity of left-leaning dissidents in solidarity with the wretched of the earth, and his gut. When confronted with a political dilemma he hadn't yet resolved to his satisfaction, he went first to his books, then to the phone, then to the airport, and then to his typewriter. He wrote in a prose that emanated precision, logic, and dispassion even as it was fueled by anger and contempt.

Hitchens also found comfort and confirmation in attending to the anti-pantheon of people whose political instincts, and personal qualities, repelled him. In particular, he paid attention to—so as not to accidentally align with—the death-dealing realpolitik of Henry Kissinger, "this deceitful and humorless toad," whose fingerprints were to be found on almost every act of American militarism or imperial indifference that Hitchens had made a career out of loathing. Kissinger sabotaged the peace and prolonged the war in Vietnam.[30] Kissinger funded the reactionary group in Chile whose violence cleared the way for the toppling of Salvador Allende. Kissinger was a consistent and cynical opponent of the national aspirations of the Palestinians.

Kissinger was also, for Hitchens, a symbol of the way that establishment Washington both evaded and celebrated the fetid workings of power.

"Yet the pudgy man standing in black tie at the *Vogue* party is not, surely, the man who ordered and sanctioned the destruction of civilian populations, the assassination of inconvenient politicians, the kidnapping and disappearance of soldiers and journalists and clerics who got in his way?" wrote Hitchens. "Oh, but he *is*. It's exactly the same man. And that may be among the most nauseating reflections of all. Kissinger is not invited and feted because of his exquisite manners or his mordant wit (his manners are in any case rather gross, and his wit consists of a quiver of borrowed and secondhand darts). No, he is sought after because his presence supplies a *frisson*: the authentic touch of raw and unapologetic power."[31]

Hitchens's steam room of heroes, allies, and villains was impressive, and it was also terribly complex: Oscar Wilde shared a bench with Noam Chomsky, Salman Rushdie, Leon Trotsky, Che Guevara, and Susan Sontag. Opposite them were Mother Teresa, Henry Kissinger, and Joseph Stalin.

The product of all these forces colliding in his soul was a sensibility that could be remarkable in its moral and political sensitivity, inspiring in its zeal, quietly unsystematic and emotional, and infuriating for those who happened to be the object of its scorn. "I'm a partisan of the pro-wit radical faction myself," he once wrote, but that neat summary underplayed the tension by a league. In his reflective mode, which he preferred for his literary criticism and his longer political essays, he paid explicit homage to ambiguity.[32] In his combative mood, which he adopted for most of his short opinion pieces, he seemed driven by a need to excise it, and to belittle those who he thought were using the idea of complexity to abdicate responsibility. In his stubborn mode he was indefensibly, and yet often admirably, stubborn. In any piece of writing longer than twenty or thirty pages, he got lost. And in public— at the many panels, debates, interviews, and lectures for which he made himself available—he could be devastating, incoherent, charming, unpleasant, or romantically outrageous, often in the same appearance.

Martin Amis, whose friendship with Hitchens became one of the constants of both men's lives, tells a story that conveys a sense of the quivering intensity of "the Hitch" toward the end of the 1980s, when Hitchens was reckoning with the death of his father and the collapse of his first marriage. It begins on a road trip the two men took in the summer of 1989 to visit Saul Bellow at his house in Vermont.

"A drive of five or six hours, but the buddy-movie, radio-on feel of the journey was part of the treat," wrote Amis in his memoir *Experience*. "Stops were made for the huge uneaten meals and many powerful drinks desiderated by the Hitch. At this time my friend was still attached by one boot to the steer of his mid-life crisis, which began in earnest at the end of 1987."[33]

Amis had agreed to take Hitchens with him to visit Bellow on the condition that there would be absolutely no "sinister balls"—a phrase they'd coined together, when writing for the *New Statesman*, for being stridently left-wing at the most ill-chosen moments. They were going, after all, as Bellow's guests. They both revered Bellow as a novelist even if they disapproved of some of his politics (in particular his support for Israel). And Hitchens was simply too compulsive to be trusted to be gracious once he got going.

Hitchens held back for a short while, but as the evening went on, and his drinking presumably did as well, he let himself go, using his friendship with Edward Said as a pretext for a fight with Bellow over Israel and Palestine.

Amis wrote: "Saul, packed down over the table, shoulders forward, legs tensed beneath his chair, became more laconic in his contributions, steadily submitting to a cataract of pure reason, matter-of-fact chapter and verse, with its interjected historical precedents, its high-decibel statistics, its fortissimo fine distinctions—Christopher's cerebral stampede.

"The silence still felt like a gnat in my ear.

" 'Well,' [Hitchens] said. 'I'm sorry if I went on a bit. But Edward is a friend of mine. And if I hadn't defended him . . . I would have felt bad.'

" 'How d'you feel *now*?' said Saul."[34]

The year 1989 was a pivotal one for Hitchens. The fall of the Soviet Union liberated him from his last real ties to the Marxist project, and although he would keep referring to himself as a socialist for another fifteen years, it became more of an affectation than a meaningful ideological tag. With the Cold War over, Hitchens found a new theme in the threat of Islamic fundamentalism, which was brought home to him by the Ayatollah Khomeini's call for his friend Salman Rushdie to be murdered.

"When the *Washington Post* telephoned me at home on Valentine's Day 1989 to ask my opinion about the Ayatollah Khomeini's *fatwah*," he wrote, "I felt at once that here was something that completely committed me. It was, if I can phrase it like this, a matter of everything I hated versus everything I loved. In the hate column: dictatorship, religion, stupidity, demagogy, censorship, bullying, and intimidation. In the love column: literature, irony, humor, the individual, and the defense of free expression. Plus, of course, friendship."[35]

The Rushdie *fatwah* also gave Hitchens another issue with which to distinguish himself from friends and rivals on the Left—many of whom, he believed, were too worried about seeming insensitive to Muslim sensibilities to be sufficiently outraged on behalf of the blasphemous Rushdie.

At home, Hitchens's marriage was in decline. "Eleni became shut in, she lost her spontaneity," Hitchens later explained to a reporter for *New York* magazine. "I felt guilty about that, that it was my fault. I resented it, too."[36] While in Los Angeles for a few days to promote his most recent book, Hitchens fell in love with Carol Blue, a friend of a friend who'd offered to host him at her apartment during his stay. When his L.A. trip was over, he flew back to D.C. and told his wife, who was pregnant at the time with their second child, that he was leaving her for Blue.

"Christopher fell in love with Carol," said Meleagrou, "and he expected me to understand. 'Don't you see? I'm really in love,' he'd say, and my reaction was, 'Bug off.' He told me he was doing me a favor. Maybe now I think he did. . . . His life is such that you either fall in line or you're left behind. I didn't want to follow anymore."[37]

Blue moved to D.C. to live with Hitchens, and the two were married in 1991. After the fallout from the divorce dissipated, Hitchens settled into a life that was a lot like the one he'd built with Meleagrou, though somewhat more upscale. Still writing for the *Nation*, he became a columnist for *Vanity Fair* and a freelancer for the higher class of literary glossies. He kept up with some of his old vendettas—still banging the drum against "that fat little fuck Henry Kissinger,"[38] for instance—but he seemed mellowed. The end of the Cold War, his increasing professional success, and his growing love of America had taken the edge off his anger, and life was good. His home was still a way station for various writers and dissidents passing through Washington, but many of those once-dissidents were now wielders of great power and influence in the world.[39]

As an essayist, Hitchens let more of his idiosyncrasies show, writing more personally about his disgust for religion, his love of literature, his vices. "Only a fool expects smoking and drinking to bring happiness, just as only a dolt expects money to do so. Like money, booze and fags are happiness," he wrote in 1992, "and people cannot be expected to pursue happiness in moderation. This distillation of ancient wisdom requires constant reassertion as the bores and prohibitionists and workhouse masters close in."[40]

In 1995 he published *The Missionary Position*, which was an almost flawless prosecution of Mother Teresa, indicting her for renting out her piety to some of the world's worst people and for propagating reactionary, theocratic beliefs that bred the misery she was then sanctified for ameliorating. "The call to go forth and multiply," he wrote, "and to take no thought for the morrow, sounds grotesque when uttered by an elderly virgin whose chief claim to reverence is that she ministers to the inevitable losers in this very lottery."[41]

Hitchens was at his best as a writer and thinker when his love or hatred for his subject was just distant enough to achieve bemusement and affection. On Oscar Wilde, for instance, he was lovely—perhaps because Wilde's failure of integrity, during the trial that brought him into disgrace, alleviated the anxiety of influence that haunted Hitchens in relation to those other men (almost always men) who were his models of unbending rectitude.

"There is a revenge that the bores and the bullies and the bigots exact on those who are too witty," Hitchens wrote of the trial that brought Wilde down. "Wilde could never hope to escape the judgment of the pompous and the hypocritical, because he could not help teasing them. I personally find it hard, if not impossible, to read the record of his trial without fighting back tears. Here was a marvelous, gay, brave, and eloquent man, being gradually worn down by inexorable, plodding oafs and heavies."[42]

Hitchens proved deceptive to his critics and admirers because his loyalties and enmities were so much more temperamental, historical, literary, and visceral than they were ideological, and because he could be ruthless when he was sure he was right or when he got caught up in the romance of himself as a partisan of the pro-wit radical faction fighting against the forces of boorishness, philistinism, prudishness, humorlessness, appeasement, and moral equivalency.

If there was any deep structure to his meanderings across space and time, it was a drive to see Great Britain held to account for its trespasses, and also to see it redeemed. That this quest was mistaken, by many for many years, as the traditional leftist antipathy to empire (particularly capitalist empire) wasn't surprising. Until the mid-1990s, he wrote most often on the ruin—in places like Zimbabwe, Cyprus, Israel, and Iraq—still echoing down from the colonial era, and on the mess that America, following clumsily in Great Britain's footsteps, was making in Asia and Latin America.

What this correlation with the Left obscured, however, was that along with his war against the delusions of empire there was a more subtle, contrapuntal war against the opposite cliché—that in the absence of empire and hegemony, the world could buy itself a Coke and sing in harmony. There was also a loyalty to those virtues that were, for men like his father, indivisible from a loyalty to the universalist vision of British civilization. Hitchens told well the story of the original sin of colonization and domination, but he told better the story of abandonment, of how Great Britain withdrew too abruptly, like a priest caught with an altar boy, with little sense of the debt it had accrued to the nations it had been screwing and little care for the consequences of such a radical abdication of authority and responsibility. Hitchens criticized America, in turn, less for aspiring to supplant Great Britain as the dominant power of the West than for lacking the style and the bone-deep certainty of superiority to carry it off properly.

Hitchens's ambivalence was both oedipal and principled. He struggled to resist the trumpet call of empire and glory—the legacy of the unreflective patriotism of his father—but he wasn't able to eradicate it. And he also believed in skepticism and contradiction as a way of life.

"But contradiction is of the essence," he wrote in *Letters to a Young Contrarian*, the closest he ever came to a personal manifesto.[43] What was fascinating to him about, say, Winston Churchill wasn't simply that Churchill was right about the Nazis when so many others were wrong, it was that he was right about the Nazis because he was the type of person who could joke around with Stalin at the expense of a nation he was about to sacrifice to Stalin's cruel empire in order to prolong the life of his own, less cruel empire. Churchill proved the great defender of liberalism against fascism because of, not despite, his own will to domination and his temperamental sympathies with fascism.[44]

Rudyard Kipling, another literary-political father to Hitchens, was both the man who serenaded Britain and America down into the coarsest delusions of world mastery, and a brilliant poet on the tragic pride of empire. Perhaps it was the imperial hubris, implied Hitchens, that ultimately fueled or birthed the tragic awareness.[45]

James Burnham showed up periodically in Hitchens's writing as a destructive but undeniably magisterial figure, "the real intellectual founder of the neo-conservative movement . . . the first important Marxist to defect all the way over to the right in his now-neglected masterpiece *The Managerial Revolution*."[46] Hitchens bestowed on Burnham his highest praise—parity with George Orwell—writing that "Only in his contest with Burnham does Orwell really engage, before his death, with the modern questions that still preoccupy us. The antagonists were well matched. Burnham liked to combat prevailing orthodoxy, had a pitiless attitude to intellectual compromise, and was an ex-Marxist with a good working knowledge of socialist thought."

Contradiction was to be embraced, wrote Hitchens, because "Ultimates and Absolutes are attempts at Perfection, which is—so to speak—a latently absolutist idea."[47] Better to look for instruction in the experience of people whose flame of inner contradiction blazed brighter than usual than to those who've submitted to a complete system. The political actors like Churchill, and the poets like Kipling, were interesting because they "achieved great and splendid effects in spite of, as well as because of, their affinity with ethical conservatism, sometimes in its radical forms."[48]

Among the greatest pleasures of the mature Hitchens was his campaign of insult against neoconservatism, a movement that was defined by its apostasy from the Left and that served as a kind of proxy for Hitchens to contend with those parts of himself that he feared might betray him if given too much sail. Neoconservatism's militarism looked, to him, like a bastard child of British imperial ideology without the savvy that was the original's saving grace. Its Zionism was tribalism in defense of further victimization of the Palestinians, who were already victimized by the Ottoman Empire and, of course, the British empire. Its moralism was Victorian rather than fin de siècle. Its sexual politics were prudish. Its cultural politics were philistine. Its religiosity was opportunistic. And its standard-bearers, with a few exceptions, were pretty offensive people.

Irving Kristol, for Hitchens, was the spindly-fingered CFO of the movement, a cynic and prude who "used to discourse about the shock of recognition when Jewish intellectuals at last met Republican businessmen and found that they could *do* things for each other."[49] David Horowitz was neoconservatism's court misfit, a tormented soul who couldn't see straight through his pain and resentment.

It was Norman Podhoretz, however, who was the object of Hitchens's greatest arias of obloquy. Hitchens wrote of "the dire Norman Podhoretz . . . perhaps the most unscrupulous man of letters of our time," "a born-again conformist with some interesting disorders of the ego." There were "the congealed regurgitations of Podhoretz," "the gruesome maturity of the once iconoclastic Norman Podhoretz," and "the third-rater's loathing for those people better equipped to face high tasks and principles."[50]

Hitchens's review of *Ex-Friends*, the second in Podhoretz's series of score-settling memoirs, was perhaps the masterpiece of abuse in a career that was built, to some degree, on Hitchens's cleverness with abuse. The book, Hitchens wrote, had "no levity—unbearable heaviness is his preferred métier—and never strays into paradox, and gives a series of chiefly posthumous but always spiteful reviews to several authors whom he may have read but certainly has not understood. This is bad manners cubed, boorishness wrenched almost into a literary form."[51]

". . . Podhoretz has found companionship and solidarity with some new chums. He mentions them shyly, as if he were back in his lonely childhood and his mother had secretly bribed them to play with him.

". . . The Russian exile writer Vassily Aksyonov—another example of the real as opposed to the bogus dissident—once wrote that Podhoretz reminded him of all the things he had left the Soviet Union to escape. He had, said Aksyonov, the mentality of a cultural commissar. . . . he has the soul of one as well. And the literary sensitivity and imagination.

"Small wonder, then, that when he needs a friend these days he has to rely on Henry Kissinger, who probably bills him for meetings."[52]

Podhoretz, for Hitchens, was an embodiment of neoconservatism's greatest betrayals—its subordination of an essentially Jewish moralistic intellectualism to the amoral military-industrial power of the WASP establishment, and its alliance, for the sake of Israel, with the fundamentalist Right.

The neoconservatives were also, from Hitchens's perspective, wrong about most of the particulars of the history with which they'd contended, and therefore a useful group to watch when trying to figure out what not to think. Wrong on Israel. Alarmist on the Soviet Union. Wrong on Nicaragua and the Contras. Wrong on Salman Rushdie, who'd made the mistake of supporting the self-determination of the Palestinians and was therefore, according to "the Podhoretz school . . . a terrorist-symp who had been caught in his own logic."[53] Wrong (with a few exceptions) on Yugoslavia and Kosovo. A better group of enemies Hitchens couldn't have hoped to find.

During the later part of the 1990s it was Bill Clinton, curiously, who was the only subject who seemed to get under Hitchens's skin as irritatingly as the neoconservatives. His grudge was principled. He disliked what he perceived as Clinton's pandering to the Right on capital punishment, welfare reform, military intervention. It was also temperamental: Clinton was too much the sweet-talker, the glad-hander, and the people-pleaser for a purist and provocateur like Hitchens. And it was a manifestly primal, almost fraternal thing for Hitchens, an anger that welled up in the space between the very different choices made by two sybaritic, brilliant, round-faced scholarship boys from bruised or broken homes who'd worked and charmed themselves into the upper classes.

Writing of Dick Morris, Clinton's Machiavellian advisor, Hitchens wrote, "Mr. Morris served for a long spell as Bill Clinton's pimp. He and Mr. Clinton shared some pretty foul evenings together, bloating and sating at public expense while consigning the poor and defenseless to yet more misery. The kinds of grossness and greed in which they indulged are perfectly cognate with one another—selfish and fleshy and hypocritical and exploitive."[54]

Even as Hitchens became, throughout the 1990s, more interested in how American military force might be wielded as a force for achieving humanitarian good, and as Clinton slowly became a cautious advocate for just such a humanitarian internationalist vision, the president was given no benefit of the doubt. Clinton was too slow and too calculating for Hitchens. Where was America, wondered Hitchens, when Hutus were slaughtering Tutsis in Rwanda? Why did America hold back as Sarajevo, once one of the most beautiful, ethnically heterogeneous, and cosmopolitan cities in the world, was torn apart by ethnic chauvinism and quasi-fascist power politics? Even when Clinton acted earlier and more decisively in Kosovo than he had in Bosnia, Hitchens never got on board with the project, choosing to snipe from the sidelines at what he saw as a cowardly refusal to commit ground troops to the fight.

In February of 1999, incensed by Clinton's continued political survival, Hitchens swore out an affidavit declaring that Sidney Blumenthal, a senior Clinton aide and an old friend of Hitchens's, had perjured himself when he'd testified to the U.S. Senate that he wasn't involved in spreading rumors to discredit Monica Lewinsky. Hitchens's impulsive act cost him Blumenthal's friendship, as well as the sympathy of many of his remaining admirers on the Left. And it was to no avail: Clinton was acquitted by the Senate the following week.

Later that year, Hitchens published *No One Left to Lie To: The Values of the Worst Family*, a defiant coda to the Blumenthal affair and a final summary of his belief that Clinton was a politician of rare toxicity.

The book's rap against Bill Clinton—that he was a phony, surrounded by phonies, who thrived through phoniness—was typical Hitchens. The tone, however, was aggrieved in a way that was striking. "There is, clearly, something very distraught in his family background," Hitchens wrote, venturing the kind of pop analysis he'd often dismissed when practiced by others. "Our physicians tell us that that thirst for approval is often the outcome of a lonely or insecure childhood."[55]

As the twenty-first century turned, Hitchens was still a man of the Left. He still wrote his column for the *Nation*, and although his crusade against Clinton had struck most of its readers as overwrought, his contempt appeared to arise from a wellspring of leftist principle. Hitchens may have been tone-deaf to the politics of impeachment—to the desire to push back against the Right, even if it meant overlooking Clinton's flaws—but he had always been impatient with such calculations. It was what had made him such an incisive critic of the Right's power lust and realpolitik. He remained an idealist, and his enemies, for the most part, remained the right ones.

Something had shifted, though. Hitchens seemed tired of being on the Left, which hadn't seen much action during the go-go 1990s, when Bill Gates, Bill Clinton, and the invisible hand of the marketplace appeared poised to solve all of our problems and to render quaint the need for a "Left" to fight against things like poverty, racism, inequality, imperialism, injustice, authoritarianism, and religious intolerance. He seemed weary of his role as the disreputable, lecherous uncle of the Movement, and he seemed bored with the Movement itself and its predictable antipathy to America, and in particular its knee-jerk opposition to the exercise of American military force.

What's the Left's answer, he began asking more and more insistently, when confronted with evil that can't be remedied by a critique of capitalist-imperialism or a withdrawal of Western military power? What should one do or say when faced with evil that might be remedied, in fact, only by an application of Western military-capitalist-imperialist power? His answer, which awaited only the right moment to deliver it, was that there were occasions when there was no choice but to get on board with power. Having preserved his moral cleanliness for decades precisely by puncturing grand narratives rather than embracing them, Hitchens was finally ready for his great cause.

September 11, 2001, and the war in Iraq, gave it to him. It was a perfect storm. He'd been writing about Iraq since the 1970s. He'd been concerned about the threat from the religious and secular fascisms of the Middle East ever since the *fatwah* against his friend Rushdie in 1989. He'd lost much of his respect for and loyalty to the Left after its tryst with Bill Clinton and what he saw as its failure to rise to the occasion in Bosnia, Rwanda, and Kosovo. In the course of his years reporting on Iraq he'd formed friendships with men like Ahmed Chalabi, the urbane Iraqi exile leader with a Ph.D. in mathematics from MIT; Paul Wolfowitz, the most genuinely idealistic of the neoconservatives who would come to populate the Bush administration; and Jalal Talabani, the charismatic Kurdish revolutionary who would later become the president of postinvasion Iraq.

In the matter of Saddam Hussein vs. the World, the difficult choice—the morally compromised one—would have been to leave Hussein in power and thus abandon the millions of suffering Iraqis to their suffering. And Hitchens, as one of his friends would later write, had "no patience with a politics of difficult choices."[56] The great cause was the fight to liberate Iraqis and to defeat Islamofascism. The great cause was to support the Kurds, whom Hitchens had befriended, insofar as you can befriend an entire people, and to stand with the resistance of exiles like Kanan Makiya, a courageous, soulful-eyed writer who'd brought Saddam Hussein's tyranny to the attention of the West in his book *Republic of Fear.*

If Hitchens had to share a bed with Norman Podhoretz, an ardent advocate of the war, then at least he didn't have to share one with realpolitikers like Brent Scowcroft and Henry Kissinger, who in the run-up to war counseled, as they always had, that the authoritarian we knew was better than the potential democrats we didn't know. At least the neocons believed in something, and at last, hoped Hitchens, America might dispose of the politics of self-interested cynicism that had tainted its foreign policy from the end of World War II up through the Clinton administration.

Hitchens ran the data through his algorithm, and the answer, with some qualifications, was war. Vaclav Havel, arguably the least sullied moral hero of the previous twenty years, had come out in support of the war. Polish dissident writer Adam Michnik, another one of Hitchens's wise men, wrote a few weeks after the invasion, "Today . . . the primary threat is terrorism by Islamist fundamentalists. War has been declared against the democratic world. It is this world, whose sins and mistakes we know all too well, that we want to defend. These are the reasons behind our absolute war on the terrorist, corrupt, intolerant regime of the despot from Baghdad."[57]

There was also history to be reckoned with. Iraq was a problem that was originally mashed together by the British empire, was exacerbated by America's encouragement of Saddam Hussein in his war with Iran, was invaded by America in the Gulf War, was abandoned back to Hussein's tyranny after the war was over, and was then punished by America with economic sanctions for another decade or so. Hitchens, born to Britain and adopted by America, felt doubly responsible, and saw in Iraq the opportunity to redeem both of his nations and their sins.

Finally, Iraq was to be one of Hitchens's Orwell moments. It was the part of the story when Hitchens saw that the fascism his country was fighting against was so great an evil that there was no choice, in the end, but to throw in on the side of flawed but redeemable liberal democracy.

"I don't quite know in what year I first knew for certain that the present war was coming," wrote George Orwell in "My Country Right or Left," an essay which served as a kind of users' manual for Hitchens in the years after 9/11. "After 1936, of course, the thing was obvious to anyone except an idiot. For several years the coming war was nightmare to me, and at times I even made speeches and wrote pamphlets against it. But the night before the Russo-German pact was announced I dreamed that the war had started. It was one of those dreams which, whatever Freudian inner meaning they may have, do sometimes reveal to you the real state of your feelings. It taught me two things, first, that I should be simply relieved when the long-dreaded war started, secondly, that I was patriotic at heart, would not sabotage or act against my own side, would support the war, would fight in it if possible. I came downstairs to find the newspaper announcing Ribbentrop's flight to Moscow. So war was coming, and the Government, even the Chamberlain Government, was assured of my loyalty."[58]

For Hitchens, the war had arrived. There was no choice but to pick a side, and the side to pick was obvious. And for Hitchens, as for Orwell, half of the fun of the refreshingly simple choice was the license it gave him to unleash the patriotism that his cosmopolitan conscience had been holding in check for decades. And who better to turn his righteous patriotic anger against than the leftists who'd for so long been Hitchens's loving but dysfunctional family. He became a professional apostate, armed with deep insight into the leftist psyche, decades of accumulated resentments, and a polemical style perfect to the role.

"Instead of internationalism, we find among the Left now a sort of affectless, neutralist, smirking isolationism," he wrote in the *Washington Post* in October of 2002, a week after he quit his column at the *Nation*. ". . . Sooner or later, one way or another, the Iraqi and Kurdish peoples will be free of Saddam Hussein. When that day comes, I am booked to have a reunion in Baghdad with several old comrades who have been through hell. We shall not be inviting anyone who spent this precious time urging democratic countries to give Saddam another chance."[59]

A month later, in a final parting shot to the *Nation*, he elaborated: "It may now seem trite to say that September 11 and other confrontations 'changed everything.' For me, it didn't so much change everything as reinforce something. I am against aggressive totalitarian states and I am resolutely opposed to religious fanaticism. I am also sickened by any attempt to call these hideous things by other names. Most especially in its horrible elicitation of readers' letters on the anniversary of September 11, *The Nation* joined the amoral side. It's the customers I want to demoralize, not just the poor editors. I say that they stand for neutralism where no such thing is possible or desirable, and I say the hell with it. I feel much better as a result—though I admit the occasional twinge."[60]

In the months after his departure from the *Nation*, and his divorce from the Left, Hitchens was at his most luminous as a writer. Writing for papers, magazines, and journals of the Left, the center, and the Right, he became the most visible and articulate of the phalanx of pro-war liberal editors and writers who did so much to legitimate the war in the eyes of Democrats, independents, and the mainstream media. America would have gone to war without Hitchens, and without the narrative he and his fellow liberal hawks spun, but it would have done so with greater doubt. He gave America not the war it was about to fight but rather the war it hoped it would be fighting—a blockbuster war, fought in defense of freedom against an enemy who'd given us no choice.

"This brings me to my closing point," he wrote in 2003, just before the invasion. "On my last visit to Kurdistan I made some friends for life, and I have kept up with them. They, and their allies in the Iraqi democratic opposition, could each tell you a story that would harrow up your soul. You'll get an idea, when the mass graves and secret prisons are opened. . . . For twelve years of compromise and dither, those inside Iraq have been kept by a cowardly international statecraft as hostages in a country used by a madman as his own laboratory and torture chamber. In the face of a modern Caligula, many of them continually risked everything to try and free their people from a system of atrocity and aggression. I feel that they were fighting all this time on my behalf. Only after a long train of blunders and hesitations and betrayals did the United States decide that it was, at long last, in the same trench as the resistance. No matter how it comes out, or how this alliance may fray, I shall never have the least serious doubt that it was the right side to have been on."[61]

As the increasingly bleak Iraq invasion went on, year after year, Hitchens stood by his war. On occasion, he would criticize the Bush administration for its incompetence, and he would note its shifting rationalizations, but he never stopped insisting that the war was just and that the arguments against it were, without exception, excuses for appeasing fascism.

His fire dimmed, though. His moral certainty, which had been so seductive when the war was still a potentiality, began to look petulant in the light of the Iraq that was happening. As generals, Republicans, and even a few neoconservatives abandoned the war as a mistake, Hitchens soldiered on. Even after it was revealed that Henry Kissinger, of all people, had become an advocate of perpetuating the war, Hitchens showed no humility. He continued to contend, in his writing, not with the strongest critiques of his position, made by the most honorable of people, but with the weakest arguments made by the silliest people.

He became an anachronism, a living but visibly dwindling remnant of a historical tendency—neoconservatism, liberal hawk–ism, Hitchens-ism—that had seemed vindicated, and had then been discredited, with tragic rapidity.

The diminution of Hitchens was perhaps most evident, to the public, on the August 25, 2005, episode of the *Daily Show* with Jon Stewart. He was the featured guest, and from the start he didn't appear quite ready for the encounter. He walked out to the desk with a bit of a hunch, seeming too small for his suit, and his new beard had subversively altered the lines of his face, depriving it of the decadent broadness that had long worked for him as a subtle tool of intimidation. The cumulative effect was that he looked as if the responsibility for defending the war in Iraq against all comers—which he'd shouldered with such exhilaration a few years before—had begun to weary him. It also seemed as though his decades of enthusiastic living might be starting to tell.

The interview turned quickly to Iraq, and over the span of the ten-minute interview Stewart was so ruthless and so disarming in his interrogation that by its end Hitchens was visibly disoriented.

"I've lost my place," he said at one point. "I really can't remember where we were just before that. This is terrible." "You tripped me up," he said by way of acknowledging why something he'd said was "a bit platitudinous." He interrupted himself, at one point, to deliver a comeback that would have been clever if only it weren't in response to a dispute they'd left behind a few minutes before.

The most devastating exchange was the final one. It began with Hitchens pointing out, as he'd done too many times before, that radical

Islamic terrorism and theocratic fascism have never needed any excuse to plan violence against America. "The people who say that the violence of these people is our fault," he said, "are masochistic and capitulationist, and they should be ignored."

"But the people who say that we shouldn't fight in Iraq *aren't* saying it's our fault," said Stewart. "That's the conflation that is most disturbing to me."

"Don't you hear," said Hitchens, "people saying we've made them . . ."

"I hear people say a lot of stupid shit," said Stewart, "but what I'm saying is that there is reasonable dissent in this country about the way this war has been conducted that has nothing to do with people believing we should cut and run from the terrorists, or we should show weakness in the face of terrorism, or that we believe that we have in some way brought this upon ourselves. They believe that this war is being conducted without transparency, without credibility, and without competence."

"But I'm sorry, Sunshine, I just watched you ridicule the president for saying that he wouldn't give a timetable . . ." said Hitchens.

"No, you misunderstood why," said Stewart. "That's not why I ridiculed the president. I ridiculed him because he refuses to answer questions from adults as though we were adults, and falls back upon platitudes and phrases and talking points."

Hitchens made another stab or two at responding, but by this point it was obvious that he'd been made to look foolish. He remained composed enough to devote the remaining few seconds to a plug for his latest book, but when he was done with that he tried to exit the stage so quickly that Stewart, it appeared, had to grab and hold him for a second or two to keep him in the frame until the commercial break began.[62]

Christopher Hitchens wasn't the typical turncoat. He wasn't a man in search of God. He wasn't betrayed by the Left. He wasn't a refugee from communism, or a dupe of leftist ideology. He wasn't alienated from popular culture, nor a passive receptacle for it. Hitchens was none of these types. He defined himself, in fact, by his refusal to be any type at all, and by his choice to be bound not by blood, nation, family, party, or ideology but only by what he perceived to be just and true.

On April 13, 2007, on his fifty-eighth birthday, Hitchens was sworn in as an American citizen. That spring he also published *God Is Not Great: How Religion Poisons Everything.* The book, like all of his longer books, was messy. It was brilliant at times, shallow at times, badly organized, gratuitously tendentious, and debaterly rather than scholarly. Out on the road promoting the book, however, Hitchens was imaginative and surprising in a way that he hadn't been for years. He brushed aside the American taboo against speaking ill of the devout as if it were no more than a minor point of etiquette—rather than one of the pressure points of American political discourse—and said those things that many of his fellow secular citizens believed but didn't have the platform or the nerve to say.

Hitchens's dislike of religion wasn't new, but the valence of it, in the wake of his defection from the Left, had changed. It was particularly discombobulating to Movement conservatives, who'd come to savor his polemical style so much when it was making the case for war in Iraq.

"The empty life of this ugly little charlatan proves only one thing, that you can get away with the most extraordinary offenses to morality and to truth in this country if you will just get yourself called reverend," Hitchens said of Jerry Falwell, the Christian conservative leader who died not long after *God Is Not Great* was released. ". . . The whole consideration of this horrible little person is offensive to very, very many of us who have some regard for truth and for morality who think that ethics do not require that lies be told to children by evil little men. . . . It's time to stop saying that because someone preaches credulity and credulousness, and claims it as a matter of faith, that we should respect them. The whole life of Falwell shows that this is an actual danger to democracy, to culture, to civilization."[63]

The book's crusade against religion also, inevitably, made the case for the war in Iraq—that it was fought on behalf of reason against the forces of religious fascism—and thus managed to upset many on the Left, who might have been heartened by Hitchens's disdain for the Christian and Zionist Right but who detested and distrusted him so much, by that point, that they were unable to entertain his attacks on Muslim fundamentalism for fear of inadvertently conceding some point about the Bush administration's foreign policy.

For Hitchens it was a kind of apotheosis. He stood alone, apart from Left and Right, in alliance only with the truth. It was also a last hurrah, and a melancholy one—because last hurrahs are by their nature melancholy, and because although Hitchens sounded sharp and agile when he was on television, he looked tired and bloated. It was sad, also, because no matter how inspiring he was, the chains of Iraq rattled behind everything he said, serving as a reminder to those who contemplated matters of posterity that he would be remembered, above all, for having gotten it wrong on the defining political question of his time.

He had help getting it wrong. The Left gave him a few too many examples of ignorance with which to dismiss the antiwar case as an exercise in moral relativism or anti-Americanism. Ahmad Chalabi, Kanan Makiya, and Paul Wolfowitz, whose ultimate loyalties were to their own interests or delusions rather than to the truth or the American public, gave him a way to believe that the American government was finally going to put aside its cynical pursuit of self-interest abroad and seek justice instead. And he was given a push by the ghost of his father and the ghosts of the unnamed legions of stolid, stoic, noble British men who for centuries had shipped out to fight for the West in the name of patriotism and civilization.

Hitchens was also betrayed by history. If the Democratic Party or the American media, both enfeebled by decades of conservative propaganda and the burden of 9/11, hadn't capitulated quite so quickly to the neoconservative narrative, Hitchens might not have had a war to champion. If Al Gore had been elected in 2000, there almost certainly would have been no Iraq War to divide Hitchens from his old colleagues and loyal leftist readers. If Henry Kissinger had come out for the war earlier rather than later, Hitchens might have thought twice. If Hitchens hadn't already been so personally invested in the cause of the Kurds, he might have viewed the war with more distance. If he'd quit drinking, or drinking so much, he might have been supple enough to disentangle his own fantasies from those of the men and women who were prosecuting the war. If George W. Bush's studied ignorance and privileged resentment had provoked Hitchens half as much as Clinton's studied empathy and phony populism once had, he might have been more wary.

Hitchens, however, ultimately failed himself. He was too much the romantic, too much the contrarian, and too much the narcissist to chart out the ways that history might fail to conform to his desires. He chose to mistake thoughtful opposition for moral cowardice and jingoism for righteousness. His bullshit detector, which had served him so well for so long, somehow failed to properly take the measure of George W. Bush. And faced with the difficulties and opportunities presented by an invasion of Iraq, Hitchens remembered only the dare, and not the caution, implicit in Marx's observation that "World history would indeed be very easy to make, if the struggle were taken up only on condition of infallibly favourable chances."

What could have saved Hitchens was blind luck. Or blind loyalty— to the Left, to his editor, to his colleagues, to his old anti-imperialism. But luck failed him, and his method, which was designed to outwit the failings of every other method, led him astray. Even Vaclav Havel can be wrong. Even George Orwell, it turns out, can be wrong, or we can be wrong about Orwell. There's no perfect refuge anywhere.

Postscript

By the time Christopher Hitchens died from esophageal cancer, in December of 2011, his best days as a writer were solidly behind him. Not that he'd become a bad writer. His last book before he died, the memoir *Hitch 22*, had some excellent writing in it. His very final essays, most of which involved a reckoning with his sickness and imminent death, had a directness to them that many readers found bracing. And there was something inspiring, almost majestic, about the way Hitchens went down. He seemed so Hitchensian—defiant, atheistic, rakish—to the emaciated end.

Yet the work itself, on its own terms, was missing something. What it meant to be Hitchensian had diminished over the last decade of his life. His writerly voice had settled into a collection of predictable rhetorical and political maneuvers, where once it had been coherent and distinctive but also fluid and surprising. He was still capable of writing well and thinking incisively when the right issue presented itself, but his capacity to hold in fruitful balance conflicting and complicated data was mostly gone.

Hitchens's writing flattened out not because it's any more difficult, in general, to think or write well from the right than from the left. Rather, it's because Christopher Hitchens lost something essential when he left the Left. Not truth, or righteousness, but tension. And there's a certain kind of political writing and thinking that can be done only by someone who is in tension. It's by putting ourselves—our highest ideals, our most atavistic impulses, our deepest loyalties—in conversation with the world, with vulnerability and conviction, that new possibilities open up. That's how we discover ourselves as intellectuals and artists. It's also how social movements are born, how societies evolve, how culture is enriched and our collective imagination is expanded.

It was from the left, it turned out, that Hitchens was able to most creatively draw on this tension. It was as a leftist—up in the balcony, like Waldorf and Statler, lobbing down wisecracks—that his critique of the Left was most sensitive and useful. And it was his allegiance to the Left that enabled him to hold captive and interrogate the deep dark part of himself that thrilled to the idea of empire. When he cut himself loose from the society of the Left, and set his inner imperialist free, there was a brief, bright release of energy and creativity. Then the essential tensions went slack.

There is no one-size-fits-all formula for how to achieve the right balance of impulses and principles, politics and habits, to do the kind of work that political thinkers do at their best. It's not about tacking artfully between extremes, or making sure to hold one's commitments with the maximal degree of skepticism, or regularly convening round-tables with one's critics and doubters. The right mixture doesn't come predictably when one is Right or Left, young or old, at the beginning or middle or end of the journey.

Whittaker Chambers's imagination was at its most capacious and subtle only once he had become a conservative, writing *Witness*. David Horowitz was at his most humane and compelling as a writer when he was saying good-bye to the Left but hadn't yet located himself anywhere else. Norman Podhoretz held fundamentally the same political commitments when he was teasing out his feelings about James Baldwin as when he wrote *Making It*, but in the former he was writing from within the tension, rather brilliantly, whereas the latter was too often an exercise in trying to write his inner conflicts out of existence.

The trick, which isn't a trick at all but rather the basic art of living, is to be grounded in a strong sense of self but attuned to one's inner frictions and fictions. It's to be passionate in one's convictions but also open to the data of experience and the evidence of error. It's to accept that there's no end to the friction and uncertainty except death. And it's to be willing to step forward, with as much courage and creativity as you can muster, when the old strategies, assumptions, and defenses simply won't do the trick anymore.

It's not the point of this book to make the case that we should all be on the Right, or the Left. I have my opinions. I'm sticking to them (for now). These six men had their own opinions, and changed them, in some cases productively and in others less so. But maybe it's the point that these lives are worth approaching with interest regardless— because there's a depth of humanity that can be achieved, by any of us, only when we reckon bravely with what's in conflict within us, rather than run away from it or deny its existence. And these are people who reckoned with themselves at the most terrifyingly fundamental level.

That we don't all like where they ended up, on the far side of their encounters, isn't beside the point. It makes the point. Growth requires risk. To turn against one's former side is to take an enormous psychological gamble. It's to let go of who you were and very possibly not find a new identity on the other side that's coherent and functional. You might alienate friends, coworkers, family, community. You might have to live your life with the haunting fear that you gave it all up for nothing. And the payoff, if there is one, is awfully hard-won and almost certainly bitter tasting.

By paying close and sustained attention to these perilous journeys, by asking ourselves where they went right and wrong, by extending our sympathies as far as they can possibly go, and imagining ourselves into lives where we could make similarly fraught choices, perhaps we can learn something that will enable us to better live our own lives, to be more aware of the possibilities—to be more bold, and more humble, somehow at the same time.

Acknowledgments

The first thing I ever officially published was a short essay on Norman Podhoretz and James Baldwin that appeared on the now-defunct web magazine TomPaine.com. It was a big moment for me as a writer. It wasn't until after that publication, in fact, that I would begin to even experiment with calling myself a writer. It was also, though I didn't know it at the time, the first concrete step along the road to what would become this book. Rick Shenkman was the editor who accepted and published the piece, who took me seriously. I still appreciate it.

In the MFA writing program at Columbia University, I had a number of exceptional professors, including Richard Locke, Michael Scammell, Patty O'Toole, and Doug Whynott. Without them I would be less of a writer, and I wouldn't have the very grounding sense I do of being heir to a coherent tradition of nonfiction writing. While there I also took a poetry workshop with Emily Fragos, who told me that I might have some talent as a poet. Her baseline vote of confidence in my facility with language meant a lot to me going forward.

Mike Janeway, who was my professor, friend, mentor, and protector at Columbia, died before I finished. I was really, really looking forward to sending him a copy of this book. I hadn't decided yet how I was going to inscribe his copy, but the thought of composing that message, and trying to distill my affection for him into a few clever sentences, gave me a lot of pleasure. I'm sad that I can't do that now. He was a rare person. I miss him.

At the *Valley Advocate*, I had the good luck to work for three years for Tom Vannah. He encouraged me to follow my interests wherever they led from the moment I sat down to interview for the job, and he never stopped encouraging me. It was at the *Advocate* that I began writing regular pieces about left-to-righters, though I didn't notice a pattern until someone said to me that maybe I should write a book on the topic.

My agent, Melissa Flashman, sold the book on the strength of her energy, skill, and enthusiasm, none of which has waned over the many years it's taken me to finish.

Having three editors during the course of writing one book isn't the ideal scenario for a writer, but I've had three smart, thoughtful, and gracious editors: Hilary Redmon, Thomas LeBien, and Jonathan Cox. Each of them has given serious attention to the book, and has been good to me.

The University of Texas at Austin, where I've worked in communications for the last eight years, has been a good professional home. I've had benevolent supervisors, supportive colleagues, and access to a world-class library.

Shirley Grogan was an immense source of support during this whole journey, and I don't know that our family could have survived it as functionally as we did without her. Jennifer Percy Dowd's comments and edits were exceptionally astute and entirely gracious.

Jason Sokol, Jeremy Sharrard, and I have been arguing and joking about the world with one another since we were kids growing up in Springfield, Massachusetts. I wouldn't be who I am, whatever that is, without them. Anthony Kyriakakis has been my guy since the day we had the good luck to be paired as roommates freshman year of Yale. I found Charles Loxton in grad school at Columbia, and haven't lost him yet. All of you know how much of me is in this book, but maybe not how much of you is in me. I can't even say how grateful I am for your friendship.

Joanne and Tim Oppenheimer, my parents, raised me on the Left. They also raised me with a healthy skepticism of the Left, and with the sense that making up my own mind was the most important thing. I never had any doubt they would love me whatever my politics. That kind of childhood is a gift for a writer and intellectual.

There's no one with whom I've spent more time talking about writing, literature, and politics than Mark Oppenheimer, my older brother. In some ways we've been an intellectual community of two. I'm incredibly grateful for that. Jonathan Oppenheimer, my younger brother, and Rachel Oppenheimer, my sister, continue to love and challenge me. It's been exciting for me to be a witness to, and part of, the lives they're building for themselves.

Asa and Jolie Grogan are the lights of my life. I always knew I wanted to have kids, but I couldn't imagine how interesting, amazing, complicated, intelligent, funny, and strange my actual kids would be until they showed up. I'm proud of this book, but they're clearly the best thing I'll ever have a hand in making.

Jessica Grogan is the most intriguing and brilliantly psychologically minded woman I know, so it's fortunate that I was married to her while writing this book. In some cases her perceptions have enriched mine. Often they've humbled me, and given me the freedom to let go of false insights and forced profundities. The book is better for her being around, and so am I. Thanks, love.

Notes

Introduction

1 Isaac Deutscher, "The Ex-Communist's Conscience: A Review of *The God That Failed*," *The Reporter*, April 1950.

1

In Spite of Noise and Confusion: Whittaker Chambers

1 Whittaker Chambers, "The Coming Struggle for Outer Space," *National Review*, November 2, 1957.

2 Whittaker Chambers, *Cold Friday* (New York: Random House, 1964), 89–144; Sam Tanenhaus, *Whittaker Chambers* (New York: Modern Library, 1998), 21–43.

3 Whittaker Chambers to William F. Buckley, August 5, 1954, in William F. Buckley, ed., *Odyssey of a Friend: Letters to William F. Buckley, Jr., 1954–1961* (New York: G.P. Putnam's Sons, 1970), 68.

4 Sam Tanenhaus, *Whittaker Chambers*, 511–12: "Over the next two years—the last of his life—Chambers was a full-time student. . . . Chambers, 'born a perpetual student,' joyously attacked his studies. Each morning he was in his basement office at dawn, preparing for class, and on weekends he studied all day long. For the first time he

excelled in the classroom. 'Straight A's,' he bragged to [Arthur] Koestler in June 1960, after completing his first year. He was delighted when his lab partner, a girl almost forty years his junior, taught him the lyrics to the pop hit, 'Itsy Bitsy Teenie Weenie Yellow Polka Dot Bikini.' The learning never stopped."

5 Eliot Weinberger, "A Spook in the House of Poetry," *Works on Paper, 1980–1986* (New York: New Directions Publishing, 1986), 95.

6 Whittaker Chambers, *Witness* (Washington, D.C.: Regnery Publishing, 1952), 91.

7 Ibid., 104.

8 Sam Tanenhaus, 6–8.

9 Whittaker Chambers, *Witness*, 102.

10 Ibid., 97.

11 Ibid., 120.

12 Meyer Zeligs, *Friendship and Fratricide* (New York: Viking Press, 1967), 36.

13 The Chamberses' neighbors in Lynbrook told an interviewer that "both Vivian and Richard had been 'over-educated' for Lynbrook; they both read books that other Lynbrook boys didn't read, etc.; also both boys very close to their mother." Interview with James Ronalds, July 9, 1968, Sam Tanenhaus Papers, Box 38, Richard Godfrey Chambers folder, Hoover Institution, Stanford University.

14 Whittaker Chambers, *Witness*, 95.

15 Anne Thaxter Eaton, "Magazines for Children in the 19th Century," *A Critical History of Children's Literature*, ed. Cornelia Meigs and Ruth Hill Viguers (New York: Macmillan Company, 1969), 280. *St. Nicholas* editor Mary Mapes Dodge described the magazine's editorial vision like this: "To give clean, genuine fun to children of all ages. To give them examples of the finest types of boyhood and girlhood. To inspire them with a fine appreciation of pictorial art. To cultivate the imagination in profitable directions. To foster a love of country, home, nature, truth, beauty, sincerity. To prepare boys and girls for life as it is. To stimulate their ambitions—but along normally progressive lines. To keep pace with a fast-moving world in all its activities.

To give reading matter which every parent may pass to his children unhesitatingly."

16 Whittaker Chamber, *Witness*, 133.

17 On the general social conditions early in the twentieth century, see, e.g., Harvey Klehr, *The American Communist Movement: Storming Heaven Itself* (New York: Twayne, 1992), 5–6; Stephanie Coontz, *The Way We Never Were* (New York, Basic Books, 1993), 5–13; David T. Courtwright, "A Century of American Narcotic Policy," in Dean R. Gerstein and Henrick J. Harwood, eds., *Treating Drug Problems, Volume 2: Commissioned Papers on Historical, Institutional, and Economic Contexts of Drug Treatment* (Washington, D.C.: National Academy Press), 1.

18 Theodore Roosevelt, "What We Can Expect of the American Boy," *St. Nicholas Magazine*, May 1900, 571–74, quote from 574.

19 Whittaker Chambers, *Witness*, 122.

20 E. B. White, "Noontime of an Advertising Man," *New Yorker*, June 25, 1949, 25–26.

21 Ibid., 149.

22 Meyer Zeligs, 36.

23 Ibid., 146–47.

24 Ibid., 154.

25 Mark Van Doren, "Jewish Students I Have Known," *Menorah Journal* 13, no. 3 (June 1927).

26 Ibid.

27 Whittaker Chambers, "Morningside," *Cold Friday* (New York: Random House, 1964), 124.

28 Mark Van Doren, *The Autobiography of Mark Van Doren*: "Not that the very first class I met was without its young man who engaged me beyond the call of duty. This was Whittaker Chambers, whose eyes were always upon me as if he thought he had found in this strange place a person who would understand him."

29 Van Doren, "Jewish Students I Have Known."

30 Meyer Zeligs, 66.

31 Chambers, "The Edwardians," *Time*, November 17, 1947, collected in Terry Teachout, ed., *Ghosts on the Roof: Selected Journalism of*

Whittaker Chambers 1931–1959 (Washington, D.C.: Regnery Gateway, 1989), 225.

32 Chambers, *Cold Friday*, 115.

33 Ibid., 116.

34 Ibid., 105: "It was very much as if I had gone to a madhouse and said, cap in hand: Please explain to me the principles of sanity and sane living. . . . Exactly the same thing would have been true, in one degree or another, if I had gone to any other of the top secular universities in the country. Nor would the colleges have been at fault. Their failure merely mirrored a much greater disaster which was the failure of Western civilization itself."

35 Whittaker Chambers, as quoted in Sam Tanenhaus, 31.

36 Michael Kimmage, *The Conservative Turn: Lionel Trilling, Whittaker Chambers, and the Lessons of Anti-Communism* (Cambridge: Harvard University, 2009), 23.

37 Whittaker Chambers, "A Play for Puppets," *Morningside*, November 1922.

38 *New York Times*, November 7, 1922, 8.

39 Whittaker Chambers, *Cold Friday*, 78.

40 Vladimir Lenin, *The Soviets at Work: The International Position of the Russian Soviet*, 5th edition (New York: Rand School of Social Justice, 1919), 3.

41 Ibid., 9.

42 Ibid., 29: "We will go ahead, trying very cautiously and patiently to test and discover real organizers, people with sober minds and practical sense, who combine loyalty to Socialism with the ability to organize quietly (and in spite of confusion and noise)."

43 Whittaker Chambers, *Cold Friday*, 135, quoted in Tanenhaus, 37.

44 Sam Tanenhaus, 44.

45 Whittaker Chambers, *Witness*, 194–95.

46 Ibid., 196.

47 Ibid., 173.

48 Ibid., 176.

49 Ibid., 178.

50 Ibid., 179–80.

51 Sam Tanenhaus, 55.

52 Whittaker Chamber, *Witness*, 187.

53 Ibid., 224.

54 Ibid., 222.

55 Ibid., 227.

56 "So absorbed were the Communists in their internal feuds that the very desire to influence the outer world had begun to atrophy: the faction struggle replaced the class struggle." Irving Howe and Lewis Coser, *The American Communist Party: A Critical History* (New York: Frederick A. Praeger, 1962), 145.

57 Quoted in John P. Diggins, *Up From Communism: Conservative Odysseys in American Intellectual Development* (New York: Columbia University Press, 1975), 140–41.

58 Whittaker Chambers, *Witness*, 251.

59 Ibid., 184.

60 Ibid., 266–67.

61 Ibid., 261.

62 Whittaker Chambers, "Can You Make Out Their Voices?" *New Masses*, March 1931; "You Have Seen the Heads," *New Masses*, April 1931; "Our Comrade Munn," *New Masses*, October 1931; "The Death of the Communists," *New Masses*, December 1931.

63 Whittaker Chambers, "The Death of the Communists," *New Masses*, December 1931.

64 Whittaker Chambers, *Witness*, 275–79.

65 Deposition of Esther Chambers, November 16, 1948. "The Alger Hiss Case: Basic Documents," Microfilm, Pt. 2, Reel 1, 489.

66 The FBI confession can be found in the Sam Tanenhaus Papers, Box 33, Folder "Whittaker Chambers' Homosexuality," Hoover Institution, Stanford University.

67 Whittaker Chambers, *Witness*, 341.

68 For more on this see Robert Conquest, *The Great Terror: A Reassessment* (New York: Oxford University Press, 2008).

69 Whittaker Chambers, *Witness*, 78.

70 Vladimir V. Tchernavin, trans. Nicholas M. Oushakoff, *I Speak for the Silent: Prisoners of the Soviets* (Boston: Hale, Cushman & Flint, 1935).

71 Ibid., 87–88.

72 Whittaker Chambers, *Witness*, 408.

73 Ibid., 79.

74 Whittaker Chambers, *Witness*, 84.

75 Ibid., 83.

76 Ibid., 63.

2

The Finest Brain: James Burnham

1 Letter to William F. Buckley, *Odyssey of a Friend*, 223.

2 Leon Trotsky, "A Petty-Bourgeois Opposition in the Socialist Workers Party," *New International*, December 1939. http://www.marxists.org /archive/trotsky/idom/dm/09-pbopp.htm.

3 W. M. Spackman, *Heyday*, in *The Complete Fiction of W. M. Spackman* (Normal, Ill.: Dalkey Archive Press, 1997), 10.

4 James Burnham, *Suicide of the West: An Essay on the Meaning and Destiny of Liberalism* (New York: The John Day Company, 1964), 99.

5 William F. Buckley, *Odyssey of a Friend*, 179.

6 "It will be seen that Burnham's predictions have not merely, when they were verifiable, turned out to be wrong, but that they have sometimes contradicted one another in a sensational way." George Orwell, "James Burnham and the Managerial Revolution," *Polemic*, May 1946. http:// www.k-1.com/Orwell/site/work/essays/burnham.html.

7 Most of the basic biographical details of Burnham's life are drawn from the one full biography of Burnham: Daniel Kelly, *James Burnham and the Struggle for the World: A Life* (Wilmington, Del.: ISI Books, 2002).

8 Frederic Richard Kilner, *Kenilworth, First Fifty Years* (Village of Kenilworth, 1947). http://archive.org/stream/kenilworthfirstf00kenirich /kenilworthfirstf00kenirich_djvu.txt.

9 James Burnham, "Riding a Morning Round-Up," *Quill*, December 1921, 20–23.

10 James Burnham, "The Stars and the Rushing Waters," *Canterbury Quarterly*, March 1923, 15.

11 James Burnham, "Do Present Conditions in America Stimulate the Production of Literature?" *Canterbury Quarterly*, May 1923, 25.

12 Quoted in a letter from J. Bryan III to Burnham, December 21, 1947, Burnham papers, Hoover Box 5: Folder 22. "I spent a weekend at Princeton back in November and a part of it (an afternoon) with Dean [Robert Kilburn] Root. Quite naturally, your name was mentioned. Said the Dean: Without any question the finest brain I have encountered in all my years at Princeton."

13 The first of the two stories, "Through a Glass Darkly," was particularly poignant on the subject. The love of a stolid young farmer for his wife can surface only at the edges of other thoughts—in his attitude toward the landscape, in his satisfaction at the progress of the farm, in thoughts about how useful she's been in persuading his neighbors to join him in a cooperative venture. When she dies, his grief proves all the more agonizing for his lack of a vocabulary with which to understand it. James Burnham, "Through a Glass Darkly," *Nassau Literary Magazine*, June 1925.

14 Quoted in Kelly, *James Burnham and the Struggle for the World*, 16.

15 David Burnham, *This Our Exile* (New York: Charles Scribner's Sons, 1931), 243–44.

16 Sidney Hook, *Out of Step: An Unquiet Life in the 20th Century* (New York: Harper & Row, 1987), 529–30.

17 *Symposium: A Critical Review*, January 1930, Vol. 1:1.

18 James Burnham, "Comment: The Wondrous Architecture of the World," *Symposium*, Spring 1931, Vol. 2, 175–76.

19 "From 1929 to 1932 . . . I felt somewhat like Paul bringing the glad news of salvation to spiritually hungry gentiles." Sidney Hook, *Out of Step*, 135. For more on Hook's intellectual background, see Christopher Phelps, *Young Sidney Hook: Marxist and Pragmatist* (Ithaca, N.Y.: Cornell University Press, 1997).

20 Sidney Hook, "Toward the Understanding of Karl Marx," *Symposium*, Fall 1931, Vol. 2, 325.

21 Ibid., 367.

22 James Burnham, "Comment," *Symposium*, Spring 1932, Vol. 3, 131.

23 James Burnham, "Book Review: The History of the Russian Revolution, Vol. I," *Symposium*, Summer 1932, Vol. 3, 379–80.

24 Ibid., 373.

25 James Burnham, "Marxism and Esthetics," *Symposium*, Spring 1933, Vol. 4, 29.

26 "Man will become immeasurably stronger, wiser and subtler," wrote Trotsky, in a passage cited by Burnham to illustrate how overwrought Marxists could become on the subject. "His body will become more harmonized, his movements more rhythmical, his voice more musical. The forms of life will become dynamically dramatic. The average human type will rise to the heights of an Aristotle, a Goethe, or a Marx. And above this ridge new peaks will rise." Leon Trotsky, *Literature and Revolution* (Chicago: Haymarket Books, 2005), 207.

27 James Burnham, "Marxism and Esthetics," *Symposium*, Spring 1933, Vol. 4, 30.

28 James Burnham and Philip Wheelwright, "Comment: Thirteen Propositions," *Symposium*, April 1933, Vol. 4, 128.

29 James Burnham, "Comment," *Symposium*, [n.d.] 1933, Vol. 4, 412.

30 Ibid., 413.

31 Sidney Hook, "James Burnham, 1905–1987: Radical, Teacher, Technician," *National Review*, September 11, 1987, 32.

32 For background on the American Workers Party, see, e.g., Sidney Hook, "The American Workers Party," *Out of Step*, 191–207; John P. Diggins, *Up From Communism: Conservative Odysseys in American Intellectual Development* (New York: Columbia University Press, 1975), 169–70; Christopher Phelps, *Young Sidney Hook*, 90–95; Peter Drucker, "The New International," *Max Shachtman and His Left* (Amherst: Humanity Books, 1994), 68–101.

33 Edmund Wilson, "Gerry Allard," *New Republic*, June 14, 1933.

34 "The tremendous historical significance of the step we are taking so boldly leaves one almost breathless upon reflection." Max Shachtman, quoted in Drucker, *Max Shachtman and His Left*, 68.

35 James Burnham (writing as John West), *New Militant*, January 18, 1936.

http://archive.org/stream/NewMilitantVol2-1936/36-newmilitant
-v2_djvu.txt.

36 Max Shachtman, *Reminiscences of Max Shachtman: Oral History*, 338–39.

37 James Burnham, "Revolutionary Fiction," *Nation*, October 9, 1935,
Vol. 141, 416–17.

38 "With full, almost naïve conviction Trotsky believed in the creative possibilities of the word, but he believed not as most Western intellectuals
have: not in some ironic or contemplative or symbolic way. The common distinction between word and deed Trotsky scorned as a sign of
philistinism, worthy—he might have added—of liberal professors and
literary dilettantes. He regarded his outpouring of brilliant composition
as the natural privilege of a thinking man, but more urgently, as the necessary work of a Marxist leader who had pledged his life to socialism.
The heritage of the Russian writers of the nineteenth century is stamped
upon his books, for he took from them the assumption that to write is
to engage in a serious political act, a gesture toward the redemption or
recreation of man." Irving Howe, "Trotsky: The Costs of History," in *The
Basic Writings of Trotsky*, quoted in Alan Wald, *The New York Intellectuals:
The Rise and Decline of the Anti-Stalinist Left from the 1930s to the 1980s*
(Chapel Hill, N.C.: University of North Carolina Press, 1987), 91–92.

39 Leon Trotsky, trans. Max Eastman, *History of the Russian Revolution*
(Chicago: Haymarket Books, 2008), 110–11.

40 "We must remember . . . that at the beginning of 1917 the Bolshevik
Party led only an insignificant number of the toilers," wrote Trotsky
in the *New Militant*. "Not only in the soldiers' soviets but also in the
workers' soviets, the Bolshevik fraction generally constituted 1 to 2
percent, at best 5 percent. The leading parties of petty-bourgeois democracy (Mensheviks and the so-called Socialist Revolutionaries) had
the following of at least 95 percent of the workers, soldiers, and peasants participating in the struggle. The leaders of these parties called
the Bolsheviks first sectarians and then . . . agents of the German
kaiser. But no, the Bolsheviks were not sectarians! All their attention
was directed to the masses, and moreover not to their top layer, but
to the deepest, most oppressed millions and tens of millions, whom

the parliamentarian babblers usually forgot. Precisely in order to lead the proletarians and the semi-proletarians of city and countryside, the Bolsheviks considered it necessary to distinguish themselves sharply from all factions and groupings of the bourgeoisie." Leon Trotsky, "Lessons of October," *New Militant*, November 30, 1935. http://www .marxists.org/archive/trotsky/1935/11/october.htm.

41 "The smallness of the group, the hardness of the road ahead only served to intensify his elation. His daydreams became ever more grandiose. He saw himself as one of a small and almost unknown band that was scorned and opposed on all sides, but which would nonetheless one day change the entire history of the world. As he walked the streets of New York or moved about at school, he kept thinking of how he was different from almost everyone he saw. He was one of a small band of people who would lead the world out of its abyss of barbarism. And he liked to think of how he, young and unnoticed, already belonged to history." James T. Farrell, "The Renegade."

42 James Burnham (as John West), "The Bands Are Playing," *New International*, July 1935. http://www.marxists.org/history/etol/writers /burnham/1935/07/bands.htm.

43 Sidney Hook, *Out of Step*, 195.

44 Max Shachtman, *Reminiscences of Max Shachtman*, 336–37.

45 As George Orwell would later write of Burnham: "It will be seen that at each point Burnham is predicting A CONTINUATION OF THE THING THAT IS HAPPENING." George Orwell, "James Burnham and the Managerial Revolution."

46 John Dewey, *Not Guilty: Report of the Commission of Inquiry into the Charges Made against Leon Trotsky in the Moscow Trials* (London: Secker & Warburg, 1938), xv.

47 Daniel Kelly, *James Burnham and the Struggle for the World: A Life*, 63–66.

48 James Burnham, "From Formula to Reality," in *Neither Capitalism nor Socialism*, E. E. Haberkern and A. Lipow, eds., 7–8.

49 James Cannon to Leon Trotsky, December 16, 1937, in James P. Cannon, *The Struggle for a Proletarian Party* (New York: Pioneer Books, 1943), 28. https://archive.org/details/struggleforprole00cannrich.

50 "The central conclusion—namely, that the confessions are false and that it is impossible to explain the confessions if they are accepted as true—is proved with genuinely scientific rigidity. It is entirely safe to predict that there will be no *rational* answers to the analyses and arguments of this study." James Burnham, introduction to *Why Did They "Confess"? A Study of the Radek-Piatakov Trial* (New York: Pioneer Publishers, 1937), 2.

51 See, e.g., James Burnham, "On the Character of the War, and the Perspectives of the Fourth Internationalists," *Socialist Workers Party Internal Bulletin*, November 6, 1939, Vol. 2: Number 2. "The task of the masses, confronted by the war, is to stop the war. This task can be accomplished by the masses only by the overthrow, within each nation, of the war-makers: that is, of their own rules and oppressors."

52 Max Eastman, "Russia and the Socialist Ideal," *Harper's*, Vol. 177, March 1938, 374–85.

53 Quoted in Diggins, *Up From Communism*, 24.

54 Leon Trotsky, "Their Morals and Ours," *New International*, June 1938.

55 James Burnham, "Max Eastman As Scientist," *New International*, June 1938. https://www.marxists.org/history/etol/writers/burnham/1938 /06/eastman.htm.

56 Max Eastman, "Burnham Dodges My Views," *New International*, August 1938. https://www.marxists.org/history/etol/writers/eastman /1938/08/burnham.htm.

57 James Burnham and Max Shachtman, "Intellectuals in Retreat," *New International*, January 1939. https://www.marxists.org/history/etol /writers/burnham/1939/intellectuals/index.htm.

58 Sidney Hook, "Reflections on the Russian Revolution," *Southern Review*, Summer 1939, Vol. 4, 429.

59 James Burnham, "A Belated Dialectician," *Partisan Review*, March 1939, 120–22.

60 Daniel Kelly, *James Burnham and the Struggle for the World*, 80.

61 "The comrades are very indignant about the Stalin-Hitler pact. It is comprehensible. They wish to get revenge on Stalin. Very good. But

today we are weak, and we cannot immediately overthrow the Kremlin. Some comrades try then to find a purely verbalistic satisfaction: they strike out from the USSR the title, 'workers state,' as Stalin deprives a disgraced functionary of the order of Lenin. I find it, my dear friend, a bit childish. Marxist sociology and hysteria are absolutely irreconcilable." Leon Trotsky, letter to Sherman Stanley, October 8, 1939, quoted in Isaac Deutscher, *The Prophet Outcast: Trotsky, 1929–1940* (London: Verso, 2003), 384–85.

62 Leon Trotsky, "The USSR in War," *New International*, September 1939. http://www.marxists.org/archive/trotsky/1939/09/ussr-war.htm.

63 Ibid. "[I]f the world proletariat should actually prove incapable of fulfilling the mission placed upon it by the course of development. . . . It is self-evident that a new 'minimum' program would be required—for the defense of the interests of the slaves of the totalitarian bureaucratic society."

64 "The petty-bourgeois intellectuals are introspective by nature. They mistake their own emotions, their uncertainties, their fears and their own egoistic concern about their personal fate for the sentiments and movements of the great masses. They measure the world's agony by their own inconsequential aches and pains." James Cannon, *The Struggle for a Proletarian Party*, 6.

65 Ibid., 119.

66 Leon Trotsky, "A Petty-Bourgeois Opposition in the Socialist Workers Party," *New International*, December 1939, in Leon Trotsky, *In Defence of Marxism* (New York: Pioneer Publishers, 1942), 44. https://archive.org/details/InDefenseOfMarxism.

67 Quoted in John P. Diggins, *Up From Communism*, 385.

68 "Trotsky must, I would feel, now propose a Special Commission to investigate and weed out all traces of anti-dialectics that have crept into the Socialist Workers Party through Burnham's activities during these years. It will, I am afraid, have plenty of work cut out for it. It might begin, for example, with the party's Declaration of Principles, its foundation programmatic document, which was, by an oversight, written by Burnham. With the war actually started, it will have to devote

particular attention to most of the pamphlets and articles on war, since most were written by Burnham. Surely it cannot overlook the political resolution for the last convention, also the product of Burnham's Aristotelian typewriter; or, for that matter, a fair percentage of all the political resolutions for conventions and conferences and plenums during the past five or six years. And not a few special articles and lead editorials in the *Appeal* and *New International*, the political document motivating the break with the Socialist Party—as well, come to think of it, as the first resolution proposing entry into the Socialist Party. . . . Let us not speak of the fact that perhaps the bulk of motions, resolutions, articles on *American politics* (the main enemy is, is it not, in our own country?) came from the same tainted source." James Burnham, "The Politics of Desperation," *New International*, January 1940. http://www .marxists.org/history/etol/writers/burnham/1940/01/poldes.htm.

69 James Burnham, "Science and Style—A Reply to Comrade Trotsky," *New International*, February 1940. http://www.marxists.org/history /etol/writers/burnham/1940/02/style.htm.

70 James Burnham, "Letter of Resignation from the Workers Party," May 21, 1940. http://www.marxists.org/history/etol/writers/burnham /1940/05/resignation.htm. "On no ideological, theoretic or political ground, then, can I recognize, or do I feel, any bond or allegiance to the Workers Party (or to any other Marxist party). That is simply the case, and I can no longer pretend about it, either to myself or to others. Unfortunately, one factor still remains. This factor is a sense of moral obligation and responsibility to my past self—seven years dominated, however, inadequately but on the whole, by Marxism or any comparable structure, cannot be wiped out by a few minutes at the typewriter—and more especially to other persons, to those with whom I have joined in loyal collaboration on both sides, and to others who have been influenced in their ideas and acts by me. Trotsky and Cannon will exploit my decision as a confirmation of their views—Burnham's quitting will be, by their remarkable but humanly understandable logic, evidence for the truth of their opinions on the character of the war, the nature of the Russian state, and the role of Russia in the war. To

many members of the Workers Party, my separation will appear as a desertion. From a moral and personal point of view, I cannot but agree that there will be a good deal of truth in this latter judgment.

"But this factor, weighed against the others, is no longer sufficient to decide my actions. Indeed, it now seems clear to me that if it had not been for these moral and personal considerations, I should properly have left the party some while ago. On the grounds of beliefs and interests (which are also a fact) I have for several years had no real place in a Marxist party. . . . Believing as I do, I cannot wish success to the Workers Party; but I can and do wish its members well. To the extent that each of us, in his own way and arena, preserves the values and truth and freedom, I hope that we shall continue to regard ourselves as comrades, whatever names we use and whatever labels may be tied around our necks."

3

When the Team's Up Against It: Ronald Reagan

1 Ronald Reagan, *An American Life: The Autobiography* (New York: Simon & Schuster, 1990), 66.
2 Whittaker Chambers, *Witness*, 9.
3 Ronald Reagan, *Where's the Rest of Me?* (New York: Duell, Sloan and Pearce, 1965), 53.
4 Ibid.
5 Ibid., 54.
6 Quoted in William Edward Leuchtenberg, *In the Shadow of FDR: From Harry Truman to George W. Bush* (Ithaca, N.Y.: Cornell University Press, 2001), 221.
7 Ron Reagan, *My Father at 100: A Memoir* (New York: Viking, 2011), 13.
8 Much of the early biographical material on Reagan comes from Anne Edwards, *Early Reagan: The Rise to Power* (New York: Morrow, 1987).
9 *Knute Rockne—All American*, DVD, directed by Lloyd Bacon (Los Angeles: Warner Brothers, 1940).

10 "As a coach, [Rockne] did more than teach our young men how to play a game. He believed truly that the noblest work of man was building the character of men. And maybe that's why he was a living legend. No man connected with football has ever achieved the stature or occupied the singular niche in the nation that he carved out for himself, not just in sport, but in our entire social structure." Ronald Reagan, 1981 Commencement Speech at Notre Dame. http://www.reagan.utexas .edu/archives/speeches/1981/51781a.htm.

11 *Knute Rockne—All American.*

12 Lou Cannon, *President Reagan: The Role of a Lifetime* (New York: Public Affairs, 2000), 190.

13 "Hot from Hollywood," *Screenland*, January 1942.

14 Quoted in Bill Adler, ed., *The Uncommon Wisdom of Ronald Reagan* (New York: Little, Brown, 1996), 30.

15 Anne Edwards, *Early Reagan*, 263–78; Garry Wills, *Reagan's America: Innocents at Home* (New York: Penguin, 2000), 192–200; Edmund Morris, *Dutch: A Memoir of Ronald Reagan* (New York: Random House, 1999), 196–217.

16 "Since Reagan's popularity was at its peak when he entered the Army, and Wyman's was growing, theirs became the quintessential wartime parting, he to the front and she to keep things up at home. . . . When Reagan returned to Los Angeles in a few weeks, for his film work, the fan magazines continued to treat him as 'off at war.' *Modern Screen* wrote: 'It's nine months now since Ronald Reagan said, "So long, Button-nose," to his wife and baby, and went off to join his regiment.'" Garry Wills, *Reagan's America*, 198.

17 Ronald Reagan, *Where's the Rest of Me?*, 143.

18 *This Is the Army*, DVD, directed by Michael Curtiz (Los Angeles: Warner Brothers, 1943).

19 Ronald Reagan, *Where's the Rest of Me?*, 119.

20 There's no independent documentation of this claim, but he made it directly to biographer Edmund Morris. Morris, *Dutch*, 733–34, footnote to p. 216.

21 The Motion Picture Alliance for the Preservation of American Ideals,

"Statement of Principles," Hollywood Renegade Archives, accessed at: http://www.cobbles.com/simpp_archive/huac_alliance.htm.

22 Edmund Morris, *Dutch*, 200–201.

23 Ronald Reagan, *Where's The Rest of Me?*, 139–41.

24 Ronald Reagan, *An American Life*, 106.

25 Edmund Morris, *Dutch*, 228.

26 In December of 1945 he volunteered to speak at a rally, organized by HICCASP, in favor of the abolition of nuclear weapons. He quietly bowed out of the rally after Warner Brothers sent a stern letter to his agent, indicating that they'd prefer he not make himself so visible politically. Instead he read the poem he'd been intending to read, Norman Corwin's "Set Your Clock at U-235," at a private dinner a few days before the rally. After describing the "stink of death . . . on the wind from Nagasaki," the poem declares that the only possible futures are extinction or cooperation: "Unless we work at it together, at a single earth . . . [T]here will be others out of the just-born and the not-yet-contracted-for who will die for our invisible daily mistakes." Norman Corwin, "Set Your Clock at U-235," quoted in Paul Vorbeck Lettow, *Ronald Reagan and His Quest to Abolish Nuclear Weapons* (New York: Random House, 2005), 5.

27 Ronald Reagan, *An American Life*, 115.

28 Quoted in Mary Beth Brown, *The Faith of Ronald Reagan* (Nashville: Thomas Nelson, 2011), 92.

29 Edmund Morris, *Dutch*, 229.

30 Ibid., 230.

31 Ronald Reagan, *Where's the Rest of Me?*, 166.

32 Ibid., 167.

33 Garry Wills, *Reagan's America*, 266.

34 Ibid., 297.

35 Ronald Reagan, *An American Life*, 108.

36 Ibid., 108.

37 Ibid.

38 Ronald Reagan, *Where's the Rest of Me?*, 171.

39 Quoted in Marc Eliot, *Reagan: The Hollywood Years* (New York: Random House, 2009), 209.

40 Seth Rosenfeld, *Subversives: The FBI's War on Student Radicals, and Reagan's Rise to Power* (New York: Farrar, Straus and Giroux, 2012), 132.

41 Garry Wills, *Reagan's America*, 298.

42 From "The Waldorf Statement," a press release issued on December 3, 1947, by the Motion Picture Association of America. http://en.wikipedia.org/wiki/Waldorf_Statement.

43 "It takes courage and desire and time for an American to work free of the tentacles of the Communist Party," went an open letter that Reagan and his MPIC allies published in the *Saturday Evening Post* and in a number of the Hollywood industry magazines. "And it takes help. But there is a way out. To any Communist Party member who may be seeking that way, we say: 'You too can be a free man again!'" Quoted in Peter Schweizer, *Reagan's War: The Epic Story of His Forty-Year Struggle and Final Triumph Over Communism* (New York: Doubleday, 2002), 21–22.

44 Ronald Reagan, *An American Life*, 115.

45 Whittaker Chambers, *Witness*, 9.

46 "What Communist has not heard those screams? They come from husbands torn forever from their wives in midnight arrests. They come, muffled, from the execution cells of the secret police, from the torture chambers of the Lubyanka, from all the citadels of terror now stretching from Berlin to Canton. They come from those freight cars loaded with men, women and children, the enemies of the Communist State, locked in, packed in, left on remote sidings to freeze to death at night in the Russian winter. They come from minds driven mad by the horrors of mass starvation ordered and enforced as a policy of the Communist state. They come from the starved skeletons, worked to death, or flogged to death (as example to others) in the freezing filth of sub-arctic labor camps. They come from children whose parents are suddenly, inexplicably taken away from them—parents they will never see again. What Communist has not heard those screams?" Ibid., 14.

47 Anne Edwards, *The Reagans: Portrait of a Marriage* (New York: St. Martin's Press, 2003), 367.

48 Nancy Reagan with William Novak, *My Turn: The Memoirs of Nancy Reagan* (New York: Random House, 1989), 125.

49   Ronald Reagan, *Where's the Rest of Me?*, 251.

50   Ibid., 175.

51   Ibid., 177.

52   Thomas W. Evans, *The Education of Ronald Reagan: The General Electric Years and the Untold Story of His Conversion to Conservatism* (New York: Columbia University Press, 2006), 65.

53   On Boulware and General Electric, see Evans, *The Education of Ronald Reagan*; Kim Philipps-Fein, *Invisible Hands: The Businessmen's Crusade Against the New Deal* (New York: W. W. Norton, 2009); Lemuel R. Boulware, *The Truth about Boulwarism: Trying to Do Right Voluntarily* (Washington, D.C.: Bureau of National Affairs, 1969).

54   Lemuel R. Boulware, *The Truth about Boulwarism*, 4.

55   Ronald Reagan, *An American Life*, 129.

56   Ronald Reagan, commencement address at Eureka College, June 7, 1957. http://www.pbs.org/wgbh/americanexperience/features/primary -resources/reagan-eureka/.

57   Quoted in Edmund Morris, *Dutch*, 309.

58   Ronald Reagan, *An American Life*, 135.

59   Ronald Reagan, "Losing Freedom by Installments," speech given to the Oregon-Columbia Chapter of the National Electrical Contractors Association, September 25, 1961, quoted in Phillips-Fein, *Invisible Hands*, 114.

60   The speech, which was recorded and released as an LP, *Ronald Reagan Speaks Out Against Socialized Medicine* (1961), was part of a campaign of the American Medical Association, Operation Coffee Cup, dedicated to defeating the legislation that eventually became Medicare.

4

Mr. Yes, Mr. No: Norman Podhoretz

1   Quoted in Marc D. Schleifer, "Here to Save Us," *Village Voice*, October 15, 1958, Vol. III, No. 51.

2   Norman Podhoretz, *Making It* (New York: Random House, 1967), 285–89.

3 Norman Podhoretz, "The Young Generation of U.S. Intellectuals," *New Leader*, March 11, 1957, 8–10.

4 The best resources for the early biography of Podhoretz are: Norman Podhoretz, *Making It* (New York: Random House, 1967); Thomas L. Jeffers, *Norman Podhoretz: A Biography* (New York: Cambridge University Press, 2010); and his essays and reviews of the early 1950s, a number of which are collected in Norman Podhoretz, *Doings & Undoings: The Fifties and After in American Writing* (New York: Farrar, Straus & Giroux, 1964).

5 On the New York intellectuals, see, e.g., Alan M. Wald, *The New York Intellectuals: The Rise and Decline of the Anti-Stalinist Left from the 1930s to the 1980s* (Chapel Hill: University of North Carolina Press, 1987); Joseph Dorman, *Arguing the World: The New York Intellectuals in Their Own Words* (New York: Free Press, 2000); Irving Howe, "The New York Intellectuals: A Chronicle and a Critique," *Commentary*, Vol. 46, October 1968, 29; and memoirs by Irving Howe, Norman Podhoretz, Alfred Kazin, and Diana Trilling, among many others.

6 Norman Podhoretz, *Commentary*, Vol. 15: "Achilles in Left Field" (Review of *The Natural*, by Bernard Malamud), *Commentary*, March 1953, 321–26; "The Language of Life" (Review of *The Adventures of Augie March*, by Saul Bellow), *Commentary*, January 1, 1953; 15, Periodicals Archive Online, 378.

7 Norman Podhoretz, "William Faulkner and the Problem of War: His Fable of Faith," *Commentary*, Vol. 16, September 1954, 227.

8 Interview with Norman Podhoretz, April 19, 2015. "I've always had a knack for anticipating trends, not by taking public opinion polls, but by looking into myself. . . . It's why I was a good editor, and one of the reasons why I was able to make such a splash with *Commentary* when I took over. . . . I had that confident sense that what was bothering me or interesting me was reflective of something larger."

9 Norman Podhoretz, "The Young Generation of U.S. Intellectuals," *New Leader*, 10.

10 Benjamin Balint, *Running Commentary: The Contentious Magazine*

that Transformed the Jewish Left into the Neoconservative Right (New York: Public Affairs, 2010), 75.

11 The encounter between Podhoretz, Ginsberg, and Kerouac is described most fully in Norman Podhoretz, *Ex-Friends: Falling Out with Allen Ginsberg, Lionel and Diana Trilling, Lillian Hellman, Hannah Arendt, and Norman Mailer* (San Francisco: Encounter Books, 2000), 29–42.

12 Allen Ginsberg, *Howl and Other Poems* (San Francisco: City Lights Books, 1959), 16.

13 "Kerouac apparently thinks that spontaneity is a matter of saying whatever comes into your head, in any order you happen to feel like saying it. It isn't the *right* words he wants (even if he knows what they might be), but the first words, or at any rate the words that most obviously announce themselves as deriving from emotion rather than cerebration, as coming from 'life' rather than 'literature,' from the guts rather than the brain." Norman Podhoretz, "Know Nothing Bohemians," *Partisan Review*, Spring 1958, 305–18.

14 As Ginsberg had vented to the *Village Voice* not long before that evening: "His criticism of Jack's spontaneous bop prosody shows that he can't tell the difference between words as rhythm and words as in diction." Marc Schleifer, "Here to Save Us," *Village Voice*, October 15, 1958.

15 Norman Podhoretz, *Ex-Friends*, 33–34.

16 "Surely the reception accorded Jack Kerouac and Allen Ginsberg, whose work combines an appearance of radicalism with a show of intense spirituality, testifies to the hunger that has grown up on all sides for something extreme, fervent, affirmative and sweeping. . . . But though one can decide which values to defend, and though one can try on ideologies like suits of clothes, one cannot choose to be passionate. It is impossible to will oneself into powerful convictions; something from the outside has to take over the mind and spirit, has to 'startle this dull pain, and make it move and live.' This dilemma today is that nothing seems to be left in our world to set an honest man's feelings on fire." Norman Podhoretz, "The New Nihilism and the Novel," *Partisan Review*, Fall 1958, Vol. XXV, 576–90.

17 Published as Norman Podhoretz, "Edmund Wilson—The Last Patrician," Parts I and II, *Reporter*, December 25, 1958, and January 8, 1959.

18 Norman Podhoretz, *Ex-Friends*, 187.

19 Norman Mailer, *Dissent*, Vol. 4, Fall 1957, 277.

20 Norman Podhoretz, *Ex-Friends*, 188.

21 See Thomas L. Jeffers, *Norman Podhoretz*, 55–58; Norman Podhoretz, *Ex-Friends*, 178–220.

22 "To follow Mailer's career . . . is to witness a special drama of development, a drama in which the deepest consciousness of the postwar period has struggled to define itself in relation to the past, and to know itself in terms of the inescapable, ineluctable present." Norman Podhoretz, "Norman Mailer: The Embattled Vision," *Partisan Review*, Summer 1959, 371–91.

23 Ibid.

24 Norman Mailer, *Dissent*, Vol. 4, Fall 1957, 290.

25 Interview with Norman Podhoretz.

26 Benjamin Balint, *Running Commentary*, 76.

27 Nathan Abrams, *Norman Podhoretz and Commentary Magazine: The Rise and Fall of the Neocons* (New York: Continuum International, 2010), 21–22.

28 Norman Podhoretz, *Making It*, 276–77.

29 Ibid., 284–85.

30 Jack Ludwig, "Orlick Miller and Company: Excerpt from a Novel in Progress," *Commentary*, Vol. 29, January 1960, 59.

31 Norman Podhoretz, *Making It*, 297.

32 Paul Goodman, *Commentary*, Vol. 29: "Youth in the Organized Society," January 1960, 95; "The Calling of American Youth," February 1960, 217; "In Search of Community," March 1960, 315.

33 "[W]e should have a society where: A premium is placed on technical improvement and on the engineering style of functional simplicity and clarity. Where the community is planned as a whole, with an organic integration of work, living, and play. Where buildings have the variety of their functions and the uniformity of the prevailing technology. Where a lot of money is spent on public goods. Where workers are technically

educated and have a say in management. Where no one drops out of society and there is an easy mobility of classes. Where production is primarily for use. Where social groups are laboratories for solving their own problems experimentally. Where democracy begins in the town meeting and a man seeks office because he has a program. Where regional variety is encouraged and there is pride in the Republic. And young men are free of conscription. Where all are citizens of the universal Republic of Reason. Where it is the policy to give an adequate voice to the unusual and unpopular opinion, and to give a trial and a market to new enterprise. Where people are not afraid to make friends. Where races are factually equal. Where vocation is sought out and cultivated as God-given capacity, to be conserved and embellished, and where the church is the spirit of its congregation. Where ordinary experience is habitually scientifically assayed by the average man. Where it is felt that the suggestion of reason is practical. And speech leads to the corresponding action. Where the popular culture is a daring and passionate culture. Where children can make themselves useful and get their own money. Where their sexuality is taken for granted. Where the community carries on its important adult business and the children fall in at their own pace. And where education is concerned with fostering human powers as they develop in the growing child." Paul Goodman, *Growing Up Absurd* (New York: New York Review of Books, 2012), 205.

34 See Nathan Abrams, *Norman Podhoretz and Commentary Magazine*, 53–57. Also interview with Norman Podhoretz: "I wasn't going where the action was, I was going where I thought the action would be."

35 Norman Podhoretz, *Making It*, 350.

36 Ibid., 333–35.

37 "I believed strongly in marital fidelity. . . . But of course I was young and the blood was hot and the temptations ever present. Resisting them was at least as hard as the 'hard business' of building a good and lasting marriage, and my friendship with Mailer made it even harder." Norman Podhoretz, *Ex-Friends*, 197–98.

38 Norman Podhoretz, *Breaking Ranks: A Political Memoir* (New York: Harper & Row, 1979), 121.

39 The basic facts of this story are confirmed in James Campbell, *Talking at the Gates: A Life of James Baldwin* (Berkeley: University of California Press, 1991), 160; and David Leeming, *James Baldwin: A Biography* (New York: Knopf, 1994), 211.

40 Norman Podhoretz, *Making It*, 342.

41 Norman Podhoretz, "My Negro Problem—and Ours," *Commentary*, Vol. 35, February 1963, 93.

42 Thomas L. Jeffers, *Norman Podhoretz*, 87–88.

43 Norman Podhoretz, "Hannah Arendt on Eichmann: A Study in the Perversity of Brilliance," *Commentary*, Vol. 36, September 1963, 201.

44 Amos Elon in Hannah Arendt, *Eichmann in Jerusalem: A Report on the Banality of Evil* (New York: Penguin, 2006), vii.

45 Norman Podhoretz, "Hannah Arendt on Eichmann: A Study in the Perversity of Brilliance," 208.

46 Norman Podhoretz, *Making It*, 351–52.

47 Nathan Glazer, "What Happened at Berkeley?" *Commentary*, Vol. 39, February 1965, 39; Bayard Rustin, "From Protest to Politics," *Commentary*, Vol. 39, February 1965, 25; Robert Penn Warren, "Two for SNCC," *Commentary*, Vol. 39, 38; David Danzig, "In Defense of Black Power," *Commentary*, Vol. 42, September 1966, 41.

48 Norman Podhoretz, *Making It*, 356.

49 Norman Podhoretz, *Ex-Friends*, 85.

50 Nathan Abrams, *Norman Podhoretz and Commentary Magazine*, 82 (n58).

51 See, e.g., Saul Maloff, "Climbing the Pole," *Newsweek*, January 8, 1968, 62; Wilfrid Sheed, "*Making It* in the Big City," *Atlantic Monthly*, April 1968, 97; Mordechai Richler, "Climbing Norman's Ladder," the *Nation*, February 5, 1968, 180; Edgar Z. Friedenberg, "Du Côté de Chez Podhoretz," *New York Review of Books*, February 1, 1968; Robert Kirsch, "Hang-ups of Podhoretz in Aping Mailer," *Los Angeles Times*, January 14, 1968, D34.

52 Stanley Kauffmann, "The Challenge of Success," *New Republic*, January 27, 1968, 27.

53 Rust Hills, "The Dirty Little Secret of Norman Podhoretz," *Esquire*, April 1968, 92.

54 Norman Mailer, "Up the Family Tree," *Partisan Review*, Vol. 25, Spring 1968, 234.

55 Diana Trilling, "On the Steps of Low Library: Liberalism & the Revolution of the Young," *Commentary*, Vol. 45, November 1968, 29.

56 "Up Against the Wall," *Columbia University Libraries Online Exhibitions*, accessed August 7, 2014. https://exhibitions.cul.columbia.edu /items/show/5524.

57 Norman Podhoretz, *Breaking Ranks*, 267.

58 Interview with Thomas L. Jeffers, quoted in Jeffers, *Norman Podhoretz*, 124.

59 Ibid., 125.

60 Interview with Norman Podhoretz.

5

The Betrayed: David Horowitz

1 David Horowitz, *Radical Son: A Generational Odyssey* (New York: Simon & Schuster, 2011), 215.

2 David Horowitz and Peter Collier, "Goodbye to All That," *Washington Post Magazine*, March 17, 1985, 8.

3 David Horowitz, "The Passion of the Jews," *Ramparts*, October 1974, 21.

4 Norman Podhoretz, "Is It Good for the Jews?" *Commentary*, 53, February 1, 1972, 12.

5 Ibid., 16.

6 David Horowitz, "The Passion of the Jews," *Ramparts*.

7 David Horowitz, *Radical Son*, 276.

8 "This whole period of my life what I was trying to do was rescue my parents' vision. I know that something had obviously gone wrong with Marxism. . . . My attitude became that because Marxism had triumphed in Russia—which is a backward country—it had been distorted, and now it was possible for the first time to have a radical movement . . . a nonservile movement where people could think, but where there was no 'Vatican' that gave down the line." Quoted in

Frank Browning, "The Strange Journey of David Horowitz," *Mother Jones*, May 1987, 27; "I wanted to avoid winding up where my parents had, embarrassed. If we were going to make a revolution, I took it very seriously that we should understand how the previous communist generation got to where it did, and avoid it." Interview with David Horowitz, April 28, 2015.

9 David Horowitz, *Radical Son*, 245.

10 Ibid., 282.

11 According to Horowitz, a number of ex-Panthers, including Huey Newton, told him that she'd been killed by the Panthers. Journalist Ken Kelley also said that Newton admitted to him that he'd ordered Van Patter killed for "refusing to clean up the party's books." Steve Wasserman, "Rage and Ruin: On the Black Panthers," *Nation*, June 24, 2013. See also Hugh Pearson, *Shadow of the Panther: Huey Newton and the Price of Black Power in America* (New York: Perseus Publishing, 1996), 272, 290, 334, and 346. The most comprehensive account of the case is "A Death in Berkeley," Kate Coleman, *Heterodoxy*, 1998. http://colemantruth.net/kate15.pdf.

12 David Horowitz, *Radical Son*, 255.

13 Ibid.

14 Interview with David Horowitz. "I just knew I couldn't be political— I couldn't act as a leftist—while these questions were unresolved."

15 David Horowitz, *Radical Son*, 255.

16 See Jason Daniel Roberts, *Disillusioned Radicals: The Intellectual Odyssey of Todd Gitlin, Ronald Radosh and David Horowitz* (dissertation, George Washington University, 2007), 91–96.

17 Peter Collier as quoted in David Horowitz, *Radical Son*, 191.

18 David Horowitz, *Radical Son*, 286.

19 David Horowitz, *The First Frontier: The Indian Wars and America's Origins* (New York: Simon & Schuster, 1978).

20 Horowitz, *Radical Son*, 286.

21 Ibid., 288.

22 Ibid., 289.

23 Ibid., 291.

24 For background on the Panthers during this period see Hugh Pearson, *The Shadow of the Panther*; Flores Forbes, *Will You Die with Me? My Life and the Black Panther Party* (New York: Atria Books, 2006); Elaine Brown, *A Taste of Power: A Black Woman's Story* (New York: Anchor Books, 1993); Kate Coleman, "The Party's Over: How Huey Newton Created a Street Gang at the Center of the Black Panther Party," *New Times*, July 10, 1978, 23.

25 David Horowitz, *Radical Son*, 266.

26 Ibid., 260.

27 Ibid., 263.

28 Ibid., 88.

29 Leszek Kolakowski and Stuart Hampshire, eds., *The Socialist Idea: A Reappraisal* (London: Quartet Books, 1974).

30 Kolakowski, "The Myth of Human Self-Identity: Unity of Civil and Political Society in Socialist Thought," *The Socialist Idea*, 18–35.

31 From the Port Huron Statement: "In a participatory democracy, the political life would be based in several root principles: that decision-making of basic social consequence be carried on by public groupings; that politics be seen positively, as the art of collectively creating an acceptable pattern of social relations; that politics has the function of bringing people out of isolation and into community, thus being a necessary, though not sufficient, means of finding meaning in personal life; that the political order should serve to clarify problems in a way instrumental to their solution; it should provide outlets for the expression of personal grievance and aspiration; opposing views should be organized so as to illuminate choices and facilitate the attainment of goals; channels should be commonly available to related men to knowledge and to power so that private problems—from bad recreation facilities to personal alienation—are formulated as general issues." Students for Democratic Society, 1962. http://www.h-net.org/~hst306/documents/huron.html.

32 David Horowitz, *Student: The Political Activities of the Berkeley Students* (New York: Ballantine Books, 1962), 17.

33 Horowitz, *Radical Son*, 275–76.

34 David Horowitz, "Unnecessary Losses (Letter to Carol Pasternak)," written April 1987, republished in David Horowitz, *Politics of Bad Faith: The Radical Assault on America's Future* (New York: Touchstone 2000), 71–72.

35 David Horowitz, *Radical Son*, 280.

36 Ibid., 305.

37 David Horowitz, "A Radical's Disenchantment," *Nation*, December 8, 1979, Vol. 229, 586–88.

38 Ibid.

39 Interview with David Horowitz. "I thought I'd be writing for the *Washington Post* and the *New York Times*."

40 Horowitz, *Radical Son*, 311–12.

41 Eve Pell, *We Used to Own the Bronx* (Albany: Excelsior Editions, 2010), 190–91.

42 Interview with David Horowitz.

43 Peter Collier and David Horowitz, *Destructive Generation: Second Thoughts about the Sixties* (New York: Encounter Books, 2005), 39.

44 Ibid., 28.

45 Ibid., 66.

46 Bob Sipchen, "Leftists Who Turned Right," *Los Angeles Times*, June 2, 1992.

47 David Horowitz, *Radical Son*, 337.

48 Peter Collier and David Horowitz, "Doing It: The Inside Story of the Rise and Fall of the Weather Underground," *Rolling Stone*, September 30, 1982.

49 Collier and Horowitz, "Whitewash," *California Magazine*, July 1983.

50 "Compassion is not what motivates the Left, which is oblivious to the human suffering its generations have caused. What motives the Left is the totalitarian Idea. The Idea that is more important than reality itself. What motives the Left is the Idea of the future in which everything is changed, everything *transcended*. The future in which the present it already *annihilated*, and its reality no longer exists." David Horowitz, "Unnecessary Losses (Letter to Carol Pasternak)," 58.

51 Horowitz, *Radical Son*, 345.

52 Interview with David Horowitz.

53 Ibid., 351.

6

A Man Alone: Christopher Hitchens

1 Martin Amis, *Experience* (New York: Vintage International 2001), 258–59.

2 "Casting our ballots for Ronald Reagan was indeed a way of finally saying goodbye to all that—to the self-aggrandizing romance with corrupt Third Worldism; to the casual indulgence of Soviet totalitarianism; to the hypocritical and self-dramatizing anti-Americanism which is the New Left's bequest to mainstream politics." Peter Collier and David Horowitz, "Goodbye to All That," *Washington Post Magazine*, March 17, 1985.

3 Christopher Hitchens, "Minority Report," *Nation*, November 7, 1987. Republished as "Third Thoughts" in Christopher Hitchens, *For the Sake of Arguments: Essays and Minority Reports* (New York: Verso, 1994), 111.

4 Ibid., 113–14.

5 Quoted in Christopher Hitchens, *Blood, Class and Empire: The Enduring Anglo-American Relationship* (New York: Nation Books, 2004), 251.

6 Christopher Hitchens, "On Not Knowing the Half of It: My Jewish Self: Homage to Telegraphist Jacobs," *Grand Street*, Vol. 7, Summer 1988, 127–28.

7 Christopher Hitchens, *Hitch-22: A Memoir* (New York: Twelve, 2010), 356.

8 Ibid., 33.

9 Lynn Barber, "Lynn Barber meets Christopher Hitchens," *Guardian*, April 14, 2002, http://www.theguardian.com/books/2002/apr/14/politics.

10 "It was, nevertheless, a good school of the second rank," wrote James Hilton in *Goodbye, Mr. Chips*, his novel about a teacher at a fictional prep school modeled on the Leys. "Several notable families supported

it; it supplied fair samples of the history-making men of the age—
judges, members of parliament, colonial administrators, a few peers
and bishops. Mostly, however, it turned out merchants, manufactur-
ers, and professional men, with a good sprinkling of country squires
and parsons. It was the sort of school which, when mentioned, would
sometimes make snobbish people confess that they rather thought
they had heard of it." James Hilton, *Goodbye, Mr. Chips* (New York:
Little, Brown and Company, 1962), 212.

11 For more on the Leys, see Geoff and Pat Loughton, *Well-regulated
minds and improper moments: A history of The Leys School* (Cambridge:
The Governors of The Leys School, 2000).

12 Christopher Hitchens (interview), *Heaven On Earth: The Rise and
Fall of Socialism* (PBS: New River Media, 2005). http://www.pbs.org
/heavenonearth/interviews_hitchens.html.

13 Christopher Hitchens, *Hitch-22*, 71.

14 Robert Anderson, *British Universities: Past and Present* (London: Ham-
bledon Continuum, 2006), 51.

15 Victor Navasky, *A Matter of Opinion* (New York: Picador, 2006), 189.

16 Rodney P. Carlisle, ed., *Encyclopedia of Politics: The Left and the Right,
Volume 1* (London: Sage Publications, 2005), 407.

17 See, e.g., Hitchens's review of a book by Ian Clegg, *Workers' Self-
Management in Algeria*, in the April–June 1972 issue of *International
Socialism* (1st series): "Generally speaking, Clegg ignores the conception of a mass workers party informed by Marxist theory. Naturally
enough, this leads him into confusion. But he has written a highly
intelligent and relevant book, which deserves the attention of all revolutionaries. It could well form the basis of a vitally needed discussion
about the proletarian movement in the Third World, as well as the
more obvious purpose which it may fulfill in illuminating the debate
on workers control." https://www.marxists.org/history/etol/newspape
/isj/1972/no051/hitchens2.htm.

18 Karl Marx, ed. Christopher Hitchens, *The Paris Commune, 1871*
(London: Sidgwick & Jackson, 1971), 10–11.

19 "A whole anthology of images survives vividly in my mind from this

time. A spontaneous riot on the broad Ramblas of Barcelona, after the last-ever use of the hideous medieval *garrotte* for the judicial murder of a Catalan anarchist named Salvador Puig Antich: the illegal Catalan flag proudly flown and a shower of gasoline bombs falling on Franco's military police. A journey to Guernica—a place name that I could hardly believe corresponded to an actual living town—to rendezvous with Basque activists. A weekend in the Latin Quarter in Paris, complete with telephone 'passwords' and anonymous handshakes in corner *zinc* bars, so that I could meet a Portuguese resistance leader named Palma Inacio who was engaged in organizing an armed battle against the dictatorship in Lisbon. Some long, hot, and fragrant days in Tyre and Sidon and points south of Beirut, meeting with militants of the 'Democratic Front' who, over lunch in olive groves, would patiently explain to me that Jews and Arabs were brothers under the skin and that only imperialism was really the problem. Standing in Freedom Square in Nicosia among a roaring crowd of demonstrators, many of whom had recently fought with gun in hand against the Greek junta's attempt to annex Cyprus." Christopher Hitchens, *Hitch-22*, 180.

20 Christopher Hitchens, interview with Sasha Abramsky, *Progressive*, February 1997, 32.

21 Clive James, *North Face of Soho: Unreliable Memoirs, Vol. 4* (London: Picador, 2006), 8.

22 Ibid., 188–89.

23 Quoted in Meryl Gordon, "The Boy Can't Help It," *New York*, April 29, 1999. http://nymag.com/nymetro/news/media/features/868/.

24 Navasky, *A Matter of Opinion*, 189.

25 Andrew Kopkind, "The Return of Cold War Liberalism," *The Thirty Years' War: Dispatches and Diversions of a Radical Journalist, 1965–1994* (London: Verso, 1995), 358.

26 Christopher Hitchens, "A Regular Bull" (review of *Whittaker Chambers: A Biography*, by Sam Tanenhaus), *London Review of Books*, July 31, 1997. Republished in Christopher Hitchens, *Unacknowledged Legislation: Writers in the Public Sphere* (New York: Verso, 2002), 122.

27 Christopher Hitchens, "On the Frontier of the Apocalypse," *Vanity*

Fair, January 2002. http://www.vanityfair.com/politics/features/2002 /01/pakistan-200201.

28 Christopher Hitchens, "On Not Knowing the Half of It: My Jewish Self: Homage to Telegraphist Jacobs," *Grand Street*, Vol. 7, Summer 1988, 127–28.

29 Ed Kashi, with an introduction by Christopher Hitchens, *When the Borders Bleed: The Struggle of the Kurds* (New York: Pantheon, 1994), 14.

30 Christopher Hitchens, *The Trial of Henry Kissinger* (New York: Verso, 2001), 150.

31 Ibid., 5.

32 Hitchens, *Letters to a Young Contrarian* (New York: Basic Books, 2001), 120.

33 Martin Amis, *Experience* (New York: Vintage, 2000), 255.

34 Ibid., 261.

35 Christopher Hitchens, *Hitch-22*, 268.

36 Meryl Gordon, "The Boy Can't Help It," *New York*. http://nymag .com/nymetro/news/media/features/868/.

37 Eleni Meleagrou as quoted in Gordon, "The Boy Can't Help It," *New York*.

38 The phrase was borrowed, by Hitchens, from Joseph Heller's *Good as Gold* (New York: Simon & Schuster, 1997), 328. Quoted in Hitchens, *The Trial of Henry Kissinger*, 150.

39 "I first met [South Korean president] Kim Dae Jung . . . when he was living in exile in Virginia, under the disapproval of the Reagan administration. . . . My Chilean friend Ariel Dorfman, who I first embraced after he read his defiant poems outside the Chilean embassy in Washington, was fourteen years later the guest of honor at reception, which I also attended, at the same embassy." Christopher Hitchens, *Letters to a Young Contrarian*, 91.

40 Christopher Hitchens, *For the Sake of Argument: Essays and Minority Reports* (London: Verso, 1993), 239.

41 Christopher Hitchens, *The Missionary Position: Mother Teresa in Theory and Practice* (New York Verso, 1995), 59.

42 Hitchens, *Unacknowledged Legislation*, 7.

43 Hitchens, *Letters to a Young Contrarian*, 17.

44 "But alone among his contemporaries, Churchill did not denounce the Nazi empire merely as a threat, actual or potential, to the British one. Nor did he speak of it as a depraved but possibly useful ally. He excoriated it as a wicked and nihilistic thing. That appears facile now, but was exceedingly uncommon then. In what was perhaps his best ever speech, delivered to the Commons five days after the Munich agreement, on October 5, 1938, Churchill gave voice to the idea that even a 'peace-loving' coexistence with Hitler had something rotten about it. 'What I find unendurable is the sense of our country falling into the power, into the orbit and influence of Nazi Germany, of our existence becoming dependent upon their good will or pleasure.'" Christopher Hitchens, "The Medals of His Defeats," *Atlantic Monthly*, April 2002, republished in Hitchens, *Love, Poverty, and War: Journeys and Essays* (New York: Nation Books, 2004), 26.

45 "Yet where Kipling excelled—and where he most deserves praise and respect—was in enjoining the British to avoid the very hubris that he had helped to inspire in them." Hitchens, "A Man of Permanent Contradictions: A Review of *The Long Recessional: The Imperial Life of Rudyard Kipling*, by David Gilmour," *Atlantic Monthly*, June 2002, republished in Hitchens, *Love, Poverty, and War*, 36.

46 Hitchens, *For the Sake of Argument*, 143.

47 Hitchens, *Letters to a Young Contrarian*, 32.

48 Ibid., 17.

49 Hitchens, *For the Sake of Argument*, 58.

50 Hitchens, *Unacknowledged Legislation*, xii, 43, 393; Christopher Hitchens, *Prepared for the Worst* (New York: Hill and Wang, 1988), 113–15, 278.

51 Hitchens, "Unmaking Friends: a review of *Ex-Friends* and *Making It*, by Norman Podhoretz," *Harper's*, June 1999. Republished in *Unacknowledged Legislation*, 389.

52 Ibid., 390–92.

53 Hitchens, "Siding with Rushdie," *London Review of Books*, October 26, 1989, Vol. 11 (20), 11–15.

54 Christopher Hitchens, *No One Left to Lie To: The Values of the Worst Family* (New York: Verso, 2000), 20.

55 Ibid., 75.

56 Michael Kazin, "The Passion of Christopher Hitchens," *Dissent*, Vol. 52, Summer 2005, 109.

57 Adam Michnik, "We, The Traitors," *Gazeta Wyborcza*, Warsaw, Poland, March 28, 2003. http://www.worldpress.org/Europe/1086.cfm.

58 George Orwell, "My Country Right or Left," *George Orwell: An Age Like This 1920–1940* (Boston: Nonpareil Books, 2000), 538–39.

59 Christopher Hitchens, "So Long, Fellow Travelers," *Washington Post*, October 20, 2002, B01.

60 Christopher Hitchens, "The Hitchens-Pollitt Papers," *Nation*, December 16, 2002. http://www.thenation.com/article/hitchens-pollitt -papers.

61 Christopher Hitchens, *A Long Short War: The Postponed Liberation of Iraq* (New York: Plume, 2003), 15.

62 *The Daily Show with Jon Stewart*, August 25, 2005. http://thedailyshow .cc.com/videos/y4xx9p/christopher-hitchens.

63 Christopher Hitchens interview with Anderson Cooper, CNN, May 16, 2007. http://youtu.be/52yTqMcwuQE, http://transcripts.cnn .com/TRANSCRIPTS/0705/15/acd.01.html.

Index

About the Author

Daniel Oppenheimer is a writer and filmmaker from Austin, Texas, whose articles and videos have been featured in the *New York Times*, TheAtlantic.com, *Tablet* magazine, the History News Network, Tom-Paine.com, and Salon.com. He has an MFA in nonfiction writing from Columbia University, was an arts writer for an alternative weekly paper in western Massachusetts, and currently holds two positions at the University of Texas at Austin: Director of Strategic Communications for the Division of Diversity and Community Engagement and Communications Manager for the Hogg Foundation for Mental Health. Oppenheimer was born in New York City, grew up in Springfield, Massachusetts, and currently lives in Austin, Texas, with his wife, Jessica, his daughter, Jolie, and his son, Asa.